STRANGE THINGS

THE STORY OF FR ALLAN MCDONALD, ADA GOODRICH FREER, AND THE SOCIETY FOR PSYCHICAL RESEARCH'S ENQUIRY INTO HIGHLAND SECOND SIGHT

JOHN L. CAMPBELL

and

TREVOR H. HALL

ROUTLEDGE & KEGAN PAUL

LONDON

First published 1968
by Routledge & Kegan Paul Ltd
Broadway House, 68–74 Carter Lane
London, E.C.4

Printed in Great Britain
by Richard Clay (The Chaucer Press) Ltd
Bungay, Suffolk

SBN 7100 6053 x

CONTENTS

III *Ada Goodrich Freer and Fr Allan McDonald's Folklore Collection* J. L. Campbell

IV '*Strange Things*'

LIST OF ILLUSTRATIONS

PREFACE

IT SEEMS desirable that something should be said of the circumstances under which this book came to be written.

When I first went to live on the island of Barra in the Outer Hebrides in 1933, many people were living who could remember Fr Allan McDonald, priest of the island of Eriskay, who had died in 1905 at the age of 46. Alike as a parish priest, a poet, and a collector of Gaelic folklore, Fr Allan McDonald had achieved a fame that lived on long after him. It therefore seemed to me extraordinary that a folklore collection as important as his should have disappeared completely. The collection seemed well worth trying to trace, and eventually, after prolonged enquiries (and in spite of the denials of two persons who actually were in possession of parts of it), I was able to trace four-fifths of it with the help of various clerical and academic friends, to whom I shall always be profoundly grateful.

The material traced consisted of eight quarto notebooks. One of these contained a collection of rare Gaelic words and expressions made in South Uist and Eriskay between 1893 and 1897; another a collection of Gaelic hymns, some traditional, some original, and some translated from English and Latin; another contained a collection of the words of waulking (labour) songs; and another, about which more will be said later, contained a collection of second sight stories and other material, including draft versions of some of Fr Allan McDonald's original Gaelic poems. Apart from these four notebooks there were four others containing general folklore—local history, folk-tales, folk-songs, folk anecdotes, proverbs, place-names, Uist and Eriskay genealogies, and so on. These were numbered I, II, V, and VI. This part of the collection had been begun in the winter of 1887–8 and had been made over the succeeding ten years. Notebooks III and IV were (and still are) missing; these had been written on Eriskay between 1893 and 1896.

An examination of the four surviving folklore notebooks and of a diary kept by Fr Allan McDonald between 1st September 1897 and 30th June 1898 revealed that a lady named Ada Goodrich Freer, well known in folklore circles as the authoress of an important book on the Hebrides called *Outer Isles*, published in 1902, and a lecturer on several occasions between 1897 and 1901 to the Folklore Society in London and other similar bodies on Hebridean folklore, had been indebted to Fr Allan McDonald's notebooks for her material to a very remarkable degree, though this was not fully realized until a catalogue of his folklore material, which was begun by myself, was completed by Miss Sheila J. Lockett, who also spent some time in checking Fr Allan McDonald's material against Miss Freer's lectures and publications for me. An outcome of this discovery was my article 'The late Fr Allan McDonald, Miss Goodrich Freer and Hebridean Folklore', published in the second volume of *Scottish Studies* in 1958 (pp. 175–88) giving examples of her indebtedness. The article had previously been rejected by several Scottish editors on the grounds that it was 'too contentious'; but the impression the exposure made at the time appears to have been minimal.[1] The present book is to a considerable extent a confirmation, and extension, of the thesis presented in that article.

The revelation that Miss Freer had been an extensive copyist of Fr Allan McDonald's folklore notebooks suggested the possibility that her literary remains, if they could be found, might well contain material copied verbatim from the two missing notebooks. But enquiries made of probable societies and institutions, including the Folklore Society, the Society for Psychical Research, and the Royal Geographical Society, of all of which Miss Freer had been a prominent member, drew a complete blank. The literary remains of Miss Freer, who had been a very well-known writer on folklore and psychical research between 1889 and 1902, authoress of many books, articles, and lectures and the person in charge of the Society for Psychical Research's enquiry into second sight in the Highlands financed by Lord Bute, in 1894, have vanished utterly. Her widowed husband, the late Rev. H. H. Spoer, then living in New York, told me by letter in 1950, the year before he died, that he and his wife had not been able to keep many papers during their travels in the Near East between 1905 and 1923, and that his wife had always returned any material she borrowed to its owners. Nevertheless, it still seems very odd that no literary remains of such a well-known writer have been preserved anywhere. The possible reason for this will be suggested in due course.

It was obvious, when Fr Allan McDonald's collection was traced, that it contained much material of interest that ought to be published. Priority was given to his collection of rare words and

[1] For example, an offprint of the article was sent to the editor of *Folklore*, but as far as I know the article was never mentioned in that journal.

expressions from the Gaelic dialect of South Uist and Eriskay, as this provided a very useful key to difficulties in Gaelic folk-tales and folk-songs collected in South Uist and Barra, and also in Fr Allan McDonald's own Gaelic poems. After arrangements to publish this work in Edinburgh had fallen through, it was accepted by the Dublin Institute for Advanced Studies and published in Dublin in 1958, under the title of *Gaelic Words from South Uist*. The next material chosen from Fr Allan McDonald's collection for publication was his own poems,[1] and after that, the ghost and second sight stories, which are published in this book (in the great majority of cases for the first time) and which it seemed particularly desirable should be published under circumstances which gave Fr Allan McDonald the fullest possible credit for their collection.

When preparing these for publication, it seemed to me that there would be little point in adding even such an interesting collection to the already large amount of material of this kind from the Scottish Highlands that is in print without saying something about the circumstances under which the collection had been made. This involved investigating, and writing the first complete account of, the Society for Psychical Research's enquiry into second sight in the Highlands and Islands of Scotland, which was financed by the third Marquess of Bute, begun in 1892, taken charge of by Miss Freer in the autumn of 1894, and after two interim reports from her in December 1894 and December 1895, mysteriously faded out of sight and came to nothing. In writing this account I have been most fortunate in being allowed access to the unpublished correspondence dealing with the enquiry in the third Marquess of Bute's papers.

My enquiries about Miss Freer herself and about what had happened to her literary remains came to a dead-end in 1953. It was not until 1964, when I happened to read Mr Trevor H. Hall's *The Strange Case of Edmund Gurney* (the story of the first secretary of the Society for Psychical Research, who committed suicide in mysterious circumstances in 1888, the year Miss Freer became an Associate of the Society), that I felt that here there was a person, a trained and critical investigator who was thoroughly well informed about the background to psychical research in England in the 1880s and 1890s, and about the strange personalities involved in it, who might know something about Miss Freer or could suggest how more might be discovered about her, and perhaps help to do so. I wrote to Mr Hall, and a large correspondence soon developed on the subject, turning eventually into a full and happy collaboration, in which Mr Hall

[1] Published in 1965, with some translations by the writer, under the title *Bàrdachd Mhgr. Ailein*, T. & A. Constable, Edinburgh.

undertook the writing of the account of Miss Freer's carefully concealed origin and of her peculiar and controversial career in psychical research between 1889, the date of her first address to the S.P.R., and 1901, when she left England for Jerusalem. This, too, is published here for the first time. I have been exceptionally fortunate in having Mr Hall as a collaborator, as it would have been quite impossible to write an adequate account of Miss Freer based on her career in folklore alone: it is significant that the remarks in three of Alexander Carmichael's letters to Fr Allan McDonald written between August 1901 and March 1902, without which evidence it would never have been known that Miss Freer had somehow come to grief and been discredited in the summer of 1901, relate to her career in psychical research, though they occur in letters of which the subject is Gaelic folklore.

I have added an appendix to this book giving illustrations of Miss Freer's often verbatim use of Fr Allan McDonald's folklore notebooks in her lectures and articles published under her name additional to the examples given in my article in *Scottish Studies* in 1958. I regret that Fr Allan McDonald's reputation as a folklorist can only be fully substantiated and restored by attacking Miss Freer's, but the very fulsome obituary accorded to her in Volume XLI of *Folklore*, coupled with the ignoring of Fr Allan McDonald's death in 1905 by that journal, makes this inevitable. Also, it must be remembered that this is not the only time that the knowledge and experience of a scholar on the spot in the Hebrides have been exploited for personal advantage by an outsider. What Fr Allan McDonald thought of it all was recorded by Miss Amy Murray in her *Father Allan's Island*,[1] when she said that although disclaiming personal ambition in the matter, 'he had been little pleased with the working up one pair of hands, at least, had given them' (*i.e.* his folklore notes). There can be no doubt whatever about whose working-up Fr Allan McDonald had in mind.

An unsatisfactory circumstance is the complete absence of any of Fr Allan McDonald's letters from the papers of his friends who one would have expected most carefully to preserve them. I refer particularly to the papers of Alexander and Ella Carmichael and of the Rev. Dr George Henderson, who was lecturer in Celtic at Glasgow University from 1906 to 1912. It is difficult to avoid the suspicion that at some time the letters from Fr Allan McDonald to such persons may have been abstracted from their papers. As regards the missing Notebooks III and IV, some of their contents are revealed from the lectures of Miss Freer and the later publications

[1] New York, 1920, p. 203.

of George Henderson, who must have had access to these notebooks during the years of his lectureship at Glasgow. This may be a clue to their present whereabouts, although they have not been so far discovered in Henderson's papers.

As for the stories of second sight collected by Fr Allan McDonald, these are given here to a great extent in the chronological order in which he recorded them. This illustrates the development of Fr Allan's contacts with his informants, and of his interest in them and in their stories. This is particularly true of the stories in his MS. notebook called 'Strange Things', after which this book is named, where one story often leads into another, and where any attempt to classify the stories under different headings would mean wrenching them from their psychological context and breaking the continuity of the record. Readers can easily find the various stories of any particular type by consulting the Motif-Index.

Owing to the large extent to which the names of persons, and places, and dates, were recorded by Fr Allan McDonald, his collection is of particular interest. In this respect it is to be hoped that by now the reproduction of the names of the persons concerned, so often concealed in the publication of such material, will not cause any offence to anyone. Mr Trevor Hall and I have every faith in the integrity of Fr Allan McDonald and of his informants, and completely open minds on the nature of their evidence, even if we sometimes think that certain apparently paranormal happenings may have natural causes, or that it is sometimes easy to find later events that may fit apparent omens. In this connection the Gaelic proverb *Cuir math air a' mhanadh, 's theagamh gun tig math as*, 'put a good interpretation on the omen, and perhaps good will come of it', may be remembered. If only a few of the anecdotes recorded by Fr Allan McDonald are first-hand, a number of others may be called good second-hand. To call such things hallucinations, as C. G. Jung has pointed out, is simply to beg the question.[1] 'Whether you believe in a demon of the air or in a factor in the unconscious that plays diabolical tricks on you is all one to me. The fact that man's imagined unity is menaced by alien powers remains the same in either case.'[2] The scholar has not yet arisen who can apply Jung's ideas on the archetypes of the collective unconscious to Highland second sight or to Gaelic folklore: it would be well worth making the attempt.

The Highlander's own view remains that of the Church: these things do exist, even though they may be due to delusion or (in the

[1] *Memories, Dreams, Reflections*, London, 1963, p. 219.

[2] C. G. Jung, *The Archetypes and the Collective Unconscious*, Collected Works, vol. IX, p. i; London, 1959, p. 105.

big cities) to trickery; but it is a very bad thing to go out of one's way to experience them. The gift of second sight is regarded as an affliction. The reader can form his own opinion of the nature of the evidence provided for it in the stories published here.

I must conclude by expressing my gratitude to the many persons whom I have had to plague with questions in the course of this enquiry, which goes back to 1950, and particularly to those who had known Miss Freer or Fr Allan McDonald, or both, personally, and who have given me their impressions of them. For impressions of Miss Freer (none particularly favourable), I am obliged to the late Lord Colum Crichton Stuart and his sister the late Lady Margaret MacRae (children of the third Marquess of Bute), the late Rev. Dr Kenneth MacLeod, the late Major Finlay S. MacKenzie, formerly proprietor of the Lochboisdale Hotel in South Uist, and to Mrs Mary Ann Campbell, née MacKinnon, of Balevulin in the Island of Tiree. All of these persons have given me written impressions of Miss Freer, and the first four gave me verbal ones as well.[1]

For memories of Fr Allan McDonald, I am indebted to Dr Kenneth MacLeod and Major F. S. MacKenzie, and also very much to the late Rt Rev. Monsignor Canon MacMaster, Fort William, who most kindly put at my disposal both Fr Allan McDonald's diary, and Miss Freer's surviving letters to Fr Allan, and who wrote for me his memories of the life of a student at Blairs and at the Scots College at Valladolid, where both he and Fr Allan McDonald were trained for the priesthood; to the late Mr Ewen MacLennan, who kept the shop on Eriskay betwen 1890 and 1900, and to the late Miss Penelope Campbell, who was housekeeper to Fr Allan McDonald at the time of his death in 1905, and who was the 'grey-eyed girl' of Amy Murray's *Father Allan's Island*. I am also indebted to the Rev. Fr Angus McQueen, the present parish priest of Eriskay, and to his predecessors there, Canon John MacCormick and Fr Colin

[1] Dr Kenneth MacLeod wrote to me on 3rd October 1950. 'You mention Miss Goodrich Freer. I only met her once, and did not like her very much. She seemed too pretentious for my taste. I must admit, however, that in the course of a long conversation, she mentioned more than once that her work for the Psychical Research Society [presumably on the Second Sight Enquiry] would have been a complete failure without Fr Allan's cooperation.'

Mrs Campbell, who remembers Miss Freer giving a lecture on botany to the pupils of Heylipol school in Tiree, was one of the prize-winners in an essay competition organized by Miss Freer there in the winter of 1896–7. The results were given in a letter from Miss Freer, published in the *Oban Times* of 10th July 1897. The subject of the competition was ghost stories, a thing which shocked Mrs Campbell's parents, and which is certainly revealing as regards Miss Freer's methods.

MacPherson, and to Dr A. MacLean and John MacInnes, M.B.E., Daliburgh, for help with my enquiries in Eriskay and South Uist.

I am indebted to Sir John Best-Shaw, Bt., for an account of his recollection of the visit of Miss Freer to the house of his father, then the Rev. C. J. M. Shaw,[1] at Swanley in the summer of 1901, and of what his mother later told him about Miss Freer many years afterwards; and to the Hon. Mrs Stirling of Keir, who was a friend of Lady Margaret MacRae's, for her recollection of the visit of her brother-in-law, Lord Encombe, to Ballechin House during Miss Freer's ghost-hunt there in the spring of 1897,[2] and to the late Professor W. A. F. Balfour-Browne for an account of his memories of his visit to Ballechin with his uncle, Sir James Crichton-Browne, and James Callendar Ross for the weekend of 7–9th May 1897. He survived until 1967. I must also express my great gratitude to the present Marquess of Bute for very kindly allowing Mr Trevor Hall and myself to see copies of the third Marquess of Bute's papers relating to psychical research, and to quote from them freely here, and to Miss Catherine Armet for going to great trouble in finding these letters and copying them for us. Without this material, our book would have been altogether the poorer and less interesting. I am also obliged to Mrs E. G. Nicholson for very kindly letting me have photocopies of the only two surviving letters from the third Marquess of Bute in the papers of the late F. W. H. Myers, who at the time in question was secretary of the Society for Psychical Research. I am also much indebted to Mr P. J. W. Kilpatrick for putting at my disposal contemporary photographs taken in South Uist and Eriskay by his grandfather, Walter Blaikie.

I must also express my gratitude to the following persons who have at various times assisted me in my researches connected with this book: in America, Professor Joseph Baylen of Georgia State College, Professor Charles R. Sanders of Duke University, North Carolina, Dr Karl Kup of the New York Public Library, Mr A. P. O'Hara, Miss Gladys Chamberlain, Miss Dorothy Kurtz, and Miss Eleanor Bell; in Great Britain, besides the persons already

[1] The Rev. C. J. M. Shaw was the 'Mr Q' of *The Alleged Haunting of B—— House*, which was first published by Lord Bute and Miss Freer in London in 1899, see p. 176.

[2] Lord Encombe's name is not to be found in *The Alleged Haunting of B—— House*, even under disguise, but F. W. H. Myers suggested him as a suitable visitor in a letter written to Lord Bute on 8th January 1897, saying, 'I have hopes of Sir John Stirling Maxwell and Lord Encombe, probably known to you and at any rate unexceptionable!' Mrs Stirling tells me that Encombe was completely sceptical about the phenomena at Ballechin.

mentioned, to the Librarians of the London Library, the Mitchell Library in Glasgow, the County Library of Dumfries, the London *Times*, the *Scotsman*, and the *Glasgow Herald*; to the Keepers of Printed Books at the Bodleian and the National Library of Scotland; to the Keepers of MSS. at Glasgow and Edinburgh Universities Library; to the Editors of the *Oban Times* and the Inverness *Courier*; to Mr Hugh Barron, secretary of the Gaelic Society of Inverness; to Major Calum Iain MacLeod, Antigonish, and to Miss E. M. Bryant, Mrs Ena Matheson, Mrs Margaret Lyons, Miss Sheila J. Lockett, and the late Miss S. R. Dowling.

I also have to express my gratitude to the various owners of Fr Allan McDonald's literary remains for permission to publish material from them. In respect of this material, one third of the royalties from this book are being given to Fr Allan McDonald's former parishes of Daliburgh and Eriskay.

Isle of Canna *John L. Campbell*

The assistance I have received in the solution of specific problems has been gratefully acknowledged in the text. I wish especially to thank, however, Dr Eric J. Dingwall, Mr Frank Beckwith, Mr George H. Brook, and Mr Herbert E. Pratt for their continuous advice and help during the whole period of the research upon which my contribution to this book is based.

Thorner, Yorkshire *Trevor H. Hall*
January, 1967

I

The S.P.R. Enquiry into Second Sight in the Scottish Highlands

B

1

FR ALLAN McDONALD AND THE ORAL TRADITION OF SOUTH UIST

ON SATURDAY, 19th July 1884, a tall, energetic, ascetic young Highland priest, Fr Allan McDonald, landed at Lochboisdale in the island of South Uist in the Outer Hebrides to take charge of the parish of Daliburgh or Dalibrog, including the island of Eriskay, to which he had been appointed by the Rt Rev. Angus Macdonald, Bishop of Argyll and the Isles in the recently restored Roman Catholic hierarchy of Scotland. In these remote and windswept islands Fr Allan, as he is still always referred to in the Highlands and Islands, was to spend the rest of his all too short life, and to win an ecclesiastical and literary reputation which has steadily grown since his death on Eriskay in October 1905.[1] No other priest of the diocese of Argyll and the Isles has had so much influence on non-Catholics as Fr Allan.

A number of accounts of South Uist have been written by various authors at various times, and varying impressions have been recorded. In 1873 Robert Buchanan wrote:

. . . *a few mountains, endless stretches of peat bogs and small lagoons, a long tract of shell-sand hillocks, all environed, eaten into, and perpetually shapen afresh by the never-resting sea . . . Like all such children of the sea they* [i.e. *the Outer Hebrides*] *flit from mood to mood, sometimes terrible, sometimes miserable, peaceful occasionally, but never highly gay. Half the year round they are misted over by the moist oceanic rains—in winter the sea strews them anew with seaweeds,*

[1] An account of Fr Allan McDonald's writings, and a list of the authors who have mentioned him or have used material from his folklore collection, is given by the writer in his *Fr Allan McDonald of Eriskay: Priest, Poet, and Folklorist*, second edition, Edinburgh, 1956. Since that time Fr Allan McDonald's dictionary, *Gaelic Words from South Uist*, Dublin, 1958, and his Gaelic poems, with some translations, *Bàrdachd Mhgr Ailein*, Edinburgh, 1965, have been published, as well as the part of his diary that was written in Gaelic, which appeared in *Gairm*.

shells, and drift timber—and for a few days in the year they bask in a glassy sea and behold the midsummer sun.[1]

Frederic Rea, who was appointed headmaster of Garrynamonie school in Fr Allan McDonald's parish in 1890, described the scene from his house in the following words:

What a view! To the south the main road wound down to the sea less than two miles away, its dancing blue stretching to a number of smaller islands, and beyond to larger ones rising into mountains. My eye

[1] *The Hebrid Isles*, London, 1883, p. 193.

ranged round from these to the west, and there lay the Atlantic, its mighty swell surging in towards us from as far as the eyes could reach. The awe I felt at this beautiful scene is with me even now as I write . . . Here and there, dotted about, could be seen the thatched stone cottages of crofters who eked out a living from their crofts, or small farms, aided by their earnings in the fishing season.[1]

The Outer Hebrides, whose very existence appears to be sometimes resented in administrative circles in Edinburgh and London, have at times been both extravagantly sentimentalized and immoderately and viciously denigrated. They are not the kind of place it is easy to be indifferent about; they grow on people, often reversing an originally unduly unfavourable first impression of desolation and backwardness.

Fr Allan McDonald arrived in South Uist with a burning enthusiasm to instruct the young, reform the old, raise the devotional standards, and improve the material conditions of his 2,300 parishioners, of whom three-fifths spoke no other language but Gaelic, and like other perfectionists in similar circumstances his immediate impressions were not entirely good ones, but he benefited greatly from the guidance and advice of a good and wise Bishop, who was himself a member of an old Highland family, the Macdonalds of Glenaladale, in dealing with the difficulties which he found.

For various reasons the Diocese of Argyll and the Isles was (and still is) the poorest of all the restored Roman Catholic dioceses in Scotland. In the 1880s and 1890s it had but one wealthy benefactor, the third Marquess of Bute, an erudite convert of whom more will be heard in these pages; his main interest lay in the performance of the full sung services of the Church in the Cathedral at Oban, a temporary structure the construction of which was financed by the Marquess on condition that this was done.[2] A far more pressing need was the improvement of church buildings and priests' houses and the provision of Gaelic devotional literature in the outlying districts of the diocese. The Gaelic-speaking Catholics in the Highlands then had a prayer-book, *Iùl a' Chrìosdaidh*, of which a new edition was published in 1885, and a not too felicitous translation of the New Testament, published in 1875; but there was still a great need for a Gaelic missal, hymnal, and for a catechism in popular language, especially in the Catholic islands of the Outer Hebrides, Benbecula, South Uist, Eriskay, and Barra.

[1] *A School in South Uist*, Routledge & Kegan Paul, London, 1964, p. 12.

[2] See Rev. Roderick Macdonald, 'The "Tin Cathedral" at Oban, 1886–1934' *Innes Review*, vol. XV, pp. 47–55, 1964.

As a boy in Fort William, then a small town on the shore of Loch Linnhe, Fr Allan had been brought up with only a smattering of Gaelic; but like some others in this position, he had conceived a great love for, and interest in the language, which he studied in his spare time when a student at Blairs and later at the Scots College at Valladolid in Spain, where the Highland students kept a holograph Gaelic magazine, to which he contributed, apparently under different pseudonyms. He was able to improve his Gaelic during two years spent under Bishop Angus Macdonald at Oban; in Uist a knowledge of Gaelic was a prime necessity for him, and in Uist he was able to improve his knowledge of Gaelic further by sessions with some of the island's traditional storytellers and other tradition bearers, from whom he was soon noting down old hymns and prayers which he felt might be put to use in future devotional publications. Eventually Fr Allan McDonald became as much at home in the rich Gaelic dialect of South Uist as if he had been born there; the Gaelic part of his diary, and his best poems, are written in that dialect. In 1889 he published a small Gaelic hymnal, including the verse paraphrase of the Mass, which is still sung in Hebridean churches; in 1893 a greatly enlarged edition of this work was printed.[1] But unfortunately Bishop Angus Macdonald was transferred from Oban to Edinburgh in 1892 and his successor gave no encouragement to this side of Fr Allan McDonald's activities, and his capabilities in this direction were not further utilized; though he left in manuscript a Gaelic translation of the Compline service.

In any case, Fr Allan McDonald's ordinary parochial work inevitably would have brought him into contact with the great but sometimes ignorantly despised Gaelic oral tradition of South Uist, of which he was intelligent enough quickly to see the immense interest, and in the winter of 1887–8 he started to note down material relating to traditional local history and folklore, encouraged by Fr Alexander Campbell (1820–93), a Uist-born priest then living in retirement on the island.[2]

Communities where an oral tradition predominates are so much out of the experience of the modern Western world that it is extremely difficult for anyone without first-hand knowledge to imagine

[1] See J. L. Campbell, 'The Sources of the Gaelic Hymnal', *Innes Review*, vol. VII, pp. 101–11, 1956.

[2] The Catholicism of South Uist, which from lack of priests had reached a low ebb by the first quarter of the seventeenth century, was rekindled by the devoted Irish Franciscan missionaries, Frs Cornelius Ward and Patrick Hegarty. See Cathaldus Giblin O.F.M., *The Irish Franciscan Mission to Scotland, 1619–1646*, Dublin, 1964. There are some interesting references to second sight in the reports.

how a language can be cultivated without being written to any extent, or what an oral literature is like, or how it is propagated and added to from generation to generation. The consciousness of the Gaelic mind may be described as possessing historical continuity and religious sense; it may be said to exist in a vertical plane. The consciousness of the modern Western world, on the other hand, may be said to exist in a horizontal plane, possessing breadth and extent, dominated by scientific materialism and a concern with purely contemporary happenings. There is a profound difference between the two mental attitudes, which represent the different spirits of different ages, and are very much in conflict.[1]

If I may quote from what I have already written on this subject:

It is always extraordinarily difficult to convey the feeling and atmosphere of a community where oral tradition and the religious sense are still very much alive to people who have only known the atmosphere of the modern ephemeral, rapidly changing world of industrial civilization. On the one hand there is a community of independent personalities whose memories of men and events are often amazingly long (in the Gaelic-speaking Outer Hebrides they go back to Viking times a thousand years ago), and where there is an ever-present sense of the reality and existence of the other world of spiritual and psychic experience; on the other hand there is a standardized world where people live in a mental jumble of newspaper headlines and B.B.C. news bulletins, forgetting yesterday's as they read or hear today's, worrying themselves constantly about far-away events which they cannot possibly control, where memories are so short that men often do not know the names of their grandparents, and where the only real world seems to be the everyday material one.[2]

It must be understood that the recital of an oral tradition, like the Gaelic tradition of South Uist, is not, except on comparatively rare occasions, a matter of public performance; it is something much more informal, belonging to the fireside, and integrated into the people's way of life. Many of the traditional songs were sung to accompany various forms of labour, such as rocking the cradle, milking the cows, waulking the home-made cloth, or rowing the boats; many of the stories related to happenings in Uist and the Highlands during the past 250 years; others belonged to the great stock of international folk-tales and anecdotes. Ballads told of the deeds of the Fingalians (the heroic company of Fionn Mac Cumhail) and of the

[1] See C. G. Jung, *Basic Postulates of Analytical Psychology*, Collected Works, vol. VIII, London, 1960, pp. 338–57.

[2] Introduction to *Tales of Barra Told by the Coddy*, Edinburgh, 1959, pp. 24–5.

Norsemen. Allusions and expressions from all these, with many pithy sayings and proverbs, constantly coloured the speech of the people. Brightly coloured, concrete and epigrammatic, Gaelic speech and Gaelic oral tradition are the reverse of the gloomy mysticism of the Celtic Twilight, practitioners of which were already beginning to find their way to South Uist and Eriskay before Fr Allan McDonald's death in October 1905; they could have become a burden had he lived much longer, for his personality attracted them, whereas he had no use for their ideas.

The background to the Gaelic oral tradition in South Uist had been the old Catholic and Jacobite family of proprietors, the MacDonalds of Clanranald, who owned the island until 1838. Connected with the ancient Lords of the Isles, they had fought for the royalist cause under Montrose, and for the Stewarts in 1715 and 1745, and had sheltered and encouraged the Irish Franciscan and Vincentian missionaries to the Hebrides in the seventeenth century. Moreover, they had been the patrons of the MacVurichs of Stadhlaigearraidh, the famous family of hereditary bards that kept up the practice of classical Gaelic court poetry well into the eighteenth century, longer than any other such family in Ireland or Scotland. They have been described as 'probably the longest-lived literary dynasty in Europe';[1] in 1781 J. F. Campbell of Islay, the famous folk-tale collector, was told by an old man in Uist that the MacVurichs had seven cart-loads of Gaelic MSS.[2]

It is difficult to make the extent of the Gaelic oral tradition of an island like South Uist credible to persons who have had no contact with such a thing. It is not a question of a few people knowing a few songs or stories by heart and reciting them occasionally at some party or concert: it is a case of numbers of people knowing forty or fifty traditional songs, or scores of stories, and not the same songs or stories, but often different ones, so that the total runs into thousands of different songs and many hundreds of different stories, not counting as different various versions of the same song or story. As the great Swedish folklorist C. W. von Sydow wrote:

Among the richest and most outstanding folk-traditions in Europe is that of the Gaels in Ireland and Scotland; and it is one of the most important objects of European folk-tale research to pay as much attention to it as possible. Its rich vitality is to be attributed partly to the

[1] Professor Derick Thomson, 'The MacMhuirich Bardic Family', *Transactions of the Gaelic Society of Inverness*, vol. XLIII, pp. 276–304.

[2] J. F. Campbell MSS., vol. XVIII, p. 131. I owe this information to Dr Alan Bruford.

fact that the people have had their present dwelling-places so long, partly that there used to be professional narrators, there being nothing analogous to them in Teutonic territory.[1]

This being the case, as one might expect, Scotland being the kind of country that it was, nothing whatever was done academically or officially in the way of paying any attention to this rich folk-tradition until under the provocation of a visit by members of the Irish Folklore Commission in 1947, the School of Scottish Studies was founded at Edinburgh University in 1951. Before that date the Gaelic oral tradition of Scotland had been condemned at various times by Scottish Calvinists, who saw it as distracting the people from the study of the Word of God; by Lowlanders and Englishmen, who saw it as encouraging the martial clan spirit of the Highlanders; by Whigs, who saw it as an aspect of Jacobitism; and by utilitarians of all three types, who saw it as something that tended to perpetuate the existence of the Gaelic language and the attachment of the Highlanders to their country, thus making them less suitable material for industrialization and emigration. More recently, a strong interest in it was considered to be a sign of narrow Scottish nationalism or even Sinn Féinism. Consequently it was left to amateurs like J. F. Campbell of Islay, Alexander Carmichael, and Fr Allan McDonald and his other friends to attempt to preserve what they could of this magnificent tradition in their own time and at their own expense.

[1] *Selected Papers on Folklore*, Copenhagen, 1948, p. 59. The reader is also referred to the paper on 'The Gaelic Oral Tradition', by Professor Derick Thomson, in *Proceedings of the Scottish Anthropological and Folklore Society*, vol. I, Edinburgh, 1954.

2

THE HIGHLAND FOLKLORISTS

ALTHOUGH THE outside world had taken some interest in Scottish Highland folklore, in its aspects of superstition, second sight, and local tradition, ever since the last quarter of the seventeenth century,[1] an interest that had been heightened by the controversy over the alleged translations by James MacPherson of the poems of Ossian in the second half of the eighteenth,[2] no systematic attempt to collect the oral Gaelic literature of the Highlands was made until the late J. F. Campbell of Islay organized the collection of folk-tales with the help of collaborators in various parts of the Highlands in the 1850s; part of this great collection was published under the title of *West Highland Tales* in 1860, in four volumes, and two more volumes have been published from Campbell's MSS. in the present century, but much more remains unpublished. J. F. Campbell, however, died in 1883, before Fr Allan McDonald went to South Uist. Campbell's contemporary, who became a personal friend of Fr Allan's, was Alexander Carmichael (1832–1912), by profession an exciseman; his great interest was the old hymns and incantations of the Hebrides, part of his collection of which, after various vicissitudes in the 1890s, were published by T. & A. Constable through the good offices of Walter Blaikie, another friend of Fr Allan's, in 1900 (two volumes: three more have appeared since Carmichael's death). Carmichael was the doyen of the little coterie of folklorists to which Fr Allan belonged; his interests in Highland traditions extended far beyond the material he published (which earned him a LL.D. from Edinburgh University and a Civil List Pension), and he left a very large collection in MS., both of his own and of his correspondents. This, with J. F. Campbell's collection, could have been the basis of

[1] For the titles of some publications connected with these aspects of Highland folklore see the chapter here on second sight.

[2] James MacPherson's first publication was *Fragments of Ancient Poetry Collected in the Highlands.* It appeared in 1760. The famous literary controversy that followed had one fortunate effect: it led to a systematic search for old Gaelic MSS. in the Highlands and to the preservation of what by then remained of them. See Professor Derick Thomson, *The Gaelic Sources of MacPherson's Ossian*, Edinburgh, 1952.

a national Scottish Gaelic folklore archive. Other members of this group were William MacKenzie, secretary of the Crofters' Commission, who read an important paper on 'Gaelic Incantations and Charms in the Hebrides' to the Gaelic Society of Inverness on 23rd March 1892 (published in Volume XVIII of its *Transactions*, pp. 97–182: some of the material in it provided by Fr Allan McDonald); the Rev. Dr George Henderson (1865–1912), later to be Lecturer in Celtic at Glasgow University, who was indebted to Fr Allan for material used in several of his publications, such as *Leabhar nan Gleann* (1898), *The Norse Influence on Celtic Scotland* (1910), and *Survivals in Belief among the Celts* (1911); and Alexander Carmichael's daughter Ella, who became the co-editor of the *Celtic Review*, published from 1904–16, and, as is well known, was the second wife of the late Professor W. J. Watson, and mother of the late Professor James Carmichael Watson, who was killed in action in 1942.

Two other writers who were indebted to Fr Allan McDonald may be mentioned here: these were Frederic Breton, who used some of Fr Allan's folklore to provide local colour for his *Heroine in Homespun*, a rather absurd two-volume novel of which the scene was South Uist, in 1893; in this Fr Allan is portrayed as 'Father MacCrimmon'; and Amy Murray, a gifted American folk-musician who visited Eriskay in September 1905, made a collection of folk-tunes there with his help, and later wrote a book about him called *Father Allan's Island*. Of a third person, Miss Ada Goodrich Freer, who first visited South Uist in 1895, won Fr Allan's confidence and personal regard to the extent that much of his collection was put at her disposal to her great personal advantage, nothing more will be said here, as much of the rest of this book is devoted to her.

Of the circle described, Fr Allan McDonald's greatest personal friend was his contemporary, George Henderson. A shy, likeable, unpretentious man, Henderson, who was a Fraser on his mother's side, was the last professional Celtic scholar in Scotland to study the Gaelic oral tradition in the field for many years. He spent some time in South Uist in the late autumn and early winter of 1892, not long after Fr Allan McDonald had had a breakdown in health, the serious effects of which were probably not immediately apparent. The two men took to each other immediately and remained fast friends for the rest of Fr Allan McDonald's life. Two letters, hitherto unpublished, which Henderson wrote to Alexander Carmichael about this visit to Uist and what he found there, are of great interest.

The Presbytery,
Dalibrog, S. Uist.
Wednesday, 11 p.m.

My dear Carmichael,

It is not possible for me to say when I should come away from here. Though I should stay months here busy as a House of Commons' Clerk I should find my hands fully occupied. Father Macdonald I like exceedingly; we are glad good friends and sit and jaunt about as suits us. I could not desire a more congenial companion; and so far as Celtic matters are concerned his taste is high and refined, while his knowledge is wide and accurate. I like the mind and the man and everybody who knows him are [sic] *bound to do the same.*

All the people here are of a literary cast; and roughly speaking, perhaps around Dalibrog itself one could summon as much talent as one would find at the Oban Mòd.[1] *I take an interest in contemporary literature and have already about a score of meritorious pieces that illustrate the life here as well as Gaelic idiom and phonetic variety. I have besides 3 long sgialachds* [*folk-tales*]*; while a long one is ready for tomorrow night and a Feinn-Duan*[2] *for Saturday—entirely new. I wish I could stay here till spring and then I would have something to speak of. We are going to Eriska on Monday; and you can easily imagine how I try to do. I am anxious my efforts in this direction may not be entirely frustrated as almost all I know of the islanders redounds to their credit. Fancy persons such as these forced to starvation point by donkeys and brutes of hireling superiors—inferior in all save sham and uppishness to the scoundrels who have no more sympathy than the stones, if one allows their actions to speak for them!*

The journey across was quiet and pleasant. Oban has some characters knocking about in it now who are quite disreputable—a mixty-maxty of mischief, slyness and rascality; but come to Uist and you see men and women who are such in more than in name, whose voices have a ring of excellence in them, and whatever faults they may have these can largely be attributed to circumstances over which they have no control.

The big farms need to be broken up and nobody needs speak of emigration of any sort till what land we have is divided among the people. One demands now-a-days of land-lords what special mark they have brought with them on their bodies or their minds to indicate to demonstration an indubitable claim to starve others and despise the image of the one Former whose shape they profess to bear?

But the chief duty is to put matter on record to point to as the marks

[1] The annual musical and literary festival of the Highland Association, An Comunn Gaidhealach.

[2] *i.e.* a Fingalian ballad.

of genuine civilisation and so uphold the claim of the downtrodden and the wretched to draw attention to a race so long suffering and hit blows & hand on a sword which will shed no blood 'ach nach fag riamh fuigheall beuma'[1]*—like Fionn's.*

But I must go to bed rejoicing in the knowledge I live among a literary people—and hope to waken with Fionn and all the other excellent Xtns from that date till now. . . .

Geo Henderson

Father Campbell does not sleep well on account of asthma; Fr Allan is well.

The visit lasted until Christmas 1892. On 26th December Henderson wrote to Carmichael from Oban, the mainland port at which he had landed on his return from Uist, as follows:

I am here at the Commercial Hotel, ready to start by [*the*] Chevalier[2] *tomorrow for Inverness: and I look to be back to the Capital*[3] *a week after New Year's Day. It would be to my taste to have stayed longer in the Isles; the more so as I have not seen so many places and persons as I should have wished. The finest things in Uist, I convince myself I have to see still; but being desirous to pass the New Year Season with familiar faces and dearest friends I came here today; all my time in S. Uist was occupied and I shall be glad if the results may in a small measure anticipate your expectations. The details I cannot enter on, but here are the lists.*

Henderson goes on to give the names of fifteen long folk-tales and nine long ballads which he had taken down. The stories included versions of such famous tales as *Fear na Habaid* ('The Man of the Habit')[4] and *Sgialachd a' Chait Chaothaich* ('The Tale of the Wild Cat'). Of the nine ballads, eight were Ossianic and one, *Am Bròn Binn* ('The Sweet Sorrow'), Arthurian.[5] In three cases two versions of the same ballad were collected, and in two others the prose introduction.[6]

[1] 'Which leaves no remnant of a blow', *i.e.* cuts right through anything it strikes, like Fionn's famous sword called 'Mac a' Luin'. See *Stories from South Uist*, London, 1961, p. 16.

[2] The steamer then sailing between Oban and Inverness by the Caledonian Canal.

[3] *i.e.* Edinburgh.

[4] A version of this story was recited by the late Duncan MacDonald, Peninerine, South Uist, at the international folklore conference held at Stornoway in October 1953.

[5] See *Miscellany presented to Kuno Meyer*, Halle, 1912, p. 18.

[6] See Appendix on p. 324 for a list of titles. Fortunately, this collection of stories and ballads has been preserved, though it has never been published.

Henderson continued:

Fr Allan is to do the Feinn Saga for me;[1] *he will transcribe the Gaelic version of 'The Raising of the Feinne' so that the incidents may be kept in sequence in order that the unity of treatment may throw light on the origin of the Feinn Mythos. I could get at least ten of this class yet. There is a first class reciter in Eriska[y], from whom no one ever took down a word,*[2] *and Iain Taillear*[3] *at Dalibrog from whom nobody ever took down a word—a man very rich in incident and variety; Smith's sons*[4] *come in after these. I should have included* Clanna Lir [*'The Children of Lear'*]*—the offset to Deirdre*[5] *or Clann Uisneach—the correspondent to the second tragic story of Ireland. Though only a fragment I am glad to have saved it to show its existence among us.*

Between MSS. given me by Fr Allan of songs by Dr Macdonnell who was at Plockton, and various Catholic pieces of merit, I have a number of songs by living poets, by [the] late Fr Allan MacLean, who died in Nova Scotia, of Alastair Mór, Lochaber, of an Oran Lua-[dha]idh, *in touching stanzas which are said to have been added by Flora Macdonald,*[6]*—all in all some 80 songs, besides others I had formerly, etc., etc.*

There is material to be got still which may serve to illustrate the life of language (phonetics); manners; customs; art; myth and legend; fable; history—indeed with a little more time, with encouragement from minds like your own I would not say to anyone to lose heart, but Work and let the Labour speak.[7]

It would be a grand thing to form a work on the scale of the West Highland Tales,[8] *say* Scottish Celtic Romances, *with notes and com-*

[1] See *Celtic Review*, vol. II, pp. 263, 351, and vol. III, p. 56, and J. L. Campbell, *Stories from South Uist*, pp. 209–14.

[2] Probably Alexander Johnston, source of the 'Feinn Saga' or rather, of this version of it, is meant.

[3] Iain mac an Tàilleir (John MacKinnon). Fr Allan McDonald later took down stories from him.

[4] Patrick Smith, South Boisdale, who had been a source for Carmichael. One of Henderson's sources was his son John.

[5] Carmichael published a version of the Deirdre story, from Barra, in 1905.

[6] Probably the waulking song beginning *Tha Seathan a nochd 'na mharbhan* ('Sean is tonight a corpse'), which one of Fr Allan McDonald's informants ascribed to Flora MacDonald: but the song has every appearance of being much older, see p. 232.

[7] There still is such material to be got in Uist, but it can hardly be said that adequate steps are being taken to collect it.

[8] The four-volume collection of Highland folk-tales made by the late J. F. Campbell of Islay, published at Edinburgh in 1860–2.

parative grammar of Romance;[1] *taking account of the development of the Feinn Saga; with some Ròlaisdean* [*'Yarns'*] *and Fables; second sight and the general result of the Celtic spirit poring on the mysteries of God. . . .*

It is a pity that Henderson was never again able to make a protracted visit to South Uist. The material he collected there in 1892 remains largely unpublished. Henderson was later to take the degree of Doctor of Philosophy at Vienna, and B.Litt. at Oxford, but whether Germanic erudition benefited his approach to Scottish Gaelic studies is a moot question. He was friendly with the Carmichaels, who hoped that he would marry Ella; but this hope was to be disappointed.

As for Fr Allan McDonald, the ultimate result of his breakdown in health in 1892 was that his Bishop separated Eriskay from Daliburgh and transferred him there in January or February 1894.[2] On Eriskay he had less parochial work to do and more time to write; but he was very isolated, and his health remained poor for the rest of his life. But he came to love the rocky island, and his most famous poem, often called *Eilean na h-Òige*, 'The Isle of Youth', was written in praise of it, and as a description of the life there.[3] When he went to Eriskay in 1894, he had filled two quarto notebooks with folklore of all kinds, and a third with traditional hymns and translations of hymns; by the time of his death in 1905 he had added to this four further quarto notebooks of folklore, another of waulking songs, another containing a collection of rare words and phrases from local Gaelic songs, stories, and colloquial speech,[4] and finally, another containing a number of second sight stories, and, among other things, a collection of flower names, of the place-names of the island of Mingulay, and some of his best poems. The whole of this collection disappeared from view within a short time after his death, and the whereabouts of any remained unknown until shortly before the last war, when the writer discovered the last named notebook on the shelves of a friend's library. Later, after the war, other volumes were traced with the help of other friends, but

[1] Presumably what Henderson means by this is a Motif-Index, such as was prepared for folk-tales generally by Aarne and Stith Thompson later.

[2] The date is often given as 1893, presumably on the authority of his obituary in the *Catholic Directory* of1906, but the parochial register of Daliburgh proves the date was early in 1894. A clock presented to him by his Daliburgh parishioners to mark the occasion still exists.

[3] A full translation of this poem can be seen in *Bàrdachd Mhgr Ailein*, Edinburgh, 1965, pp. 122–30.

[4] See p. xi.

Notebooks III and IV remain missing, though some of the contents are known.

It is with the stories about second sight in the notebook last described, which Fr Allan titled 'Strange Things', and with similar stories in his first two notebooks, that we have to deal here: for the first time the tale of how 'Strange Things' came to be collected will be told, and for the first time the stories themselves in it will be printed.

3

SECOND SIGHT IN THE SCOTTISH HIGHLANDS

'THE MOST known and the most general superstition of the Gaels,' wrote the Swiss scientist Necker de Saussure,[1] 'is that which they call *Taishitaraugh* [*Taibhseadaireachd*] and the English, *Second Sight*. It is the faculty of discerning objects invisible to other persons. Those who were gifted with it were called Seers, and in Gaelic *Taishatrim* [*Taibhseadairean*].' De Saussure, who was sceptical about the faculty himself, goes on to quote Martin Martin's description of the seers and their visions in his book on the Western Islands of Scotland, which was first published in 1703. De Saussure also mentions, as did Thomas Pennant before him, what is one of the most famous cases of second sight—Lord President Forbes foretelling at the time of the battle of Prestonpans that the Jacobite rising of 1745 would end at Culloden.[2]

The great Oxford Celtic scholar, Edward Lhuyd, who visited Argyllshire in the autumn of 1699, describes some of the usual prognostications as follows:

Men with the second sight see a man with a light like the light of the glow-worm, or with fish [*scales*] *over his hair and his clothes, if he is to be drowned; bloody, if he is to be wounded; in his shroud if he is to die in his bed; with his sweetheart on his right hand if he is to marry* [*her*], *but on his left hand if he is not to win his sweetheart.*

In Mishnish in Mull there was a man who was said to see a man carrying a creel-ful of cheese from his house, although he was eight

[1] L. A. Necker de Saussure, *A Voyage to the Hebrides*, London, 1822, pp. 92–3. The original French reads 'La plus connue et la plus générale des superstitions des Gaëls est celle qu'ils nomment *Taishitaraugh*, et les Anglais *Second Sight*, seconde vue. C'est la faculté de discerner les objets invisibles. Ceux qui en étoient doués s'appelloient *Seers* en Gaëlic *Taishatrin* qui signifie *voyants*.' (*Voyage en Écosse et aux Iles Hébrides*, vol. III, Geneva, 1821, p. 240.)

[2] *Ibid*., p. 245; and Thomas Pennant, *A Tour in Scotland*, vol. I, fifth edition, London, 1790, p. 200.

miles from home; and since he recognised him, he went back [*and*] *caught hold of him.*[1]

Martin Martin himself defined second sight as follows:

The Second-Sight *is a singular Faculty of Seeing an otherwise invisible Object, without any previous Means us'd by the Person that sees it for that end; the Vision makes such a lively impression upon the Seers, that they neither see nor think of any thing else, except the Vision, as long as it continues: and then they appear pensive or jovial, according to the Object which was represented to them.*[2]

He goes on to discuss the faculty, giving about thirty cases, mostly from the Isle of Skye, and an account of the significance of the signs perceived by the seers, such as was given by Lhuyd. As the cases described by Martin are very similar to those recorded by Fr Allan McDonald and printed here, there is no need to dwell on them. Martin (who otherwise frequently reprobated Hebridean 'superstitions', particularly if they offended his religious convictions) had a complete belief in second sight, and goes on to answer the objections of sceptics to the existence of such a faculty. These he gives as three. First, that the seers are 'visionary and melancholy People' (or, as we would say, persons liable to hallucinations). This Martin denies, saying that 'it is observ'd among 'em, that a Man drunk never sees the Second Sight; and he that is a Visionary, would discover himself in other things as well as in that; and such as see it, are not judged to be Visionaries by any of their Friends or Acquaintance'.

The second objection was, 'There is none among the Learned able to oblige the World with a satisfying account of those Visions, therefore it is not to be believed.' To this Martin replied tartly that 'If every thing for which the Learned are not able to give a satisfying account be condemn'd as impossible, we may find many other things generally believed, that must be rejected as false by this Rule,'[3] words which remind one of the way in which Jung wrote of the 'shallow positivism' with which Freud rejected the possibility of psychic phenomena.[4]

[1] J. L. Campbell and Derick Thomson, *Edward Lhuyd in the Scottish Highlands*, Oxford, 1963, pp. 54–5. The passage in question was translated from the Welsh by Professor Derick Thomson. Lhuyd got this information from the Rev. John Beaton, last learned member of the famous family that had been hereditary physicians in the Isles for many generations.

[2] Martin Martin, *A Description of the Western Islands of Scotland*, second edition, London, 1716, p. 300.

[3] *Ibid.*, p. 308.

[4] C. G. Jung, *Memories, Dreams, Reflections*, Routledge & Kegan Paul, London, 1963, p. 152.

The third objection Martin recorded was that 'The Seers are Imposters, and the people who believe them are credulous, and easily imposed upon.' To this he replied that 'The Seers are generally illiterate, and well meaning People, and altogether devoid of design, nor could I ever learn that any of them made the least gain by it, neither is it reputable among 'em to have that Faculty: because the People of the Isles are not so credulous as to believe implicitly, before the thing foretold is accomplished; but when it actually comes to pass afterwards, it is not in their power to deny it, without offering violence to their Senses and Reason.'[1] Martin went on to point out that the faculty was not confined to one corner of the Hebrides, nor even to the isles themselves, but was also known in other places, such as Wales, the Isle of Man, and Holland.

In fact, a great deal of interest has been taken in Highland second sight, and many cases have been described, ever since the second half of the seventeenth century, when men of learning, such as Edward Lhuyd, John Aubrey, Robert Wodrow, and Robert Boyle, began to perceive that the Gaelic-speaking Highlands of Scotland were a remarkably interesting repository of archaic customs and beliefs, and began to gather information about them. The information given to them about second sight included the following points: even by 1700 it was said that it was not so common as it used to be; it was 'a trouble to most of them who are subject to it, and they would be rid of it [at] any rate if they could';[2] it was not a gift acquired in consequence of any pact with the Evil One, being of its nature spontaneous (this was a matter of some importance in the seventeenth century, when trials for witchcraft still occurred in Scotland: had it been held that the seers owed their powers to any such pacts, they could have been in serious trouble). Whether the gift of second sight was hereditary or not is something on which the authorities were not in agreement.[3]

[1] *A Description of the Western Islands of Scotland*, p. 309.

[2] Lord Tarbat, letter to the Hon. Robert Boyle, p. 92. Printed as an Appendix to Andrew Lang's edition of Robert Kirk's *Secret Commonwealth*, Stirling, 1933, third edition. The letter is titled 'A Succint Accompt of the Predictions made by Seers whereof himself was Ear and Eye-witness'.

[3] The literature on Highland second sight is extensive. Besides the works already referred to here, there may be mentioned: John Aubrey's *Miscellanies*, London, 1721; 'Theophilus Insulanus', 'Treatises on the Second Sight' (*Miscellanea Scotica*, Glasgow, 1819, vol. III); J. G. Campbell, *Superstitions of the Scottish Highlands*, Glasgow, 1900 (mostly material from the island of Tiree); *Witchcraft and Second Sight*, Glasgow, 1902; Rev. John Frazer, 'Deuteroscopia, or a Brief Discourse, concerning the Second Sight' (first printed in 1820 in *A Collection of Rare and Curious Tracts on Witchcraft and the Second Sight*; Mrs Grant, *Essays on the Superstitions of the Highlanders of Scotland*, London,

Very little had been added to the debate between Martin Martin and the sceptics of over two hundred and fifty years ago, although many more alleged cases of second sight have been recorded since his time. It was therefore to be expected that sooner or later the phenomenon of Highland second sight and the seers themselves would receive attention from the investigators of supposedly paranormal phenomena in which interest had been steadily increasing in England in the second half of the nineteenth century; and so it came to pass.

1811. In fact, the phenomenon is mentioned in most of the books that have been written about the Scottish Highlands. The Irish Franciscan missionaries to the Hebrides mention several instances of it in their reports to Rome from the Isles between 1624 and 1640.

4

THE S.P.R.'s ENQUIRY INTO SECOND SIGHT IN THE SCOTTISH HIGHLANDS

ON THE 18th of August 1894 the following report appeared in the columns of the *Oban Times*, the leading local paper of the Western Highlands and Islands of Scotland:

'SECOND SIGHT' IN THE HIGHLANDS

We understand that several members of the Society for Psychical Research are at present on a tour of the West Highlands and Islands collecting information from the natives in regard to that peculiar faculty said to be possessed by many people, especially in the Highlands, and popularly known as 'second sight', as well as kindred subjects. While in Oban, two of the lady members interviewed a number of people reputed to have some experience in the matter, and were particularly interested in the details of the famous 'Evil Eye' case, which came before Sheriff Substitute MacLachlan about twelve months ago—a full report of which duly appeared in the Oban Times. *Among the party was the lady editor of* Borderland *and the Rev. Mr Dewar, North Bute, Secretary for the Society in Scotland. It is reported that the tour has been inaugurated at the instance of the Marquis of Bute, who is one of the Vice-Presidents of the Society.*

We shall hear a great deal more about the apparently self-styled 'lady editor of *Borderland*', a person whose name was Ada Goodrich Freer and who in fact was only assistant editor to W. T. Stead on this occult quarterly, which was published from 1893 to 1897.[1] But first of all it is necessary to explain what the Society for Psychical Research was, and how its members came to be involved in seeking for instances of 'second sight' in the Scottish Highlands.

The Society for Psychical Research had been founded by a number of persons, mostly Cambridge intellectuals, in 1882, 'for the purpose of making an organized and systematic attempt to

[1] Not from 1896 to 1899, as was later incorrectly stated in Miss Freer's *Who's Who* entries.

investigate various sorts of debateable phenomena which are *prima facie* inexplicable on any generally recognized hypothesis'. The work which it proposed to undertake was described as:

> *1. An examination of the nature and extent of any influence which may be exerted by one mind upon another, otherwise than through the recognized sensory channels.*
> *2. The study of hypnotism and mesmerism; and an inquiry into the alleged phenomena of clairvoyance.*
> *3. An inquiry as to the existence of relations, hitherto unrecognized by science, between living organisms and magnetic and electric forces, and also between living and inanimate bodies.*
> *4. A careful investigation of any reports, resting on strong testimony, of apparitions occurring at the moment of death or otherwise, and of disturbances in houses reputed to be haunted.*
> *5. An inquiry into various alleged physical phenomena commonly called 'spiritualistic'.*
> *6. The collection and collation of existing materials bearing on the history of these subjects.*[1]

After the death, in mysterious circumstances, of Edmund Gurney, the first secretary of the Society, in 1888,[2] the secretaryship was undertaken jointly by two leading members of the Society, F. W. H. Myers and Frank Podmore, both of whose names are prominent in the contemporary literature of psychical research.

In 1889 John, third Marquess of Bute (1847–1900), a wealthy, erudite Catholic convert of widely ranging intellectual interests, became a member of the Society for Psychical Research (henceforward to be referred to as the S.P.R.). In 1890 he was made one of the Vice-Presidents of the Society, of which the President was then Arthur J. Balfour, M.P., F.R.S., and other leading members were Lord Rayleigh, F.R.S., Professor W. F. Barratt, F.R.S.E., the Earl of Crawford and Balcarres, K.T., F.R.S., William Crookes, F.R.S., Walter Leaf, Litt.D., Professor Oliver J. Lodge, F.R.S., F. W. H. Myers, and Professor and Mrs Henry Sidgwick.

In the same year as the Marquess of Bute had become a member the S.P.R. had begun a large scale 'Census of Hallucinations'—the term 'hallucinations' having been defined by Edmund Gurney as 'precepts which lack, but which can only by distinct reflection be recognized as lacking, the objective basis which they suggest'.[3]

[1] Quoted from the 'Objects of the Society' as given in the S.P.R. *Journal* for 1893.

[2] See Trevor Hall, *The Strange Case of Edmund Gurney*, London, 1964.

[3] Quoted by F. W. H. Myers at a General Meeting of the S.P.R. held on 27th

Considering the literature that was already extant on the subject, going back to the seventeenth century and including the cases noted by, or reported to, such writers as John Aubrey, Martin Martin, Edward Lhuyd, and the Rev. John Frazer, Episcopalian minister of Tiree, it was natural that the S.P.R. should want to include an enquiry into Highland second sight in its 'census of hallucinations'. As recently as 1885 Lord Archibald Campbell, of the ducal house of Argyll, had published in his *Records of Argyll* several striking instances of second sight from the island of Tiree, which since the last quarter of the seventeenth century had been owned by his family.

Surviving unpublished correspondence shows that F. W. H. Myers paid a visit to Rothesay on the Isle of Bute, where the Marquess of Bute had a seat named Mount Stuart, in February 1892, during which he had met the Rev. Peter Dewar, who was minister of North Bute from the time of his ordination in April 1881 until his death in 1927. Dewar, who was the last minister to preach in Gaelic in Bute, was locally a well-known and affectionately regarded personality.

Myers was obviously pleased with him. The idea of the Second Sight Enquiry in the Highlands, and the proposal that Dewar should act as the secretary of it, appears to have matured in the autumn of 1892, for Myers wrote to Lord Bute on 28th November of that year as follows:

I enclose letter from Dewar, and letters of his friends. I am struck by their almost complete unanimity in encouraging the proposed quest. All that Dewar suggests seems to me reasonable. From the point of view of the S.P.R. the only objection seems to be the expense; which would probably be about £50 per annum (including Dewar's postage) for 2 or 3 years. The S.P.R. only keeps its head above water by frequent gifts in various ways from Sidgwick and a few others, and could not at present guarantee Dewar.

Dewar's letter was as follows:

The Manse
North Bute
Rothesay
25th November 1892

Dear Mr Myers,

I have, within the last ten days, not only made the proposed second sight inquiry, the subject of patient reflection but I have also consulted

---

April 1894. C. G. Jung has pointed out in his book on *Flying Saucers* that the word 'hallucination' bears the stamp of a pathological concept, and that a more suitable term is 'vision'. (Footnote to p. 1.)

with friends in the Church[1] *who are intimately acquainted with the Highlands and who have all strong pronounced Celtic sympathies. These friends are Professor MacKinnon of the Celtic Chair in the University of Edinburgh, Doctor Donald Macleod, Editor of Good Works,*[2] *The Very Rev. Dr Cameron Lees of St Giles Cathedral, Edinburgh; the Rev. Dr K. MacKenzie minister of Kingussie; the Rev. Dr Masson, minister of Gaelic Church, Edinburgh; Rev. A. Gordon, minister of St Andrews Church, Edinbro', Rev. W. MacPherson, minister of South Church, Greenock, and Sir Charles Dalrymple Bart.*[3]

Although their replies written in the intimacies of private friendship were only meant to meet my own eye, still they may be of interest to you as indicating the various views taken by prominent men of the subject of the proposed Enquiry and of some of the difficulties to be faced in grappling with it, and accordingly I enclose their letters for your perusal.

And now for my own views on the subject. Having a difficult parish to work (without any curate to help me) owing to its wide extent and the scattered character of its rural population; having to minister in two churches[4] *about two miles distant, to two separate congregations every Sunday, and to attend to all the other manifold duties of a parish minister, I greatly fear that I could not, were I to take charge of the Enquiry, devote more than one day in the week to correspondence in connection with it. Perhaps you would consider such an arrangement as this unsatisfactory. Of course after a twelve months I might have more leisure, but the pressure of work on a parish minister in the Church of Scotland is nowadays severe. If my eldest brother, the minister of Applecross, the Rev. Duncan Dewar, were asked by the Society*[5] *to associate himself with me in connection with the Enquiry and if he consented to do so there might be a subdivision of labour and the Enquiry would, in all likelihood, be more satisfactory. He has more leisure on his hands than I have and having been, for the last 28 years, successively minister of three Highland parishes, he is fuller of Celtic Lore than I can profess to be.*

I anticipate there will be difficulty in getting any considerable number

[1] *i.e.* the Church of Scotland.

[2] The well-known Church of Scotland magazine.

[3] M.P. for Buteshire 1868–85, and after 1886 for Ipswich. Born Charles Dalrymple Fergusson, he had changed his name on succeeding to the estates of his great grandfather, Sir David Dalrymple, Bt.

[4] St Colmoc's in Rothesay and St Ninian's in Port Bannatyne. The latter had been built through Dewar's own efforts. The memorial stone was laid by Sir Charles Dalrymple, Bt., on 24th July 1886.

[5] *i.e.* the S.P.R.

of ministers and landowners in the Highlands to answer the questions that may be addressed to them in the printed Schedule. I speak from experience. The majority, I fear, will regard the Enquiry in anything but a serious light and act accordingly. Of course I have not the slightest idea as to the extent to which the supposed faculty and a belief in its existence prevails. Some of the favourite ministers of the last century were credited with it. The Highlander is naturally taciturn and reticent. He won't unbend unless he happens to meet a congenial soul, who can enter sympathetically into his moods, and converse with him in his mother tongue.[1]

To pursue an Enquiry of this kind, with any hope of success, one would require, I imagine, not only to issue Schedules of Enquiry and conduct correspondence, but also to become something of a peripatetic and interview informants in their own haunts and homes. I would be quite willing to devote six weeks annually to peregrinating the Highlands and personally interviewing informants provided that my travelling expenses were paid and that I were allowed a sum of £3 to provide good pulpit supply during every Sunday I was absent from my own pulpit in connection with the work of the Enquiry. All the rest would be a labour of love. I leave myself entirely in the hands of Lord Bute, Professor Sidgwick and yourself. If, after the explanation given you still wish me to take charge of the Enquiry, I shall be happy to do so as I feel really interested in the subject and am only sorry that I have not more time to devote to it.

I presume the circular letter sent out with the Schedules would be printed and that I could occasionally employ a clerk to address them. With the circular letter and the Schedule it would be advisable to enclose to ministers and landowners a copy of 'Objects' of the Society. I feel deeply sensible of the compliment that has been paid me in asking me to take charge of the proposed second sight Enquiry.

Peter Dewar

These letters appear to have impressed Lord Bute, for the next communication from Myers, one acknowledging a donation of £150 from Lord Bute, was written on 5th December 1892:

I beg to thank you most gratefully and sincerely, on the part of the S.P.R., for the extremely munificent gift of £150 just received, for the purpose of conducting an enquiry into second sight and cognate phenomena in Scotland. I will do my best to see that the money is carefully

[1] Dewar was the last minister of North Bute to preach in Gaelic: on 9th November 1895 the Kirk Session petitioned the Presbytery of Dunoon to remove the parish from the 'Gaelic essential' list. Miss Freer, who later superseded Dewar in charge of the Enquiry, could not speak Gaelic.

spent, and that neither Dewar nor I are pauperized *by the magnitude of the gift! I propose to place the money to the account of the S.P.R., at the [illegible] Bank, and to ask our Treasurer to invest £100 of it in Consols as it is impossible that more than £50 will be wanted for the first year, and the rest may as well roll up £2 3/4 more. This will also indicate to Mr Dewar that the sum is to be carefully and slowly expended.*

I will send him your instructions, which appear to be exactly right; and if any matter of importance as to either policy or expenditure arises I will refer him to you. I am at present away from home; but after talking to the Sidgwicks I will write again as to the form of the circular, etc.

Six days later Myers wrote to Lord Bute that he and Professor and Mrs Sidgwick had 'concocted a draft circular' which was sent for Lord Bute's approval, with a suggestion that Bute should join the Council and the Literary Committee of the S.P.R. (This was declined.) Lord Bute was asked to show the circular to Dewar and return it with any suggestions before the next meeting of this Committee, which was to be on 19th December. Not surprisingly the circular did not reach Lord Bute in time to be returned to London by this date. On 17th December Myers wrote that the Literary Committee of the S.P.R. would pass its resolutions on the 19th provisionally on Bute's later approval.

Myers went on to say that what he dreaded was 'that the second sight evidence may be found too largely amongst *fishermen* and other uneducated persons', thus revealing the prevailing notion that the only really reliable witnesses to paranormal phenomena were professional men of sound character and sufficient means to be immune to the temptation of committing practical jokes or faking phenomena for personal profit. Applied to Highland second sight, which has always locally been regarded in the nature of a spontaneous personal affliction and out of which it was hardly possible to make either personal profit or social advancement, this criterion was only applicable to the *interpretation* of allegedly paranormal occurrences,[1] not to their *observation*, for which the unlettered Gaelic-speaking Highlander had as much capacity as anyone, and, if the tradition of second sight was to be relied on, more opportunities than anyone.

Myers' letter of 17th December 1892 continued with a list of prominent persons who might be friendly to the Enquiry—Sir

[1] As when a late well-known Gaelic storyteller told the writer a story of witchcraft which was obviously the impression he had been given by a demonstration of conjuring.

Herbert Maxwell, Sir John Stirling-Maxwell, Lady Archibald Campbell (who will be referred to again), Princess Louise, Duchess of Argyll, and her son the Marquess of Lorne, and Lady Frances Balfour. The Duke of Argyll himself (George Douglas Campbell, 1823–1900) is described as 'entirely hostile', and Lord Kelvin as 'as hostile as so good and gentle and great a man can be'. 'It will be interesting to see how other notable Scotchmen comport themselves.' 'I trust,' wrote Myers six days later, 'that in a few months we shall have got hold,—amid doubtless many disappointments—of some curious things.'

5

THE S.P.R.'s SECOND SIGHT CIRCULAR

THE CIRCULAR and Schedule of Questions on Highland second sight were printed in January of 1893. On 12th January Myers wrote to Lord Bute thanking him for his criticism of the proof of the Circular. On the 27th of the same month Dewar wrote to Bute enclosing the proof of the Schedule, and saying he had asked Dr Walter Leaf of the S.P.R. to push on with the printing of both Circulars and Schedules as rapidly as possible, 'so that I may start the Enquiry as early as possible next week'. Dewar also thanked Bute for his hospitality during Dewar's visit to Falkland, which had given him an opportunity to acquaint himself better with the special points the enquiry on second sight should consider. On 1st February 1893 Myers wrote to Lord Bute that two thousand copies of both the Circular and the Schedule were being printed and would be sent to Dewar within a few days. At this point it is suitable that both these documents should be reproduced in full.

SOCIETY FOR PSYCHICAL RESEARCH CIRCULAR LETTER NO. VI

January 1893

Dear Sir,

At a meeting of the Literary Committee of the Society for Psychical Research, held on Monday, December 19th 1892, it was resolved that a Sub-Committee be constituted for the purpose of conducting an inquiry into Second-Sight in Scotland; and that this Sub-Committee consist of Messrs. W. Leaf, Litt.D., F. W. H. Myers, M.A., and the Rev. P. Dewar, M.A., Hon. Sec.

The Committee, constituted as above described, has now entered on its work; and it is plain that our success must depend upon our enlisting the aid of as many correspondents as possible, possessed of local knowledge and influence in the various districts of Scotland. I therefore venture to ask you whether, either from your own experience or from that of others, you can furnish us with any well-attested—if possible first-hand—*cases of second sight; that is to say, cases where knowledge of any fact in the past, present, or future appears to have been obtained in any way other than through the normal exercise of the ordinary senses. Your replies to the appended schedule of questions would be esteemed a great favour.*

We should be glad also to receive any negative *accounts that may be instructive in indicating causes of error in narratives of second sight, or showing how knowledge supposed to have been acquired through second-sight may have been reached by ordinary means.*

It is desired for this inquiry, as for all others conducted by the Society for Psychical Research, that it shall be carried on in an impartial and scientific spirit, in the hope, not of proving or disproving any given theory, but simply of discovering truth by the collection and analysis of facts which have never hitherto been treated in that thorough manner which their importance (if true) certainly demands in an age like our own. We trust that the Proceedings *already published by the S.P.R. may serve to show that, while the actual evidence for any statement will be strictly examined, no well-attested narrative will be set aside on account of any strange or unusual features which it may contain.*

All communications must be accompanied by true names and addresses, as a guarantee of good faith; but no names will be published without consent; and any injunctions as to the treatment of MSS. sent to us will be carefully attended to.

It is proposed that the evidence received, after due analysis, should be submitted to the Council of the S.P.R. in the form of Reports, and that such Reports (if judged of sufficient interest), should be published in the Proceedings *of the Society.*

All communications should be addressed to the Rev. P. Dewar, The Manse, North Bute, Rothesay, N.B.

I am, dear Sir
Faithfully yours
Peter Dewar

The Schedule to Circular Letter No. VI of the S.P.R. reads:

1. Is 'Second Sight' ~~*still*~~ *believed in by the people of your neighbourhood?*
2. Have you yourself seen or heard of any cases which appear to imply such a gift? If so, will you send me the facts?
3. Can you refer me to anyone who has had personal experience, and who would be disposed to make a statement to me on the subject?
4. Do you know of any persons who feel an interest, and would be disposed to help, in this enquiry?

The word 'still' in the first question was deleted in accordance with Lord Bute's wish.

Nearly two thousand copies of this Circular Letter and Schedule of Questions, together with the Objects of the S.P.R. already printed here, were promptly sent out by the industrious Mr Dewar, as described in the following letter to Lord Bute, written on 10th February 1893:

Yesterday I received from the London printers the circular letters etc. (copies of which I enclose) in connection with the Second Sight Enquiry, and I am now prosecuting with vigour the work of compiling lists of addresses, and of addressing envelopes etc. To save time I have engaged the Village Schoolmaster and the Inspector of Poor to assist me for several hours every day. We have already overtaken something like half of the work.

In accordance with your Lordship's suggestion in your letter to Myers of date December 1st 1892, we are sending letters etc to all the clergy (Established, Catholic etc.); doctors, Police (Inspectors and Sergeants); Sheriffs; Sheriff Substitutes; Fiscals; and Factors; to the leading Schoolmasters; and to the more likely of the Proprietors in the Counties in Caithness, Sutherland, Ross and Cromarty, Moray, Argyll, Inverness, Bute and Perth. If your Lordship has any further suggestion or instruction to give, I shall be very happy to attend to it. I extremely regret the Schedule was printed before Dr Leaf got my letter asking that the word 'still' in query No. 1 should be deleted. I am going over the Schedules carefully and drawing my pen through the word.

Myers must have expected far quicker results from this Circular than anyone familiar with the Scottish Highlands would, for on 16th March 1893 he wrote to Bute, 'I am sorry to hear from Dewar that he has not got much harvest yet; but I dare say people will need time to understand and answer.' Dewar himself wrote to Bute a day later:

Of 1900 second sight schedules issued, only 54 have as yet been returned, duly filled up. To the question is Second Sight believed [*in*] *in their neighbourhood 26 return an affirmative and 28 a negative answer. But even those who reply affirmatively have not yet furnished me with any well-attested* first-hand *case. Several have given me the names and addresses of those who are reputed to be Seers. In every case I have communicated with these—but as yet have had no reply. Mr William Mackenzie, Secretary of the Crofter Commission, has promised to collect information for me on Second Sight.*

One of Her Majesty's Assistant Inspectors of Schools (Mr D.

MacLeod, Inverness) tells me the belief in second sight is universally current in Sutherlandshire, and he has kindly promised to collect information in Sutherlandshire as well as in Skye and elsewhere. One of the Procurators Fiscal wrote me from Lochmaddy that he believes there could be got by judicious investigation a vast fund of information of a kind which might be considered trustworthy, but that for anyone to undertake to collection [sic] *of all the information bearing on the subject which could be had in his district would be to undertake a vast labour. I have had notes of some second hand cases sent me, but they are evidentially weak. . . .*

Following Dewar's letter of 17th March 1893, nothing more is heard on the subject of the Second Sight Enquiry until the end of the year, when Myers wrote to Bute:

I can't make out what Dewar is doing. No answer comes from him. I hope he is not ill. If he cannot get on with the quest, ought we to give you back what remains of your generous gift?

Talking of second sight, the Rev. A. Stewart, The Manse, Nether Lochaber, Onich, has been writing under the nom de plume *of 'Nether Lochaber', an interesting series of papers in the* Inverness Courier. *He testifies to a good deal of second sight still going on in his parts. . . .*

Apart from spending his vacation in 1893 travelling around the Highlands and Islands to interview persons to whom the S.P.R.'s Schedule of Questions had been sent—and funds were not then yet available for such an expedition—it is difficult to have seen what Dewar could have done besides wait for more replies to come in. On 26th January 1894 he acknowledged gratefully the gift of £50 from Bute, adding, 'I do hope the summer tour may be fruitful of genuine and good results and I shall not fail to inform your Lordship from time to time of the progress made in the Enquiry although I can see it will be beset with difficulties.' At the same time Walter Leaf wrote to Lord Bute from London on 27th January:

Mr Dewar has sent me the papers of which he speaks—they certainly give an idea of the peculiar difficulties of the enquiry. It is clear that by correspondence alone we shall get nothing worthy of the name of evidence, and that a personal visit to some of the likeliest places is the only hopeful method. From the replies to circulars, Tiree and Islay suggest themselves as hopeful regions.

Mr Dewar estimates the expense of a two months' journey for himself (including salary of a substitute) at about £80. I confess this seems a rather large sum, and it would be greatly increased if he took Mr

Carmichael with him.[1] *I am now writing to ask Mr Dewar if he knows the conditions on which the latter would come. But I think it is certain that we could not send both for two months with the balance of your fund. Perhaps* one *month, in Tiree, say, would be enough to enable us to judge if the enquiry is hopeful enough to justify further enquiry.*

The fact was that the original questionnaire had failed to elicit even second-hand evidence for instances of second sight in any number. It was decided to reprint the Schedule of Questions and send them to all addressees who had not answered, together with a personal letter from Lord Bute appealing for help in the Enquiry. This new Circular was referred to by Dewar in this same letter: 'perhaps your Lordship's proposed circular might be issued in the course of next month'. Much was hoped for from Lord Bute's personal influence. Myers had written to him on 16th May 1890 (the earliest letter extant): 'Your intercession with possible informants is certainly very potent! When not thus backed up a large percentage of psychical inquiries remain—I grieve to say—altogether unanswered.'

So the personal touch was introduced. On 13th February 1894 Dewar wrote to Lord Bute:

I am in receipt of your letter of the 10th inst. and of the newspaper cuttings for which I thank your Lordship. I am writing Dr Leaf to push on with the printing of your circular. Last year the schedule and circular were issued to 720 ministers, 260 Doctors of Medicine, 118 Factors, 66 Inspectors and Serjeants of Police, 22 Sheriffs, 51 Fiscals, 21 secretaries of Highland Clan Associations, 23 Scottish members of [*the*] *S.P.R., 22 Inspectors and Sub-Inspectors of Schools, 21 to members of the Celtic Class in Edinburgh University, 304 to Teachers, 31 to Newspaper Editors in the North, 350 to Landowners etc.*

The compiling of the addresses of all these was a matter of much difficulty, but I have preserved them in some large notebooks so that the new circular can be issued more expeditiously. I presume it is your Lordship's wish that all who have not replied to the first circular and schedule should get copies of them sent to them along with your Lordship's circular. In that case we should have to get reprinted afresh 2000 copies of [*the*] *original circular—2000 copies of* [*the*] *second sight schedule—2000 copies of your own circular. I presume it will be quite unnecessary to send to the people in the North a second time copies of*

[1] Alexander Carmichael, later well known as the collector and translator of *Carmina Gadelica*, Edinburgh, 1900. Dewar's letter of 13th February 1894 shows that Carmichael refused to go on this expedition.

'The Objects of the Society'[1] *and of 'The principal contents of the Proceedings of the Society'. I enclose copies of the original circular and schedule. If your Lordship thinks it desirable to have either the one or the other reprinted in another form—perhaps you will now kindly indicate your wish on the subject. I recollect that after they were unfortunately out of the printer's hands last year, you expressed the opinion that the circular might be issued in a more attractive form. I think also you should kindly indicate the form that your own circular should assume, and I am writing Dr Leaf to send you a 'proof' before finally printing off.*

I wrote Mr Andrew Lang thanking him for his letter to the 'Northern Chronicle' and asking him if he would have any objection to its being re-printed and issued along with our circulars, if such a course should be thought advisable. He told me that Dr Stewart of Nether Lochaber had sent him some second-sight tales and I begged him to send them to me if he thought them worth following up. . . . [*Alexander*] *Carmichael as you will see from the enclosed note is to give no help. This I regret as he knows the Western Highlanders so well. . . .*

So the S.P.R.'s Schedule of Questions on Highland second sight went out again, this time accompanied by Lord Bute's Circular, of which unfortunately no copy appears to have been preserved. On 17th March 1894 Dewar wrote to Bute a letter which contains the first reference to Fr Allan McDonald and his collection:

I thank your Lordship very much for your kind note of the 16th inst. just come to hand. I am delighted that Bishop Smith[2] *has so kindly evinced such an enlightened and scientific interest in our 2nd sight enquiry and I shall be grateful for any introduction he may be so good as to give me to the priests in the Western islands.*

I heard of the Revd. Alan Macdonald [sic] *rather more than a year ago through Mr William Mackenzie, secretary of the Crofter Commission, who is an enthusiastic collector of Celtic Folk-lore. I wrote Mr Macdonald to bespeak his kindly interest in the second sight inquiry, and received from him a cordial invitation to stay with him and prosecute inquiries in Dalibrog.*[3] *I have not yet accepted Mr Macdonald's invitation as I thought it would be better to wait to see what might be the result of your Lordship's circular in the way of indicating the most probable fruitful field for inquiry—but I mean to accept Mr*

[1] *i.e.* the S.P.R.

[2] The Bishop of the R.C. Diocese of Argyll and the Isles at the time.

[3] MS. Daliborg? By this date Fr Allan McDonald had been transferred to Eriskay.

Macdonald's invitation and to avail myself of all the assistance he may be disposed to give.

It is very good of your Lordship to indicate a way in which my visit to him might prove agreeable and useful. If he permits me, I shall have a look through his folk-lore MSS. I think there must be much in Celtic folklore that is worthy of permanent preservation; for the superstitions, the customs, the tales, the songs, the hymns, the proverbial sayings of a people so often throw such an interesting and instructive and unexpected light upon its history. They seem to be more alive to this fact in England than we are in Scotland, and I have been surprised recently to hear how many English counties have Societies for the Collection and Examination of traditional customs and institutions and beliefs—the results being annually or biennially published in [*the*] *form of Antiquarian and Folk-lore pamphlets. I think your Lordship would do a real service to the Sciences of Anthropology and Antiquarian research by encouraging the collection and publication of material relating to Celtic Folk-lore. Of course the material would need to be carefully sifted. The rapid spread of the English language in the Highlands is causing Celtic Folklore to die daily from our midst—and if material is not collected now, the opportunity will never recur. . . .*

A week later Leaf wrote to Lord Bute to thank him on behalf of the S.P.R. for a 'further generous gift'. On 13th March Dewar wrote Lord Bute that he was sending circulars to two hundred newspaper editors throughout Scotland, including the *Scotsman*, *Herald*, and *Leader*. He refers also to a circular of Andrew Lang's published in the *Glasgow Evening Times*. 'Your Lordship's circular has done good. Replies continue to come in—some of them of a very interesting character—one particularly so from the parish priest of Beauly[1]—and my hands are kept full with correspondence. Although the cases are remote, and the evidence for the majority of them cannot, I fear, be made first-class, the inquiry is assuming a more hopeful character.' Dewar also expressed the intention of calling on the Rev. Charles Macdonald, formerly parish priest of Moidart, then living in retirement at Helensburgh.

On 25th April 1894 Dewar wrote to Lord Bute that:

Something like 157 Second Sight Schedules have been returned, 115 of which return negative answers, and there are 42 replies which are more or less affirmative. They have brought to light several cases of the telepathic order, and I have put myself into communication with the alleged percipients with the view of obtaining first-hand accounts and corroborative evidence which alone can make them scientifically valuable.

[1] The Rev. Canon John Cameron, parish priest of Beauly from 1886 to 1912.

6

'MISS X' TAKES OVER

BY THE late spring of 1894 it was obvious that the S.P.R.'s Schedule of Questions and Lord Bute's personal appeal had accomplished as much as this method of approach could achieve. It was clearly going to be necessary to send somebody to the Highlands to investigate matters on the spot, and to interview persons who had replied to the Schedule and anyone else who was interested, particularly the alleged seers, if possible.

The obvious choice would have been Dewar himself. He had put an immense amount of work into compiling a list of suitable addressees, sending out the Schedule and Circulars, and studying the replies. He was a Gaelic-speaker with a first-hand knowledge of the Highlands, possessing friends among both Church of Scotland and Roman Catholic clergy. But he was also a Presbyterian minister, which might have a slightly inhibitory effect on certain possible informants; he had a parish to look after, and was in the process of becoming engaged to be married. The S.P.R. leaders clearly wanted to have someone in closer personal contact with London and themselves to go to report on the situation.

The precise circumstances under which Miss Ada Goodrich Freer, at this time publicly known as 'Miss X', was chosen for this mission are not known, but they are not difficult to guess. Miss Freer, the story of whose peculiar career in psychical research and in folklore is told elsewhere in this book by my collaborator and myself, was in 1894 a well-known member of the S.P.R., on friendly terms with the Society's leaders, particularly Myers and the Sidgwicks, and at the same time assistant editor to W. T. Stead on the occult quarterly *Borderland*. This, it may be said, was something in the nature of making the best of both worlds, as in the eyes of Stead the S.P.R. was unduly sceptical, particularly of spiritualist phenomena, whereas in the eyes of some of the S.P.R. leaders at least, *Borderland* was unduly credulous and sensational.

Miss Freer was later to report to the S.P.R. on her visits to the Highlands and Islands on this quest on 7th December 1894 and 6th December 1895: these reports also appear at considerably greater length in *Borderland* of January 1895 and 1896 respectively. Little credit is given to Dewar for his help in the Enquiry: one would only think he had acted as Lord Bute's amanuensis. In fact, he paved the way for Miss Freer's expeditions to the Isles, giving her invaluable introductions in Tiree and North and South Uist, including one to Fr Allan McDonald, as is clear from the following letters.

The first reference to Miss Freer (Miss X) in this correspondence occurs in a letter from Dewar to Lord Bute written on 22nd May 1894:

I think your Lordship is quite right in thinking that it would be highly improper for me to travel with Miss X. I shall write to the clergyman and Factor in Tiree to give her every assistance in their power. I have written Mr Myers suggesting that if Miss X has time, she might make inquiries in Mull, Jura, Islay, and Ballachulish, and that I would prosecute inquiries in Skye, Uist, and Lewis. . . .

A week later Dewar wrote to Lord Bute:

I enclose for your Lordship's perusal a letter from Miss A. Goodrich-Freer, which yesterday came to hand. Miss Freer seems to be a bright, energetic, sprightly young lady and enters with great heartiness into the projected tour to Tiree and the Western Isles. I am glad she is to be accompanied by a lady friend and I think we may expect good results to flow from her visit to the Highlands. I hope Mr Myers has impressed on her the harm that may be done if any of our cases should be published in Borderland.[1]

Should I make arrangements for her staying at the Hotel at Tiree or should I allow her to make whatever arrangements she may deem to be best?

Miss Freer's letter was as follows:

2 Westbourne Park Road
London
25th May 1894

Dear Mr Dewar,

I have this morning received with great interest and pleasure a letter which you have addressed to Mr Myers, and which he was so good as to forward to me.

I gather that you know the proposition which has been made to me, and that, therefore, I need not enter into particulars. Before definitely accepting the suggestion, I should be glad of some information from

[1] Which is just what Miss Freer did do, see pp. 60–66.

yourself, if you will be so good as to give it to me. I should like to know how far the enquiries have gone, and what point they have reached. Though I feel much flattered that my help should be asked, I should like to be able to feel that there is some prospect of my being of use—perhaps I should say of special use—in the matter. So far as the collection of evidence is concerned, there must be many persons quite as competent, if not more so, to deal with it as myself.

As to any special gifts or powers, as you probably know very well, they are far too capricious in their operation to be depended upon; and I am not sure that mine are not even more so than those of others. But I would be a most grateful and willing learner, *and would do my utmost to utilize, in this interest, any powers that I may already possess. I myself am of Scotch blood (Aberdeen), and belong to a family which has possessed the gift of second sight for many generations.*[1]

As to material details, it would be necessary, for the satisfaction of my friends, that I should have a companion, who would of course pay her own share of the expenses, and would be a great help to me in many ways. I am not at all exacting as to manner of life, so long as fresh eggs and milk, perhaps fish, are to be had: and my walking, averages sixteen miles a day. I delight in outdoor life, and can ride and swim. I am accustomed to the Yorkshire peasantry, and should probably be able to make friends with the people.

On the whole, however, I feel that you *are the most important factor of the enterprise—important for me, that is—as I should depend on you for information and advice. I have many friends in Scotland, who, I think, would supplement your kind offer to ensure every possible facility, including the Rev. H. MacPherson of Skye and the family of the Duke of Argyle.*

I have no acquaintance with Gaelic, but have a good ear, and pick up languages pretty easily. Among other details, I might mention that my friend and I are not only good sailors, but can ourselves manage a boat.

If I can only be assured that there is some prospect of my being really useful, I should accept the scheme with very great pleasure, as being congenial in every respect.

Thank you for all your kind promises of help, made through Mr Myers; and believe me

Very truly yours,
A. Goodrich-Freer (= X)

[1] This apparently quite unfounded claim to Scottish ancestry had been made by Miss Freer in her article on crystal-gazing nearly a year earlier in *Borderland* (I 127). The passage was omitted when the article was reprinted in 1899 in her *Essays in Psychical Research.*

It may surprise the reader to learn that the 'bright, sprightly, energetic young lady' who wrote this letter had just passed her thirty-seventh birthday. On 28th May she wrote to Lord Bute, who was then in London, requesting an interview. This was given on 30th May. It is clear that this was the first personal meeting between the two, although Bute himself had joined the S.P.R. in 1889. On 4th June Dewar wrote:

On reaching home from Edinburgh where I had been attending the meetings of the General Assembly, I found your kind note of the 30th ult. awaiting me. I am very pleased to hear that your Lordship has had an interview with Miss Goodrich-Freer on the subject of her projected tour to the Western Isles, and that you have formed a high opinion of her gifts and graces. I feel considerably relieved to hear that her association with Borderland *does not imply that she is an adherent of Steadism.*

As your Lordship seems to think it desirable, I shall pay a visit to Tiree on hearing from her that she has reached there. I think a Lady in her position by settling down quietly for a week or two in a promising district and making friends with the people, will obtain from them personal information as to cases of second sight which they might not care to communicate to a clergyman. I have succeeded in getting from one of the Tiree Seers a note of his personal experiences which are rather interesting. . . .

I have recently been informed that there are second sighted people on Lord Howard's[1] *estate in Moidart. I think that is a district Miss Goodrich-Freer might explore.*

On 9th July Miss Freer, whose interview with Lord Bute had been so satisfactory, wrote to Bute:

I am sending you a hasty line just before we start to say that personally, *I heartily endorse your Lordship's suggestion that any enforced service on the part of Mr Dewar would not—probably—be agreeable to me, nor profitable to the Society! I think I might quite suitably impress upon him that I regard* my *time as wholly at the disposal of the Soc: for Psy: Research, so long as I am existing, in great part, at the Society's expense—owing to your Lordship's liberality—and perhaps the hint may suggest to him that we are in the same boat and might be supposed to have the same standard of morality.*

Whatever the precise nature of the hint conveyed to Mr Dewar, it is clear from succeeding correspondence that Miss Freer, who at

[1] Lord Bute's father-in-law.

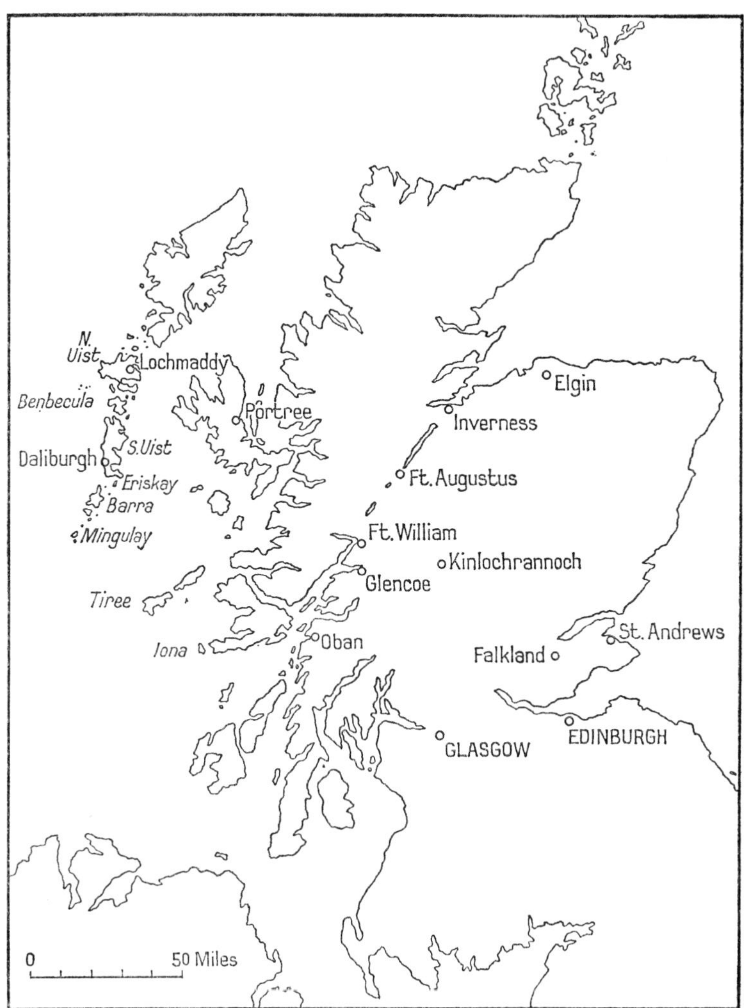

Places in Scotland visited by Ada Goodrich Freer in connection with the S.P.R. Second Sight Enquiry.

this time was in fact existing in great part at *Borderland*'s expense owing to W. T. Stead's liberality, and who owed her entire introduction to the Highlands and to the subject of Highland second sight to Dewar's indefatigable kindness, set herself steadfastly to undermine Dewar's position as secretary to the Enquiry. In her letters to

Lord Bute and to Myers, Miss Freer repeatedly asserts that she does not really need Dewar's assistance, that a Presbyterian minister is not really the right kind of person to be associated with an enquiry into second sight, and that Presbyterianism is irreconcilably opposed to the whole subject anyway.

Dewar, on the other hand, gave her devoted assistance. On 13th July he wrote to Lord Bute:

I had a deeply interesting interview with Miss Goodrich Freer at Glasgow on Wednesday,[1] *and handed her the most important communications on second sight that had reached me from different parts of the Highlands, so that she might peruse them as soon as she reached Tiree and get, as she expressed it, into the atmosphere of the subject. Miss Maund*[2] *and myself accompanied Miss Freer and Miss Moore*[3] *part of the way on her journey to Oban yesterday, and I got her letters of introduction to the different pursers on board the Highland fleet of steamers so she might receive every help and courtesy and kindness.*

Miss Freer thought she would be able to study my second sight papers by Wednesday of next week[4] *when I join her at Tiree, and then we shall set to work together. I can see she is pre-eminently qualified for the mission she has so heroically undertaken, as her powers of sympathy seem to me to be supernormal, and she will get into living sympathetic touch with the people in a way that no others can, and thus will be able to win their confidence. I propose that she should not confine herself exclusively to Tiree, but that she should visit Iona, the districts of Moidart and Arndmurchan* [sic] *and the Isle of Skye, which are all districts in which our enquiries may be so far as I can judge fruitfully prosecuted.*

Miss Freer thinks she can stay in the Highlands until the end of August—and I am most anxious she should stay as long as she conveniently can. Miss Maund is anxious that our enquiries should not suffer from my engagement with her, and I shall stay in the north until the middle of August and longer if necessary. I hope to be in Portree on the 25th, and with the Revd. A. Macdonald of Eriska on the 30th July. I have written Bishop Smith and if he happens to be in Oban on the 16th or 17th, I shall endeavour to have the pleasure of an interview with him. . . .

Miss Freer was not long in making her first private report to

[1] *i.e.* 11th July 1894. [2] Dewar's fiancée.

[3] Miss Constance Moore (1857–1945), daughter of Canon Daniel Moore, Prebendary of St Paul's, who was to be Miss Freer's companion on her travels for the next seven years.

[4] *i.e.* 18th July.

Lord Bute. On 18th July she wrote to him from Scarinish in Tiree on S.P.R. notepaper:

My dear Lord Marquis,

Now that we have been here five days I think you may like to know the prospects of our quest.

I feel quite satisfied that Tiree was the right place to come to, and I feel, on the whole, encouraged as to results. I have already got into touch with the few educated people on the Island, the Factor, Doctor, Minister,—the sister of a former minister,[1] *and best of all, with a very intelligent farmer who is nearer to the people than the others, and who happily is inclined to be very friendly and really enjoys exchanging stories.*

Some of these stories are delightful, just the kind I most wanted,—those, that is, that best fit in with my own ideas and experiences. What remains is to get all those at first hand, and this, I doubt not, is only a work of time,—for I have collected the names and addresses of six second sighted men on the island, and have made acquaintance with two of them.

We spend all our time walking and boating—chatting with every one we meet, and all receive us courteously. Our walking powers seem to astonish the natives and they have a way of expressing their good-will by offerings of 'Tups' of milk and of rides in carts and we never refuse anything. Two pounds of 'goodies' which I brought with me and which are not yet exhausted, have enlisted the sympathies of the children and I have a dog, of a kind unknown here, which affords an unfailing basis of conversation with the men. Most have some *English, and I have acquired a few phrases of Gaelic—just enough to express good feeling.*

We saw Mr Dewar in Glasgow where we stayed a night on purpose to confer with him. He was good enough to hand over all papers referring to our enquiry, so that I am now en rapport with all that has been done.

This is, on the whole, encouraging and I feel that there is plenty of work for me in various places; at the same time it will I think be best to do Tiree thoroughly, *rather than half a dozen places imperfectly, so I make no plans, but just go on from day to day, and so far, each day has contributed something.*

[1] The Church of Scotland minister on Tiree in the summer of 1894 was the Rev. Hector MacKinnon, M.A., a native of the parish. He had succeeded in 1892 the Rev. John Gregorson Campbell, the former minister referred to, who made a most important collection of Tiree folklore. Fortunately Miss Freer did not manage to get this collection into her hands. His sister was Mrs Wallace.

In 1883 the Factor (really Sub-Factor) of Tiree was Hugh Macdiarmid, and the doctor was Alexander Buchanan. These gave evidence to the Crofters' Commission that year, as did Lachlan MacPhail, farmer, Kilmoluag.

Our accommodation and food are very primitive, but that does not trouble me at all, as everything is clean: my companion sometimes gets hungry, as she is less used to country fare.

We saw Miss Maunde[1] *in Glasgow. She seems a very sensible person, Mr Dewar's senior, I should think, and very kind and motherly. She is very anxious not to interfere with his work, and wished him to come* with *us if I desired it, but I thought he would be more useful later, so he is to come tonight for a few days before following her south.*

So far as I *am concerned there is no need for him to stay. All these gentlemen on the island have offered their services as interpreters, and as the people know them they might serve the purpose even better than Mr Dewar, who however is most kind and obliging.*

The atmosphere, (*using the word in its psychic sense*) *of the island is, I should think, very conducive to second sight. So far I have had no experiences—the surroundings have been too new and exciting. I had a curious vision in Holyrood which interested me greatly though not of course of evidential value,—of the kind Mr Myers would call retro-cognitive.*

If anything of marked interest occurs I shall acquaint your Lordship further.

Very truly yours.
A. Goodrich-Freer

Aithne na bliadhna aig fear na h-aon oidhche![2] Miss Freer had been only five days in Tiree when she wrote this letter, and admits she knew no Gaelic, yet she is already completely *au fait*, and can dispense with the assistance of Mr Dewar. Her next letter, written after she had returned to the mainland after a three weeks visit to the island, heightens the impression. The reader may be struck by one thing in particular: that even though Miss Freer in writing privately to Lord Bute, who is financing her expedition, frequently says she is meeting men who have second sight, she very rarely identifies them in any way.

On 8th August Miss Freer wrote an expanded account of her Tiree visit to Lord Bute from the Loch Leven Hotel at Ballachulish:

My dear Lord Marquis,

I feel that you may have thought me somewhat remiss in not having replied earlier to your very kind letter. But indeed, absurd as it may

[1] Rev. Peter Dewar's fiancée.

[2] A Gaelic proverb which means literally 'the man of a single night has a year's knowledge', *i.e.* thinks he has. Applied to the tourist who thinks he knows everything about a place after a few days spent in it.

sound, I have found no time for more than postcards even to my people at home.

Our work has been intensely absorbing in every way—both of time and interest, and we seem never to have a leisure moment. Interviewing the Highlander is not a rapid process and one has to give up all thought of anything but the work in hand.

I wish I could in any degree convey to your Lordship the intensity of the interest of the work. The field of enquiry is a splendid one, far exceeding my utmost hopes:—I only wish it were in my power to come and settle among these Highlanders for some months at least. We get on capitally together, they have shown us everywhere the greatest courtesy and friendliness—the one thing lacking is time.

At all costs, if in any way possible, I intend to return to Tiree and to this neighbourhood—Lochaber, another year. I mean it in the most serious sense, when I say, that I feel my vocation is here, and that for the 'Sensitive' this country with its atmosphere, its traditions, and its practical teaching, is the place for study.

And now you will ask me what I have accomplished? I think it very likely that many, reading with an eye to mere quantity, the notes which I am preparing for your Lordship and which you will, I hope, receive in a day or two—would answer 'Little or nothing'. I find however that those on the spot, the many, many, who were very sceptical of our success, who knew the difficulties of our quest—are astonished at our results, at the confidence which the people have shown us,—at the number of experiences we have collected.

I myself am well content—for myself, full of hope and confidence for much that is in store for us,—but I am obliged to acknowledge that of evidence, as such, I have as yet got very little.

At the end of three weeks in Tiree, I found myself no nearer to the possibility of obtaining evidence of the S.P.R. standard, than on the first day; added experience only convinced me of the truth of the advice of those whose experience was life-long—that any attempt to obtain such would absolutely wreck our prospects, and I finally accepted the advice of several whose friendliness and wisdom I had tested—which was, to go away and return another year—when the people would receive me as an old friend—when I should be, so to speak, several points further on in their esteem than when I left.

I did all I could (or rather I should say we, for Miss Moore was extremely popular with them) to earn their friendship and I am proud to say we succeeded. Our lack of Gaelic stood but little in our way, for the Highlander is so courteous that someone was always ready to help us, and most of the fishermen (our best informants) have been sailors and can speak English.

I think I have filled most of the pipes in Tiree, for I always had one pocket full of 'baccy' and when a boat came in and the men sat down in the sun to dry their nets and mend their sails, we used to steal in among them, and get them to 'yarn' to us,—never forcing our subject, but sure, if we waited long enough, that the talk would work round to what we wanted. As a rule their politeness obliged them to treat—at the beginning—of topics adapted to our comprehension,—the Queen, and 'Jack the Ripper'—being supposed to be our favourite heroes. Sometimes we went out in the fishing boats and got them to sing us Gaelic songs, and so round to talk of their experiences. The old women we could generally catch at the loom, or the spinning wheel, and we have bought wool and blankets and petticoats enough to last a life time.

We got hold of the younger folk by taking photographs of the babies and carrying sweets in our pockets for the bairns. Mr Dewar's kindness helped us to gain the interest of the clergy and students at home for their holidays in the island—and the farmers and larger crofters were hospitable and kindly too.

I shall hope to send you a resumé of our results before long—meantime I should like to say briefly, that they are of a kind which I find the more interesting and instructive that they are throughout on the lines of my own experience—both personal and in the way of observation of others. They are mainly premonitions, visual and audile, they are spontaneous in kind, the gift is commonly hereditary, rarely communicated—almost always regarded as sacred, and regarded with reverence, —usually found in people of a distinctly religious, meditative cast of mind,—men mainly who live out of doors and are much alone, who take broad, simple views of life, self communing, lovers of nature, little regardful of small commonplaces. All this I deeply sympathise with.

But I must not run on—more of all this later. I think you will understand why I left, and that it seemed after all the wisest course.

The factor, two ministers, two University students, the Doctor, one enthusiastically interested farmer, and others, will now work the ground we have ploughed, and we have planned some little pleasures for the poor in the winter which may help to keep our memory green.

A minor reason for leaving was that the food difficulty had come to a climax and combined with 8 or 10 hours a day in the open air, and often 12 to 16 miles of walking[1] *had made us both really weak and ill.*

[1] The island of Tiree is roughly eleven miles long and in breadth varies from one to six miles. Miss Freer and Miss Moore were staying at Scarinish, which is about seven miles from the west and four miles from the east end of the island. These walks of twelve or sixteen miles are therefore hardly credible. No responsible folklore collector would expect to accomplish anything by trying to cover the ground in such a manner and in such a short time.

A wild orgie of cutlets and fresh fruit at Bunessan[1] *on our way here, began the work of restoration and we are almost right again—but when one remembers that in* time *measurement Tiree is as far from Glasgow as London is, and that there is little to be had nearer, one can hardly wonder at short supplies, and that everything is at famine prices.*

In Oban we have enlisted a great deal of sympathy and have converted many active opponents. Here, I have a warm friend in the quarry and on Sat: am to have a smoking and 'cailing'[2] *party when quarry work is over—my party consisting entirely of the descendants of one Mackenzie who was a Seer 100 years ago.*

From 'Nether Lochaber'[3] *I have a splendid story never recorded before. We go walks together and he is excellent company. . . .*

May I just add how very sensible I am of the fact that it is—ultimately—to your Lordship that I owe all that I have learnt or rather, all the opportunities I have had of learning, during the past month what I could never have otherwise acquired. I hope that you will not measure my efforts by mere statistical results. There are many who know, and could witness that our efforts have been unremitting literally *ceaseless.*

Most truly yours,
A. Goodrich-Freer

Miss Freer's next letter to Lord Bute was written from the Loch Leven Hotel at Ballachulish, near Glencoe, on 15th August:

A kind note from you has just reached me via Tiree. The receipt and despatch of letters has been attended with some delay and difficulty, but I found this one at Oban whither I went yesterday to have an interview with Mr Dewar. The opening of the new railway[4] *has so much disconcerted the steam boats as to add very much to the difficulties of locomotion and I had to stay at Oban all night, which I grudged as a waste of valuable time. For this reason, and because I had an unexpected opportunity of investigating a phenomenon which has interested Mr A. Lang, my extended report for your Lordship has not been written. I am going to ask you to accept in the meantime, a letter which I*

[1] A small port in the Ross of Mull. Miss Freer and Miss Moore may have landed there for a brief visit to Iona.

[2] What Miss Freer means is a 'céilidhing' party. The word *céilidh* in Gaelic means an informal fireside gathering for conversation, during which oral Gaelic literature, songs, and stories, are often sung and told.

[3] The Rev. Alexander Stewart (1829–1901), minister of Ballachulish for the last fifty years of his life, a much-loved personality who made many contributions to the preservation of local lore under the pen-name of 'Nether Lochaber'.

[4] The railway between Oban and Ballachulish. It was closed in 1966.

propose to write on my way—to Mr Myers who is anxious for news, and time will not admit of two separate reports.[1]

The letter you forward from Robert Cameron is just what I wanted in the way of additional information as to his Mother[2] *who I am exceedingly anxious to see, and I propose to set out today in her direction taking Fort Augustus—whence Father Oswald sends two good cases—on the way.*

Mr Dewar is very anxious that we should proceed to Skye and South Uist and Moidart—and an Aunt of Dr Leaf's kindly sends an invitation to Dunvegan Castle,[3] *and I am* unspeakably *disappointed that the claims of* Borderland *(my Secretary on whom I have been depending, clamours for a holiday) require my return at the end of the month. Personally I would make any sacrifice to go on, so convinced am I of the possibilities and importance of our quest.*

With many apologies for haste
I am very truly your Lordship's
Ada Goodrich-Freer

I believe I have to thank your Lordship for The Petty Seer *which is intensely interesting. The Church history of Scotland, seems to me, with all its associations, one of the most suggestive and pathetic conceivable, and the glimpses one gets in this book are delightful.*

On 6th September 1894 Miss Freer wrote a letter to Lord Bute, shortly after her return to London, of which the concluding two paragraphs referred to the Second Sight Enquiry.

Mr Dewar perhaps mentioned to you, I think I asked him to do so, that I learnt in Oban a month ago that there would be no entries for your prize and several persons said then, one (a most interesting psychical baker) writes again today, how much they hoped that the offer would be repeated another year and the competition thrown open. *Oban* (pace *the Westminster Gazette which wants to know what in the world we expect to find* there) *is an excellent field of enquiry, and such an essay might lead to the accumulation of valuable evidence—especially if it could be so arranged that the authors' names should not be revealed.*

[1] This letter is printed in full below, see p. 48. It was sent on by Myers to Bute and kept by him.

[2] This refers to Mrs Cameron, the seeress of Kinlochrannoch, see p. 53.

[3] In Skye, seat of the chiefs of the MacLeods of Harris for many centuries. It is not clear who was the 'aunt'. Norman MacLeod of Macleod married Emily Caroline Isham in 1881; his brother, Sir Reginald MacLeod, had married Lady Agnes Northcote, daughter of the first Earl of Iddesleigh, in 1887. Walter Leaf's mother's maiden name was Isabella Ellen Tyas; his wife was a daughter of J. A. Symonds.

The prize essay referred to needs some explanation. On 2nd May 1894 John Mackintosh, the Secretary of An Comunn Gàidhealach (the Highland Association), which had been founded in 1891 for the preservation of the Gaelic language, its literature and music, in Scotland, approached Lord Bute with the suggestion that he might join a number of donors of special prizes for competitions at the Association's annual *Mòd*, a festival that had been founded on the lines of the Welsh Eisteddfod, and which was held at Oban in 1894. The most prominent of these donors was then Lord Archibald Campbell, who was giving the sum of £10 for 'solos accompanied by the Highland Harp or "Clarsach" '. Mackintosh suggested that Lord Bute might like to donate a gold medal as a special prize to be competed for by soloists, 'for which those who have already received first place two years in succession in the solo competition for amateurs might be allowed to compete' as well as professionals.

Lord Bute's reply was to offer 'a prize of £10 for the best essay on Second Sight in the Highlands, based on actual observation by a Doctor of Medicine'. This was apparently to be *in English.* It is really not very surprising there were no entries for this competition in 1894, and apparently none either in 1895, when Lord Bute doubled the sum offered, but did not accept Miss Freer's suggestion, which was also made by the secretary of the Association in April 1895, that the competition should be made an open one and not restricted to medical men.

Miss Freer continued her letter with self-exculpation over the report of the Second Sight Enquiry which had appeared in the *Oban Times* of 18th August, and which has been quoted earlier:[1, 2]

We never discussed our errand in any hotels or with strangers, or with any *one, except for business purposes, and then never on speculation, only with those we thought would be useful. I never posted any letter with the* Borderland *stamp, or allowed any to be sent to me, and I think I may safely say that no one in either my office or Mr Stead's (to whom I frankly explained the position) knew of my mission.*[3] *The account, and my connection with* Borderland *first appeared in the* Oban Times, *and was out before I could interfere, though I managed to modify an article in the* Express. *It originated I believe in Mr Dewar's conversation on board* The Fingal *on his way to Tiree. He did not then know my wishes on the subject and was not to blame.*[4]

[1] See p. 21.

[2] Letter of 15th August from Ballachulish to Lord Bute.

[3] See p. 38.

[4] Letter of 6th September from 2 Westbourne Park Road, London, to Lord Bute.

If Miss Freer really believed that anything so conspicuous as a mission to investigate second sight composed of two English ladies and a Church of Scotland minister could have failed to attract comment in the Highlands of Scotland, she was a good deal more innocent and more ignorant of rural life than she would have liked us to think. The reader will notice the black mark against Mr Dewar: he is 'not to blame', but his indiscretion is duly recorded.

Myers, who obviously took a keen personal interest in Miss Freer's visit to the Highlands for the Enquiry, wrote to Lord Bute on 1st August saying that he was glad she was combining business and pleasure so successfully. On 16th August he wrote to Bute, saying that:

I feel that the enquiry is being prosecuted in exactly the right spirit; a spirit at once scientific and sympathetic; and I am exceedingly glad that you instituted it, and very hopeful as to the ultimate result.

Myers added that no doubt by now there was enough matter available to make an interesting first report, although Miss Freer would have to consider whether any publication now might hinder her chances next year. On 21st August, Myers wrote to Bute enclosing the following long letter Miss Freer had written him about the expedition on the 15th of the same month:

S.S. Chevalier between Onich and Fort William
15th August 1894

My dear Mr Myers,[1]

I am writing on board the Steamer so please forgive starts and jumps. I have been leading so active a life these last few weeks, that I begin to look on journeys as quite leisure times!

I was glad to hear that you were back in England, as I think it is time I gave some account of myself. When I get back to town I will have my notes transcribed by my Secretary, and send them to you and to Lord Bute. Meanwhile you will like to have some idea of what I have been doing.

Please meditate for a moment on the facts,—that you have known me for some time and that you know I am not *a fool,—that it is in the interest, let us say, of my vanity to represent my mission as a success, that probably* no *one is more deeply interested in the subject of my*

[1] The formal mode of address used by Miss Freer here to Myers, whom she obviously knew very well, shows that her letter was written with the intention that it should be shown to Lord Bute.

enquiry than I myself or more anxious for its advancement, further please believe, as all concerned will assure you, that I have worked ceaselessly and in defiance of any prejudices of conventionality, in defiance of fatigue,—having literally taken but one day 'off'.

Now (if you can,) try to believe that it is not my fault if the facts I have accumulated, are but in small degree evidential. *I believe that they are in almost all cases facts, but they are not,* as yet *facts to take to a jury.*

I believe that they may be made so—in time, and I believe that they involve some exceedingly interesting deductions.

To my thinking—I am sorry for it but it was nobody's fault—this journey has accomplished the work which the Schedules *ought to have accomplished,—if people had been ready for them. The main result is that in each of my three centres (and I believe that the experience of Mr Dewar, with whom I had a meeting last night, agrees with mine on this point) I have left several intelligent, deeply-interested observers whose interest has been, through this process, either freshly aroused or based on a new footing, and who will carry on what I have begun. Some of our best helpers have been those who either ignored our Schedules, or sent negative answers—both facts being the result, in many cases, rather of sincerity than of indifference.*

We have a good deal of indirect evidence, such as the fact of a prediction being common talk long before it was fulfilled, and so on, but the difficulty of getting direct evidence proceeds from several causes.

1. *We dare not show a notebook. The 'conditions' as the Spiritualists say, are so delicate, that this would be fatal. 'A chiel's amang ye takin' notes and faith he'll prent 'em' would ruin us.*
2. *They have the most inconvenient superstition about telling of a premonition; unless the gift is very highly developed, to tell of a thing before-hand imperils the gift—so much so that I am quite accustomed to hear of people who had the power once of second sight, 'but they told it and got cured'.*
3. *And even those who are confirmed seers will always prefer to tell you of his* [sic] *neighbour's powers—sometimes permitting the neighbour to tell of his—it is 'better luck'.*

Also I can assure you, one has to go through some stiff preliminaries to get at it at all. *The real standing enemy to the enquiry—don't tell Mr Dewar I said so!—is Presbyterianism. It has always seemed to me destructive of all that is loftiest in Human Nature, and any traditional respect I had for it has died out* absolutely *these few weeks. Our work has really been easiest at Ballachulish where the population is all Roman or Anglican*[1] *except a few followers of that dear old gossip 'Nether Lochaber', Dr Stewart.*[2]

At this point quotation of Miss Freer's long letter may be suspended for some comment. First of all, it must be said that the assertions made are largely preposterous. It is true enough that Highlanders have had, and still do have, good cause to be suspicious of the stranger who comes among them with a notebook asking leading questions and writing down the answers, especially if the stranger is not a Gaelic-speaker. Only too often experience has shown that such persons were gathering material either to present the local inhabitants in a false or ridiculous light, or to obtain at little cost to themselves material for literary exploitation. Often enough both purposes have been combined. But no inhabitant of the Highlands would have commented upon this in the absurd bogus Scottish dialect which Miss Freer put in inverted commas.

So far as the seers themselves were concerned, in 1894 most of them were still monoglot Gaelic-speakers, and it may legitimately be questioned whether Miss Freer's information did not mostly derive from answers to the S.P.R.'s Schedule of Questions rather than from personal contact with the seers themselves. What must be understood is that what is called second sight is and was considered in the Highlands and Islands to have been an affliction rather than a 'gift'. Personally I have never heard or read of seers supposing they would lose the 'gift' if they divulged their premonitions. In fact, the difficulties alleged in the second and third paragraphs here look much more like the excuses made to Miss Freer by persons alleged to have second sight for their unwillingness to discuss their experiences with her. And with regard to her comments on Presbyterianism, it is worth recording here that the outstanding collector of the folklore of Tiree, which Miss Freer had just visited, was the Church of Scotland (Presbyterian) minister J. Gregorson Campbell.

The letter continues:

By the way, another difficulty—I hope I am not talking treason,—is the mischief that has been done by Lady A. Campbell. I venture to think that good *witnesses have fought shy of her,—these Highland folk are so earnest so serious that her attitude does not suit them, but where she has handled a case, I venture to think she has spoilt it, so that I avoid her footsteps. This was especially the case in Tiree where the other*

[1] *Recte* Scottish Episcopalian.

[2] The Rev. Alexander Stewart, minister of Ballachulish from 1851 to 1907, a much loved minister and a well-known writer on the traditions of Lochaber, see also p. 31.

people considered she 'made a fool' of those she examined and where for a time they were shy of us in consequence. It is a process that requires the utmost care and tact.

The impertinent nature of these remarks may be appreciated when it is pointed out that Lord Archibald Campbell was a member of the ducal family of Argyll, and his wife, Janey Sevilla, a Callander of Ardkinglass in Argyll, had herself been ward of her husband's father, the eighth Duke, before their marriage. At the time this letter was written, Lord and Lady Campbell lived at Coombe Hill Farm near Kingston in Surrey. Lord Archibald himself was a member of the Folklore Society and was well known for the 'Waifs and Strays' volumes of Highland traditional lore of which he had been editor and patron. In 1885 he had published *Records of Argyll*. As this book contained several second sight stories from Tiree, of which island the Argyll family had been proprietors since the late seventeenth century, one might have expected that the S.P.R. would have consulted Lord Archibald before sending Miss Freer to investigate second sight there. Lady Archibald, who herself became a member of the S.P.R., wrote an article printed in the *Nineteenth Century* of September 1897 (a month after the same magazine had published Miss Freer's defence of the Ballechin House ghost-hunt) entitled 'From Tyree to Glencoe', in which she remarked that 'were the members of the Psychical Society to win the confidence of the natives of Tyree by talking to them in Gaelic, they would get some curious information to add to their already voluminous testimony as to the reality of second sight in other countries'.[1] Lady Archibald's knowledge of Gaelic may not have been perfect, but it was certainly better than Miss Freer's.

Miss Freer's letter continues:

By the way I ought to give thanks for my special opportunities; over and over again I have secured witnesses who would otherwise have been dumb by convincing them that I was one of themselves. I had an assignation, at dusk, in Glencoe, with the great Seer, the sixth in succession of his race—a young quarryman[2]—but though I went seven miles in a heavy down-pour, and sacrificed my dinner—he didn't turn up,—to my great disappointment. He had been a little doubtful from the first, because I wouldn't say I was sure *to see anything, a proof of want of faith on my part and therefore unworthiness of my office! I could*

[1] *Nineteenth Century*, September 1897, p. 455. The article covers the identical districts as Miss Freer's 1894 visit, and must have been written with it in mind.

[2] This may have been the Ewen McColl referred to by Lady Archibald Campbell in her *Nineteenth Century* article, see *op. cit.*, p. 459.

only say that as I had already had a vision in Glencoe (to which I don't attach great importance—as one doesn't know how much to subtract for expectation and self-suggestion) which was correct as to past details of which I knew nothing—on the same spot on which he had also seen figures, it would be interesting to revive and compare experiences.

This is a rambling letter and is becoming portentously long, but I want to touch on one more point.

It is to me intensely interesting to find in the stories of so remote a spot as Tiree, of such remote periods as some of the old folks tell of (one of 87 who cherishes stories received direct from a certain Ewen MacColl who died an old man, 60 years ago) that however different their material,—their unit of thought so to speak—the super-normal part of the stories run on lines with which we are familiar,—premonition often externalized in sight or sound,—thought transference,—information subconsciously acquired. The stories of return after death are very very few, and of hauntings few.

Then the visions, etc. are spontaneous, *never intentionally induced, not under command, the power is not to be acquired, (they pooh-pooh the 'methods' for the most part)—almost always hereditary,—is mainly associated with the religious temperament especially with lovers of nature,—and is mostly found among men. I have taken great pains to enquire into the thought habits of the Seers and find that without exception, so far as I have seen, they are visualisers of a very intense degree. We have had much talk of Crystal-Gazing and I hope many will try it.*

I have gleaned a good deal of experience for future procedure. Any further enquiries should be pursued earlier in the year, when the people are more at leisure—not later than May or June. (For another, though minor reason, just now in the season, everything is shockingly dear! We have done our best to economize in every detail but have already spent £40. Bal[l]achulish was the worst take-in as to money,—the Bishop of Argyll's Hotel 12/6 a day and utter discomfort,—worse than Tiree!) When I come again,—and I cannot let this drop if I can help it—I should—now I know the way, take cottage lodgings, by which means I should really see more of the people, than by my present method of haunting the stables and chumming with the fishermen and miners.[1]

I am quite convinced that there is a first rate harvest to be reaped here to which nothing the S.P.R. has yet touched, can compare. I believe it would be an excellent thing to spend at least six months in the Islands, and another six in Lochaber,—and I would give much to be able to do it. Mr Dewar has been all that is kind and helpful—nothing could exceed his desire to be useful and I feel much indebted to his help.

[1] Presumably the Ballachulish slate quarriers are meant.

Nevertheless, another time I should prefer to break the ground myself, as in Tiree his arrival was a distinct check, not in the least from his personality but solely because the presence of a Minister at once imported a party feeling which I had to struggle against. Poor Miss Moore, who is nothing if not orthodox, had to accompany me to 'kirk' and to take tea with the Miss Baptist Ministers, and go out in a boat with the young men from the Independent Manse—all to show that there was nothing invidious in Psychical Research! All's well that ends well, and I've got a trunk full of 'keep-sakes' from the natives of all classes and opinions. So too in Oban. In Ballachulish, Onich and Glencoe I was a Seer among Seers and found that the most helpful attitude. And all being well next time I can spare a few weeks I mean to go again.

My own experiences have not been important. I recognized that the atmosphere was all that one could desire, but I have lived in such a whirl of action, and a good deal of anxiety and fatigue and these have not been favourable. But I have had some few telepathic and retrocognitive experiences, duly recorded.

Now we are on our way to Fort Augustus to see Father Oswald (thanks for additional case from him) and thence to see Mrs Cameron, the wise woman of Rannoch,[1] *who if not already* exploitée, *and unfortunately she has some celebrity, should be of extreme interest. Thence on Sat*[urday][2] *to Falkland, by desire of Lord Bute. (Letters to be sent to c/o Major Wood, The Palace.) I have a very great deal more to say but I must stop sometime. Are you likely to be within reach of London during the first week in September?*

Very truly yours,
A. Goodrich-Freer

I think that anyone who reads this letter cannot fail to be impressed by the astounding self-assurance of the writer, who implicitly claims to be completely *au fait* with Highland second sight and Highland seers after only a month spent in the country; and by the deftness, worthy of a rising politician, with which she torpedoes the claims of her potential rivals, Lady Archibald Campbell and the Rev. Peter Dewar.[3] As for the Seer of Glencoe, he was clearly glad

[1] A Highland clairvoyante who specialized in finding drowned bodies, see Angus MacLellan, *The Furrow Behind Me*, London, 1962, pp. 43 and 197.

[2] Presumably 25th August.

[3] It is significant that in the discussion that followed Miss Freer's lecture to the Viking Club on 26th November 1897 on 'The Norsemen in the Hebrides', the President remarked that the inability of Miss Freer's interpreter (unnamed) to understand Hebridean Gaelic was due to his bad Perthshire Gaelic! Dewar was born in Perthshire. The assertion must have come from Miss Freer.

to find an excuse for avoiding the proposed assignation with the Sassenach lady visitor.

Dewar himself had been on a visit to Skye, North and South Uist, and Eriskay, about which more later, after leaving Miss Freer in Tiree. On 17th August he wrote Lord Bute that he had had an interview with Miss Freer at Oban on 14th August: it was presumably then that the report which was printed in the *Oban Times* of 18th August, and which is reproduced here on p. 21, was given to the Press. Dewar says he and Miss Freer had agreed that only an interim report could be given to the S.P.R. on the Enquiry at this point, as subsequent investigations might cause them to modify the opinions they had formed on fundamental matters. Dewar also said that he had entrusted to Miss Freer's charge 'all the Schedules and correspondence which have remained in my possession ever since the enquiry was set on foot'. He proposed later, when the papers were returned to him (which was apparently never done), to commit his own views to writing and send them to Dr Walter Leaf for consideration ('along with whatever evidence may have been collected by Miss Freer and myself') by Dr Walter Leaf and Myers before submission to the S.P.R. Council. Dewar stressed his agreement with Lord Bute that it was of vital importance to secure as many intelligent local correspondents and co-operators as possible, so that work could be continuous. This had been the method used by J. F. Campbell of Islay in making his great collection of Highland folk-tales, and any modern folklorist would be in agreement with it. Dewar said he thought he had succeeded in thoroughly interesting all the clergy of Tiree, the minister of Bracadale, Snizort, Portree, Waternish, Broadford and Kilmuir in Skye, the ministers and priests of North and South Uist, 'and of my very good friends Fathers Macdonald of Eriskay and Macdonald, late of Moidart and now of Helensburgh' (the latter of whom died later in the same year, 1894). He also suggested it would be a good thing if the S.P.R.'s publication *Phantasms of the Living*[1] (which had been issued in 1886 over the names of Edmund Gurney, F. W. H. Myers, and Frank Podmore) were 'circulated amongst the clergy of the Highlands'.

Miss Freer continued her journey, travelling to Fort Augustus, then on to Kinlochrannoch in Perthshire, and then to the ancient palace of Falkland in Fife, which Lord Bute had purchased in 1887. In her letter of 8th August to Bute she had referred to this visit, apparently made at Bute's suggestion, and said that she would be 'glad to do my utmost—or perhaps should say to refrain to the

[1] See Trevor Hall, *The Strange Case of Edmund Gurney*, London, 1864, pp. 70–8.

utmost from doing anything to await impressions and results'. Psychical impressions are meant. They were duly experienced, and were recounted to Lord Bute at great length in a letter written from Falkland on 21st August. They were apparently accepted without question, for from this time on until his stroke in August 1899 put an end to Lord Bute's many activities, Miss Freer clearly enjoyed his complete confidence, and considerable patronage, as a clairvoyante. On 8th October Myers wrote to Bute that: 'I saw Miss X the other day; extremely interested in the Hebrides investigation, which she hopes to make more and more thorough. I think you have got the right woman and in the right place!'

7

FR ALLAN McDONALD IS DISCOVERED

MEANWHILE, THE Rev. Peter Dewar was busily engaged in preparing the ground for the Enquiry, travelling through Ardnamurchan, Moidart, and Skye, to South Uist. And it was he, and not Miss Freer, who discovered Fr Allan McDonald and his folklore collection, and brought them to the knowledge of a wider world than the little coterie of Gaelic scholars and folklorists with whom Fr Allan McDonald had been previously associated. Dewar's report on his journey, on Fr Allan McDonald and the Eriskay seers, is best given in his own words, as written to Lord Bute from the Chapel House on Eriskay on Wednesday, 8th August—curiously enough the same day as Miss Freer's first letter from Ballachulish.

After leaving Tiree I spent several days in the Ardnamurchan district making enquiries, but found it was not so nearly hopeful a field for Psychical Research as Moidart, and I have suggested to Miss Freer that she might sojourn there for a week or two after visiting the Ballachullish and Oban district [sic]. *I have been for a week making enquiries in Skye, but I found the people extremely reticent and uncommunicative. Several of the clergymen and doctors however promised to interest themselves in the Enquiry and send me notes of any cases they considered to be well-authenticated.*

A much more promising field than Skye or even Tiree is North and South Uist. I spent some time in Lochmaddy and saw the Parish Minister, the Procurator Fiscal and some of the leading merchants. I find that it is only after I have personally visited people having local influence in the Highlands that they become fully alive to the scientific importance of our Enquiry—feel truly interested in it and promise cooperation. The Fiscal and one of the Lochmaddy merchants has undertaken to send me some striking cases of second sight that they consider to be well attested. They were of opinion that the cases of second sight in Uist are so numerous that to investigate them in a satisfactory manner one would need to settle down in the district for a couple of months, make friends with the people, the priests and the parish ministers, and move from locality to locality and island to island.

The Rev. Allan Macdonald, under whose hospitable roof I have been staying since Friday[1]*, is precisely of the same opinion. Father Macdonald I find to be a cultured, devout and charming person. He has lived all his life in the Highlands—and deeply loves the Highlanders; their beliefs—their traditions—their songs and their lore. He seems to me to be a thorough master of the Gaelic Language, and has been so good as to present me with a collection of Gaelic Hymns which he edited and published a few years ago.*[2] *Several of the hymns in this collection are his own composition and seem to me to be very beautiful. He takes a great interest in our second sight Enquiry—an interest of an enlightened and scientific character—and gave me every assistance in the way of interviewing several of the noted Eriskay Seers.*

The cases one meets with in Eriskay are cases of lights of a supernormal character—foreshadowing deaths; phantasmal funeral processions seen in many instances months before the deaths they seem to presage;[3] *processions of the dead by which the Seers sometimes are met and carried in an unconscious state, for considerable distances:*[4] *phantasmal writings*[5] *or the hum of phantasmal voices engaged in conversation heard some days or even weeks before a death; chests containing grave clothes (kept by the people in view of any emergency that might occur) being seen to open and shut with a loud noise a few days before neighbours called to beg the loan of a winding sheet or shroud;*[6] *phantom ships seen by fishermen on a certain part of the coast where subsequently —(in some cases a considerable period of time thereafter) vessels of an exactly similar description were wrecked and the lives of the crew lost;*[7] *lovers being met in the twilight, and roughly handled by the apparitions of living maidens to whom they were previously engaged or with whom they had at one time 'kept company', but whom they subsequently deserted in favour of a more attractive rival.*[8] *The apparitions of the dead seem to be very common in North and South Uist. The apparitions of the living, in a time of crisis, or at the moment of death are, so far as*

[1] *i.e.* 3rd August. 8th August was a Wednesday.

[2] The first edition of the Gaelic hymn book was published in 1889: a greatly enlarged edition was published in 1893.

[3] It seems clear that at least some of these items derive from Fr Allan McDonald's notebooks rather than from Dewar's conversations with seers on Eriskay: for phantom funerals see 'Strange Things', Nos. 7 and 35 here.

[4] See the 'Early Collection', Nos. 37–40 here; 'Strange Things', No. 52.

[5] See the 'Early Collection', Nos. 23 and 27.

[6] See 'Strange Things', No. 1.

[7] See the 'Early Collection', No. 47.

[8] See *ibid.*, No. 48.

I could gather, almost unknown—a fact which astonishes me very much —considering what an overwhelming number of our published cases[1] *are of this character.*

On board The Staffa, *Wednesday evening.*

I think that next year an Enquiry of a sifting character should be carried on in North and South Uist; Benbecula; Barra and Lewis, perhaps also in Sutherlandshire. One, I find, needs to cultivate friendly relations with the people, win their confidence, awaken them to a sense of the scientific importance of the Enquiry—enlist the sympathies of doctors, priests and parish ministers and teachers by personal intercourse, before progress can be made or any valuable results gained. All this is largely a question of patience—perseverance—tact but above all of time. *It is no use marching into the house of a reputed Seer armed with pencil and notebook and submitting him to a searching cross-examination; for when one does so he simply lapses into a dogged silence.*

Another difficulty that perpetually confronts one is the difficulty of getting Highlanders to fix the date of their experiences. Very few of them can afford the luxury of a chronometer; almost none of them make notes, or can make notes, of their experiences at the time of their occurrence. I have not met one individual who has kept a diary. In the case of an Enquiry like ours where so much depends on dates, *the evidence, as* evidence, *cannot but be regarded from a scientific point of view as vague and unsatisfactory. Still, I would fain hope that before the Enquiry is concluded some valuable information may be gained.*

I had the pleasure of meeting Mr Shaw of New Cumnock at Loch Boisdale on my way to Eriskay, and of inspecting the handsome new Hospital erected by Lady Bute at Dalibrog. It should prove a great boon to the poor people of North and South Uist. I return to 47 Rose Street, Garnethill, Glasgow, on this day week and go south with my fiancée to Runswick, Yorkshire, on the 16th; remaining there till the beginning of September when I resume parish work at North Bute. I hope to have an interview at Oban with Miss Freer on my way south.

I hope your Lordship may be able to read this letter. It is finished on board The Staffa.[2]

Dewar's letter of 17th August 1894 to Lord Bute contained some further information Bute had asked for:

With reference to the auxiliary information to which your Lordship refers I have found

[1] *i.e.* of the Society for Psychical Research's published cases. The allusion is probably to the book *Phantasms of the Living,* which had been published by the S.P.R. a few years previously.

[2] The mail-boat then serving the Uists.

(1) that Seers have the idea that if 'they commit themselves' (as they phrase it) by communicating with the apparitions they meet by speech disastrous results to themselves, as a general rule, will inevitably follow. Hence they often walk side by side with apparitions for a considerable distance in solemn silence.[1]

(2) They know little or nothing of the use of the crystal or of hypnotism. In fact they are inclined to look on both as 'black arts'!

(3) They have as yet heard nothing of automatic writing or of the alleged phenomena of spiritualism.

(4) The test whereby they try the spirits is, so far as I could gather, by invoking the presence of the three persons of the blessed Trinity to be betwixt them and every evil influence.

The expedient you suggest as to the best means of meeting the date difficulty[2] *seems to me admirable. I suggested to Father Macdonald, before leaving Eriskay, that he might get Seers to communicate with him, and he promised, if they did so, to record the date and the details of their experiences. I found that in the case of the great majority of visions of funerals there is nothing distinctive to differentiate one from the other so that they (the Seers) are unable to tell beforehand* whose *funeral is foreshadowed. I am rather inclined to think that when Seers are carried along by a 'procession of the dead'*[3] *they fall into the trance state. But the phenomenon is so curious and interesting that I shall make further enquiries. It will give me great pleasure to call on your Lordship when I return to my parish and to talk over with you some of the most interesting cases of which I took notes, which I shall extend.*

[1] See the 'Early Collection' here, No. 26.

[2] *i.e.* the difficulty of getting the Gaelic-speaking seers to record the dates of their experiences.

[3] See Nos. 38–41 of the 'Early Collection', and No. 52 of 'Strange Things'.

8

'MISS X' MAKES HER FIRST INTERIM REPORT

MISS FREER read her first interim report on the Second Sight Enquiry to the S.P.R. at Westminster Town Hall on Friday, 7th December 1894, with Dr Leaf in the chair. Her lecture was reported in January 1895 in the S.P.R.'s *Journal* (vol. VII, p. 2), and by Miss Freer herself at considerably greater length in *Borderland* the same month (vol. II, pp. 56–9), notwithstanding the fact that Myers was supposed to have 'impressed on her the harm that may be done if any of our cases are reported in *Borderland*'.[1] As the *Borderland* version of Miss Freer's report is considerably fuller than that published in the S.P.R.'s *Journal*, it is used for quotation here.

Miss Freer began by remarking that on account of the fact that the faculty of second sight was surrounded with awe and reverence, 'first hand testimony can be obtained only by living among the people and cultivating personal relations with them. This Miss X, accompanied by a friend, tried to do during some weeks of the past autumn, both among the islands of the Hebrides and in some of the more retired glens of the mainland.'

The liberality of the Marquis of Bute has enabled the S.P.R. to institute some formal inquiries in Scotland upon the subject of Second Sight, extending over a period of some eighteen months preceding Miss X's visit, and which served, at least, to indicate the difficulty of the inquiry, and the reluctance of the Highlanders to commit themselves upon the question.

Miss Freer went on to say that the Rev. Peter Dewar had undertaken the office of honorary secretary, and had sent out nearly two thousand copies of the Schedule of questions to supposedly suitable persons. There is not a single word of recognition of Dewar's other labours on behalf of the Enquiry nor of the help that he had afforded her in various ways, including important introductions and the handing over to her of all the correspondence and replies connected with

[1] See p. 36.

the schedule. This Miss Freer quotes, saying that on the first occasion 'Out of these [2000] but sixty were returned duly filled up, and but half of these answered' the questions in the affirmative. Miss Freer went on to say that when the schedules were reissued with Bute's covering circular letter, two hundred and ten replies were received, 'of which sixty-four answers were more or less affirmative'.

It is interesting to compare this statement of the results of the Enquiry with the much more cautious remarks of Dewar in his letters of 17th March 1893 and 25th April 1894 to Lord Bute, quoted earlier in this book. The reader will remember that Dewar reported that by the first date only 54 replies had been received to the questionnaire and of these only 26 had answered the first question 'is "Second Sight" believed in by the people of your neighbourhood' in the affirmative; '*but even those who reply affirmatively have not yet furnished me with any well-attested first-hand cases*'. In the second case Dewar had reported that 157 replies had been received by 25th April 1894, of which only 42 were 'more or less affirmative'. Dewar had gone on to say he was taking steps to get into touch with alleged percipients 'with the view to obtaining first hand accounts and corroborative evidence, which alone can make them scientifically valuable'.

Even allowing for the possibility that Miss Freer's figures of 60 and 210 replies are achieved by including answers received after the dates on which Dewar made up his returns, the fact remains that she made no mention to the S.P.R. of Dewar's cautious reservations on the lack of first-hand evidence in either of her reports in 1894 or 1895. This certainly ought to have been done.

Miss Freer went on to describe the alleged difficulties of the Enquiry—the awe with which Highlanders supposedly regarded second sight, their disinclination for, or lack of habit in, expressing themselves in writing, the hostile influences of the modern educational system and of Presbyterianism. There was a good deal of truth in all this, no doubt, but ignorant of the Highlands as Miss Freer was, she quite failed to see that the most fundamental difficulty of all was the deeply rooted disinclination of Highlanders to answer leading questions put to them by strangers, particularly in writing. In the Scottish Highlands, leading questions were, and often still are, associated either with oppressive measures, rules and regulations, emanating from an authority outside the Highlands, or else with efforts of 'clever' visitors to make the 'natives' look foolish. Leading questions to a Highlander are about as popular as queries from the Inspector of Taxes regarding sources of income are with the average citizen. Of this Miss Freer showed very little signs of awareness.

Miss Freer remarked, continuing, that hints had been thrown out that information might be forthcoming personally in preference to in writing, and that there were certain traditional methods of acquiring second sight. 'These hints led, in the end, to a request from the committee [of the S.P.R.] appointed to carry out the investigation, that Miss X would undertake to visit such localities as appeared likely to yield some reward for the necessary time and trouble.'

The invitation had been gladly accepted, and accompanied by a friend [Miss Constance Moore] and a dog [Scamp] Miss Freer had set out from London early in July for 'a small island in the Hebrides' that had been 'fixed upon as our centre', *i.e.* Tiree. The date of her departure from London, 11th July, was later given in her book *Outer Isles*, where significantly nothing whatever was said about the purpose of her journey. Miss Freer and her friend took with them an ordnance map of Scotland on which they had marked with coloured chalks the places from which reports of second sight had been received. 'To our great satisfaction the entire Highlands were soon sufficiently suffused with the colour of promise to raise our spirits very considerably.'

'Among the various discouragements offered to us, was the fact that we were entirely ignorant of Gaelic.' This is an important admission, in view of the knowledge of Gaelic implied in Miss Freer's later folklore writings. A knowledge of Gaelic would nowadays be considered an essential qualification in any student of any aspect of the Gaelic oral tradition. But Miss Freer shrugged this off. Bilingual sailors, ministers, and doctors, she says, were always available to interpret. But where interpreters are necessary, the right atmosphere for gaining intimate personal reminiscences of second sight does not exist, and in the 1890s even when an interpreter was not necessary bilingual Highlanders used English for pure formal purposes only, preferring to discuss personal matters in Gaelic.

Miss Freer made the claim that though she and her friend had made no talk about the purpose of her visit, their reputation had preceded them. 'This was rather an unwelcome discovery, the more so that a somewhat exaggerated account of our personal psychic powers soon became current, and we had to live down various reports as to our exercise of magic and witchcraft.' This was really trying to have things both ways, as in her letter of 15th August to Myers, Miss Freer had claimed that what enabled her to be accepted by the Highland seers was the fact that she was a seer herself. She goes on in her interim report to assert that:

On the whole, this had a good effect upon the evidence—a slight feeling of awe, a recognition of power as adepts in their own line, saved us from having palmed off upon us the kind of story, which not on the islands, but in the more frequented parts, is reserved for the amateur who likes a little folklore.'

It is not surprising that in South Uist and Eriskay Miss Freer is still remembered today under the nickname of *Cailleach bheag nam Bòcan,* a mildly mocking appellation that is difficult to translate succinctly but which conveys the idea of 'the little middle-aged lady who is preoccupied with ghosts', or that she was darkly suspected of spiritualism there.

Miss Freer remarked that 'we look forward to repeating our visit with even greater satisfaction than that with which we first undertook the Trust' and that 'we hope at our next visit to bring all our stories up to the evidential standard which we have yet reached in certain cases only'. 'We were much impressed by the apparent trustworthiness of the traditions. We made a point of hearing each story as many times over, from as many witnesses as possible, and were greatly struck by the absence of variation in detail.' The critic will ask how on earth this kind of thing could have been done by a stranger to the Highlands, ignorant of Gaelic, in three or four different districts within the space of six weeks. 'We kept a careful diary of our conversations, and whenever possible we both heard each witness and compared notes the same day, as soon afterwards as possible.' Where is this diary of Highland conversations, kept by Miss Freer in the 1890s, today, if it ever really existed?

There follows a description of Tiree, a definition of second sight as held by the seers themselves to be 'a kind of extension of vision, a seeing of something not visible to those not specially gifted'.[1] Then come eight second sight stories of which the provenance is carefully concealed: it is impossible to say whether they were actually collected by Miss Freer herself, or had previously been communicated to the Rev. Peter Dewar. That the material was actually Dewar's is proved by a letter written by Dewar to Myers on 11th October 1895 in which Dewar said, 'In July 1894 I handed over to her [Miss Freer] such documentary evidence as came into my possession, but Dr Leaf agreed with me in thinking it was of but slight scientific value.... I have no material on second sight which would be suitable for an address to the S.P.R. Such as there was, has, I gather, *been already communicated to the S.P.R. by Miss X.*' (My italics.) The inaccuracies in one of the stories will be discussed later.

[1] Which is not different from Martin Martin's definition in 1703! See p. 18.

Miss Freer summed up her interim conclusions as follows:

(*1*) *The evidence of the Seers themselves seems to point to the theory that 'Second Sight' is, in many cases, a sort of extension or exaltation of the normal faculties, the 'prophecies' being, in many instances, closely analogous to the cases of crystal vision, automatic writing, and other forms of externalizing an idea, which may be due to memory and unconscious observations, especially of such signs as might easily escape the notice of the more occupied ordinary consciousness.*

(*2*) *Though such a faculty is quite unrecognized by the Seers themselves, there seems little doubt that Thought Transference plays an important part in the experiences they relate.*

(*3*) *Careful enquiry into their habits of thought showed the Highland Seers, whom Miss X had an opportunity of questioning*[1] (*some twenty, at least*), *to be strong visualizers; this, in relation not only to their visions, but to their ordinary mental habits.*

(*4*) *In many stories, the same feature recurred—namely, the vision of a bright light* (*usually in connection with some incident in the story*), *followed by unconscious deportation of the Seer—suggesting a conceivable clue in the possibility of self-hypnotization and change of place while unconscious of surroundings.*

(*5*) *Miss X failed to find any indication of belief that the visions are due to the agency of the Departed; and the suggestion of Spirit Return was invariably rejected with strong expressions of dislike. The very few whose experiences suggested active external agency attributed such agency to the Devil.*

(*6*) *Miss X found traces of certain methods of divination or automatism, possibly mixed with*[2] *remains of forms of evocation, such as gazing into liquids carefully compounded, 'getting news' from the sea at certain stages of the moon, and the like. She also received certain formulae for the acquisition of Second Sight; but in no case did the people themselves seem to attach much importance to methods of any kind.*

(*7*) *On the contrary, they reject experiment, and believe that the gift is hereditary* [*and spontaneous in its exercise*],[3] *as indeed, among them appears to be the case.*

The reference to the possibility of 'thought-transference' playing an important part in the seers' experiences should be noted. It was reiterated by Miss Freer in her second interim report to the S.P.R.

[1] And whom she is careful not to name!

[2] 'mixed with possible' in the S.P.R.'s *Journal* version.

[3] The words between square brackets occur in the S.P.R. *Journal* version, but not in the *Borderland* one.

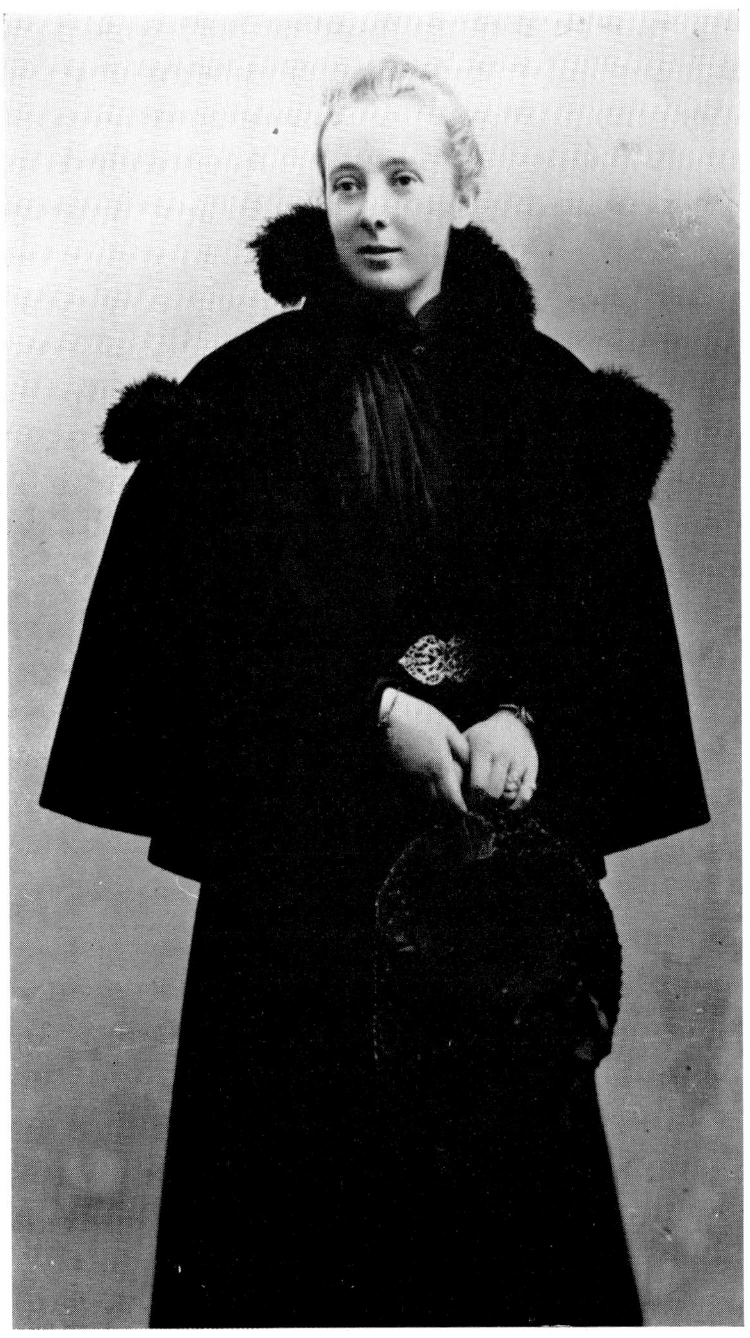

1. 'Miss X' November 1894. The only photograph of Ada Goodrich Freer in the files of the Society for Psychical Research, by whose courtesy this copy is reproduced.

2. Ballechin House in 1897. Reading from left to right, the group consists of L. C. Powles, Mrs Walker, Miss Ruth Langton, and Miss Constance Moore. These persons were together at Ballechin between 22nd and 26th February 1897. The photograph, which was probably taken by Miss Freer, is reproduced from a print pasted inside the cover of Fr Allan McDonald's notebook 'Strange

a year later, when she said that 'many of the stories might be fairly explained by the hypothesis of Thought-Transference, and the Highlanders themselves seemed aware of its possibilities'.[1] Yet less than two years later we find her writing, in her farewell article in *Borderland*,[2] that 'in seeking for evidence in the Western Highlands of the existence of second sight . . . my great obstruction was that there had lately passed through the land a member of the S.P.R. with a notebook, who exploited the evidence and told the people "It was all telepathy". The Free Kirk minister had said it was the de'il, which was bad enough,[3] but telepathy was worse as suggestive of the unknown.' It is difficult to know what to make of this in view of Miss Freer's earlier assertions quoted here, and of the fact that the 'good man' referred to is not identified. Seemingly it could only have been Myers himself (who had visited Bute in 1892), the Rev. Peter Dewar, or Dr Wallace, who had quoted sceptical remarks made to him by an inhabitant of Iona in the discussion after her second report. But by October 1897 Miss Freer had quarrelled with the leaders of the S.P.R. over their failure to support her in the controversy about the Ballechin House ghost-hunt in the columns of *The Times*, and over their increasing interest in the famous American medium Mrs Piper.[4]

As printed in the S.P.R. *Journal* for January 1895, the meeting at which Miss Freer's first interim report was read ended with the Chairman, Walter Leaf, being reported as having spoken

of the difficulties which he anticipated in raising the evidence for second sight to such a level as was required by the Society. Not the least of these difficulties, in his opinion, would be the entire neglect of dates, which he expected would be found so soon as the endeavour was made to get accurate details. In enquiries which had been made in Brittany, a well-known home of 'second sight', this difficulty had proved insuperable.

In Miss Freer's account of the meeting, printed in *Borderland*[5] the same month, this paragraph appears as follows:

The Chairman, Dr Walter Leaf (who is also a member of the Committee of Inquiry into Second Sight), in thanking Miss X for her address, and congratulating the Society on the fact that the investigation

[1] *Borderland*, vol. III, p. 57 (January 1896).

[2] *Borderland*, vol. IV, p. 367 (October 1897).

[3] No worse than Miss Freer's Hieland English!

[4] See Miss Freer's article on 'Psychical Research and an Alleged Haunted House', in the *Nineteenth Century*, August 1897, from which it is perfectly clear that the attention the leading members of the S.P.R. were giving to Mrs Piper and her séances was resented.

[5] *Borderland*, vol. II, p. 59 (1895).

had fallen into such competent hands, contributed the interesting fact that he was in a position to judge of the difficulties of the inquiry and to estimate Miss X's success in the matter, having himself undertaken a similar task in regard to Second Sight in Brittany.

It is characteristic that the words about the difficulties of 'raising the evidence for second sight to the level required by the S.P.R.' were omitted in the version printed in *Borderland.*

Any independent checking of the stories related by Miss Freer was rendered practically impossible by her habit of suppressing the names of persons and places involved in them. The only instance in which such a check can be made does not inspire confidence. This is the story of the seer on the Island of Tiree who foresaw the soldiers who were sent to the island about twenty years later at the time of the land agitation. Miss Freer, who does not name the seer, who she says died before his vision was fulfilled, tells us that:

In 1889, during the Crofters' agitation, their (i.e. *the soldiers'*) *presence became necessary on the occasion of the installation of new owners in a certain farm lying beyond the Island House, and to which they proceeded along the very road where they had been seen in vision.*[1]

This, says Miss Freer, had been coincidentally confirmed when some weeks later she met on the mainland two of the party who had visited Tiree in 1889, who corroborated the account of their movements.

This encounter would have been in August 1894. The memories of Miss Freer's unnamed informants must have been short, because in a much more detailed and authoritative account of the whole affair the date of the landing of soldiers on Tiree is given as 30th July 1886, the seer is identified as James MacLaren and is said to have been alive at the time, and the occasion of the trouble is described as a land raid on the farm of Greenhill, then vacant between two tenancies, followed by a technical deforcement of the servers of an interdict on the raiding crofters and cottars who had put their cattle to graze on the farm.[2] The military occupation of Tiree, by nature one of the quietest and most peaceful of the islands in the Hebrides, by a force of 250 marines and sixteen policemen at the national expense for a whole month, was a ridiculous panic measure on the part of the authorities, egged on by grossly exaggerated unfavourable reports of the actions and attitude of the Gaelic-speaking population that appeared at the time in the sensational Press.

[1] *Borderland,* vol. II, p. 58.

[2] James Cameron, chapter on 'Tiree under Military Law', in *The Old and the New Highlands and Hebrides,* pp. 89–100.

9

'MISS X' REACHES ERISKAY

MISS FREER'S first interim report on the Second Sight Enquiry evidently impressed the S.P.R. favourably. On 19th January 1895 Dewar wrote to Lord Bute saying that he had heard from Dr Leaf and Mr Bennett that Miss Freer's report had excited much interest. Dewar also referred again to his having given Miss Freer all the correspondence relating to the Enquiry in the autumn of 1894.

Miss Freer herself wrote to Lord Bute on the 2nd February 1895 that:

The theory about publishing results of the Scotch enquiry is that it should be kept quiet until I have carried it further, as I hope to do. Mr Myers thinks I ought to be able to produce a serious book on the subject but I should not like to rush into print with immature conclusions.

I have not received any cases from Mr Dewar so that I have only the results of my own seven weeks' work, and far more than that is, or should be requisite. From the delay that ensued in paying out my expenses, about £45 for two persons (my companion paid for her own travelling) for seven weeks I gather that the S.P.R. funds are low, and that another time I must provide for myself which however I am willing to do. How the S.P.R. spends its large income and its frequent legacies and donations, considering that no one is ever paid for work, I don't know, but that is not my business!

The complaint about Dewar's not having sent any memoranda was repeated on 20th July, although, as has been seen, Dewar had written to Lord Bute at great length on his 1894 Hebridean tour on 8th August of that year. It was not true that Miss Freer had only the results of her seven weeks work in 1894; Dewar had given her not only all the replies to the second sight questionnaire but also the papers connected with the case of Mrs Cameron, the seeress of Kinlochrannoch.[1]

Miss Freer's remarks about the financing of her trip to the Highlands seem decidedly disingenuous. She was well enough aware that Lord Bute was financing the Enquiry: she had alluded to its in-

[1] Letter, Rev. Peter Dewar to Lord Bute, 3rd June 1895.

debtedness to his liberality in her first interim report, already quoted. What her remarks therefore imply is that the S.P.R. was not disbursing Bute's donation promptly insofar as her expenses were concerned. This may have been her justification for requesting a loan on her visit to Falkland at the end of her 1894 tour: the matter is discussed by Mr Trevor Hall elsewhere in this book.[1]

Miss Freer, in any case, was indebted to the Rev. Peter Dewar for making advance arrangements on her behalf, not only in Tiree in 1894 but also in North and South Uist in 1895. On the 20th July Dewar, who the previous month had visited Mrs Cameron at Kinlochrannoch on behalf of Lord Bute, wrote to Bute that:

I shall arrange for Miss Freer visiting Uist and write the Revd. A. Macdonald and other kinds friends in Lochmaddy and Lochboisdale who will take her by the hand.

On 5th July Miss Freer wrote to Lord Bute that she was to 'discuss the Scotch journey with Myers tomorrow'. There was difficulty about a companion; Miss Moore could not go this time, having to look after an invalid father. Miss Freer could find 'no *woman* so interested. Mrs Grundy disallows a man of whom I would find plenty.' On 20th July Miss Freer wrote:

Of course I will not fail to let you know of the progress of my work in Scotland, to which I am most eagerly looking forward.

I am waiting to make any plans till I hear from Mr Dewar of his enquiries in Skye last year, as that seems my next likely hunting ground.

Dewar cannot be blamed for the delaying of Miss Freer's 1895 trip to the Hebrides, however. During the week before 14th August Miss Freer wrote to Lord Bute in a letter of which the first part has been lost:

I hope to be off on Wednesday. I have been waiting partly for my companion, having at last, I hope, got hold of the right person, a Miss Bates, a great traveller and clever authoress who has investigated spiritualism in America, and of whose escort Mr Myers highly approves!

I find that my article on St Winifrede[2] *has met with high approval among the priests of the S*[*ociety of*] *J*[*esus*] *and I hope may help me with some of those I shall meet in Scotland, in Uist and elsewhere. I am quite convinced that I shall get nothing out of Presbyterians. They* are *what they* call *Catholic and Anglican Churchmen, 'priest-ridden'.*

[1] See p. 139.

[2] See *Essays in Psychical Research*, London, 1899, p. 261.

I propose to have another try for written evidence in Tiree but have not much hope.[1] *We work gradually northward leaving Oban about August 28.*

I should have been in Tiree now, by myself, but have been ill, for the first time in all my experience made ill by psychic phenomena!

The matter is private but may interest you. I received a long communication lasting over five hours, professedly from Sir Richard Burton whom I never knew, and containing a great number of facts which have since been verified in every detail, which no sub-conscious memory or observation can explain. The whole thing is very curious and interesting but has left me quite prostrate, and I am only just beginning to feel capable of travel . . .

The 'Burton Messages', which are discussed by Mr Trevor Hall on pp. 146–151 of this book, were 'communicated' through 'Miss X' by automatic writing at the 'country house' of her friends 'Mr and Mrs D.' on 25th and 26th July 1895, and by ouija board, crystal-gazing, and 'hearing' at the house of Lady Burton at Mortlake on 5th August, and were described by 'Miss X' (Miss Freer) at great length in *Borderland*, vol. III, pp. 157–72. There is no mention of Miss Freer's having been left prostrate, in her article, but undoubtedly the writing of it must have been an exhausting effort.[2] She and her companion did not reach Oban until about 18th August. From there she wrote to Lord Bute at some length:

Windsor Hotel, Oban
26th August 1895

My dear Lord Marquis,

In view of being, after this week, more or less beyond the reach of posts I am writing to tell your Lordship that we expect to be off northwards next Friday. I have taken counsel with MacBrayne's Manager as to the sequence of my tour as on the one hand I don't want to be hurried nor on the other to be planté là.

I have a few cases in Skye, some in Uist, Eriskay, Barra, and Tiree,

[1] This is a contrast to her early enthusiastic letters from Tiree.

[2] Miss Freer's accuracy, and secretiveness, can be judged from the remark (*Borderland*, vol. III, p. 167) that shortly after her séance with Lady Burton she 'left England for nearly three months'. Readers would think she had gone, not to Scotland, but abroad. In any case, her next letter from London to Lord Bute was dated 19th October, so her absence was one of only a day or two over two months. Myers wrote Bute on 13th August that Miss Freer had told him she was leaving for Scotland on the 15th. The 15th was a Thursday. In the letter just quoted Miss Freer ended by saying that she proposed to rest for a few days on her way north at the Hon. Mrs Greville Nugent's house at Ecclefechan.

and have written to Mr Chisholm and the Doctor who filled up the Census papers.

I have been here over a week working up some clues which have arisen since my last visit mainly through the kindness of Mrs Malcolm of Poltalloch on Loch Awe and of Mr McIsaac who you may remember is the reviser of the Gaelic of Lord Archie Campbell's Argyllshire series. I have also renewed my acquaintance with the Seer of Glencoe, and of the Clergy there (Anglicans, or rather I should say Episcopalians!) who have been very kind in helping . . . .

If you have any directions or suggestions for me, I shall be grateful for them and as my stay in each place depends on what I find there, perhaps it would be well to send to Poste Restante, Oban, as my address will be telegraphed there at each point. If I settle *anywhere I will write again.*

Truly yours
Ada Goodrich-Freer

'Mountaineer'
2nd September

My dear Lord Marquis,

I am writing without a table, with a Swan pen, and an 'Author's Block' on board the Steamer. My apology for this unconventional stationary.

Your kind note has just reached me. The weather has been so tremendously rough that even MacBrayne's Agents advised us not to start on Thursday, so I went up to Ballachulish instead where we were most kindly entertained by the Bishop of Argyll for three days.

I visited all the Seers I made friends with last year, so as to keep alive their interest, and among new facts found, to my great pleasure, that a form of mirror gazing I had heard of in central Europe only, is practised by 'Witches' in Scotland.

I think almost any collection might easily be better than Lord A. Campbell's![1] *It has been my misfortune to follow him both in Tiree and Lochaber, and to have to live him down in both places, before I could get anything of value!*

It will interest me immensely to carry out your suggestions. The few stories Mr Dewar brought away from Mr MacDonald were not very interesting, but the fault may have been (from want of experience) in their selection, and if he, Mr MacDonald, should allow me to see his collection I would report upon it as a whole. I heard of him the other day as a very interesting man from one who knows him well, Dr Stewart. . . .

[1] This impertinent remark apparently refers to Lord Archibald Campbell's *Records of Argyll*, published by Blackwood's in 1885. Among much local tradition, it contains some second sight stories from Tiree.

I picked up some very interesting healing traditions in Lochaber, but could find no one now exercising the healing gift.

I heard from Lady Victoria Campbell this morning. She is hoping to spend the winter in Tiree. . . .

[*There follow comments on Lord Archibald Campbell's plan to march pipers down Glencoe.*]

The Cluiney [?] *-Haldanes gave a dinner party on my account that I might meet the neighbourhood and their own Pipe Band performed while we were at dinner. Having heard of my quest, the Bishop's piper, a Cameron—opened with 'Mount Stuart' as a compliment to your Lordship!*

During this week, Poste Restante, Barra, by Oban will find me.

Sincerely yours,
Ada Goodrich-Freer

Though Miss Freer had written in her letter of 15th August 1894 to Myers that any further enquiries should be pursued earlier in the year, when the people had more leisure, this time she had started for the Highlands more than a month later. Her progress to and from the Hebrides was reported in the *Oban Times*, where on Saturday, 7th September, we find:

Miss Goodrich-Freer, who last year visited the Highlands with other members of the Psychological Society [sic] *collecting information regarding second sight, was in Oban last week on her way to the Outer Hebrides with the same object in view. Miss Goodrich-Freer is an acknowledged authority on the subject of second sight and kindred subjects.*

This is the first time that 'Miss X's' real name appeared in print. In fact, she had held a Press interview at Oban, for on the 17th of the same month Dewar wrote to Lord Bute that:

From last week's Rothesay Chronicle *I notice that Miss Goodrich-Freer has been according newspaper editors in Oban this year, as she did last year, the honour of an interview on the prospects of the Second Sight Enquiry in the Highlands. I wrote Dr McRury of Barra, Revd A. Macdonald of Eriskay, and some friends in Uist to kindly aid her in the research. I have not heard from her since she left London, when she wrote that she had made all her arrangements. I hope she has been successful in her quest, and that results of permanent scienti[fi]c value to the cause of Psychical Research have been obtained.*

News must have come from South Uist to Dewar or Lord Bute immediately after this, for on 21st September Dewar wrote:

I am most sincerely sorry to hear that the state of the health of the Revd A. Macdonald of Eriskay is thought to be so serious, for he has thrown himself heart and soul into the work of his sacred calling, and is a man of fine qualities of head and heart. I shall never forget his kindness and courtesy to me last summer, when I stayed for several days under his hospitable roof. He not only was so good as to accompany me to the homes of several members of his flock, and to encourage them in every way frankly and freely to state their second sight experiences, but he even allowed me to copy notes of interesting cases jotted down some years previously in his private note-book.[1]

I hope the Bishop will arrange to relieve him of duty for a time, as a sojourn in the sunny south and a generous regimen might even yet be the means of restoring his health. I could see that he must have suffered considerable hardship in Eriskay, which is not only insular but extremely isolated.[2]

Miss Freer proceeded to Barra, the Uists, and Skye. Unfortunately no letter written by her to Lord Bute between 2nd September and 2nd October 1895 appears to survive, and we are therefore without any account of her first impressions of South Uist and Eriskay or of her first meeting with Fr Allan McDonald. She was probably the source of the information about his bad health, on which Dewar comments. That Miss Freer's attitude towards Fr Allan McDonald and his folklore collection was, originally at least, patronizing and acquisitive is abundantly proved by her next letter, and by the correspondence about his MSS. which follows it. On 2nd October she wrote to Lord Bute from the Lochmaddy hotel in North Uist:

Thank you for two kind notes received today.

I am more than glad that you are willing to give help to Father Alan Macdonald [sic] *as to his MSS. I hope that he will decide to sell them to you out-right so that, with your permission, they may afford, apart from any separate publication, material for our present enquiry, as I did not make notes of what he* told *me, knowing that the matter already existed in MS. I venture to think that the offer should be made* pro-*spectively, as well as* retro-*spectively as he told me that he had much unwritten material.*

If it seemed desirable I would willingly take up my abode in Eriskay for any necessary period, if he and his sister would receive me, later. Naturally he has no experience as to what is, or is not, valuable in his collection.

I have just had the pleasure of sending him some port wine and essence of beef from London. Good men—as good as that—are scarce! . . .

[1] It was from Dewar that Miss Freer first learnt about Fr Allan's notebooks, see p. 70.

[2] There was then only one postal delivery at Eriskay a week.

Skye proved a very happy hunting ground. The Clan Macdonald were all assembled for Lady Eroll Hay's wedding[1] *and with Highland hospitality took me to their hearths and homes and would have entertained me for a year and a day had I had that time to spare. However, I had time enough to start enquiries in various directions, and Dr Keith Macdonald especially, has become enthusiastic. I have promised, if possible, to visit them all next year. There is a young laird there, Nicol Martin, said to belong to a family which anti-dates even the MacLeods, who took an immense amount of trouble in the matter, and drove me 30 one day miles* [sic] *story-hunting.*

I have one story of premonition of marriage and dozens of phantasmal shrouds, such as you ask about!

Thank you for advice about Borderland. *I have abandoned the current number and find that Mr Stead has taken fright in consequence. He writes today to sound me as to the conditions of my return. Of course he is furious at the check to his book, a new experience to him!*

I have let my London house and am so much the more in a position to make my own terms as to Borderland. *The question has come to be one of conscience, as well as of taste!*

The remaining points with which your Lordship's letters deal is that of my movements. I returned here yesterday. Mr Chisholm, who was so kind in his offers of help, is very willing, but personally so unpopular in the Island, that I have been glad to strike a fresh vein. I have now had enough experience to acquire some flair *in such matters! I have now made friends with a certain Gillies, an old soldier, and some schoolmasters and am off tomorrow to the other side of the Island, for which I must give myself at least four days, leaving here at latest on Sunday night and giving up Stornoway altogether. . . .*

I had a curious bit of second sight myself in Skye which caused a small sensation and was useful 'pour encourager les autres', a prevision on Monday last, of a carriage accident which occurred on the wedding day—Wednesday. . . .

Sincerely yours
Ada Goodrich-Freer

I hear from Lady Victoria Campbell that she is now in Tiree. I grieve that time fails me to go there again. It would have been worth while.

It is clear from this letter that Miss Freer had persuaded Lord Bute to offer to purchase Fr Allan McDonald's MS. folklore collection as it then existed—presumably the first four notebooks of the

[1] Mrs Otta Swire tells me that the wedding thus referred to was that of Sir Lewis John Erroll Hay, Bt. and Miss Lizabel MacDonald of Skaebost, which took place at Portree on 25th September 1895.

series[1]—and also whatever matter of interest he might collect in the future. Fr Allan McDonald apparently replied with a counter-suggestion of which the precise nature is unknown, as the letter containing it was returned by Lord Bute, after it had been shown to him, to Miss Freer, and has disappeared with her other papers. But from Miss Freer's comments in her accompanying letter of 19th October 1895 it may be fairly surmised that what Fr Allan McDonald suggested was something in the nature of support for the publication of a book about Hebridean folklore and folk-tales in general, such as had been suggested by George Henderson in 1892.[2] He may well have been influenced by the fact that George Henderson had a strong interest in the Fingalian stories taken down during his visit to Eriskay in the early winter of 1892, and Alexander Carmichael an equally strong interest in much of the other material he had collected. The proposal, whatever its precise nature was, was immediately vetoed by Miss Freer.

. . . .I have received the enclosed letter from Father Allan, from which I gather that the scheme proposed to him has been misunderstood, either by himself or by his correspondent. Such work as he suggests is already being done by the Gaelic Society,[3] by Lord A. Campbell—by the Viking Society and other existing agencies with various degrees of success—If such work were possible or were deemed necessary, it would be pleasant enough in the doing, but I doubt its appreciation by the public. Of course I have not replied without instructions. I fancy he must have been asked to write a book on the Hebrides, whereas I imagine your Lordship's intention was to suggest the purchase of the notes he has already made.

Carmichael's work I believe is good from the literary point of view, but my experience of him is, that he clings to every half penny of its value! and I doubt his willingness to collaborate with anyone! . . .

Lord Bute himself, while possessed of the qualities of generosity, imagination, and intellectual curiosity, was inclined to be impatient of opposition and irritated by counter-suggestions put forward to his plans.[4] He commented petulantly on Fr Allan McDonald's proposals in a letter from Cardiff Castle, a copy of which has fortunately been preserved in his papers:

[1] See p. 15. [2] See p. 14.

[3] Presumably the Gaelic Society of Inverness, see p. 82.

[4] Bute's official biographer, the Rt Rev. Sir David Hunter Blair, O.S.B., remarked of Bute that 'the candid biographer must admit that, with all his admirable qualities, he was not of a temperament that could easily or patiently brook opposition to his matured views' (*The Marquess of Bute*, London, 1921, p. 186).

The Revd. A. MacD[onald] is very tiresome—When one has given a great deal of thought, time and trouble to a thing, and after the most mature consideration is met by a contrary proposal, one is naturally vexed. Besides, I have so much to do that I cannot spend hours and days in writing about things I will have nothing to do with. He must either accept my proposals or not. C'est à prendre ou à laisser.

I refuse absolutely and finally to have anything to do with such a work as he proposes, and which was a thing that of course had never entered my head. I will not have anything to do with other collaborators than you and him.

The material was entirely and exclusively confined to that bearing on psychical matters, but it was to include not only what he has but also what he may hereafter obtain. You told me he had unwritten matter already.

The Bishop and I agreed that your kind offer to edit these materials ought to be accepted—and the Rev. A. MacD. now assents to the same thing. So that is at an end, if you are still of the same mind. But I must ask you to tell me what your terms would be. These things are always better settled beforehand.

The Bishop had to submit to [the] Rev. A. MacD[onald] the following questions (supposing him prepared to allow the use of his material):— Would he prefer

A. To sell me the material out and out for as much (say) as £100, or other sum that might be agreed on? or
B. Would he prefer to retain the material, collaborating with you in your editing at my expense so much of it as you might judge desirable, and he receiving from me £50 to meet expenses of his own?

I can imagine nothing simpler than this. I had thought it all out, and the question is final. He could have answered alphabetically 'A' or 'B', and I neither can nor will go into matters with which I have never dreamt of having anything to do.

You may settle it with him i.e. *whether A or B, if you are still disposed. But I own that it makes my heart sink when in reply to a question so clear, he does nothing but write you the wearisome mess of irrelevant trash about a thing I never dreamt of and definitely refuse even to entertain, which you sent me and I return. But I must beg never to be pestered with it again. If I am, I cannot promise to take any notice of it.*

Under psychical matters I include those having to do with religion, omens, magic etc.

Miss Freer promptly replied from Holy Trinity Vicarage, Paddington, on 24th October:

Dear Lord Marquis,

I am very sorry that I had to bore you with Father A. Macdonald's irrelevancies but as I *had never communicated with him in the matter, and did not know what line the Bishop had taken, I felt bound to bring the matter before your Lordship. I will write to him on the lines you indicate. Your proposal is extremely liberal and as you leave the matter in my hands, I will see that he shall be brought to the point.*

As to my own share (if any is necessary) in the matter it is not a question of fee. My sole desire was to forward psychic research, and incidentally to help a man who is in poverty and suffering. As you know, our rule in the S.P.R. is never to receive anything but expenses and had I had any thought of my own advantage I should not myself have made the proposition. . . .

Her next communication on the subject to Lord Bute, dated 11th November 1895, makes her attitude to Fr Allan McDonald, and to his fellow-countrymen, with whom she later claimed to be connected,[1] quite plain:

. . . . Father A. Macdonald has by this time received a very definite letter from me to which he must give an answer which will settle everything. I have no doubt of his taking his instructions as sent. The only way to get on with Highlanders is to say *what you want. They always obey. . . .*

Miss Freer next wrote a letter to Lord Bute's secretary which betrays her determination to get hold of what Fr Allan McDonald had collected in the past and might collect in the future, and to do so at a cut rate—Lord Bute's suggestion of giving Fr Allan £50 for his future expenses is reduced by her to £10. It is hardly necessary to say that she had no qualifications for revising or editing Fr Allan's collection as a whole; on the other hand, if it were a matter of choosing the best attested second sight stories recorded in English in it, and classifying them under various headings, any intelligent amanuensis could have done that, or better still, Fr Allan McDonald could have been asked to do it himself.

27 Cleveland Gardens
29th November 1895

Dear Mr Anderson,

I hear with much regret that his Lordship is not well and I therefore hope that I am doing right in communicating directly with you upon a little matter of business.

Doubtless you know that an offer has been made via *Bishop* [*Smith*]

[1] See pp. 82, and 89.

to the Rev. Allan Macdonald in regard to some MS. collections which he has made of Second Sight stories and the like.

The original suggestion as to payment seemed to me 1. disproportionately liberal, 2. possibly disappointing in results; as an out and out purchase seemed less likely to be of use than a method which should keep Father M. at our service *in this connection,—besides minor reasons with which I need not trouble you.*

His Lordship left the matter in my hands and I write to tell you the present position of affairs.

a. Mr Macdonald has sent me all [*the*] *MSS. he at present possesses. They are somewhat confused and contain a good deal irrelevant to our purpose, but are very interesting.*

b. He is willing to continue collecting in his own island and the other Catholic Islands.

c. I propose to receive and revise his MSS. and if they seem suitable for publication to edit them in some form which may seem desirable at a later stage. My work to be of course honorary, but Lord Bute was good enough to suggest that I should apply to him for any necessary expenses —such for example as going to Eriskay (apart from the S.S. enquiry) if desirable, to deal directly *with Father Allan.*

d. Payment to Father A. to be on the usual literary terms, on publication, but Father Allan McD. to receive, at once, £10 for immediate expenses.

I enclose a copy of what he says in a letter to me, and shall be glad of any directions and suggestions.

Truly yours,
A. Goodrich-Freer

Copy of passage in letter from the Rev. A. Macdonald, November 26, in answer to a letter from me making the final proposals quoted in the accompanying letter.

You ask for my views on the question—of collecting evidence I suppose.

I am most willing to forward you from time to time all such cases as I may collect, and I am most willing also to collect in Barra, S. Uist and Benbecula. There is no plan so agreeable to me as to forward notes to you and to leave them to your discretion. I hope Lord Bute will find that plan satisfactory.

The reader will note that Fr Allan McDonald's reply, if it was authentically transmitted by Miss Freer, makes no reference to any sale of his existing manuscripts. It simply indicates his willingness to collect future instances of second sight in the Catholic islands for

Lord Bute and forward them to Miss Freer. Fr Allan McDonald's main collection remained his property until it was sold to Walter Blaikie nearly ten years later. He duly began his collection of second sight stories, entitled 'Strange Things', which is printed here, on 26th November 1895—the first items bear this date—but his main collection had passed meanwhile into the hands of Miss Freer, and she was soon to exploit it to gain herself an undeserved reputation as a Hebridean folklorist. Ironically enough, 'Strange Things' never passed into her hands; the Second Sight Enquiry petered out while the MS. was still in Fr Allan McDonald's possession.

The £10 Miss Freer suggested for Fr Allan McDonald's expenses was not received immediately. On 16th January 1896 Miss Freer wrote to Lord Bute's secretary:

At the beginning of December I wrote to you as to the MSS. of the Rev. Allan Macdonald which Lord Bute had instructed me to deal with. I ventured to suggest that being a very poor priest he should have £10 on acc: for his expenses.

I have received no reply and do not know how to proceed. His Lordship did not wish to be troubled in the matter, but as he gave me carte blanche *as to procedure, I have allowed Mr Macdonald to continue his researches.*

Shall I send him my own cheque, or will you send the amount to me—or to him? Address Presbytery, Isle of Eriskay, Loch Boisdale, and he can only be reached once a week, on a Thursday, so the letter should reach Loch Boisdale on a Wednesday.

The cheque was sent. On 27th January Miss Freer wrote:

Thanks for cheque received. I am very glad to have some one to share my responsibility in this matter. Lord Bute's liberality in leaving the entire question à discretion *threatened to stop proceedings altogether!*

'I have allowed Mr Macdonald to continue his researches'!! One can here see the growth of that overweening pride and self-assertiveness which brought down so much criticism and disapproval on the head of 'Miss X' over the Burton, Clandon, and Ballechin affairs, which are described here in later chapters by Mr Trevor Hall.

10

'MISS X' MAKES HER SECOND INTERIM REPORT

MEANWHILE, THE *Oban Times* had reported the return of Miss Freer from the isles on 12th October 1895:

Miss Goodrich Freer, a prominent member of the Society for Psychical Research, and who has for some time been travelling in the Hebrides collecting information regarding second-sight and kindred subjects, was in Oban during the week on her way south. This lady visited North and South Uist and part of Skye, and has secured a large amount of curious and interesting information from the islanders, which will doubtless in time be made public. Miss Freer has expressed her great admiration of the Highlands and its people, and of the kindness and hospitality she experienced in the course of her tour she will always retain a pleasant recollection.

She had also visited Barra, as is clear from an anecdote Fr Allan recorded as having occurred while she was there that year. Meanwhile, the generous Lord Bute had given the S.P.R. a further sum of £100 towards the Enquiry.[1] Bute apparently suggested that Dewar should be invited to give an address on Highland second sight and the Enquiry to the S.P.R., for on 14th October Myers wrote to Bute enclosing Dewar's letter declining the invitation with appreciation and thanks, partly on domestic grounds (his wife, whom he had married a year earlier, was then expecting her first child), partly because Miss Freer had already used the material he had collected in her first report (see page 63). Dewar remarked that 'in Scotland there is a great deal of prejudice and apathy still to be overcome'. Dewar had earlier, 31st August 1894, written to Bute referring to newspaper ridicule of the Enquiry,[2] and saying that he himself had been subjected to ridicule 'at the hands of men who should know better' and that 'a goodly number of parishioners and of the mem-

[1] *Journal*, S.P.R., vol. VII, 1895, p. 130.

[2] See leading article on 'An Taibhsear', in the *Glasgow Evening News*, 10th April 1894, gently mocking the Enquiry.

bers of my congregation have indicated to me that I ought to be more usefully employed'.

Miss Freer made her second interim report on the Second Sight Enquiry to 'a very crowded general meeting' of the Society for Psychical Research on 6th December 1895 in the Westminster Town Hall, with Professor H. Sidgwick in the chair. The meeting, and her address, were reported at length in *Borderland* of January 1896. The second interim report did little more than reiterate the findings of the first—it even repeated a second sight anecdote that Miss Freer had related before, that of the man who tried unsuccessfully to falsify a seer's prediction that he would be a pall-bearer at a funeral at which he would be carrying an overcoat.[1] It does however amply illustrate the growth in Miss Freer's self-confidence, and also the capacity for arranging and presenting her material, however obtained, which was later to be shown in her folk-lore lectures based on Fr Allan McDonald's collection. There is no reference to Dewar; the schedule of questions issued in 1893–4, 'through the liberality of the Marquis of Bute', is stated to have 'failed to elicit much information'; but Miss Freer 'had been happy in securing help and sympathy in her work among all classes in the Highlands, and by one means or another had never yet been refused a first hand narrative from any Seer she had been fortunate to discover'. She had 'lost no opportunity of interesting, whenever possible, all educated residents in the Islands and Highlands with whom she had been brought into contact'. The only difficulty had been obtaining evidence to substantiate the stories of the seers. 'Highland reticence, Highland indifference to method and system, Highland repudiation of meddling with a neighbour's affairs, might be overcome' but establishing exact dates was a matter of extreme difficulty. In any case, 'Miss X did not encumber her address with details as to evidence, reserving all such matter for a more formal occasion than this of a mere *interim* report.'

Ten anecdotes were given, with the names of persons and places suppressed—not that it is particularly difficult for a reader to guess the identity of 'the Island of S——' or 'A——shire'. Miss Freer asserted that the 'natives' distinguished 'at least three kinds of second sight, the Gaelic names for which might be rendered as (1) second sight (proper), (2) sight by "wish", and (3) sight by "vision", or, as we should perhaps say (1) visualized clairvoyance or premonition, (2) experimental clairvoyance, and (3) symbolic vision.'

The Gaelic for 'second sight' is *an dà shealladh*, 'the two sights'.

[1] See *Borderland*, vol. II, p. 59 (1895); vol. III, p. 59 (1896).

3. Left to right: Walter Blaikie, Miss Constance Moore holding 'Scamp', Miss Ada Goodrich Freer, and Fr Allan McDonald. Photograph taken on Eriskay in August 1898 with Walter Blaikie's camera, possibly operated by the Hon. Everard Feilding.

4. Haun, Eriskay, in 1898. South Uist is seen across Eriskay Sound in the background. Photograph taken by Walter Blaikie.

The writer is unaware of the existence of Gaelic terms meaning literally 'sight by wish' and 'sight by vision'. It is clear from the examples Miss Freer gives that what she means by 'sight by wish' is 'divination', for which the Gaelic is *fiosachd* or *frìth*, and what she means by 'sight by vision' is 'forewarning', for which the Gaelic is *manadh*. Examples of all three kinds will be found among the stories collected by Fr Allan McDonald that are printed in this book; the reader in search of them can find them through the Motif-Index.

Miss Freer concluded her remarks by saying that in search of her material she had 'sought out the most remote spots accessible' [actually Dewar had found them for her!] and 'had gleaned her information from the fisherman in his herring boat, and the travelling "merchant" in his gig, in the blacksmith's forge, and the manse kitchen; she had received help and hospitality from the Roman priest and the Presbyterian minister [this was true enough] from the laird, the police, and the poor-house official. . . . She looked forward to the future prosecution of her inquiry, as she looked back on the months already spent among those she proudly [and quite imaginatively!] claimed as her fellow-countrymen, with unmixed pleasure and cordial appreciation of all they have of grand and noble to show, to share, and to teach.'

What a pity that the information gained by Miss Freer in the fishermen's boats, the merchants' gigs, and at the blacksmiths' forges, if it really amounted to more than the material received by the Rev. Peter Dewar in answer to the schedule of questions or noted by Fr Allan McDonald in his earlier notebooks, along with the 'details as to evidence' and the 'careful diary of our conversations',[1] has not been preserved, after all the expense Lord Bute incurred over the survey and all the interest the S.P.R. took in it! Only one hint of scepticism was heard at this meeting to hear the second interim report, that of Dr A. R. Wallace, who said that 'he had followed "Miss X" in Iona, and had communicated to a native (*sic*) his speculation as to the success of her inquiry in that island. The reply had been that she very likely had succeeded, as 'they were as good liars in that island as in any other'.[2] To this 'Miss X' replied that they were 'probably better' owing to contamination by 'English and Lowland tourists'—but the point had been made.

[1] *Borderland*, vol. II, p. 57 (January 1895). [2] *Op. cit.*, p. 61.

11

THE FAILURE OF THE SECOND SIGHT ENQUIRY

IN JANUARY of 1896 Miss Freer gave up, or was relieved of, her assistant editorship of *Borderland.* No doubt the duties connected with it had already been delegated, in view of her innumerable outside activities, including the Second Sight Enquiry. In order to promote this, Miss Freer gave a lecture to the Gaelic Society of Inverness on 30th April.[1] This lecture was ultimately printed in Volume XXI of the Society's *Transactions,* but it was also immediately printed in the local paper, the Inverness *Courier*—and immediately criticized there.

It is particularly striking that the lecture, as reported in the *Courier* of 5th May 1896, is entirely different from what later appeared in the Gaelic Society's *Transactions,* even as regards the title, which in the *Courier* is given as 'Second Sight and Psychical Research' and in the *Transactions* as 'Second Sight in the Highlands'. In the *Courier* Miss Freer, who gave the lecture under her own name, was introduced as 'co-editor of Mr Stead's publication entitled *Borderland*' (which in fact she had ceased to be) and was described as having 'a pleasing presence and an excellent command of language'. The lecture was reported to have 'extended over little short of two hours'. As reported, Miss Freer began her remarks by saying that she 'was proud that she was to a very great degree by blood a Highlander, in spite of her misfortune of having been born in England'. This claim was reiterated in the version of the lecture printed in the Gaelic Society's *Transactions,* where Miss Freer also referred to 'us Celts', and herself as 'a woman of leisure'. These remarks were untrue.

As reported in the *Courier,* the lecture continued with many anecdotes of second sight in the Highlands, one being that of the Bracadale (Skye) shepherd's restless crook, an implement the uncanny movements of which presaged its ultimate use to save a man from drowning. In the course of the lecture Miss Freer alluded to

[1] She refers to the Society's invitation to give this address, in a letter to Lord Bute dated 18th January 1896.

the séances she had had with Lady Burton the preceding summer. After she had finished her lecture, various persons present told second sight stories such as have always been current in the Highlands.

At least one sceptic, familiar with what the London Press had had to say about the Burton séances, must have been present in the audience, for the lecture, as reported in the *Courier*, was followed immediately by a letter signed 'A Member', in which Miss Freer was described as 'Mr Stead's medium', and a scathing attack on the Burton séances in the *World* was quoted at some length. The writer went on to say that 'the lecture on "Second Sight" was the most ridiculous thing that the Gaelic Society has perpetrated, and I doubt if the Society could survive another such performance. For that reason I hope that the clever "little lady"[1] will not come back.' This attack produced an immediate reply from Miss Freer, written from Rusack's Marine Hotel in St Andrews on 8th May 1896, asserting that a main object of both her lecture to the Society and her article in *Borderland* on the Burton séances had been 'to disavow the necessity for supposing any connection between the phenomena of Second Sight and the hypothesis of spiritualism', denying that she was 'a medium' (although she had not repudiated this suggestion when it came from Mrs Piper in 1889,[2] and had certainly acted as one with Lady Burton); and ending by saying that she was 'responsible for none of the opinions expressed in *Borderland* but those which appear above the signature of Yours faithfully, A. Goodrich-Freer ("X")'. This was the first time she had publicly admitted the identity of 'Miss X' in print.

When the lecture was revised by Miss Freer in the autumn of 1897 for printing in the Gaelic Society's *Transactions*, both a diagram which Miss Freer had used to demonstrate the space–time co-ordinates of second sight, and the second sight stories themselves, were dropped, Miss Freer remarking in a letter that was printed along with the lecture that: 'I think that such persons as are likely to be interested by what I had to say can probably supply more and better stories than I.'

The result is that, as printed in the Gaelic Society's *Transactions*, the lecture contains little more than the account of the Second Sight Enquiry, promoted by the S.P.R. and financed through the liberality of Lord Bute, which had already appeared in the pages of the S.P.R. *Journal* and in *Borderland*. This is coupled with an appeal to members of the Gaelic Society of Inverness for more material. As so

[1] This suggests that the writer was familiar with Miss Freer's Gaelic nickname, 'Cailleach bheag nam bòcan'.

[2] See *Borderland*, vol. I, p. 226.

printed, the lecture would seem to be about the dullest ever to appear in the Society's *Transactions*. It is not easy to understand why it should have been published at all, for Volume XXI of the Society's *Transactions* did not appear until the summer of 1899, almost coinciding with the publication by Miss Freer and Lord Bute of their book *The Alleged Haunting of B—— House*, in which Miss Freer defended the Ballechin ghost-hunt, and criticized the S.P.R., and Myers in particular, for yielding to attacks on it in *The Times* in June 1897, and refusing to print her report on it in the Society's *Proceedings*. Presumably the Gaelic Society of Inverness was unaware that by 1899 the Second Sight Enquiry was dead, killed by this quarrel between Miss Freer and the leaders of the S.P.R., unless she still hoped, when in the autumn of 1897 she revised her address for publication in the Society's *Transactions*, to continue the Enquiry independently with the help of Lord Bute.

From St Andrews, where Lord Bute, who was Rector of the University, had archaeological interests, Miss Freer went on to Edinburgh. On 15th May she wrote to Lord Bute from Sanquhar:

I went to Edinbro for a day or two and did various bits of S.P.R. business. I saw Lady Victoria Campbell who gave me some help as to Tiree, and also a Tiree minister whose information as to the real source of any difficulties that have occurred is most invaluable. Also Mr Taylor Innes, with whom I talked for three hours, I hope to his soul's good, as he ended by proposing to do pennance [sic] *in a white sheet for the mischief he has wrought the S.P.R. in his articles in the* Nineteenth Century. . . .[1]

Miss Freer then returned to London, and on 27th June wrote to Lord Bute that she was 'deep in *Borderland* work'. On 30th July 1896 Myers wrote to Bute:

I hear from Miss Freer that she is shortly going to the Highlands and I believe *that the fund which you have generously devoted to that enquiry is running very low:—so it will be kind if you will either replenish it, or tell us that it is* not *to be replenished!*

Lord Bute must have responded promptly, and favourably, for on 5th August Myers wrote:

Thank you most sincerely for your very generous reinforcement of the Second Sight Fund. I do not really know whether so large a sum will

[1] Taylor Innes had severely criticized the S.P.R. publication 'Phantasms of the Living' in the *Nineteenth Century* in 1887 and 1891, on the ground that the stories therein lacked evidential substantiation in nearly every case, see Trevor H. Hall, *The Strange Case of Edmund Gurney*, London, 1964, pp. 76–7.

still be needed; Miss X is careful*; but she seems to be meaning to make rather a long tour this summer in the Highlands. Accurate* account *is kept of her expenditure.*

Miss Freer travelled north in the middle of August. Her immediate purpose was to consult Alexander Carmichael, who by this time was the doyen of Scottish Gaelic folklorists. Her visit is referred to both in a letter from her to Lord Bute, and in a letter from Carmichael to Fr Allan McDonald. On 19th August Carmichael wrote:

Miss Freer came to us last evening. Mr Henderson is home and we see him often but not half so often as we would like. He was with us last evening and of course is charmed as we all are with Miss Freer . . .

Ella[1] *went a week ago to St Abb's with friends. She came home yesterday to help to entertain Miss Freer. When Miss Freer leaves Ella will go back to her friends at St Abb's for a few weeks more till her classes begin . . .*

Miss Freer had been in communication with Carmichael previously, for in a letter to Fr Allan McDonald, apparently dated 2nd July 1896, Carmichael remarks that: 'I did not know that you were so ill till Miss Freer told me.' This may refer to Fr Allan's illness in the autumn of 1895, as the previous existing letter from Carmichael is dated on 7th November of that year.

Miss Freer wrote to Lord Bute on 20th August: the letter is headed 'Edinbro':

I am here to consult Mr Carmichael, who you may know as a Highland archaeologist, on my proceedings. No one I have ever met is so full of information on the western Highlands. Today I go to Oban and thence to Skye.

I saw the Archbishop[2] *here yesterday and was very glad to hear him say he entirely believed in the Second Sight. As a Highlander I knew the* man *must, but I was glad to hear the Ecclesiastic say so.*

Mrs MacDonell—Keppoch—has given me some first hand cases to look up on the braes of Lochaber. The Bishop's house will shelter me at Ballachulish. My best Tiree informant and good friend has just been appointed to the Kirk in Glencoe, so I can interview him[3] *. . .*

[1] Carmichael's daughter.

[2] Archbishop Angus Macdonald, formerly Bishop of Argyll and the Isles (1878–92), in which capacity he had had a considerable correspondence with Lord Bute, some of which can be read in the Rev. Roderick MacDonald's article on 'The "Tin" Cathedral at Oban', in the *Innes Review*, vol. XV, pp. 47–55.

[3] The Rev. Dugald MacFarlane was ordained and appointed to the Church of Scotland parish of Glencoe in July 1896; transferred to Arrochar in January 1902; in later years he was well known in Gaelic circles in Scotland.

On 27th August Carmichael wrote to Fr Allan McDonald: 'You will see Miss Freer soon and I heartily envy you.' She had made, as usual, a favourable first impression.

Miss Freer reached Oban towards the end of August 1896. On 5th September the *Oban Times* reported that:

Miss Goodrich Freer a member of the Psychical Society of London was in Oban during the week. This lady it may be remembered has for several years paid periodical visits to the Western Highlands and Islands to gather much curious and interesting information from the people regarding second sight, witchcraft and kindred subjects. Miss Freer is at present on her way to Tiree, the Uists, and neighbouring islands.

On 19th September the *Oban Times* published a report from its Tiree correspondent that Miss Freer had 'paid a visit to the island last week on her way to the Outer Islands and likely has collected a number of second sight and ghost stories among the people. Miss Freer appears to be a favourite among Highland people.' A week later it was reported from Tiree that Miss Freer had offered four prizes of £1, 10*s*, 7*s* 6*d*, and 5*s*, to be competed for by children at all the Tiree schools, for the four best stories as told at 'A Winter Evening or Ceilidh in Tiree', the stories to be written 'in Gaelic and English'.

The results of this competition were announced by Miss Freer in a letter printed in the *Oban Times* of 10th July 1897, in which she admitted she was unable to judge the merits of the Gaelic essays but had submitted them to an 'accomplished Gaelic scholar'. Miss Freer regretted that the award of prizes had been delayed 'first through illness from a somewhat serious accident and later by my absence from England', a rather peculiar way of referring to the months she spent at Ballechin House in the early spring of the same year and to her accident when she was thrown out of a trap at Aberfeldy railway station on 22nd February.[1] The names of the prize-winners were given as A. MacKinnon, John MacKechnie, Kate MacIntyre, Archibald Cameron, John MacLean, Mary MacKinnon, and Hugh MacLean. Of these, one at least, Mary MacKinnon, now Mrs Campbell, is still alive and remembers Miss Freer coming to deliver a lecture on the botany of Tiree to Heylipol school there. In a letter to the writer Mrs Campbell describes how the headmaster of the school later received a letter from Miss Freer offering prizes to senior pupils for the best essay on 'ghosts and visitations'. Mrs Campbell says that her mother strongly disapproved of an essay competition on such a subject, but as it was school work, she was allowed to enter: the ghost stories she subsequently was told by an

[1] See *The Alleged Haunting of B—— House*, 1900 edition, p. 118.

uncle left her 'scared to go upstairs alone' in her own home for many years. The essays were used by Miss Freer to compose the fourth chapter of her book *Outer Isles*, of which more later, but the names of the writers are not given there.

On returning to Oban from her trip to the isles, of which no more is known for this year (1896) as Lord Bute was in bad health in the autumn of that year and no letters written to him by Miss Freer after that of 20th August, already quoted, now exist, Miss Freer found the following comments on her activities quoted from the *Glasgow Evening News* in the *Oban Times* of 26th September:

GHOST HUNTING IN THE HIGHLANDS

Miss Goodrich Freer of the Psychical Research Society was last week tiptoeing round the Hebrides in a careful and gallant attempt to surprise real Highland ghosts at work; capture a possessor of the second sight, or collect any other sort of evidence on the occult phenomena of the Outer Isles. She has with her a snap-shot camera, without which no modern ghost hunter can be considered completely equipped, and, as the lady acts in conjunction with Mr W. T. Stead as well as with the S.P.R., we may ultimately look to the Borderland *for spook interviews in Gaelic with process blocks. 'Miss Freer,' says a contemporary, 'has collected a number of second sight and ghost stories among the people.' No doubt. An Outer Hebridean with an appreciative listener can cover a lot of mythology at a sitting, for the practice of orally perpetuating the folklore of the West is still common at evening Ceilidhs or gossip parties from Arisaig on the mainland to Barra Isle.*

But the stranger who would benefit from these quaint recitals must be possessed of winning ways and a knowledge of the language spoken in Eden,[1] *for the natives, garrulous enough among themselves, filling up the long winter evenings round the peat fire with the most ingenious history,* sgeul[2] *and song, close like oysters and become as taciturn in the presence of a stranger who by race, training and prejudice cannot be expected to have the right sort of sympathy with old romance and fancy.*

Supposing Miss Freer is the proper sort of investigator, however, and able to inspire the natives of Harris, say, with the utmost confidence, she must not too readily imagine that their stories of ghosts, fairies, supernatural cantrips, are absolutely believed by the people who narrate them. Nine times out of ten, the narrator has but the novelist's belief in his own creation or at most the convenient illusion of a spectator at a play. In the case of the tenth man who, as an Irishman would say, is nearly always a woman, the ghosts are very real things; the rappings as

[1] *i.e.* Gaelic. [2] Folk-tales.

Alex. Smith found in Skye, are solemnly portentous, the second sight is a thing to swear by on the Bible. In Morvern and some parts of Skye, they still leave out a cogie of warm milk at night for the little brownie who is thereby rewarded for taking care of the cows. There have been foolish people—notoriously the clergy—who have hinted that the brownie had often human friends with whom to share the milk, but, be that as it may, who would risk the inevitable loss of a cow from the herd, by refusing such a trifling tribute?

Also the uisge-each [sic][1] *as Miss Fiona MacLeod calls the water-horse in Gaelic which will bring a blush to the cheek of Celtic modesty, still cavorts in Hebridean meadows at nightfall, and Loch Ness is full of water-bulls. But none of these manifestations is, we fear, for a lady interviewer with a kodak. To them must be brought the eye of faith and an hereditary nose for the uncanny gifts that stenography and the snap-shot lens are poor substitutes for.*

It is interesting to see how this comparatively mild and good-natured criticism put Miss Freer immediately on the defensive, and provoked her to write the following letter to the *Oban Times* in defence of the Enquiry. The reader will not fail to notice a number of inexactitudes in her letter: thus, the account given of the sending out of the schedules enquiring into second sight omits the second circularization; so far from her interest in the phenomena having nothing to do with journalism as represented by W. T. Stead, she had published two full versions of her first and second reports on second sight in the Highlands in Stead's quarterly *Borderland*; and her claims to be a 'person of leisure' possessed of strong racial sympathies with the Highlanders are disposed of elsewhere in this book.[2] Readers will also notice the hostile references to spiritualism, the forerunners of more serious quarrels between Miss Freer (who was herself suspected of being a spiritualist in the Isles) and the spiritualists between 1897 and 1899. The letter was printed with the heading:

MISS GOODRICH FREER AND SECOND SIGHT IN THE HIGHLANDS

Royal Hotel, Oban
8th October 1896

Sir,

On my return from regions where newspapers are scarce I turn with added interest to the Oban Times. *Will you allow me to make a state-*

[1] Presumably this refers to the bad Gaelic of 'Fiona MacLeod' (William Sharp), a notorious cultivator of the Celtic Twilight in the 1890s.

[2] See pp. 103–104.

ment in connection with a paragraph I found quoted from some Glasgow newspaper as to my inquiry into second sight in the Highlands?

My interest in the phenomena has absolutely nothing to do with journalism as represented by Mr W. T. Stead or any other editor to whose periodicals I may at any time contribute. The enquiry was initiated by the Society for Psychical Research at the suggestion of its Vice-President, the Marquis of Bute, whose liberality enabled them in 1892 to send out two thousand schedules of enquiry into the Gaelic speaking Highlands, the Rev. Peter Dewar of North Bute acting as secretary.

The method did not prove successful, only about sixty replies being received. It then became obvious that such an investigation could only be pursued on the spot by some person of leisure cognisant of the subject and possessed of strong racial and personal sympathies with the Highlanders themselves.

For lack of any one better, and in no sense officially but purely from sincere interest in every aspect of the question at issue, I volunteered to do my best in the matter and have now spent the autumn months of the past three years in the Highlands and Western Islands to my great pleasure and profit, and I hope the advancement of the enquiry.

The phenomena of second sight is one of special interest to Psychical Research because it is, so far, unexplained. At the present stage of my enquiry and my knowledge of psychical phenomena, I have personally no hesitation in saying that, when all allowance is made for possible exaggeration, mal-observation and imperfection of record, a residuum is left impossible to explain or to explain away. The subject of premonition is one of which we, at present, know little, which the unobservant alone deny, and on which the unintelligent alone dogmatise. Thought transference, sub-conscious activity, subliminal observation, the modern machinery by which the supernormal is in these days reduced to the normal are powerless to transform our Highland second sight to the common-place of science; and the superstition of spiritualism has, happily, so far let it alone.

I cannot conclude without once more expressing my most cordial gratitude for the unfailing courtesy, friendliness and helpfulness which (in spite of some adventurous discomforts especially in the recent gales) have added year by year to the delight I feel in my return to the Western Highlands.

I am etc.
A. Goodrich-Freer

And that is all we ever hear about the Second Sight Enquiry except for a letter from Myers to Miss Freer written on 15th April 1897, and quoted by Miss Freer in her book *The Alleged Haunting of B—— House* in 1899,[1] saying that if she had not got her material on the Ballechin House phenomena ready for publication in the next number of the S.P.R.'s *Journal*, 'should you have your Second-Sight material ready then?'

It never was presented; no final report on the Enquiry ever appeared in the pages of the S.P.R. *Journal* or anywhere else. Miss Freer, accompanied by Miss Constance Moore paid, a visit to South Uist and Eriskay while Everard Feilding and Walter Blaikie were there, in August 1898,[2] and reported to Lord Bute from the Roxburghe Hotel in Edinburgh on 4th September that they had even visited Mingulay and Barra Head 'delightfully primitive from the fact that the extreme difficulty of landing makes a visit very unusual. We collected a good many new Second Sight views and opinions and interviewed a great many Seers' (who, as always, are not named!). 'As usual our great allies were the priests—Presbyterianism and Second Sight cannot go together.' Fr Allan McDonald is not mentioned in the letter, which goes on to animadvert on an unsuitable priest appointed to Daliburgh by Bishop Smith, and the management or mismanagement of the hospital Lord and Lady Bute had founded there. But as far as any positive results were concerned, although Lord Bute's generous support had provided Miss Freer with three expense-paid visits to the Highlands and Islands, and thus given her access to the replies to the S.P.R.'s Schedule of Questions on second sight and to Fr Allan McDonald's notebooks, nothing had been achieved in the way of scientific proof or vindication of the existence of the faculty of second sight in the Scottish Highlands. This failure was later admitted by the Secretary of the S.P.R. to the writer of the article on 'Second Sight in Skye', in *Cameron's Handbook to the Isle of Skye*, published in Glasgow shortly before 1914 in the following words:

An enquiry into Second Sight in the Highlands was instituted by the Society some years ago, but it proved to be most unsatisfactory. Second-hand traditions were numerous but it was very difficult to obtain direct evidence principally on account of native reticence and the reverent awe with which the faculty is regarded. But what little real evidence was obtained showed that the experiences were closely analogous to cases of

[1] P. 186 (in second edition).

[2] Letters of Walter Blaikie to Fr Allan McDonald, 20th August and 12th September 1898. It was on this occasion that the group photograph of Miss Freer, Miss Moore, Fr Allan McDonald, and Walter Blaikie himself, which is reproduced in this book, was taken.

It is not known how this 1898 Hebridean trip of Miss Freer's, or her visit to Tiree in June 1901, was financed. The 1898 trip was her last visit to South Uist.

crystal vision and automatic writing and that telepathy played an important part in them, and that the special faculty of the Highland seer seemed to be that of premonition.[1]

This was in reply to a letter from the writer of the handbook drawing the attention of the S.P.R. to the existence of belief in second sight in the Isle of Skye. The writer made the following comment on this letter from the Secretary of the S.P.R.:

Although the result of the writer's investigations on the spot do not permit him to endorse the view expressed on behalf of the Society for Psychical Research, yet it is valuable to have this direct and unmistakable declaration from it. It is not altogether a confession of failure to explain the phenomena of second sight, but it is not very remote from it, and the reason of failure is not far to seek. It is because those whom the Society has entrusted with its investigations don't understand the language of the people. I cannot conceive success in collecting 'Second Sight' evidence to bear scientific scrutiny unless the investigator knows the Gaelic language. This acquisition is a sine qua non*; without it all enquiry except that of the most superficial kind will be fruitless.*

The S.P.R.'s Enquiry cannot be said to have added anything to what is already known of the subject from the older literature, apart from evidence that in the 1890s second sight was still believed in in certain districts, mostly in the islands. It is indeed surprising that Miss Freer, the person to whom it was entrusted, who had previously shown in her paper on crystal-gazing read to the S.P.R. on 10th May 1889 that she possessed very considerable ability for discovering, arranging, and presenting information on this kind of subject, apparently made no effort to study and analyse the material on second sight in the Highlands which had been recorded by such earlier writers as Necker de Saussure, Martin Martin, and Lord Tarbat, to whom reference has already been made. A monoglot English-speaker with no previous knowledge of the Highlands, Miss Freer had in fact no particular qualifications for taking charge of such an enquiry apart from her claim to be a clairvoyante herself and therefore able to win the confidence of the Highland seers. This was really no qualification for conducting a scientific investigation into second sight at all, for even if her claim were genuine—and subsequent chapters will show that it was certainly dubious—it left Miss Freer's encounters with the seers open to the possibility of

[1] P. 120. The author of the handbook may have been James Cameron, a Glasgow journalist who wrote *The Old and the New Highlands and Hebrides*, published at Kirkcaldy in 1912. It is interesting to find the Secretary of the S.P.R. admitting the failure of an enquiry on which the S.P.R. today possesses no file.

mutual suggestion, the dangers of which are well known in psychical research.

What was wanted for the Enquiry, apart from the absence of newspaper publicity, was a trained psychical researcher with a knowledge of Gaelic, of psychology, and of the values of evidence. To the Highlanders themselves, Miss Freer must have appeared as just another Sassenach busybody. Indeed, it is doubtful if it would have been possible for anybody to have obtained the kind of substantiation in the form of dates, signed statements, and personal witnesses, from a people of whom at that time many knew little or no English and whose only timepiece was often the cockerel crowing in the morning. It is obvious that if psychical powers do exist most strongly among an unsophisticated people like the old-fashioned Highlanders, this is just the milieu where precise scientific evidence of their existence is going to be most difficult to obtain.

One thing must be said on behalf of Lord Bute and the S.P.R. However amateurish Miss Freer's handling of the Enquiry, and however uncritical the S.P.R.'s acceptance of her two reports may have been, the Society deserves the credit of having been the first learned body outside the Highlands themselves to see that there was something unusually interesting surviving in the Gaelic oral tradition, and to make some kind of systematic attempt to investigate and record it, which could only have been done with Lord Bute's very generous financial help.

It may fairly be assumed that it was Miss Freer's resentment of the S.P.R.'s disavowal of the Ballechin House ghost-hunt that brought the Second Sight Enquiry to an end: for the story of Ballechin,[1] and of Miss Freer's real origin and remarkable career in psychical research between 1889 and 1901, we must turn to Mr Trevor Hall's account in the following chapters.

[1] Ballechin is pronounced with the stress on the second syllable, indicating derivation from the Gaelic *Bail' Eachainn*, 'Hector's Farm'.

II

The Strange Story of Ada Goodrich Freer

1

THE MYSTERY OF 'MISS X'

IN DECEMBER 1964 Dr John Lorne Campbell sent me a copy of his booklet, *The Late Fr Allan McDonald, Miss Goodrich Freer and Hebridean Folklore.*[1] This essay showed that a substantial part of the literary remains of Fr Allan McDonald of Eriskay, which Dr Campbell was preparing for publication, had been unscrupulously used by the late Miss Freer over her own name in the furtherance of her literary career as a self-styled authority on Scottish Gaelic folklore.

Dr Campbell asked whether I had any information in my library regarding Miss Freer. His enquiry had been prompted by the reading of my book on the mysterious circumstances surrounding the death in 1888 of Edmund Gurney,[2] the Hon. Secretary of the Society for Psychical Research, an organization of which Miss Freer had been a prominent member from the year of Gurney's death to the turn of the century. I was asked if I knew anything of Miss Freer's personal life and antecedents, and of the activities in psychical research with which she had been preoccupied before embarking upon her career as a folklorist. In particular, Dr Campbell enquired whether I could throw any light upon an incident which had taken place in the village of Swanley, Kent, in which Miss Freer had been involved, evidently not to her credit, and to which Dr Campbell had discovered an unpublished reference in Fr Allan's papers. This occurrence, whatever it was, had soon been followed by Miss Freer's relinquishment of her membership of the S.P.R., and her departure from England to Jerusalem at the end of 1901.[3]

At the time I received Dr Campbell's letter my knowledge of

[1] Reprinted from *Scottish Studies*, 1958, vol. II, pp. 175–88.

[2] *The Strange Case of Edmund Gurney*, London, 1964.

[3] It is true that Miss Freer's last entry in the membership lists of the S.P.R. was in January 1903, but she had undoubtedly left England before then. This is clear from an unpublished letter from Miss Ruth Landon to Fr Allan of 15th December 1901, in which she referred to the fact that Miss Freer was already on her way to Port Said. The preface to Miss Freer's book, *Outer Isles*, was written in Jerusalem in May 1902.

Miss Freer was little more than superficial. I was aware that she had been an early and highly regarded member of the S.P.R., had made substantial contributions to the Society's *Proceedings*, and had written two books on psychical research, *The Alleged Haunting of B[allechin] House* (with Lord Bute, a Vice-President of the S.P.R.) and *Essays in Psychical Research*, both published in 1899.[1] I knew that Miss Freer had been the assistant editor of the spiritualist periodical *Borderland*. Her photograph had shown her to be an attractive woman, and I had been told that in some circles an affair between Miss Freer and F. W. H. Myers, one of the founders of the S.P.R., had been suspected.

An interesting discovery involving Miss Freer had been made during my investigation of the life and death of Edmund Gurney. Just as Eleanor and Arthur Sidgwick, the biographers of Henry Sidgwick, the first President of the S.P.R., in *Henry Sidgwick, A Memoir* (London, 1906), had suppressed that part of his 'Journal' in which Sidgwick had revealed his doubts about the supposed accidental circumstances of Gurney's death, so had they also thought it expedient to conceal from the reader Sidgwick's references to certain incidents connecting Miss Freer and F. W. H. Myers.[2] This was about the limit of my original knowledge of the lady in whom Dr Campbell was interested, except that I think I recalled at the time, from a note in the late Harry Price's *Short-Title Catalogue of Works on Psychical Research, etc.* (London, 1929), that at a later period of her life Miss Freer had married Dr Hans H. Spoer. Biographical enquiry is, however, very congenial to me, and I welcomed the opportunity of offering such assistance as I could in solving the problems which Dr Campbell had outlined in his letter.

A considerable correspondence soon developed between Dr Campbell and myself, which ultimately led to the kind suggestion that we should collaborate in the preparation of this book. The matter was of great interest to me for more than one reason. First, it has been invariably urged by believers in psychical phenomena that educated, intellectually gifted, and socially accomplished persons like Miss Freer, who claim so-called supernormal powers, can never in the nature of things be fraudulent, because of the lack of any obvious motive. The consistent attitude of researchers in this field, since the formation of the S.P.R. in 1882 to the present day, is that

[1] A second and revised edition of *The Alleged Haunting of B—— House* was published in 1900.

[2] The extracts from the MS. of Henry Sidgwick's 'Journal', now in the Library of Trinity College, Cambridge, were very kindly made for me by Dr A. R. G. Owen. They are referred to in more detail later.

stories by such individuals of their experiences, however improbable and uncorroborated, must be accepted without question.[1] The case of Miss Freer, whose accounts of her crystal visions, shell-hearing, and telepathic abilities were accepted with implicit belief and enthusiastic praise by leaders of the S.P.R. of the stature of Professor Henry Sidgwick and F. W. H. Myers, seems to be an appropriate subject for enquiry in this connexion. Secondly, a study of the career of this lady, and her relationships with those eminent Victorians who were interested in occult matters, adds significantly to our knowledge of the melancholy history of psychical research in England during the period from the climacteric of the death of Edmund Gurney to the end of the nineteenth century.

The circumstances of the birth and early life of Ada Goodrich Freer are of importance to our understanding of the motives and psychology of this extraordinary woman. She enjoyed the advantage, apparently throughout her adult life, of appearing to be at least ten years younger than her actual age, with personal attractions which seem to have been almost hypnotic in their effect, and which she used irresistibly and ruthlessly upon those whom she thought could be of use to her.[2] These qualities were combined with remarkable energy and a formidable intelligence. There is a good deal of evidence to suggest, however, that she suffered from *folie de grandeur*. As an example, she quarrelled bitterly with F. W. H. Myers in 1897, and he became seriously ill early in 1898. Miss Freer wrote to Lord Bute on 28th March 1898, pointing out that Myers had never been ill in his life before and that 'those who hate or oppose me always come to grief'. She claimed that she could quote a score of other cases in which this had happened, and that she had in consequence and in charity to exercise restraint in forming dislikes for people.[3] She was indeed a strange person, and it is therefore unfortunate that she was consistently both deceitful and secretive about her antecedents and upbringing, thereby making this part of the enquiry both protracted and difficult, and in some respects still incomplete.

[1] For an authoritative comment on what Dr E. J. Dingwall has called 'this naïve belief', the reader is referred to his 'British Investigation of Spontaneous Cases', *International Journal of Parapsychology*, 1961, vol. II, pp. 89–97. It is discussed on pp. 63 ff. of my *The Strange Case of Edmund Gurney*.

[2] In an unpublished letter of 13th July 1894 the Rev. Peter Dewar, in the first flush of his enthusiasm for Miss Freer, wrote to Lord Bute that her powers of sympathy seemed to him to be supernormal, and that she could get into living, sympathetic touch with people as no others could do. Fr Allan McDonald wrote of Miss Freer in his diary on 9th September 1897, 'My acquaintance with her has been an education of mind and soul, and has thrown sunshine over the last two years of my life.'

[3] An unpublished letter.

When Miss Freer (then Mrs H. H. Spoer) entered St Luke's Hospital, New York, on 20th December 1930 suffering from 'hypertensive heart disease', to die there on 24th February 1931, her age was recorded as fifty-six. This information, suggesting that she was born in 1874, was presumably given either by Miss Freer herself or her husband. As Dr Spoer was sixteen years younger than his wife, he himself may have been misinformed regarding her age. It is admittedly hard to credit that Dr Spoer could really have believed that his wife was fifty-six when she was actually seventy-three, but the fact that the former incorrect age is also recorded at Cedar Lawn Cemetery, Patterson, New Jersey, where Miss Freer is buried, would suggest that this was so. On the other hand, it seems probable, to say the least of it, that Dr Spoer knew that the statement on his wife's death certificate that she had lived in the United States for twenty-six years was untrue to the extent of at least eighteen years, for they came to America together as man and wife certainly not earlier than 1923.[1]

Official and semi-official sources offer little information about Miss Freer's personal life. In none of her twenty-five entries in *Who's Who* did she disclose anything whatsoever of her date or place of birth, her parentage or place of education. The single piece of biographical information offered is that she married Dr Spoer in 1905. The same withholding of any clue as to whom she was or where she came from is repeated in her many books, and in the whole of her voluminous writings in *Folklore*, *The Occult Review*, *Borderland*, *The Nineteenth Century*, the *Proceedings* and the *Journal* of the Society for Psychical Research, and the other periodicals to which she contributed. Indeed, during the initial ten years of her published work on psychical research and kindred subjects from 1889 she preferred at first to remain completely anonymous, later using the pseudonym 'Miss X'.

Previously unpublished correspondence, now available to Dr Campbell and myself, is no more helpful in this regard than the printed sources. According to the late Lady Margaret MacRae (formerly Lady Margaret Crichton-Stuart), the daughter of Miss Freer's patron Lord Bute, the family was informed by Miss Freer that she was a relative of Sir Bartle Freer [*sic*].[2] On the other hand,

[1] They had been married for twenty-six years, and it is possible that Dr Spoer incorrectly thought of his wife as having been an American citizen for that length of time.

[2] Sir Henry Bartle Edward Frere (1815–84), K.C.B., G.C.S.I., D.C.L. (Oxon.), LL.D. (Cantab.), F.R.S., statesman and Governor of Bombay, was commonly called Sir Bartle Frere. He ranks twenty columns in the *Dictionary of National Biography*. His statue on the Thames Embankment was un-

Miss Freer (who by that time was calling herself Goodrich-Freer) told Lord Bute in her letter of 9th December 1895 that 'my father and all my deceased family were Goodrich'. It seems impossible to reconcile this statement with the fact that investigation has shown that her father was George Freer and that her mother's maiden name was Adcock. Miss Freer's second forename derived from her paternal grandmother, who before her marriage to William Freer was Ann Goodrich, the daughter of a wheelwright in Rutland.

These facts regarding Miss Freer's parentage also throw the gravest doubt upon her story to Lord and Lady Bute in 1898 that Dr John Bacchus Dykes (1823–76), the distinguished musician and divine, was her uncle.[1] Before her marriage to Dr Dykes, his wife was Miss Susan Kingston, the daughter of George Kingston of Malton. Dr Dykes's mother's maiden name was Elizabeth Huntington, the daughter of a Hull surgeon. The biography of Dr Dykes contains no reference whatever to any Freer, Adcock, or Goodrich.[2] What it does reveal is that Fr Thomas Dykes, who embraced the Roman Catholic faith in 1851 and became a Jesuit priest, was the elder brother of Dr J. B. Dykes, who Miss Freer claimed as her uncle. Yet, in a letter to Lord Bute of 5th March 1897 she stated that Fr Thomas Dykes was her cousin.

The suspicion that these claims by Miss Freer to intimate connexions with distinguished families may have been manufactured to impress Lord Bute and others is not diminished by another very odd story told by her. Paulet is, of course, the family name of the Marquess of Winchester. At the end of 1895 Miss Freer wrote to Lord Bute to say that she had received a paranormal message at the moment of his death from 'my dear old friend Stuart Paulet, who was brought up with me and has been far more of a brother to me than my own ever were'.[3] She did not learn of his death by normal means, she added, until four days after her experience. She wrote

[1] This story was vaguely supported by a claim by Miss Freer in her essay, 'The Mystic Musician', that in earlier years she had lived in the household of a distinguished musician (*Borderland*, 1894–5, vol. II, p. 422).

[2] J. T. Fowler, *Life and Letters of John Bacchus Dykes, M.A., Mus.Doc.*, London, 1897.

[3] Neither Burke, Debrett, nor Walford make mention of any Stuart Paulet. The Lists of Members of Oxford and Cambridge Universities of the period also fail to record anyone of this name. No obituary has been traced.

---

veiled by the Prince of Wales in 1888. On 10th October 1844 he married Miss Catherine Arthur, the daughter of Sir George Arthur of Bombay. Quite apart from the difference in the names, I am not aware of a shred of evidence to connect him with Miss Freer.

that five years previously, in 1890, she and Paulet had quarrelled and as a result he had left England, a somewhat dramatic departure for which his parents had blamed Miss Freer. Paulet was, said Miss Freer, 'impulsive and romantic'. She said that in 1887 she and Paulet had been through a crisis in their religious opinions, 'as most thoughtful young people do'. Miss Freer was thirty in 1887.

A useful background to the truth or otherwise of these assertions by Miss Freer about herself to Lord Bute and his family was her claim to have been one of the first women to become a Fellow of the Royal Society. This was recorded by Lord Colum Crichton-Stuart, Lord Bute's son, in a letter to the late Miss S. R. Dowling in terms that make it plain that Miss Freer had convinced the Bute family that she did enjoy this distinction. The facts in regard to the election of women to Fellowship of the Royal Society are of interest in this connexion, and I am indebted to the Society and its Librarian for kindly supplying them.

In January 1902 a certificate of candidature in favour of Mrs H. Ayrton was received and declined in the face of legal advice that the Society could not elect women under its Charters and Statutes. This first became possible under the Sex Disqualification (Removal) Act 1919, but it was not until 1944 that the Statutes of the Royal Society were actually amended to enable women to be elected. Miss Freer was never an F.R.S., and had indeed been dead thirteen years before she could have become one. The first two ladies to be appointed Fellows were Dr Kathleen Lonsdale (now Dame Kathleen Lonsdale) and the late Dr Marjory Stephenson. Both were elected in 1945.

Confidence in Miss Freer's adherence to the truth in her correspondence with her patron Lord Bute is not increased by her assertion in her letter of 23rd March 1896 that her brother was at Oxford with Lord Onslow. The circumstances of the upbringing of Miss Freer and her brothers, to be discussed later in this chapter, were not such as would make it seem probable that any of them were at Oxford. However that may be, the facts are that those of Miss Freer's brothers who did not die in infancy, Benjamin, George, Arthur, and Ernest, were born respectively in 1849, 1851, 1854, and 1858. William Hillier Onslow (1853–1911), the fourth Earl, entered Exeter College, Oxford, on 15th April 1871 and left in 1872 after rather more than a year without sitting for any of the university examinations.[1] The *Oxford University Calendar* of 1872, which

[1] J. Foster, *Alumni Oxonienses*, Oxford, 1888, vol. III, p. 1043, and *Dictionary of National Biography*.

shows Lord Onslow as a commoner of Exeter, also lists a Benjamin John Michael Freer as an undergraduate and bible clerk of Oriel. If casual enquiry was limited to this single source, therefore, it might seem possible that Miss Freer's story could have been true, although it is fair to point out that her eldest brother, born in Uppingham, Rutland, on 16th June 1849, was simply 'Benjamin Freer', according to his birth certificate.

On the assumption that Miss Freer took the risk of fabricating her statement to Lord Bute after an examination of the *Oxford University Calendar* for the two years of Lord Onslow's short period at the university (and if she did not, then the coincidence that a Benjamin Freer was actually at Oxford at the relevant time is an extraordinary one), it is a pity that she did not take the additional precaution of also consulting Foster's *Alumni Oxonienses*. This work of reference would have told her that additional information was in print, which could have been seen by Lord Bute, which demolished her story completely. Benjamin John Michael Freer was not Miss Freer's brother but the second son of Thomas Freer of Kirk Braddan in the Isle of Man.[1] The extraordinary fact is that he entered Oriel College in 1855 at the age of eighteen, and was still an undergraduate in 1872 at the age of thirty-five.

There remains one puzzling aspect of what appears to have been a singularly reckless piece of deception on the part of Miss Freer. It will be recalled that in an earlier letter to Lord Bute of 9th December 1895 she had falsely claimed that her father's name was really Goodrich. Of the eleven members of the university of this name one only, Laurence Charles Goodrich, was at Oxford, and indeed at Exeter College, at the same time as Lord Onslow. Miss Freer had no brother named Laurence, of course. Laurence Goodrich was the fifth son of James Pitt Goodrich, gentleman, of Maisemore, Gloucestershire, and entered Exeter College on 21st January 1871.[2] He was clearly not Miss Freer's brother, and it seems difficult to believe, moreover, that the Maisemore family had any close connexion with Miss Freer's paternal grandmother, Ann Goodrich, the daughter of a wheelwright in Rutland. However this may be, the fact that there was a Goodrich of good family at Exeter College with Lord Onslow at the relevant time makes one wonder whether Miss Freer intended Lord Bute to believe that her brother at Oxford was Laurence Goodrich or Benjamin Freer. Her previous story that her father's name was Goodrich supported one claimant, while the fact that she

[1] *Alumni Oxonienses*, vol. II, p. 494. The Treasurer of Oriel College has very kindly confirmed the facts regarding B. J. M. Freer.

[2] *Alumni Oxonienses*, vol. III, p. 538.

had a brother named Benjamin supported the other. We can take the matter no further.[1]

Such information as has been published about the date of Miss Freer's birth has been both varied and incorrect. The Folklore Society, which she joined in 1893, believed that she was born in 1870,[2] presumably from particulars supplied by her when she applied for membership. Her card in the Catalogue of the Library of Congress, on the other hand, records her year of birth as 1865,[3] as do her entries in the *Literary Year-Book and Bookman's Directory*. As has been said, the particulars supplied to St Luke's Hospital, New York, and repeated in Miss Freer's death certificate, indicate her year of birth as 1874. Ada Goodrich Freer was, in fact, born on 15th May 1857.[4]

The earliest book of reference that I have been able to discover containing her name is the List of Members of the Society for Psychical Research. She joined this organization on 28th January 1888 as an Associate, first describing herself simply as 'Miss Freer'.[5] When she was awarded the distinction of Honorary Associateship and relieved of her subscription in 1893, in recognition of what was regarded as her outstanding work for the Society, this was amended to 'Miss A. Goodrich Freer'. By August of the same year, however, she began to hyphenate her name as 'Goodrich-Freer' in the

[1] The incident that caused Miss Freer to assert that her family name was really Goodrich was a séance held in London at which the medium was Mrs Everitt, whose career had begun as early as 1855. Miss Freer wrote scornfully to Lord Bute about this séance, referring to the medium's 'cockney twang' and to the 'silly drivel' of her communications. 'The grand test offered, was that though I was introduced as Miss X, the spirits called me "Freer", and brought me messages of the "Be good" type from deceased Freers, the fact being that my Father and all my deceased family were Goodrich!' The cynical reader may well suspect that Mrs Everitt may have revealed some embarrassing truth about Miss Freer's origin at this séance, which might well have surprised Lord Bute, had it reached his ears without previous contradiction.

[2] This date is given in her obituary, published by the Society in its official journal, *Folklore*, 1931, vol. XLI, pp. 299–301. The obituary was written by the Editor at the time, A. R. Wright, F.S.A., who remarked that it was greatly to be desired that a biography should be written of a life so noteworthy. He can scarcely have realized how difficult such a task might be.

[3] This date is given in the printed catalogue as '1865–'.

[4] This name is recorded on her birth certificate, where her parents are shown as George and Mary Freer. On her New York death certificate, however, her father's name is enlarged to George Goodrich Freer. The fact that she was born in Uppingham, Rutland, was not revealed.

[5] *Journal*, S.P.R., February 1888, p. 221. Her promotion was rapid. In the first List of Members published after her election, made as at May 1889, in *Proceedings*, 1888–9, vol. V, she was already shown as a full member.

membership list. In 1907, when her name first appeared in *Who's Who*, she added an extra initial and was there shown as 'A. M. Goodrich-Freer', this being repeated in all her subsequent entries, which continued until 1931, the year of her death. In the British Museum Catalogue her name is given as 'Ada M. Goodrich Freer'.[1] She started to call herself 'Adela Goodrich-Freer' in the *Literary Year-Book and Bookman's Directory* in 1907, having described herself as 'Ada Goodrich-Freer' in the issues up to 1906. In the Library of Congress Catalog she is described as 'Adela M. Goodrich-Freer'.

On her death certificate her name is recorded as 'Adela Monica Spoer', while in her obituary in *Folklore* she is referred to as '[Mrs] Adela Monica Goodrich-Freer Spoer (1870–1931)'. It seems probable that in her later years she was known by her invented name of Monica, for her tombstone is inscribed 'A. Monica, née Goodrich-Freer, wife of H. Henry Spoer'.[2]

During the investigation of Miss Freer's life it has become apparent that little reliance can be placed upon her statements in regard to her antecedents and upbringing (with the names of persons and places consistently omitted or disguised under mere initials) implying that she came from a distinguished and well-to-do family in the North of England and was of Scottish descent. I myself doubt the truth of either of these suggestions. So far as Ada Freer's alleged Scottish forebears are concerned, it may be pointed out that her father, grandfather, and great-grandfather were all residents of the town of Uppingham, in Rutland, in the English Midlands. She herself was born there, a fact which she concealed throughout the whole of her adult life. Although, according to the present rector, none of the family survive there today, the Freers were established in Uppingham from the middle of the eighteenth century at the latest. We find from the church register, for example, that on 12th December 1751 Henry Exton married Susanna Freer, followed by numerous and regular entries of baptisms, marriages, and burials of Freers in Uppingham during the intervening years to 1812, when William Freer, Ada's grandfather and the son of John Freer, a carpenter, married Ann Goodrich. The reader may think that if the Scottish ancestors existed, they were too remote adequately to justify, for example, Miss Freer's statement to the Rev.

[1] *British Museum General Catalogue of Printed Books*, vol. 79, London, 1961.

[2] It is of interest that Fr Allan McDonald wrote in his diary on 4th May 1898 'St Monica's [day]. Said Mass for Miss Freer.' This suggests that she had an interest in St Monica for a number of years before adopting the name.

Peter Dewar, in a letter dated 25th May 1894[1] on the subject of her extreme suitability for the Scottish Second Sight Enquiry, that she was 'of Scotch blood (Aberdeen), and [I] belong to a family which has possessed the gift of second sight for many generations', or her claim in her lecture to the Gaelic Society of Inverness in April 1896 that she spoke as a Highlander to Highlanders,[2] or her published remark in the same year that she proudly claimed the Scots as her fellow-countrymen.[3] It may be pointed out in this connexion that these observations in regard to her alleged Scottish descent were all made during the period when she was seeking or enjoying the patronage of the wealthy Lord Bute,[4] a convinced Scottish nationalist and an advocate of Scottish home rule, who had devoted much time to a long and intensive study of Scottish history and institutions.

The well-to-do 'county' family background claimed by Miss Freer also seems to fall to pieces when examined. The index to the *Victoria History of the County of Rutland* (London, 1936), which contains every family of any importance in England's smallest county, makes no mention of the names of either Freer or Goodrich. I see no reason for stretching the imagination to suppose that either Dr Frier, a master at Oakham School in 1649, or the Rev. Thomas Frere (d. 1667), Rector of Whitwell, had any direct connexion with the Freers of Uppingham, a family of tradesmen. Neither of the two issues of *The Visitation of the County of Rutland*, published in London by the Harleian Society in 1870 and 1922, contains the name Freer, either in their indexes or in the quite exhaustive lists of families whose pedigrees are there traced. It would seem, moreover, that as late as the end of the eighteenth century some of the Uppingham Freers were without education. When George Chilton, a soldier of the Durham Regiment of Militia, married Sarah Freer of Uppingham on 9th December 1799 both bride and bridegroom signed the church register with an 'X'.

One cannot avoid, indeed, the melancholy conclusion that many of Miss Freer's references to herself were calculated to mislead her readers. She wrote, for example:

[1] Quoted at length by Dr Campbell on p. 36.

[2] She did not say that she was born in Scotland, and indeed conceded that she was 'born south of the Tweed', less fortunately than her forebears (*Transactions of the Gaelic Society of Inverness*, vol. XXI, p. 106).

[3] *Borderland*, 1896, vol. III, p. 61.

[4] In a letter to her mother, the Marchioness of Bute, of 1st June 1901, Lady Margaret MacRae wrote, 'How cross she [Miss Freer] would be if she thought you didn't think her Scotch. She isn't a bit, but always says she is, and her Scottish stories and accent would make a cow laugh.'

I belong to no effete race, but to a family which for physique and longevity might challenge any in the annals of Mr Francis Galton;—a family which has never lived in cities, and which, for many generations, has expended its energies and ambitions on horses and hounds.[1]

So far as longevity is concerned, it is pertinent to point out that Miss Freer's father and mother died at the ages of forty-six and forty-five respectively, while her grandmother only lived to be thirty-eight. Her aunt died at twenty-seven. Her sister Ann and two of her brothers died in infancy. On the subject of the absorption of 'many generations' of her forebears in horses and hounds, it is relevant to mention that Miss Freer's grandfather was a wheelwright, and her great-grandfather a carpenter. It is true that Miss Freer's father was a veterinary surgeon,[2] but whether that was the impression Miss Freer intended to convey by her reference to horses and hounds is, I fancy, open to question. It seems to me more likely to be part of the pattern of the grooms and gardeners who told her ghost stories as a child, the dear old family servants she had known all her life and the other ingredients of the vague, affluent, country-house background she created for her autobiographical asides.

It is unfortunate and somewhat remarkable that, apart from her many letters to Lord Bute, now available for the first time, virtually all original papers and correspondence relating to Miss Freer seem to have disappeared. From 1893 to 1897 Miss Freer was employed by W. T. Stead as his assistant editor of the occult magazine *Borderland*, but the correspondence between Stead and Miss Freer, and indeed all the papers connected with *Borderland*, seem to have vanished completely, according to Stead's biographer, Professor J. O. Baylen, of the University of Mississippi.[3] The Folklore Society, of which she was a member for nearly thirty-eight years, knows

[1] *Proceedings*, S.P.R., 1892, vol. VIII, p. 484. Miss Freer was probably referring to Sir Francis Galton's *Human Faculty* (London, 1883), and to *Natural Inheritance* (London, 1889) by the same author.

[2] In her letter of 24th January 1896 to Lord Bute, Miss Freer wrote that her father had studied medicine before his elder brother died, 'but never took his degree or practised', thus implying that he was a person of leisure and inherited wealth.

[3] Professor Baylen has written to Dr Campbell to say that it almost looks as if what material there may have been among the Stead papers relating to Miss Freer has been removed by someone at some time. If this is so, then such removal must have taken place after the publication of Frederic Whyte's *The Life of W. T. Stead*, 2 vols., London, 1925, for in this book there are several references to correspondence between Stead and Miss Freer. It is, incidentally, curious that in another life of Stead, published in 1913, *My Father*, written by Stead's daughter, Miss Estelle W. Stead, there is no mention of Miss Freer at all, although the publication of *Borderland* is discussed at some length.

virtually nothing about her which is not available in *Who's Who*. Her obituary in *Folklore* gives no details of her early life, and contains many errors of fact in addition to the mistake of thirteen years in her date of birth. Not long before his death in 1951 Dr H. H. Spoer wrote to Dr Campbell to say that all his wife's papers had been lost or destroyed in the course of their travels in the Near East.

She was a leading member of the Society for Psychical Research from 1888 until 1902, and her photograph is included in the Society's album, 'English Portraits', of the distinguished members and associates of early years. She claimed to be an officer of the Society [1] and a member of several of its Committees.[2] She presented several long papers to the Society on crystal-gazing, telepathic experiences, clairvoyance, and similar subjects, under the chairmanship of various presidents, including Henry Sidgwick and William Crookes. She had been intimately acquainted with F. W. H. Myers, one of the founders of the Society, and had known well other presidents such as Mrs Henry Sidgwick and Andrew Lang. Among many other activities and writings, she was the Council's representative for the three investigations into second sight in the Highlands and the Islands of Scotland in 1894, 1895, and 1896, paid for by Lord Bute, a Vice-President of the S.P.R. She was the medium through whom the famous messages, allegedly from the spirit of Sir Richard Burton, were received in 1895, and about which she lectured to the Society. She was mainly responsible for the enquiry into the alleged haunting of Ballechin House, in Perthshire, in 1897. Yet all the files dealing with these and other matters connected with Miss Freer have disappeared. The present officers of the Society say that they do not now possess any documents relating to her apart from the single photograph mentioned. The fact that no obituary was published in either the *Journal* or the *Proceedings* of the Society is presumably explained by the fact that although to the end of her life Miss Freer claimed to be a member in her entries in *Who's Who*, she had in reality ceased to have any connexion with the S.P.R. for nearly thirty years at the time of her death.

[1] A. Goodrich-Freer and John, Marquess of Bute, *The Alleged Haunting of B—— House*, new and revised edition, London, 1900, p. xiii.

[2] A. Goodrich-Freer, *Essays in Psychical Research*, London, 1899, p. 16.

2

MISS FREER'S ANTECEDENTS

THE MORE immediate history of Miss Freer's forebcars began on 13th July 1812 in Uppingham. On that day William Freer, a wheelwright and the son of an Uppingham carpenter named John Freer, married Ann, daughter of Thomas and Elizabeth Goodrich. Ann died in Uppingham on 14th January 1828 aged thirty-eight, after having given birth to many children. After Ann's death William married again, and his second wife was buried in the same grave in Uppingham churchyard as Ann. On 25th December 1852 William married yet again. His third wife was another Ann, daughter of an Uppingham labourer, John Kirby. William did not long survive this marriage and died on 7th August 1853.

While it is true that the Victorians produced larger families than we do today, the alacrity with which both Miss Freer's grandfather and father entered into further unions so soon after bereavements suggests that one attribute of the family was unusual sexual vigour, which may offer some explanation of Miss Freer's extraordinary energy. In her letter to the Rev. Peter Dewar in 1894, published for the first time elsewhere in this book,[1] she said that she delighted in an outdoor life and could ride, swim, and sail a boat, which may well be true, although her unfortunate lack of adherence to the truth about herself in her writings could cause the sceptic to doubt her statement that she rose early each day and walked six to twelve miles in all weathers[2] as a relief from her intellectual preoccupations. There can be no doubt at all, however, on the evidence of her published work and correspondence, about the immensity of her labours, the extreme diligence and ability with which she studied the unusual subjects to which she devoted most of her life, and the

[1] See p. 36.

[2] *Proceedings*, S.P.R., 1892, vol. VIII, p. 484. On 25th May of the previous year she told the Rev. Peter Dewar, in the same letter referred to above, that her walking averaged sixteen miles a day! And if this amount of physical exercise was not enough, Miss Freer claimed in an article extolling the virtues of horticulture as an appropriate activity for educated persons, published in *The Nineteenth Century*, November 1899, that she had been an enthusiastic practical gardener from her earliest childhood.

persistence with which she pursued her social and literary ambitions.

George Freer was born in 1820 and was one of William Freer's children by his first wife Ann Goodrich. On 16th September 1847 he married Mary, the daughter of Josiah Adcock, also of Uppingham, by whom he had eight children, whose birth certificates are before me as I write. They were: Benjamin, b. 1849; Ann, b. 1850, who died in the same year; George, b. 1851; Arthur, b. 1854; Ada Goodrich, b. 1857; Ernest, b. 1858; an unnamed twin with Ernest, who lived only one hour; and William Howard, b. 1860, who also died in infancy. It is curious that Ada was the only child who was given the name of Goodrich.

Mary Freer died at the age of forty-five, of tuberculosis, on 10th December 1862, so that at the age of five years Ada Goodrich Freer became motherless, in company with her four surviving brothers, Benjamin, George, Arthur, and Ernest. We may note in passing that a lady named Elizabeth Stokes, and not George Freer, was the informant of Mary's death to the registrar on 12th December 1862 having also been present at the death two days previously. In November 1863 Hannah, daughter of an Uppingham drover named John Cave, evidently became pregnant by the widowed George Freer. They were married on 20th March 1864 and their child Mary was born on 1st August, living only nine months. On 8th January 1866 a second child of this union, Howard, was born. His father survived him by a matter of days only, for George died on 21st January 1866 aged forty-six. Ada Goodrich Freer and her brothers had lost both father and mother in the space of little over four years.

The Freers were not well off, and indeed according to the Probate Registries in both London and Leicester, Miss Freer's parents left neither money nor real estate. The position of their five surviving children would not be an easy one, for it is reasonable to suppose that Hannah Freer, the drover's daughter, would be reluctant to take responsibility for the bringing-up of the children of the first wife of George Freer, to whom she had been married less than two years before his death.

It follows that Miss Freer's claim in her subsequent writings that she was 'brought up by an elderly relative with early Victorian standards'[1] could well be true, and is indeed confirmed in general terms by her niece, Mrs K. M. Connors, whom I located after not inconsiderable enquiry and correspondence. Mrs Connors, who was born in 1884, and is the daughter of Benjamin Freer, is the last

[1] Quoted from a contribution by Miss Freer to Edith K. Harper's *Stead: The Man*, London, 1918, p. 63.

surviving close relative I have been able to find after a protracted investigation in England, South Africa, and finally New Zealand, where Mrs Connors lives. She has told me that Benjamin Freer, who was seventeen when his father died, 'did his best to bring up his three brothers', presumably with help from local relatives. The responsibility for Ada's education and upbringing, however, was assumed by 'an aunt who had a boarding school for young ladies', but most unfortunately Mrs Connors never knew (or has forgotten) the name of this relative and the location of the school. It was not in or near Uppingham, and Mrs Connors believed that it was located in Yorkshire. She has told me that her parents never discussed 'Aunt Ada' because of 'family dislikes'. I have no doubt myself, on the evidence of Miss Freer's literary skill, that the 'elderly relative' did provide her with an excellent education.

Miss Freer was able to make a most favourable impression upon the eminent Victorians with whom by 1888 onwards she was in contact, mainly through the introduction of F. W. H. Myers, including Henry and Eleanor Sidgwick, Lord Bute, and others, because of her social accomplishments, charm, good looks, and curiously youthful appearance. There can be no doubt about her attractive personality. In 1888, when she was thirty-one, F. W. H. Myers wrote privately of her beautiful grey eyes and believed her to be in her middle twenties, as did W. T. Stead, who first met her in 1891 when she was thirty-four.[1] The Rev. Peter Dewar, in a letter to Lord Bute quoted at length on p. 40, remarked that her 'powers of sympathy seemed to me to be supernormal', while in the same year he referred with pleasure to Bute's own 'high opinion of her gifts and graces'. The enthusiastic first opinions of Alexander Carmichael, the distinguished author of *Carmina Gadelica*, and George Henderson, later Lecturer in Celtic at Glasgow University, expressed in letters from Carmichael to Fr Allan McDonald in August 1896, have already been quoted.[2] That Miss Freer was aware of her attractions for the opposite sex is revealed by a comment in her letter to Lord Bute of 5th July 1895 about the difficulty of finding a woman companion for her second visit to the Highlands and the Isles as a result of her friend Miss Constance Moore's necessary attendance upon her invalid father. Miss Freer said that plenty of men would be glad to accompany her, but that Mrs Grundy would not permit it.

[1] F. Whyte, *Life of W. T. Stead*, vol. II, p. 38.

[2] See pp. 85–86. Carmichael wrote that Henderson 'is charmed, as we all are, with Miss Freer', adding two weeks later that Fr Allan would soon be seeing her himself and that Carmichael heartily envied him. Miss Freer was nearly forty at this period, but looked very much younger.

I do not think that there can be any doubt that those she met, and so completely charmed, accepted her own assessment of her intellectual abilities and social and educational background. W. T. Stead, after his first meeting with her in 1891, wrote that she 'lives in Society, has had a first-class education, and is perfectly self-possessed'.[1] Two years later, when he was announcing the publication of *Borderland*, he amplified this opinion and quoted the views of others:

I should not have attempted the publication of this quarterly had I not been fortunate enough to secure the assistance and collaboration of a lady who, of all others, is most competent to execute my idea. For some years past every reader of the Proceedings of the Psychical Research Society has been well aware of the contributions of a lady who in the papers is always referred to as Miss X. In all the investigations of the Society into the phenomena of telepathy, crystal-vision and shell-hearing, together with many other departments of research, Miss X constantly appears and re-appears as one of the most trustworthy, careful and exact of all their inquirers. Her papers on crystal-vision are the classic upon the subject, for Miss X was the pioneer of the Society in this most promising field of research. This has been repeatedly recognized both at home and abroad by the leading authorities. M. Janet, for instance, who is probably the most eminent of French investigators into psychical phenomena, told the International Congress of Experimental Psychology, which met in London in 1892, that his attention was first turned to the subject of crystal-vision by reading Miss X's papers, and he cordially attested the exactitude and importance of her observations. Herr Max Dessoir, writing in the Monist, *declared that Miss X 'possesses a highly critical mind, is well acquainted with the common sources of error in this department of investigation, and her testimony is, in his* [sic] *opinion, more valuable than that of all the early authors put together'. Miss X is a lady of good birth and education, familiar to her finger-tips with almost all the phases of the phenomena under consideration, and capable of following the evidence and arguments in three or four laguages. I am extremely glad that the publication of* Borderland *promises to supply a sphere in which the exceptional talents and rare natural gifts of Miss X may be utilized to the best advantages for the purpose of psychical research.*[2]

It was perhaps inappropriate for Miss Freer herself to quote, as she did, a letter from an acquaintance describing her as 'refined, edu-

[1] *Life of W. T. Stead*, vol. II, p. 38.
[2] *Review of Reviews*, 1893, vol. VII, p. 678.

cated, and well-connected',[1] but there can be little doubt that this was the public image of herself she had created. Much had happened to her since her days in Uppingham, days that she was evidently anxious to conceal for the rest of her life.

Who was the 'fairy godmother' who gave Miss Freer these advantages? And if Mrs Connors' memories of what happened many years ago are well founded, where was the school for young ladies that was the source of Miss Freer's excellent education and social graces? One thing seems certain, and that is that Miss Freer was just as determined to conceal the identity of the elderly relative and her school as she was anxious to hide the modest circumstances of her birth in Uppingham. It would have been simple and becoming for her to state the facts, instead of imposing upon her readers the mass of vague hints with which her writings are so liberally embellished, to the exclusion of even the smallest fragment of definite information. She could so easily and generously have said, 'After the death of both my parents I was brought up by my aunt, Miss So-and-so, who had a school for girls at So-and-so, and to whom I shall be indebted all my life for the advantage of a very good education.' She never did. The reader may think that a probable reason for this secretiveness is that the kindly relative who did so much for the orphaned Ada Freer did not measure up to the social background which, by 1888, she wished her new friends in the oligarchy of the Society for Psychical Research to associate with her. It seems probable that the country house with its grooms and gardeners, the supposed scene of her upbringing, existed only in her imagination, like her Scottish descent.

I think it likely that her complementary pose in print as 'a woman of leisure'[2] and independent wealth was also assumed. Certainly she was not possessed of any private fortune, for when she died the value of her estate was sworn as less than $1,000 by her husband. In the early 1890s she was seeking paid employment from both W. T. Stead and the Swanley Horticultural College, very privately advertising her services in occult matters,[3] and at the same time obtaining

[1] *Essays in Psychical Research*, p. 188.

[2] *Transactions of the Gaelic Society of Inverness*, 1896, vol. XXI, p. 110. This was clearly untrue on the basis of her appointment as the paid assistant editor of the spiritualist paper *Borderland* alone. She received a salary of £200 per annum from W. T. Stead, the proprietor, which was not insubstantial remuneration for a woman at the end of the nineteenth century.

[3] I do not think there can be any doubt that the advertiser in the first volume of *Borderland*, from the address of the private office used by Miss Freer in Pall Mall East and describing herself as 'A Lady with considerable psychical experience', with 'Terms on Application', was Miss Freer.

loans on occasions from Stead and Lord Bute. The mystery presented by her monetary affairs, however, is that for a year or two prior to this her position seems to have been quite different. In the late 1880s, when she was closely associated with F. W. H. Myers, she was living, apparently alone in London, at St Stephen's Ladies' Home in Westbourne Grove Terrace, ostensibly without any need to earn her living. For a period she seemed to be able to devote unlimited time to experimenting with automatic writing, crystal-gazing, and similar subjects, under the guidance of Myers, and to preparing long papers on these matters, which Myers read to the S.P.R. and published in the *Proceedings*, while strictly preserving the anonymity of the writer. Miss Freer said that she did the work on at least one of these papers while actually staying in the house of Myers' elderly mother. From this it would seem either that Myers was privately supporting his protégée until about 1891, when he recommended her to W. T. Stead as a paid literary assistant and later as the assistant editor of *Borderland*, or that she had some private source of income which ceased after a few years. Certainly money became a matter of serious importance to her from the early 1890s onwards, and it is noteworthy that by 1895 she had become a permanent guest at the house of her friend, Miss Constance Moore, with whom she was to live until she left England in 1901.

A point in favour of these arguments is that enquiry has not resulted in the discovery of any 'elderly relative' of Miss Freer who might be presumed to be socially distinguished or wealthy. Due to the kindness and diligence of the Rector of Uppingham, Canon S. C. Woodward, and the Deputy Superintendent Registrar of Uppingham District, Mrs Rosalie M. Russell, very full searches have been made among the records of the local families of Freer, Goodrich, and Adcock for an aunt of Miss Freer who could possess these qualifications, but without success.

The essential details of the Uppingham Freers have already been studied. Thomas Goodrich, like William Freer, was a wheelwright, and both he and his wife Elizabeth died in Uppingham without any recorded issue other than their daughter Ann, Ada's paternal grandmother. Josiah Adcock, a butcher who died in 1860, and his wife Ann, Ada's maternal grandparents, had only two daughters of whom particulars are recorded in Uppingham and its environs; Mary, Ada's mother, who married George Freer, and her sister Charlotte, who died unmarried in 1848 at the age of twenty-seven. So far as I have been able to ascertain, the line of Uppingham Adcocks ceased in 1862. Ann Adcock, widow of Josiah, died on 2nd November of that year, while Mary Freer died a few weeks later on 10th December.

Faced with these failures, an attempt has been made to pinpoint the district where the 'aunt' and her school might have been located, by examining the allusions to her childhood days with which Miss Freer's writings are plentifully sprinkled. Experience has shown that these reminiscences must be read with reservations. Miss Freer wrote, for example:

It was my privilege when a child in the schoolroom to spend an occasional half-holiday in very good company. The Carlyles were there, and lively little Miss Jewsbury, and many others whom I would fain remember and whom I should better appreciate in these latter days, for in sooth, I then thought them all noisy and mostly shrill, and as the Sunday afternoons wore away in talk which I but little understood, the chances dwindled of my being taken to hear the music at St Mark's, Chelsea, and, after all, I liked that best—that and the artist who drew pictures for me. I have some of them now, and I hope he is at least a Royal Academician by this time, though as they are not signed and I forget his name, I shall not profit by his promotion![1]

Jane Welsh Carlyle died in 1866, so that this charming story, suggesting that Miss Freer was acquainted during Mrs Carlyle's lifetime with the social and literary scene in London, would by itself contradict her various claims to have been born in 1865, 1870, and 1874. As she was born in 1857, however, it could have been true, and we have to consider it despite Mrs Connors' belief that Miss Freer was educated in Yorkshire, with which this account is at variance. Thomas and Jane Carlyle were, of course, established in Cheyne Row, Chelsea, many years before the death of Mrs Carlyle, so that it will be seen that Miss Freer's story of those pleasant afternoons spent in their company during her half-holidays from the schoolroom, if true, would place her early upbringing and education by her relative, in London. I am inclined to think, however, that this single reference to London as the location was pure invention, for it is confirmed neither by Mrs Connors nor by the rest of Miss Freer's colourful asides on this subject, the latter being reasonably consistent. She wrote, for example, in connexion with her capacity for crystal-gazing, discovered and developed under the guidance of F. W. H. Myers, that 'as a child far away in the north' she used to climb from rock to rock until she reached a moorland tarn in which she could see visions of distant lands and water-maidens with beckoning hands, and referred to 'the accident of a north-country upbringing'.[2] She said that she had lived from her earliest years

[1] *Borderland*, 1893–4, vol. I, p. 117.

[2] A. Goodrich-Freer, 'Hobson Jobson', *Nineteenth Century*, April 1902, p. 585.

'among the people of a northern village'.[1] In her introduction to an edition of Susan Ferrier's novels that she published in 1902 she referred to herself as 'we of the north'. It is clear that these allusions (and especially to the moorland tarn) could not apply to London or to the gentle, pastoral contours of Rutland in the English Midlands. If they meant anything at all, they referred to the location of her upbringing and education by her relative during the period of her schooldays, from about 1866, when she became an orphan, to probably the mid-1870s.

It may, of course, be urged that Miss Freer was such a proven fabricator of stories about herself that any endeavour to make sense of these pointers is like trying to follow the trail of a fish in water. On the other hand, her repeated claims to have been brought up in the north have some slight independent support from a comment by Frederic Whyte in his book on W. T. Stead. Whyte said that in 1891 'an old friend of Stead's, the Rev. Henry Kendal [*sic*] of Darlington' told Stead that Miss Freer, whom he knew well, was 'a depository of endless stores of authentic information as to apparitions'.[2] Henry Kendall was, of course, the minister of the Darlington Congregational Church from 1859 to 1893. Darlington is in Durham, just over the boundary with Yorkshire. Mrs Connors' memory of what happened to Miss Freer, moreover, seems to me to be confirmed up to a point by two facts that are established. The research in Uppingham has shown that Miss Freer was an orphan by 1866 and was, therefore, not brought up by her parents, while the quality of her literary work indicates her standard of education. It may be said, too, that while her anxiety to ingratiate herself with the wealthy Lord Bute offered an obvious motive for her claim to an 'inherited Highland sympathy with the mysterious', as it was styled in her obituary,[3] it is not apparent what she had to gain by stating that she had been brought up in the north of England if this was not true.

Other stories by Miss Freer suggest that her more general references to the north could be narrowed to Yorkshire, and indeed to the West Riding. When she was emphasizing her extreme suitability for the Scottish Second Sight Enquiry to Lord Bute and the Rev. Peter Dewar in 1894 she said (somewhat loftily, it might be thought) that she was accustomed to the Yorkshire peasantry, and that her patron could, therefore, assume that she would know exactly how to deal with the people of the Highlands and the Isles. In an unpublished letter to Lord Bute of 17th January 1896 she said that her

[1] *Borderland*, 1895, vol. II, pp. 263–4.
[2] *The Life of W. T. Stead*, vol. II, p. 38.
[3] *Folklore*, 1931, vol. XLI, p. 299.

Yorkshire home was 'in the heart of the Quaker country'.[1] She evidently knew York Minster sufficiently well to refer to it very appropriately as 'overwhelming',[2] and she was familiar enough with Yorkshire terms to refer to the 'Boggarts of Yorkshire'.[3] She wrote of an old country house in the Vale of York with which she was familiar.[4] She referred to the 'welcome West Riding accents' of a chance acquaintance,[5] and spoke of second sight 'in the West Riding of Yorkshire' in a lecture to the Scottish Society of Literature and Art in 1901.[6] There were also two references at least by Miss Freer, vague though they were, to country dominated by hills and moors. One of these occurred in her lecture reported in the *Oban Times* already quoted, while her description of herself 'as a child far away in the north', climbing from rock to rock until she reached a moorland tarn, will be remembered.

Finally, in an article 'Folklore and Psychical Research', in which she answered some criticisms of the S.P.R. made by Mr Edward Clodd in his presidential address to the Folklore Society in 1895, Miss Freer described her 'northern village'. She wrote:

I admit some prejudice on my part, having been, according to my lights, a folk-lorist from my earliest years, the natural result of living among the people of a northern village, rich in tradition and story, where mumming plays were of triennial occurrence, and Dolmens and Menhirs, and Roll-right stones, and rocks with cup-markings, and Celtic inscriptions, and Roman altars, and Saxon crosses, were things of every day.

Can I not to this day quote pages of Racine, and Pearson on the Creed, and dreary 'sacred' poetry learnt in bitter punishment for happy, never-to-be-forgotten hours, when perched in an apple-tree or on a manger, I drank in from groom and gardener many a story of local witches and boggarts and rocking stones and cromlechs?[7]

[1] While the early strength of the Quaker movement in Yorkshire cannot be disputed (see W. C. Braithwaite, *The Beginnings of Quakerism*, London, 1923, pp. 368–70), there is, in my view, no special area of the county where the Quakers established themselves above all others. There were important groups in most of the larger towns of the West Riding, such as Leeds, Huddersfield, Halifax, and Wakefield. Bradford was a considerable stronghold (A. R. Hodgson, *The Society of Friends in Bradford. A Record of 270 Years*, Bradford, 1926). So, also, was York, where the great Quaker families engaged in the manufacture of chocolate wielded considerable influence. The Quaker public school at Ackworth is near Pontefract, in the south of the West Riding.

[2] *Essays in Psychical Research*, p. 42.

[3] *Ibid.*, p. 80. [4] *Ibid.*, p. 93. [5] *Ibid.*, p. 280.

[6] *Oban Times*, 23rd November 1901.

[7] *Borderland*, 1895, vol. II, pp. 263–4.

It could be argued that this collection of asides by Miss Freer may well be deliberately misleading and therefore valueless, and that in any event the location of her upbringing and education is not of sufficient importance to justify any serious speculation on the basis of the available information. On the other hand, it seems to me that however purposefully imprecise Miss Freer undoubtedly was in her references to a West Riding upbringing, these allusions do at least form a sufficiently consistent pattern of informed half-truths to merit some consideration. I confess, moreover, that to anyone interested in the antiquities of Yorkshire, her description of her 'northern village' can hardly fail to be of great interest and worthy of some examination.

It is noteworthy that after her single quoted reference in 1895 to the folklore and antiquities of her 'northern village' Miss Freer never again discussed in print the origin of her early interest in such matters, so far as I am aware. This is surprising, for she wrote voluminously and professionally on these subjects in subsequent years. It might be thought that the village of her upbringing, 'rich in tradition and story', would have provided a familiar, convenient, and immediate field for description and personal comment by so able a writer as Miss Freer. There must, it would seem, have been some good reason why the scenes of her later writings on folklore and kindred subjects in Great Britain were limited to the Highlands and the Islands of Scotland, which she knew only from her several brief visits for psychical research purposes, with the added disadvantage that she was unacquainted with Gaelic. As her picture of her 'northern village' was undoubtedly overdrawn, it is possible that some of her more obvious errors were drawn to her attention, causing her embarrassment and a resultant decision that it would be prudent not to refer to the subject again.

One of Miss Freer's more patent mistakes was to claim that there were 'Roll-right stones' in her village in the north. These curiosities are, of course, specifically the circle of stones three to five feet high near the villages of Great and Little Rollright in Oxfordshire.[1] Another glaring error was her reference to mumming plays 'of triennial occurrence', which are non-existent. The leading authority on this subject, Mr Alex Helm, a member of the Council of the Folklore Society, further informs me that the only truly traditional

[1] For a description of the Rollright stones see James Fergusson, *Rude Stone Monuments in all Countries*, London, 1872, pp. 124–6. They are illustrated in a photograph opposite p. 168 of J. Cannan's *Oxfordshire*, London, 1952. See also A. J. Evans, M.A., F.S.A., 'The Rollright Stones and their Folklore', *Folklore*, March, 1895, pp. 5–51.

ceremony in the country celebrated every third year is the painting and re-raising of the village maypole at Barwick-in-Elmet,[1] only a few miles from my own 'northern village' of Thorner in the West Riding of Yorkshire.

In assessing the worth of Miss Freer's description of the scene of her upbringing, expert help has been available to me from an old friend, Mr Hartley Thwaite, J.P., F.S.A., of the Yorkshire Archaeological Society, who has confirmed that her effusive account, with its plethora of antiquities, cannot apply accurately to any single known location in the British Isles. The extreme rarity of Celtic inscriptions, I am informed, enables these to be pinpointed geographically with precision. They do not exist anywhere to our present knowledge in company with the multiplicity of the other types of historic remains, described by Miss Freer as 'things of every day'. Her mention of the Celtic inscriptions and the Rollright stones is sufficient to indicate that her knowledge of archaeology was very superficial.

If Miss Freer's description is considered tolerantly, however, ignoring the more flagrant mistakes I have mentioned and making due allowance for her somewhat vivid imagination and lack of expertise, it is of great interest to anyone familiar, even in the most amateur sense, with the archaeological history of Yorkshire. It seemed to me, too, that if the account of the 'northern village' had any truth in it, the problem of locating it could be approached in an alternative way. If Mrs Connors' recollection was accurate so far as it went, directories of the period might contain a record of the school for young ladies existing in the 1860s, when Miss Freer's aunt assumed the responsibility for her upbringing. In following this tenuous clue, I had no choice but to assume that the school-owning aunt was unmarried and that her name was Freer, or in the alternative either Adcock or Goodrich, these latter being the maiden names of Miss Freer's mother and grandmother.

Miss Freer's description at first seemed to me possibly to point to the village of Aldborough, near Boroughbridge, on the boundary of the West and North Ridings of Yorkshire. Certainly no other

[1] Rev. F. S. Colman, *A History of the Parish of Barwick-in-Elmet in the County of York*, Leeds, 1908, pp. 19–25. Miss Freer could not have been describing Barwick-in-Elmet, for this village, while proud of a remarkable and extensive series of ancient earth-works, possesses none of the antiquities listed by her and is situated in level pastoral country. It is an odd coincidence that Thomas Dykes, the grandfather of Dr John Bacchus Dykes mentioned in the previous chapter, was briefly curate of Barwick-in-Elmet in 1789–91 (*ibid.*, p. 86) before becoming vicar of St John's Church, Hull. The Dykes had no later connexion with Barwick-in-Elmet.

village in this part of England contains more of the features mentioned by Miss Freer. Aldborough was the Iseur of the ancient Britons and the Isurium of the Romans. From the point of view of a person writing in London, Aldborough is certainly 'a northern village, rich in tradition and story'.[1] There is both a Saxon cross and a Roman altar there. The most striking point of identification, however, is the presence, a mile away, of the three menhirs, or 'Devil's Arrows', situated in two fields in Boroughbridge. These three monoliths vary from eighteen to twenty-two feet in height, and archaeologists seem uncertain whether they are of British or Roman origin. Menhirs in groups like these[2] are exceedingly rare, and indeed the only other menhir in Yorkshire known to me is the single example at Rudston, a village in the East Riding near the coastal town of Bridlington. Neither Roman altars nor Saxon crosses are plentiful, and the occurrence at Aldborough of these curiosities close to the well-known 'Devil's Arrows' is probably unique, and is certainly so in the north of England. On the other hand, Aldborough is situated in flat pastoral country. There are no moorland tarns.

Aldborough has been visited. It would have been very pleasant to pin down Miss Freer's childhood village to this discovery, but an investigation has not been fruitful. Some temporary interest was aroused by the discovery that Henry Goodricke was the vicar of Aldborough from 1750 to 1801, but he left no descendants of whom there are any records in the district. The vicar of Aldborough, Rev. S. A. Atherley, has most kindly searched his records for me, as has his colleague at Boroughbridge, but without result. Reference books and directories of the period give some details of the inhabitants of Aldborough and Boroughbridge and of private schools, but unfortunately the names of Goodrich, Freer, and Adcock are conspicuous by their absence.

The ancient village of Adel, near Leeds, now almost a suburb of Yorkshire's largest city, qualified on some points, for it possesses the remains of three Roman altars and some notable Saxon anti-

[1] T. S. Turner, in his *History of Aldborough and Boroughbridge, Containing an Account of the Roman Antiquities, Devil's Arrows, Churches, Halls and Other Curiosities*, London, 1853, says that there are few places in England where one can enjoy the historical past with greater pleasure than the village of Aldborough, while it is said in *The Tourist's Companion*, Ripon, 1818, that Aldborough has always arrested the attention and engaged the particular notice of antiquaries.

[2] Not to be confused with cromlechs, which are not uncommon in Yorkshire. Menhirs, literally 'Long stones', are monumental standing stones of substantial height.

quities.[1] Although it was interesting to discover that Isaac Freer of Arthington, a nearby village, is buried at Adel,[2] it soon became clear that this could not be Miss Freer's 'northern village'. Isaac died on 24th March 1696 and is the last Freer recorded in Adel. Directories of the period showed no school that fitted, and Adel has no menhirs or moorland tarns.

Ilkley, an inland resort of great beauty on the river Wharfe, with fine moorland scenery, was the Olicana of the Romans. It has three carved Saxon crosses in the churchyard. Its present population of some 19,000 started to grow from small beginnings in the middle of the nineteenth century, with the advent of the railways. Less than 500 people lived there in the first half of that century,[3] and it was still being described as a village in Kelly's *Post Office Directory of the West Riding of Yorkshire* in the 1860s and 1870s.

In their great book on Ilkley[4] Dr R. Collyer and J. H. Turner describe the antiquities to be found on Rombalds Moor (popularly called Ilkley Moor) which immediately adjoins the southern outskirts of the town. These included 'cup-marked rocks' and a 'despoiled rocking stone and cromlech'.[5] The 'circle, sixteen yards in diameter, composed of twelve upright stones, three or four feet high',[6] known as the Twelve Apostles, might have been mistaken by the uninformed Miss Freer for menhirs, as might 'Cowper's Cross', an upright stone modernly (in 1868) fashioned into a Calvary Cross,[7] or the 'two pyramidal idol rocks, and a rock bearing cup marks on the margin',[8] on the highest part of the moor. There are, in addition, barrows, pit dwellings, burial mounds, cairns, and other relics on Rombalds Moor.

The Roman altar discovered at Ilkley is illustrated on p. 17 of *Ilkley: Ancient and Modern*, while the three ancient Saxon crosses now in Ilkley churchyard are shown on p. 41. The reader may think,

[1] See Henry T. Simpson, *Archaelogia Adelensia, or a History of the Parish of Adel*, London, 1879, and George Lewthwaite, *Adel: Its Norman Church . . . and Other Early Antiquities*, Lincoln, Leeds, and London, 1887.

[2] *The Registers of the Parish Church of Adel* (*Publications of the Thoresby Society*), Leeds, 1895, vol. V, p. 128. Mr Vincent Sternberg, one of the principal actors in the ghostly drama of the Leeds Library, discussed in my *New Light on Old Ghosts*, is buried at Adel.

[3] Thomas Allen, *A New and Complete History of the County of York*, London, 1832, vol. VI, p. 143.

[4] Robert Collyer and J. Horsfall Turner, *Ilkley: Ancient and Modern*, Otley, 1885.

[5] *Ibid.*, p. lxxx.

[6] *Ibid.*, p. lxxxiii.

[7] The authors were quoting from a pamphlet printed in Wakefield in 1868, *Rambles on Rombalds Moor*, by C. Forrest and W. Grainge.

[8] *Ibid.*, p. lxxxiv.

against the background of the reservations to which I have drawn attention in previous pages, that there are some quite striking correspondences between Ilkley as it was in the nineteenth century and Miss Freer's description of her 'northern village'. Moorland tarns are shown on both ancient and modern maps of Ilkley, and some of these are in quite close proximity to the town.

While the archaeological enquiry was being pursued, *Kelly's Post Office Directory of the West Riding of Yorkshire* was searched, and disclosed the very interesting information that a Miss Ann Adcock had a private boarding school for girls in Ilkley from 1861 to about the middle of the 1870s. I could trace no other entry of a private boarding school for girls in the whole of the West Riding in the name of Freer, Adcock, or Goodrich.

Kelly's *Directory* gave no address for Miss Adcock's establishment for young ladies. Slater's *Royal National Commercial Directory of the County of York*, 1864, however, gave the school as being situated at Ilkley Hall. Local guide-books of the period[1] were examined at Ilkley, together with Shuttleworth's *New Map of Ilkley*, 1874. These, together with the 1875 issue of Slater's *Directory* at the British Museum, provided some additional information.

The 1863 edition of Shuttleworth, under 'Boarding Schools for Young Ladies', listed Miss Adcock's establishment as being at The Hall, Ilkley, while the 1865 issue gave the location as Bilberry Bank, Crossbeck Road. Slater showed the address as Ilkley Hall in 1864, and Crossbeck Road in 1875. Denton gave the Bilberry Bank address in his local guide-book in 1871. This information showed that Miss Adcock moved her school in or about 1864, some two years before Miss Freer became an orphan, from Ilkley Hall, a sizeable property in its own grounds and an impressive address for a boarding school, to Bilberry Bank, a much smaller semi-detached house with a steeply sloping garden backing directly on to the moor[2] in those days.

This sounds very much as if Miss Adcock's young lady pupils were diminishing in numbers by 1864, which is rather confirmed by the fact that the last record of the school's existence is in the issue of Slater published in 1875, when it seems to have finally closed down altogether. The reason for the school losing ground and the move to much smaller premises may well have been increased competition

[1] Notably *Shuttleworth's Guide-book to Ilkley and Vicinity*, published at Ilkley in 1863, with a second edition in 1865, and *Denton's Ilkley Directory, Guide Book and Almanac*, Ilkley, 1871.

[2] Bilberry Bank and the adjoining house Moorlands (the names are very descriptive of the situation) are shown on the map of 1874, but no longer exist today.

from rival schools being established in Ilkley at this period, due to the very suitable situation for girls' boarding schools of this beautiful and healthful district. Shuttleworth, in the second edition of his guide-book, listed three other schools similar to that of Miss Adcock, all in the same part of Ilkley.

If the reader considers that it is probable that Miss Ann Adcock was the 'elderly relative', and that Miss Freer's schooldays were indeed spent among the Saxon crosses, the rocks with cup-markings, the rocking stones and cromlechs, the stone circles, Roman altars, and moorland tarns of Ilkley, then he may think that the other indications, already discussed, that Miss Freer had no background of wealth are rather confirmed by what little we know of Miss Adcock and her school. Miss Freer's parents had no money, and it would seem that the 'elderly relative', if she was Miss Adcock, was not possessed of any substantial means. This opinion is supported by the results of another line of enquiry.

I asked an old schoolfellow, Mr John Lancaster, of the West Riding Registry of Deeds, if he would look at his records during the relevant period. He kindly did so, and after an extensive search had to report that the name of Ann Adcock does not appear at all in his indexes of Ilkley. As registration of all property transactions was compulsory in the West Riding in the latter part of the nineteenth century, this means that Miss Adcock was the owner of neither Ilkley Hall nor Bilberry Bank, and that as leases of twenty-one years and more were also required to be registered, it follows that her tenancies were only of short duration, as is indicated by the facts previously assembled. Miss Adcock was not a property owner.

Another interesting discovery is that Miss Adcock was not a member of any old-established Ilkley family. The name Adcock does not appear at all in William Cooper's *The Parish Registers of Ilkley, 1597–1812*, which was privately printed in 1927 for the Yorkshire Parish Register Society, nor was Miss Adcock recorded as a resident of Ilkley in the directories to which reference has already been made, except for the period when she had her school. This suggests that she came to the small community of Ilkley from some other part of England shortly before 1860, which would make it possible for her to have been a member of the Adcock family resident in the Leicestershire, Northamptonshire, and Rutland district at that time.

What happened to Miss Adcock when she gave up her school in the mid-1870s is a mystery which I have not been able to solve.[1]

[1] One reason why we know so little about Miss Adcock's school is that it is not mentioned, either by advertisement or in any other way, in any issue of *The Ilkley Gazette* during the relevant period.

Miss Margaret E. Hutchin, the Superintendent Registrar of the Wharfedale Registration District, has most kindly established for me that Miss Adcock neither married nor died in this part of Yorkshire during the last thirty years of the nineteenth century. My colleague Mr H. E. Pratt has spent many diligent Saturday mornings at Somerset House going completely through the whole of the indexes throughout the same period over the whole country with the same object. Some forty certificates of deaths or marriages have been taken out and examined, quite apart from the scrutiny of other entries in the indexes relating to Ann Adcocks who could be ruled out on account of impossible ages, such as those in their teens or eighties when the school was established about 1860. A large proportion of the deceased Ann Adcocks were, of course, married women who did not qualify. It is disappointing, however, that among those remaining we could discover no Ann Adcock who was described as a retired schoolmistress, or who could be convincingly identified with Miss Adcock of Ilkley. It would have been very agreeable to complete this small fringe investigation in a definite and satisfying way, but so far we have not been able to do so with any degree of confidence. As I have remarked to Dr Campbell on more than one occasion, Miss Adcock seems to have obliterated her trail almost as successfully as Miss Freer. She may or may not have been the 'elderly relative', and my hope is that this book may conceivably come to the notice of somebody who can supply the essential information for which we have looked for so long, and which Miss Freer could have given in a single sentence had she thought fit to do so.[1]

As Miss Freer was born in 1857, she would be eighteen in 1875, when her schooldays may be presumed to have been over. How was her time spent between 1875 and the later 1880s, when she was living in London, came under the notice of F. W. H. Myers, and ultimately joined the S.P.R.? We cannot answer this question with any certainty, because we have no information beyond a variety of vague statements made by Miss Freer herself which may or may not be true. Many of these comments are contained in her long anonymous paper, 'A Record of Telepathic and Other Experiences',[2] read to the S.P.R. for her by F. W. H. Myers on 25th October 1889. If the

[1] One can only speculate whether Ann Adcock may have been the 'old lady in the spirit wearing a cap who is fond of you—your grandmother' whom Mrs Piper described to Miss Freer in a séance on 7th December 1889, and whom Mrs Piper said was 'named Anne'. Miss Freer said this was a correct description of a friend whom she was 'in the habit of calling Granny' (*Borderland*, I, 227).

[2] *Proceedings*, S.P.R., 1889–90, vol. VI, pp. 358–97.

'elderly relative' was still alive she does not seem to have taken much part in Miss Freer's reminiscences of her life during this period.

She stayed, she said, 'in a country vicarage in the North', at a date unstated, where the children of the house were her constant playfellows (p. 371), while in 1875 she was a guest in 'a country house in the Midland counties' (p. 372). She enjoyed supernormal experiences during both these visits, which seems to have been her invariable habit wherever she went.

On p. 363 of her paper she said that when she was a child of thirteen she was taken to see a college, to which it was proposed to send her later to complete her studies. She saw an apparition in an empty classroom (it was during the vacation period), and when in later years she took her place in the college she met a girl whom she called 'N', the original of the apparition, and established a friendship with her 'which has never changed'. If this story is true, it may be that Miss Freer's education continued until 1878 or so, when she was twenty-one. Who 'N' was, I do not know. If we bring ourselves to believe Miss Freer to a limited degree, it cannot have been her devoted friend Miss Constance Moore, for according to Miss Freer's letter to Fr Allan McDonald of 28th October 1901, she and Miss Moore had been 'twenty-one years together', which would mean that their intimate friendship did not start until 1880.

On the assumption that Miss Freer's paper was not entirely fiction, it seems to me that Miss Moore must have been 'D', a friend with whom Miss Freer was staying in a country house in 1882, where the latter had a remarkable premonition (p. 374), although 'D' does not seem to have been her companion when Miss Freer was staying at another 'house in the country' in August 1887 (p. 372), nor when she was living 'in a private boarding-house' in August 1885, recovering from an illness and accompanied by someone (the elderly relative?) who was too deaf to hear passing conversation. Miss Freer said (p. 358) that 'during the last few years' she had formed an 'intimate friendship' with 'D', and that between their two minds telepathic communications occurred with such frequency that they had come to regard them as a matter of course.[1] She added (p. 362) that as 'D' had scarcely any other psychical experiences, this success probably depended upon their propinquity and

[1] It must be recorded, however, that in a letter to Lord Bute of 25th January 1896 Miss Freer said that Miss Moore 'scorns the whole subject' of psychical research. Mr (later Sir) John Ritchie Findlay, in a letter to Lord Bute of 3rd March 1897, describing his experiences during his stay at Ballechin House, said that 'Miss Moore, on the other hand, struck me as being a person of sound common sense, and her evidence I should value beyond that of all the others, who are pre-disposed by temperament to such experiences.'

common interests. For three months of the year 1888 Miss Freer stated that she and 'D' were living under the same roof (p. 377), and from the description of other incidents they seem to have lived within very easy reach of one another during the remainder of that year. In January 1889, moreover, the two friends were living together again, for Miss Freer described how they were reading their letters together which had just been delivered, and she was able to surprise 'D' by divining correctly the Christian name of the latter's correspondent as 'Wilhelmina', by seeing this in 'letters of light' against a dark background near the fireplace (p. 365). All this clearly suggests that if Miss Freer and Miss Moore had been 'twenty-one years together' in 1901, then Miss Moore and 'D' were one and the same person. Certainly they were together from 1895 onwards, when Miss Freer moved into Miss Moore's home, Holy Trinity Vicarage, Paddington, the house of the latter's father, the Rev. Daniel Moore.

It is for the reader to decide what credence he attaches to Miss Freer's accounts of her life as a young woman, which included a statement in 1894 that some time prior to 1890 she had been living with friends in Baltimore.[1] This occurred in a curious story which to me at least (surprisingly in the case of Miss Freer's writings) is not easy to follow. It concerned the psychometry of a cat's hair, a young woman with 'terrible headaches', and the alleged death of an elderly aunt of the family with whom Miss Freer was staying. All this is vague and unsatisfactory of course, and we are not really on firm ground until January 1888, when Miss Freer joined the S.P.R. We know that by then Miss Freer was living in London at St Stephen's Ladies' Home, and that this address remained unchanged in successive lists of members for some years. She certainly stayed for periods in other people's houses, including the home of the elderly mother of F. W. H. Myers, but St Stephen's Ladies' Home seems to have been her permanent address.

The foregoing pages do not seek to show that Miss Freer did not enjoy a more advantageous upbringing than her brothers whom she left behind in Uppingham. I think that there is no doubt that she did. What has been demonstrated, I venture to think, is that her secretiveness and her addiction to misleading statements about herself, which she continued to display virtually to her death, enabled her to conceal the details of much of her life very effectively indeed. More importantly, the reader may think that attention has been

[1] *Borderland*, January, 1894, vol. I, p. 229. But it is just possible that this story though quoted by Miss Freer in the first person, relates an experience of someone else, who is not named.

drawn to material by which we can estimate the likely truth of Miss Freer's stories of her psychical experiences, which occupied so many pages of the *Proceedings* of the S.P.R., and enabled her quite rapidly to become a leading member of that organization at an important period in its history.

3

MISS FREER AND THE S.P.R.

AFTER EDMUND GURNEY, a man of brilliance and complete integrity, had taken his life in a Brighton hotel in June 1888,[1] his work as Honorary Secretary of the S.P.R. was taken over jointly by Frederic W. H. Myers and Frank Podmore. It is hard to avoid the melancholy conclusion that with Gurney's critical counsel silenced by his death, there was a deterioration in the standards of evidence adopted by the leaders of the Society in the cases they printed in their *Proceedings*. In July 1889, for example, F. W. H. Myers published, as a genuine case of haunting, the story of the Leeds Library ghost,[2] without disclosing that in January and February of the same year he had received letters from two of the principal witnesses which threw the gravest doubts upon the whole affair.[3] The suppression of these two letters was repeated in 1903, when the Leeds Library case was reprinted without amendment in Myers' book, published after his death.[4] Those familiar with the work and

[1] After *The Strange Case of Edmund Gurney* appeared in 1964, some additional evidence from the past became available, supporting my theory that Gurney's suicide was concealed by the S.P.R. leaders. *The Diary of Alice James*, originally privately printed in four copies in 1894, was published in 1965 with an introduction by Dr L. Edel. Alice James was the sister of William and Henry James. William James was a friend of Gurney, Myers, and Sidgwick and became President of the S.P.R. On 5th August 1889, shortly after William James had arrived in England, Miss James wrote in her diary, 'They say there is little doubt that Mr Edmund Gurney committed suicide. What a pity to hide it; every educated person who kills himself does something towards lessening the superstition' (1965 edition, p. 52).

[2] F. W. H. Myers, 'On Recognised Apparitions Occurring More than a Year After Death', *Proceedings*, S.P.R. 1889–90, vol. VI, pp. 13–65.

[3] The two letters concerned, written to Myers by Mr (later Sir) John Y. W. Macalister and the Rev. Charles Hargrove, are still in the files of the S.P.R. Their surprising contents are discussed in my *New Light on Old Ghosts*, London, 1965, pp. 35–53.

[4] *Human Personality and Its Survival of Bodily Death*, London, 1903, vol. II, pp. 380–1. The book was edited by Dr Richard Hodgson and Miss Alice Johnson, two prominent members of the S.P.R. Another example of Miss Johnson's concealment of evidence, that of her pamphlet on the Smith/Blackburn 'mind-reading' fiasco, printed in 1909, is documented and discussed in my book on Edmund Gurney.

character of Edmund Gurney may think that such a concealment of vital facts would not have occurred when he was Honorary Secretary of the Society and editor of its *Proceedings*.[1]

Miss Freer became prominent in the affairs of the S.P.R. during this period of increasing credulity on the part of its leaders, and what seems, indeed, to have been their determination to prove at all costs the existence and reality of psychic phenomena. The climate of the Society could hardly have been more appropriate for the enthusiastic reception and publication of Miss Freer's engaging accounts of her childhood visions, her crystal-gazing, and her telepathic experiences in the unnamed country houses and rectories in which she claimed to have stayed. The fact that not a shred of corroborative evidence, nor even of identification of places and persons, was offered in connexion with any of these wonders meant that the stories could be published without fear of them being checked, with a consequent precipitation of the kind of disaster that had followed the earlier printing of cases like that of Sir Edmund Hornby.[2] This affair, in which the Society had unfortunately given names and dates, had been exposed, after publication, as such nonsense that the S.P.R. had no choice but to withdraw the part of the volume of *Proceedings* in which the Hornby case had been included, and issue a reprint with another story substituted, occupying exactly the same amount of space.

There can be no doubt that from first joining the Society in 1888, Miss Freer made a most favourable impression upon the oligarchy of the S.P.R. Professor Henry Sidgwick, one of the Society's founders and its original President, in his first reference to her wrote in his private 'Journal' or diary, on 31st July 1888, of a curious incident connected with Miss Freer, whom he described as 'a friend of Fred Myers'. Apparently F. W. H. Myers or Miss Freer (or both) had told Sidgwick, some five weeks after the event, that on Sunday, 24th June 1888, the day after Gurney had been

[1] Myers became Joint Hon. Secretary of the S.P.R. after Gurney's death, and it seems inevitable that the policy of the Society would be influenced by his pronounced sympathy with the claims of spiritualism. This attitude of Myers, and the published opinions of him by contemporaries such as Lady Constance Battersea, Lady Caroline Jebb, and Sir Joseph Thompson, is discussed on pp. 37–48 of my *The Strange Case of Edmund Gurney*. It is plain from the unpublished correspondence between Lord Bute, a Vice-President of the S.P.R., and the Rev. Peter Dewar, that as late as 1894 it was regarded as regrettable that Myers was still attracted to 'the camp of spiritualism' and to patently fraudulent mediums.

[2] The Hornby imbroglio is described on pp. 65–8 of my book on Edmund Gurney.

found dead behind the locked door of a Brighton hotel bedroom, Miss Freer had a spontaneous and vivid supernormal conviction that some calamity had happened connected with her friend Myers, who was of course a close colleague of Gurney. Sidgwick was evidently much impressed by this example of Miss Freer's claim to clairvoyant ability, for he wrote that she had already experienced a number of similar telepathic impressions, and added of the Myers incident, 'What can this mean?' He had apparently no doubts about Miss Freer's truthfulness and sincerity, for he added, 'We think her a perfectly trustworthy witness.' When Eleanor and Arthur Sidgwick, Sidgwick's widow and brother, who were both prominent S.P.R. members, published the 'Journal' in *Henry Sidgwick, A Memoir* (London, 1906) they chose to omit the entire entry for 31st July 1888, which described both this incident and Sidgwick's views on the strange circumstances of Gurney's death. A few weeks later, in his 'Journal' of 10th September 1888, Sidgwick underlined his approval of Miss Freer. 'She is bright and clever and by no means credulous: altogether my impression of the evidential value of her remarkable series of experiences is raised.' As in the case of the earlier comment by Sidgwick, his biographers, in transcribing this entry in 1906, chose to suppress both Miss Freer's identity and Sidgwick's praise of her qualities, which it is difficult not to connect with other evidence, both published and unpublished, which suggests that the S.P.R. leaders may have revised their opinion of Miss Freer somewhat drastically in later years. It was not possible, however, to extinguish in 1906 approving comments by Sidgwick that had already been published. In 1894, for example, after taking the chair at a meeting of the S.P.R. at Westminster Town Hall on 8th June, at which Miss Freer read a paper, 'The Apparent Sources of Supernormal Experiences', Sidgwick praised the lecturer warmly indeed:

The Chairman, in expressing the thanks of the meeting to Miss X., remarked that it was rare to find the capacity for supernormal perception combined with the power of self-observation and analysis, the carefulness and promptitude in recording experiences, and the appreciation of the importance of different kinds of evidence, which Miss X's paper showed.[1]

[1] *Journal*, S.P.R., June 1894, p. 261. W. T. Stead proudly quoted Sidgwick in full, adding, 'A compliment from Professor Sidgwick is a compliment indeed, and those who read the "Notes" in our present issue will see how thoroughly it was deserved by my able and gifted assistant' (*Borderland*, July 1894, vol. I, p. 400).

5. John, 3rd Marquess of Bute, wearing St Andrews University rectorial robes.

6. Gravestone of Ada Goodrich Freer (Mrs Spoer) at Cedar Lawn Cemetery, Paterson, New Jersey, U.S.A.
Photo. Dorothy Kurtz.

7. Fr Allan McDonald.

The date and circumstances of the first meeting between Miss Freer and F. W. H. Myers are not known to me, but there can be little doubt that he admired her and that he was on much more intimate terms with her than were any of his colleagues. He seems to have introduced her to psychical research and the Society, to whose members he personally read her first two anonymous papers, 'Recent Experiments in Crystal-Vision' on 10th May 1889[1] and 'A Record of Telepathic and Other Experiences' on 25th October of the same year.[2] He was mainly responsible for her appointment as a paid assistant to W. T. Stead, the owner and editor of the spiritualist journal *Borderland*, and for other favours. We know from unpublished correspondence that it was through Myers that she was introduced in 1894 to Lord Bute, a Vice-President of the S.P.R. who became Miss Freer's generous patron. I have not been given access to Myers' papers, but Mr R. D. Stein, who presumably has, claims that according to a note by Myers, the couple first met in January 1888, when Myers wrote privately of Miss Freer's beautiful grey eyes, and said that she was in her middle twenties.[3] I cannot test the worth of this statement, for Mr Stein's article lacks any documentation, contains some errors of fact, and is completely wrong on one main point which is very relevant to any speculation regarding the relationship between Myers and Ada Freer. We are more likely to suspect a man who had indulged in a three-year liaison with his own cousin's wife, of seeking further sexual adventures than one who had not. The matter which Mr Stein has elected to raise in this connexion is an exchange of letters between Mr W. H. Salter, Dr A. Gauld of the S.P.R., and myself. It is fortunate that I have preserved this correspondence.

Mrs Marshall, the wife of Myers' first cousin and the mother of five young children, drowned herself in Ullswater in 1876, after trying to cut her throat with scissors, following a three-year passionate love-affair with Myers. Mr Stein mistakenly asserts that Mr Salter, one of the earliest S.P.R. members still living, a Past President, and the Society's Honorary Secretary for over twenty years,

[1] *Proceedings*, S.P.R., 1888–9, vol. V, pp. 486–521.

[2] *Ibid.*, 1889–90, vol. VI, pp. 358–97.

[3] R. D. Stein, 'In Defence of F. W. H. Myers', *Fate*, Douglas, I.O.M., September 1965, pp. 47–61. This essay was, in essence, a violent criticism of Mr A. S. Jarman's recent study of the effect of Myers' relationship with Mrs A. E. Marshall, upon his attitude towards psychical research and the proof of survival, 'Failure of a Quest', *Tomorrow*, vol. 12, No. 1, pp. 17–29, and *Dr Gauld and Mr Myers*, London, 1964. Mr Stein's paper was marred by some mistakes, and Mr Jarman's reply (*Fate*, January 1966, pp. 26 ff.) makes entertaining reading.

and Dr A. Gauld, Myers' biographer, with the Myers papers at their disposal, wrote to me to ask if I had 'gleaned any information on Annie's pregnancy' in connexion with the tragedy. The exact reverse of this unlikely if flattering picture of myself as a fountain of knowledge is true. The facts are that I first read of Mrs Marshall's death, without any details or mention of suicide, in Mr Salter's 'F. W. H. Myers' Posthumous Message' (*Proceedings*, S.P.R., vol. LII, pp. 1–32). After seeing the death certificate and the inquest reports, I wrote spontaneously to Mr Salter, who in his reply openly spoke of Mrs Marshall's pregnancy at the time of her death as an established fact. This again was completely new information to me. When I later wrote to Dr Gauld, he told me that the secret had been passed to Mr Salter by S.P.R. leaders of the last generation, including Mrs E. M. Sidgwick, Sir Lawrence Jones, and Mr J. G. Piddington.

Whether Miss Freer was ever more than what Sidgwick called 'a friend of Fred Myers', we may never know with certainty. That Myers was a confessed sensualist and womanizer before his marriage to Eveleen Tennant in 1880 is not in dispute,[1] but it is fair to point out that many a 'lecher' (as Dr Gauld once described Myers to me) becomes a model husband. On the other hand, we must remember that Professor C. D. Broad has told us that Eveleen Myers was 'a singularly egotistical and rather unscrupulous person' and that Myers had marital difficulties.[2]

Any affair with Miss Freer would involve an assumption of Myers' infidelity to his marriage vows. In this connexion it is of interest to see that Mr Stein believes that Myers' love poem 'A Sister of Phyllis', which was included in his *Fragments of Inner Life*, privately circulated in a few copies after his death, was written about his brief association with a young widowed medium, Mrs Constance Julia Turner, in April 1890, when Myers had been married for ten years. Dr A. Gauld shares this view,[3] which has been put forward in opposition to the suggestion of Mr A. S. Jarman that the poem concerned Myers' earlier affair with Mrs A. E. Marshall.

'A Sister of Phyllis' contains expressions of Myers' admiration for the slenderness and fairness of the young woman concerned (whoever she was) and of 'The blue, the gold, of eyes, of hair', and the following lines, to which Mr Jarman has attached significance:

I spake; she listened; woman-wise
Her self-surrendering answer came.

[1] See, for example, the comments of Miss Helen Gurney and Lady Caroline Jebb, quoted on pp. 33, 38, 39, etc., of *The Strange Case of Edmund Gurney*.

[2] *Swan On a Black Sea*, edited by Signe Toksvig, with a Foreword by C. D. Broad, London, 1965, p. xix.

[3] *Journal*, S.P.R., June 1964, pp. 319–20.

It is fair to point out that Dr Gauld, while conceding that Myers 'several times went out by the sea alone with Constance, and he took her out again on 1st June [1890] when he was passing through Folkestone', nevertheless insists that there is no evidence 'for supposing that Myers was physically involved with Constance', or that the lines about her 'self-surrendering answer' necessarily refer to her seduction by Myers.[1] Dr Gauld may be right in these assumptions. On the other hand, if, as he thinks, the poem quoted does refer to Myers' association with Mrs Turner, then it is not easy to believe that there was not at least an emotional relationship between them.

In later years Miss Freer quarrelled bitterly with Myers, and in her published criticism of him, to be discussed later, the emotional overtones were fairly obvious. Despite her attractions, she did not marry until she was forty-eight, four years after Myers died, and at the time of his final illness and death she suffered a severe nervous and physical breakdown. Clearly, I think, there was a special relationship of some sort between the two, but how deeply it went is a matter for the judgment of the reader when he has considered the evidence. In this connexion the very odd business of Miss Freer's violent reaction to Myers taking Miss Chaston, a woman seven years younger than Miss Freer, to Ballechin House in 1897, and the diligent curiosity of Sir James Crichton-Browne and Lord Bute to find out who and what Miss Chaston really was, to be discussed later, is very relevant. Whatever the truth of the matter may

[1] *Journal*, S.P.R., June 1964, pp. 319–20. On the subject of Mr Stein's errors of fact, in his essay, it may be pointed out that his observation that the death of Constance Turner took place at Folkestone (p. 57) is quite wrong. Mrs Turner died on 10th August 1890, a few months after her meetings with Myers, at Abbey Lands, Weston-on-Trent, in the Midlands, her death being reported by her sister and fellow medium, Mrs Everett, of the same address. And as regards the accuracy of Dr Alan Gauld, the editor of the S.P.R. *Journal*, in his criticism of Mr Jarman, it may be pointed out that his explanation of why Mrs Marshall's body was taken for burial by her father to her old home at Thornton-le-Dale in Yorkshire, and not interred in Cumberland where her married life had been spent, was wholly wrong. Dr Gauld said (*Journal*, S.P.R., June 1964, p. 322) that 'prior to the Burial Laws Amendment Act of 1880, the burial of suicides presented difficulties, which Mr Hill could have overcome by burying his daughter in the parish of which he was himself rector'. Dr Gauld overlooked the fact that the verdict at the inquest contained the saving clause 'being of unsound mind' in regard to Mrs Marshall's suicide, which removed all burial difficulties, and he was evidently unaware, through failure to consult *Crockford*, that at the date of the tragedy Mr Hill had not been the rector of Thornton-le-Dale for nearly twenty years. The point is not lacking in importance. Dr Gauld was trying to counter Mr Jarman's argument that the removal of Mrs Marshall's body to distant Yorkshire by her father confirmed the very reasonable belief, for which there was other evidence, that Mrs Marshall and her husband became estranged during her affair with Myers.

be, the observation by Mr Stein that Myers and Miss Freer first met in 1888 does appear to be at variance with what seem to be the rather strong indications that they were in close contact with each other some years earlier. Clearly, anything Miss Freer wrote requires corroboration, but it is relevant to point out that she published a number of statements on this question during Myers' lifetime, which he could have contradicted if he had thought it appropriate to do so.

Miss Freer's work, albeit anonymously, first achieved prominence in psychical research circles by her unsigned paper on crystal-gazing, read to the Society for her by Myers in the Spring of 1889, and printed in full in the *Proceedings*. It was, she recorded, Myers who first put a crystal ball into her hands, asking her whether she had ever before experimented with anything of the kind. According to her, pictures soon presented themselves, and Myers allowed her to keep the 'treasured crystal', and for more than a year she experimented and gave the subject her most serious attention. She undertook, she said, a prolonged scholarly study of the history of the whole subject in the British Museum and elsewhere, and an investigation of all the literature, both ancient and modern, that she could find which touched upon crystal-gazing. This work, she recorded, was done as early as 1887, a statement which, if true, would in itself dispose of the suggestion that she and Myers first met in 1888.[1]

Some confirmation is available of this dating of her interest in crystal-gazing, in that before Myers introduced Miss Freer to this subject they had already done work together in automatic writing, in which Myers was keenly interested. She wrote during Myers' lifetime that her first experiments in this subject were undertaken 'in 1885 or 1886' at his urgent published plea.[2] This 'earnest appeal', as Myers called it, was printed by him at the end of a long paper on automatic writing dated 30th January 1885. He asked for first-hand testimony from spiritualists in England and America who were automatists, to be sent to him at the S.P.R. in London or to his home address.[3] He said that an earlier appeal in spiritualist papers had produced only meagre results. It seems more probable, on the face of it, that Miss Freer's response to this invitation would be 'in 1885 or 1886' rather than as late as 1888. If this first contact was indeed in, say, 1886, and was followed by the year's work on crystal-gazing in 1887, then the sequence of events would fit together very well, as will be seen.

[1] *Borderland*, 1895, vol. II, p. 263. [2] *Ibid.*, 1896, vol. III, p. 169.

[3] F. W. H. Myers, 'Automatic Writing', *Proceedings*, S.P.R., 1885, vol. III, pp. 1–63.

In this connexion it is important to bear in mind that although the paper on crystal-gazing was not read to the Society and printed in its *Proceedings* until the Spring of 1889, it was in fact submitted to the S.P.R. in 1888, as Sidgwick said in his Foreword to the later paper on telepathy, also written by Miss Freer and read to the S.P.R. by Myers on 25th October 1889.[1] This was to be expected, when it is recalled that Miss Freer was a newcomer to the Society and that this was her first published work, however highly it may have been recommended by Myers. Sidgwick was obviously referring to the long and intricate first section of the crystal-gazing paper dealing with the history of the subject, which had required many months of literary study, in that the final section, presumably added as an afterthought at Myers' suggestion, consisted of some examples of Miss Freer's experiences stated to be copied from her notebooks, some of which ran into early 1889.

In the light of the foregoing it seems to me that Miss Freer's timetable of these events is more probable than the suggestion that she first met Myers in 1888, for an impossibly tight schedule would be involved if we try to fit the automatic writing, the crystal-gazing experiments, and the writing of the paper on that subject into that one year. Of this latter work she wrote:

When, in 1887, I devoted a considerable amount of leisure to investigating the subject [*of crystal-gazing*], *I was mainly indebted for material, in what was then a somewhat remote research, to my acquaintance with folk-lore, and to those authors, classical and mediaeval, upon whom the writers on folk-lore mainly depend. It was necessary, not only to search the annals of Greece and Rome, of civilised Asia, of Egypt, and of mediaeval Europe, but to examine scores of pamphlets and rare tracts in various languages (as well as, of course, the recognised authorities) dealing with the peasant tales of Scandinavia and Russia, with legends and myths of American Indians and Pacific Islanders, with the tribes of Australia and New Zealand, and Southern Africa.*[2]

These were large claims; but it can be said that her paper on this subject, immense in its length, was impressive in its obvious

[1] In this paper, prepared after the one on crystal-gazing, Miss Freer wrote (and Myers read out to the S.P.R.) that she was writing up some of her telepathic experiences for him as early as January 1888, which in itself makes it additionally difficult to believe that they first met in that year (*Proceedings*, S.P.R., 1889–90, vol. VI, p. 370).

[2] *Borderland*, 1895, vol. II, p. 263. And it was Myers, according to her, who first introduced her to the subject by placing a crystal ball into her hands, an event which must have taken place some time before she began her investigations.

diligence and presentation of her material. It covered thirty-six closely printed pages of the S.P.R. *Proceedings*, and contained no less than eighty footnotes and references. She quoted many writers, both ancient and modern, famous and obscure, in her account of the history of the subject. If the work at the British Museum was done in 1887, and did take a year as she claimed, which might well have been, then this would bring the submission of the completed paper to the S.P.R. to 1888, as Sidgwick said. It is relevant also that Miss Freer stated that the greater part of the writing of the paper was done in the house of Myers' mother, which suggests in itself an earlier and a greater degree of familiarity with Myers than with the other S.P.R. leaders, as does the fact that in July 1888, some months after she had joined the Society, Sidgwick was still referring to her as 'a friend of Fred Myers', rather than as a member of the S.P.R.

The personal experiences in crystal vision and telepathy, told in Miss Freer's two papers on these subjects in 1889, were purely anecdotal. She had been able, she said, to obtain from the crystal the address, which she had inadvertently destroyed, of a person to whom she wished to write. As she had no other information, she wrote, she 'risked posting my letter to the address so strangely supplied'. The letter reached its destination.[1] She was successful in finding a missing medical prescription, which had been 'accidentally folded within one of E's letters, where it had remained, I have reason to believe, for more than four years'. The crystal provided the information as to its whereabouts.[2] A lost household key was similarly discovered after Miss Freer had 'applied to the crystal for information'.[3] Not a shred of evidence was offered regarding the location of these occurrences or the names of the persons involved. Indeed, when Miss Freer described how she was able to see in her crystal the details of the new decorations of a friend's house, her caution was such that not only did she conceal the name of the friend or where she lived but even the year in which the alleged incident took place.[4]

Miss Freer's second anonymous S.P.R. paper, this time dealing with her telepathic experiences, was even longer than her earlier contribution, occupying no less than forty pages of the *Proceedings*. As before, it was read to the Society by Myers, and Sidgwick provided a short Foreword. The style did not differ from that of the earlier paper. Her readers learned that Miss Freer had been enjoying psychical experiences 'extending over a life-time' from the age

[1] *Proceedings*, S.P.R., 1888–9, vol. V, p. 507.
[2] *Ibid.*, p. 509. [3] *Ibid.*, p. 509. [4] *Ibid.*, p. 512.

of three.[1] When she was fifteen she had been able telepathically to summon a friend who was eighty miles away. The friend arrived in a few hours.[2] As a child she had abandoned her 'favourite amusement of chess', she said, because her ability to foresee her opponents' intentions gave her such an advantage that her schoolboy friend had fallen into the reprehensible habit of betting on her invariable success.[3] She was able, by telepathy, to save the house of her friend 'D' from being burnt down.[4] As in the case of her crystal visions, Miss Freer refrained from giving either the names of the friends involved or the location of any of the incidents, so that neither criticism nor comment was, or is, possible. This was perhaps one of the reasons why these stories were so acceptable to the S.P.R. leaders, and why so many pages of the *Proceedings* were gratefully devoted to their publication. However this may be, there is no doubt that if this was the kind of material welcomed by the Society, then Miss Freer was willing to provide it in quantity at this period. This was additionally demonstrated by her contribution to Myers' series of immense papers on what he called 'The Subliminal Consciousness'.

The fifth of these papers was read by Myers to the Society at the Westminster Town Hall on 28th October 1892 and published in the *Proceedings*.[5] Many pages were written by Miss Freer, who by now was using her pseudonym of 'Miss X'. Myers, in introducing her contribution, said that her phenomena were continuing steadily and increasing in value with each year of their continuance. They were also enlarging in scope, for as Myers revealed (p. 492), Miss Freer had now added the ability to receive psychical messages through seashells to her other talents. She herself explained this new gift and how she acquired it:

I have naturally exceedingly acute and sensitive hearing, which was developed by four years of scientific musical education, and it was with some hope that I possessed myself of a smooth-lipped cowrie of a size convenient to hold in the palm of the hand, applied it to my ear, and waited.[6]

[1] *Proceedings*, S.P.R., 1889–90, vol. VI, pp. 359–60. She commenced her paper with a general claim to supernormal ability, saying that throughout the whole of her life she had 'possessed some power of telepathic percipience, or susceptibility to the action of other minds, and at the same time some power of influencing them in a similar way'.

[2] *Ibid.*, p. 361. [3] *Ibid.*, p. 361. [4] *Ibid.*, pp. 367–8.

[5] F. W. H. Myers, 'The Subliminal Consciousness, V', *Proceedings*, S.P.R., 1892, vol. VIII, pp. 436–535. This section alone occupied a hundred pages of *Proceedings*. In the same volume two earlier sections had already been printed, covering over seventy pages. [6] *Ibid.*, p. 493.

Results were rapidly forthcoming, and some of these were included in Myers' paper. He said on p. 492 that he hoped that Miss X's example as a successful shell-hearer would be followed by others interested in the subject. Only one of Miss Freer's anecdotes is worth repeating here, because of its connexion with George Albert Smith, Myers' private secretary. This young man, who in my opinion was indirectly responsible for Gurney's suicide, was later to be revealed as a ruthless trickster by his confederate Douglas Blackburn. At this time, however, Smith was contentedly receiving a salary from the S.P.R. leaders in exchange for deceiving them, before taking up once more his career as a showman in Brighton.[1] It is of some interest, therefore, to discover that Miss Freer and Smith were on friendly terms.[2]

According to Miss Freer's section of Myers' paper, Smith had visited her to engage in some successful thought-reading experiments. He left Miss Freer about seven p.m. After dinner Miss Freer took up her shell, which began to repeat some of Smith's engaging conversation earlier in the evening, in his voice, describing a walk over the rocks by the sea at Ramsgate in Kent. This was interrupted by the shell, still in Smith's voice, asking the curious and quite irrelevant question, 'Are you a vegetarian, then?' Miss Freer at once sat down and wrote a letter to Smith about this incident, to which Smith replied with equal promptitude. After leaving Miss Freer, he wrote, he had met an acquaintance whom he called 'Mr M',[3] who alluded in conversation to a vegetarian restaurant he knew, which caused Smith to ask the question Miss Freer heard in the shell. Smith said that the words quoted by Miss Freer were exactly those he had used, and there was no doubt 'that the shell spoke the truth'.[4] The only help I can offer to the reader in assessing the worth of this remarkable story is to remind him that Dr E. J. Dingwall has recently described the late George Albert Smith as 'an individual in whom well-informed persons today place only the slightest confidence'.[5] This opinion of Smith was held as early as

[1] The careers of Smith and Blackburn are described in my *The Strange Case of Edmund Gurney*.

[2] Professor J. O. Baylen has discovered among the papers of W. T. Stead a letter from F. W. H. Myers to Stead at this period, dated 5th December 1892, which refers to Miss Freer and Smith. Myers wrote, 'I thought that some of the cases which Miss Freer allowed me to see in MS. looked very good; and we will gladly help in working them up, if it prove possible. G. A. Smith, I think, has been instructed by Miss Freer on that point.'

[3] The identity of 'Mr M' was not revealed.

[4] *Proceedings*, S.P.R., 1892, vol. VIII, pp. 494–95.

[5] *Mediums of the 19th Century*, New York, 1963, vol. I, p. xv. This book is a reprint, with an introduction by Dr Dingwall, of Frank Podmore's *Modern*

1899, even before Douglas Blackburn's revelations were published. Mr R. P. Ellis, writing in *The Ethical World* on the early S.P.R. experiments in thought transference, observed:

The Creery children are exposed; and for some time now, it is well to remember, a Mr G. A. Smith is the link between Mrs Sidgwick, the usual controller of the experiments, and the indifferent class of individuals to whom he 'telepathically' transmits numbers and the like.

The percipients, the 'indifferent class of individuals', were a group of working-class youths in Brighton, friends of Smith, who were paid by the S.P.R. for the experiments, which depended entirely upon the integrity of Smith and the boys. Mr Ellis said of Smith:

Unknown as that gentleman is to the world, one may reasonably ask, on general grounds:

'Who is Smith? Ah! who is he,
That all the world should trust him?'

By 1892, as we shall see, Miss Freer had much to interest her besides the preparation of long papers for the S.P.R., however enthusiastic their reception may have been. To anticipate a little, however, it may be said that her last contribution to the *Proceedings* in any way comparable with her earlier efforts was printed in 1895, with the now customary introduction by Henry Sidgwick.[1] The paper was somewhat shorter than the previous ones, and was published over the pseudonym of 'Miss X', which Miss Freer had now been habitually using for two or three years.

One story in this paper is of some interest, as it possibly illustrates the methods used by Miss Freer in building up these psychical reminiscences. She was reading *Love's Labour Lost* [*sic*] in bed before rising, she wrote, when suddenly 'the picture I had conjured up disappeared, and gave place to the village street of my northern home'. Miss Freer added that the scene was out of date in that the rough stone cottages of her childhood days, in one of which an old family servant had lived, had now been displaced by a block of handsome stone buildings. She experienced an inexplicable sense of loss and distress, and tears sprang to her eyes. She knew that some

[1] 'On the Apparent Sources of Subliminal Messages', *Proceedings*, S.P.R., 1895, vol. XI, pp. 114–44.

Spiritualism, London, 1902. Dr Dingwall knew Smith, who lived to a great age. Attempts to put forward the contrary view against the weight of evidence available, notably by Mr Fraser Nicol, seem to have arisen from a lack of acquaintance with the literature.

tragedy had occurred. A moment later there was sad but complete confirmation of this 'subliminal message'. Miss Freer's maid entered the bedroom with the morning tea, together with a letter from a friend. The letter told Miss Freer that her 'dear old servant', the inhabitant of one of the cottages, a servant whom Miss Freer 'had known all my life, had died suddenly, and that my friends had just returned from the funeral service'.[1] It is almost superfluous to say that the reader was offered no clue of any kind as to the identity of the northern village, the dear old servant, or the sympathetic correspondent.

If this story had any ingredient of truth in it, then the scene with which Miss Freer had been familiar, the home of the servant she had known all her life, must have been in the town of Uppingham in the Midlands, where the first years of her life were spent, and not in a northern village at all. If, at any rate, we make this assumption, the result is not lacking in interest. The Freer family had lived in High Street in Uppingham until 1890, when Benjamin Freer, after living for a time at the White Hart, moved into nearby Orange Lane, which is now Orange Street. High Street is dominated by Uppingham School, which was much extended in the nineteenth century and may very appropriately be described as a 'block of handsome stone buildings'. If the reader is of the opinion that the superstructure of this engaging story was built up in this way, then the typical touches by Miss Freer regarding her reading of Shakespeare in bed before rising and the ministrations of her maid will not have escaped him.

[1] *Op. cit.*, pp. 138–9.

4

MISS FREER, *BORDERLAND*, AND THE BURTON CASE

AS I have had occasion to say earlier, Miss Freer seems on the face of it to have enjoyed some degree of financial independence during the first years of her association with Myers. By the early 1890s, however, she had become interested in obtaining money from any source available to her. Certainly by September 1894, on the evidence of Sir William Huggins, she felt it necessary to borrow from Lord Bute, who was already paying through the S.P.R. for her Scottish tour.[1] She became employed in a minor and part-time administrative capacity from 1893 by the Swanley Horticultural College. In 1895 she moved as a permanent guest into the home of her friend Miss Constance Moore, daughter of the Rev. Daniel Moore, at Holy Trinity vicarage, Paddington, London, thereby presumably reducing her living expenses.[2] Most importantly she became, apparently from 1892 at latest, the paid assistant of W. T. Stead, who in the following year was to begin the publication of the spiritualist quarterly *Borderland*, of which Miss Freer became assistant editor.

William Thomas Stead (1849–1912), the radical journalist and author, editor of the *Pall Mall Gazette* and the *Review of Reviews*, had been introduced to the attractions of spiritualism in 1880 and

[1] On 2nd February 1895 she complained to Lord Bute of the difficulty in which she had been placed by the S.P.R.'s delay in paying some of her expenses, amounting to £45, from money provided by Bute, adding that she had no idea how the S.P.R. spent 'its large income and its frequent legacies and donations'. Whether this criticism had any foundation in fact, or whether it was merely a hint that a further loan from Bute would be agreeable, I do not know.

[2] Daniel Moore (1809–99) was the Vicar of Holy Trinity, Paddington, and Rural Dean of Paddington until 1895. He was Chaplain-Ordinary to Queen Victoria and Prebendary of St Paul's. He was the son of George Moore, a Coventry ribbon manufacturer, and his wife, Hannah Shaw, the daughter of another industrialist. When Miss Freer came to live in his house he was eighty-five. When the Moores removed to 27 Cleveland Gardens, Hyde Park, Miss Freer moved with them, remaining there until she and Miss Constance Moore set up house together at The Laurels, Bushey Heath, Hertfordshire.

had become an ardent believer.[1] He met Miss Freer in the autumn of 1891, and like most men who came into contact with her at this period, Stead was immediately captivated. He wrote of her to a friend:

I have just lunched with a young lady who has seen five of her relations and friends who have appeared to her at the moment of death. She has already seen an indefinite number of others, and sees in the crystal—in short, has a personal practical experience of almost every kind of phenomenal apparition, and is not in the least spoiled by it. She is, I think, about 25, and is devoted to good works; lives in Society, has had a first-class education, and is perfectly self-possessed.[2]

According to Miss Freer, it was through Myers that her first meeting with Stead was arranged. She wrote:

It must have been in the summer of 1891 that I first came into touch with my revered and valued friend W. T. Stead. I had recently contributed to the pages of the Proceedings of the Society for Psychical Research *a paper upon 'Some Experiments in Crystal Gazing'* [sic]. *This, in deference to prejudice on the part of my family had been strictly anonymous, and indeed the greater part of it was written not at home, but when upon a visit to Mrs Frederic Myers, the mother of Mr F. W. H. Myers, though it was the result of prolonged study at the British Museum and elsewhere.*

I received a letter from Mr Myers asking permission to reveal my identity to the well-known journalist, who had not been altogether in sympathy with the work of the Society, but who desired nevertheless to make my acquaintance. Mr Myers added that Mr Stead was engaged upon the work afterwards published as Real Ghost Stories, *and was therefore in communication with a great number of people who might be of use to psychical research, and to whom Mr Myers suggested I might be the means of 'bringing into line'.*

I wrote to Mr Stead that I hoped to call upon him when we returned

[1] Estelle Stead, *My Father, Personal and Spiritual Reminiscences*, London 1913, pp. 95–103. According to Miss Stead, it was Mr Mark Fooks who first introduced Stead to psychic matters. Stead attended his first séance in 1881, when he was told by the medium that he would become 'the St Paul of Spiritualism'. Although Miss Stead describes the founding and publication of *Borderland* in some detail, Miss Freer's name is mentioned nowhere in her book.

[2] *The Life of W. T. Stead*, vol. II, p. 38. Whyte said of Stead (*ibid.*, vol. I, p. 247) that he was always an easy prey for adventuresses. Of his acquaintance with Mrs Gordon-Baillie, 'the fair seductress', in the late 1880s, Stead's biographer wrote that had it been safe for this lady to stay in London, 'the consequences to Stead's private purse might have been serious indeed; he was always an easy prey even to less accomplished swindlers'.

to London in the Autumn, and on 10th October I paid a visit to Mowbray House, Norfolk Street, which is memorable to me in many ways. It was an adventure for a girl[1] *brought up by an elderly relative with early Victorian standards, to find herself in the presence of a non-conformist journalist, in a London office; an adventure undertaken secretly so far as my home was concerned, though with the knowledge of the friends whom I was visiting, and who had sent with me a trusted family servant . . .*

He wished me to collaborate in the book he was writing, and to lunch with him at Gatti's, in the Strand one day a week to discuss progress. I was obliged to decline, but offered to contribute anonymously, to the book, in which, as a matter of fact, there was eventually a good deal of my work . . .

Within a few months changes occurred which freed me from the more extreme of the conventional austerities he so much deprecated, although, when in the following spring I agreed to become joint editor of an Occult Journal, it was still necessary that I should be known only as 'Miss X', and that arrangements should be made which should obviate the necessity for my frequenting Mowbray House, and taking my place as a member of the staff. Rooms were taken in Pall Mall East, and a married lady engaged as my secretary. I was to visit the office occasionally only, and to see no one except by appointment. Nothing could have been kinder or more generous than the spirit in which Mr Stead met this necessity of circumstance, a kindness all the more generous in that he was wholly out of sympathy with the social restrictions in question. In a certain sense they annoyed him; he was specially annoyed that I declined to have my portrait published in Borderland. *There was, however, from the journalistic point of view a certain value in the mystery in which the personality of 'Miss X' was enshrouded . . .*

It was the last number of the year [during the third year of Borderland] *and my Chief signified his appreciation by sending me for a Christmas present a deed of gift of all property in* Borderland, *to take effect in the year 1900, 'by which time', he was kind enough to add, my commercial education would be as complete as my literary experience. I showed the document to the late Marquis of Bute, whose interest in psychical research is well known, and he congratulated me heartily, proposing himself as a partner, and saying, 'It shall be the biggest thing of the kind in Europe.'*[2] Borderland, *however, did not live to*

[1] Miss Freer was thirty-four years old in October 1891.

[2] Professor J. O. Baylen says that Stead's papers do not mention this alleged deed of gift. Miss Freer's 109 letters to Lord Bute, covering the period from their first meeting in May 1894 to July 1899, shortly before Bute's first apoplectic seizure in August of that year, are completely silent on the subject. Stead left nothing to Miss Freer in his will.

1900 and the Marquis passed away during that year. During this same absence [Stead was abroad] Mr Stead asked me to take charge of certain of his private benefactions and to see to their administration. It was a further revelation of his wonderful charity and large-heartedness. They were a curious collection of people, these recipients of his bounty, and after careful study of the paper connected with their stories and antecedents, and some observation of the people themselves, I could not but feel that in some cases he was being badly imposed upon. He was deeply hurt when I suggested to him, on his return, that the liberal sums expended should be administered by the Charity Organisation Society.[1]

This tribute to Miss Freer's 'revered and valued friend W. T. Stead' was written after the death of both Stead and Lord Bute, both of whom had been Miss Freer's generous patrons and between whom there had been little sympathy. The unpublished correspondence between Miss Freer and Lord Bute, and between Lord Bute and the Rev. Peter Dewar, shows that Stead's kindness had aroused no loyalty in Miss Freer. As early as June 1894, when she saw the better opportunity offered by the patronage of Lord Bute, with whom she had established herself in the previous month, she found it convenient to deny emphatically that she was 'an adherent of Steadism'. On 2nd February 1895 she told Bute that 'The stuff that passes for Astrology in *Borderland* is beneath criticism', and on 2nd October of the same year she confided to her new patron that the embarrassment of her paid appointment with *Borderland* had become a matter of conscience with her as well as of taste. On 15th December 1895 she wrote, possibly hopefully and certainly rather oddly in view of her subsequent letters, that her agreement with Stead was not legally binding and that after 'a harried and hurried week' with Stead she had settled her affairs with him at 'considerable money loss' to herself.

In the event the prickings of conscience were evidently not effective, for she continued with her salaried work for Stead, while her criticisms of him to Lord Bute became more positive. On 6th January 1896, the year in which she afterwards said in print that Stead had been especially generous to her, she wrote to Bute that the next issue of *Borderland* would contain, to her regret, 'some dissenting profanities of Mr Stead's', but that for the sake of the public she was doing her best with the magazine. Later in the same month, on 25th January, she told Bute that Stead was publishing statements in *Borderland* that he knew to be false. On 30th March

[1] Quoted from a contribution by Miss Freer to E. K. Harper, *Stead: The Man*, London, 1918, pp. 63–8.

1896 she wrote to Bute (possibly hopefully), 'My *Borderland* affairs, *i.e.* my relations with the magazine, are very disagreeable to me, but I cannot afford to break them as I should lose £200 a year'. One wonders, in parenthesis, what Lord Bute thought of this statement in the light of Miss Freer's letter to him of 9th July 1894, two months after their first meeting, when she had already been employed by Stead for three years. She wrote, 'I regard my time as wholly at the disposal of the Society for Psychical Research [with which Stead had no connexion] so long as I am existing, in great part, at the Society's expense owing to your Lordship's liberality.' And if the story of Stead's extreme generosity to her in 1896 (the third year of *Borderland*) had any truth in it, a letter from her published in the *Oban Times* on 17th October of that year,[1] extolling the value of the S.P.R. Second Sight Enquiry and the liberality of Lord Bute, was singularly unkind to Stead. She wrote, 'My interest in the phenomena has absolutely nothing to do with journalism as represented by Mr W. T. Stead, or any other editor to whose periodicals I may at any time contribute.' This was untrue as well as ungenerous. She was the assistant editor of *Borderland* under her pseudonym of 'Miss X', and not merely a contributor to it. At this particular time, moreover, Stead was abroad and she was running the paper herself on his behalf. It may be added that after *Borderland* had ceased publication in 1897, and the embarrassment of her salary of £200 a year from Stead had been discontinued, Miss Freer's criticisms of him to Lord Bute did not abate. In a letter to Lord Bute of 9th May 1898, for example, she advised that friends of his with alleged mediumistic gifts should not be allowed to fall into the hands of Stead, who would merely exploit them.

With the knowledge of Miss Freer's private opinion of Stead at his disposal, the reader is in a position to follow the development of her association with the proprietor of *Borderland* from the date of their first meeting, as described by her, in the summer of 1891. By October and November 1891 Stead and Miss Freer were meeting continually in London, and Frederic Whyte, Stead's biographer, evidently had access to some of Stead's hurried notes to her at this time, although very oddly these letters and all other such papers connected with Miss Freer have since disappeared. There can be no doubt about Stead's admiration for her qualities and his belief in her alleged spiritualistic abilities. He wrote to her on 12th November 1891, 'I telepathed madly to you this morning to come at 12 o'clock.' On 16th December of the same year he wrote, 'I recognize with great satisfaction the methodical neatness with which you do your

[1] Quoted in full by Dr Campbell, see pp. 88–89.

work, and I heartily wish that you could infuse a little bit of that eminent virtue into my veins.'[1]

The first number of *Borderland* appeared in July 1893. In his introductory article Stead described Miss Freer as 'my assistant editor, Miss X'. Myers was delighted, and Stead printed a letter from him in the same issue, saying that Myers observed with pleasure that the lady known in S.P.R. *Proceedings* as 'Miss X' had consented to aid Stead in his task.[2]

Dr Campbell once wrote to me that *Borderland* may be not unfairly described as a chronicle of the incredible, written by and for the credulous. Certainly the following statement by Stead about Miss Freer, published in the first issue, is of great interest to the student of the psychology of testimony:

However incredible it may appear, I can, and do constantly, receive messages from my assistant editor, Miss X, as accurately and as constantly as I receive telegrams from those with whom I do business, without the employment of any wires or any instrument. Whenever I wish to know where she is, whether she can keep an appointment, or how she is progressing with her work, I simply ask the question and my hand automatically writes out the answer.

There is no consciousness on her part that I have asked the question, and received her answer. Distance does not affect the messages, they are received equally when she is asleep or awake . . . How it is done I do not pretend to know. That it is done is certain. It is no longer an experiment, it is a practical, every-day addition to the conveniences of human intercourse.[3]

As might have been expected, this statement aroused much published scepticism. The magazine *Black and White*, in its issue of 22nd July 1893, suggested sarcastically that despite these miracles, in certain stagnant and unprogressive offices the sixpenny telegram might still be useful. The *Glasgow Herald* on 17th July 1893 said that it was very difficult to accept the story of the alleged powers of the remarkable assistant editor 'Miss X', adding, 'Mr Stead may, as we have said, be perfectly honest in this matter, but if he is, then so much the worse for Mr Stead'.

These and other criticisms did not prevent Stead persisting in his claim that there was complete and continuous *rapport* between Miss Freer and himself. He wrote in the same volume of *Borderland*:

[1] *The Life of W. T. Stead*, vol. II, p. 38.

[2] *Borderland*, 1893–4, vol. I, p. 15.

[3] *Ibid.*, p. 6.

CERTIFIED COPY OF AN ENTRY OF BIRTH

The statutory fee for this certificate is 3s. 9d. Where a search is necessary to find the entry, a search fee is payable in addition.

GIVEN AT THE GENERAL REGISTER OFFICE, SOMERSET HOUSE, LONDON.

Application Number PAS 25496/67

Form A502 (S.13408) Dd.163861 30M 6/66 Hw.-RE-30

REGISTRATION DISTRICT Uppingham

1857. BIRTH in the Sub-district of Uppingham in the Counties of Rutland Leicester & Northampton

Columns:—	1	2	3	4	5	6	7	8	9	10*
No.	When and where born	Name, if any	Sex	Name, and surname of father	Name, surname, and maiden surname of mother	Occupation of father	Signature, description, and residence of informant	When registered	Signature of registrar	Name entered after registration
107	Fifteenth May 1857 Uppingham	Ada Goodrich	Girl	George Freer	Mary Freer formerly Adcock	Veterinary Surgeon	George Freer Father Uppingham	Twenty Fifth June 1857	John Bell Registrar	—

CERTIFIED to be a true copy of an entry in the certified copy of a Register of Births in the District above mentioned.

*See note overleaf.

Given at the GENERAL REGISTER OFFICE, SOMERSET HOUSE, LONDON, under the Seal of the said Office, the 6th day of April 1967.

BC 594944

This certificate is issued in pursuance of the Births and Deaths Registration Act 1953.
Section 34 provides that any certified copy of an entry purporting to be sealed or stamped with the seal of the General Register Office shall be received as evidence of the birth or death to which it relates without any further or other proof of the entry, and no certified copy purporting to be given in the said Office shall be of any force or effect unless it is sealed or stamped as aforesaid.
CAUTION.—Any person who (1) falsifies any of the particulars on this certificate, or (2) uses a falsified certificate as true, knowing it to be false, is liable to prosecution.

8. Miss Freer's birth certificate.

Form 15 H

1 PLACE OF DEATH

BOROUGH OF Manhattan

Name of Institution 64 Hawkes Hospital

STATE OF NEW YORK

Department of Health of The City of New York

BUREAU OF RECORDS

STANDARD CERTIFICATE OF DEATH

Register No. 5914

2 FULL NAME Adela Monica Freer

3 SEX	4 COLOR OR RACE	5 SINGLE, MARRIED, WIDOWED or DIVORCED (Write the word)
Female	white	Married

6 DATE OF BIRTH ...., 1........ (Month) (Day) (Year)

7 AGE 56 yrs. ...... mos. ...... ds. If LESS than 1 day, ... hrs. or ...... min.

8 OCCUPATION

(a) Trade, profession or particular kind of work Housewife

(b) General nature of industry, business or establishment in which employed (or employer)

(c) No. of years so occupied

9 BIRTHPLACE (State or country) England

(9A) How long in U. S. (if of foreign birth) 26 yrs (9B) How long resident in City of New York 3½ yrs.

PARENTS OF DECEASED

10 NAME OF FATHER George Goodrich Freer

11 BIRTHPLACE OF FATHER (State or country) England

12 MAIDEN NAME OF MOTHER Mary Adcock

13 BIRTHPLACE OF MOTHER (State or country) England

14 Special INFORMATION required in deaths in hospitals and institutions and in deaths of non-residents and recent residents.

Former or usual residence 2540-30th St. Astoria, L.I.

Where was disease contracted, if not at place of death?

MARGIN RESERVED FOR BINDING

NO MUTILATED CERTIFICATE WILL BE RECEIVED

15 DATE OF DEATH February 24, 1931 (Month) (Day) (Year)

16 I hereby certify that the foregoing particulars (Nos. 1 to 15 inclusive) are correct as near as the same can be ascertained, and I further certify that deceased was admitted to this institution on December 2[illegible], 1930, that I last saw her alive on the 24 day of February 1931, that she died on the 24 day of February 1931, about 2 o'clock A. M. ~~or P. M.~~, and that I am unable to state definitely the cause of death; the diagnosis during her last illness was:

Hypertensive Heart Disease

duration 20+ yrs. ...... mos. ...... ds.

Contributory (Secondary) Myocarditis with failure

duration 10+ yrs. ...... mos. ...... ds.

Witness my hand this 24th day of February 1931

Signature [illegible] Keating M.D.

House [illegible] Surg.

17 I hereby certify that I have this ...... day of .... 19...., performed an autopsy upon the body of said deceased, and that the cause of h.... death was as follows:

Signature .... M.D.

Pathologist .... Hospital

FILED	18 PLACE OF BURIAL Cedar Lawn Cemetery, Patterson, New Jersey	DATE OF BURIAL Feb. 26 1931
	19 UNDERTAKER R. F. Lockridge	ADDRESS 118 62 9 [illegible]

9. Miss Freer's death certificate.

When Miss X, my assistant editor on Borderland, *returned from her recent interesting expedition in search of the gifted seers of the Highlands, she wrote telepathically with my hand, a long report covering three closely written quarto pages, describing the result of her visits, her plans and intentions in the future, reporting upon the condition of the office and its work, and discussing questions of practical business. All this was written out with my hand at Wimbledon, while Miss X was in town. I had not seen her for nearly six weeks, during which time I had not once written to her. When I met her I read over to her her telepathic message. When I had finished, she said, 'You have made one mistake. You say, "So-and-so is very painstaking, but very stupid." That is not my opinion. So-and-so is very painstaking, but only occasionally stupid.' And that was the only error in three closely-written quarto pages!*[1]

Whyte quotes a story by Stead about his psychic lady friend, clearly Miss Freer, who had promised to lunch with him in London. Wishing to know definitely whether she would keep the appointment, he placed his pen on a piece of paper and mentally asked her the question. She replied telepathically, and Stead's hand wrote out a disturbing message. A man alone in a railway carriage with her had made improper advances to her:

I was alarmed and repelled him. He refused to go away and tried to kiss me. I was furious. We had a struggle. I seized his umbrella and struck him, but it broke and I was beginning to fear he would master me, when the train began to slow up before arriving at Guildford station. He got frightened, let go of me, and before the train reached the platform he jumped out and ran away. I was very much upset.[2]

Miss Freer's appointment as assistant editor of *Borderland* in 1893 was a milestone in her career. This was her opportunity to spread her wings, and she immediately became a substantial contributor of long articles, reviews, and editorials under her pseudonym of 'Miss X'. She was an able and a prolific writer and succeeded, for a time at least, in the difficult task of obtaining the best of both worlds in occult matters. She assumed, on the one hand, the respectability of a mild impartiality and agnosticism, while at the same time showing a kindly tolerance for the fantastic claims of the spiritualists and making the most of her own allegedly supernormal experiences. The reader may think, moreover, from the following advertisement, which appeared in the first volume of *Borderland* over the address of Miss Freer's very private office in Pall Mall, that although Stead

[1] *Op. cit.*, p. 50 [2] *The Life of W. T. Stead*, vol. I, p. 326.

undoubtedly paid her generously, she was not disinclined to make a little extra money privately if she could:

A Lady, with considerable psychical experience, not a Spiritualist, will be happy to advise, by correspondence, in the conduct of experiments in Thought-Transference, Crystal-Gazing, Automatic Writing, and other forms of Automatism. Terms on application. Letters addressed to 'Psychic', Borderland *Office, 18 Pall Mall East, will be forwarded.*[1]

In my view, further light is thrown on the financial relationship between Stead and Miss Freer at this period by an incident mentioned by Myers in one of his papers on 'The Subliminal Consciousness'. I do not think that there can be any doubt that the lady friend of Stead's upon whom Myers said he would 'bestow the name of Miss Summers' in 1893 was Miss Freer. She was, as we know, strictly preserving her anonymity at that time. Myers said that 'Miss Summers' was 'the most important of Stead's telepathic correspondents', and that Stead 'almost every day received communication' by automatic writing from his friend. 'Miss Summers,' wrote Myers, moreover, 'was engaged on literary work of a kind needing much care and accuracy.' The identification with Miss Freer can scarcely be doubted. This being so, it is of interest to discover from Myers that when in September 1893 'Miss Summers' was temporarily short of money, Stead generously assisted.[2]

The pages of *Borderland* reveal much of the strange personality of Miss Freer, and of the social and intellectual world in which she lived between 1893 and 1897, the years of the magazine's existence. In *Borderland*, too, can be found much more detailed reports of her visits to the Highlands and the Islands of Scotland in connexion with the Second Sight Enquiry by the S.P.R. than appeared in the *Journal* of that organization. These journeys, in which she was usually accompanied by her ever-faithful friend Miss Constance Moore, have been discussed in detail by Dr Campbell. Their importance from my point of view is that they establish the fact that by 1894 Miss Freer had contrived to secure for herself another wealthy patron, Lord Bute, who paid for these expeditions. It will be convenient, however, to include a general comment upon the relationship between Miss Freer and this wealthy and distinguished if eccentric Vice-President of the S.P.R. in a later discussion of the controversial Clandon affair.

A case of which *Borderland* and the S.P.R. made much was that of the 'Burton Messages', in which Miss Freer was the medium in a

[1] *Borderland*, 1893–4, vol. I, p. 383.

[2] *Proceedings*, S.P.R., 1893–4, vol. IX, pp. 52–4.

series of séances in July and August 1895, and produced by means of alleged automatic writing a number of messages supposed to emanate from the spirit of Lady Burton's husband, Sir Richard Francis Burton, the famous explorer and scholar who had died on 20th October 1890. After the first of these experiences Miss Freer wrote to Lord Bute to say that it 'has left me quite prostrate, and I am only just beginning to feel capable of travel'. On 26th August she wrote:

Lady Burton is deeply impressed by the characteristic language and the curious details, and has already altered her will on the strength of certain statements of which I hardly understand the import. As one issue is that she has left me Sir Richard's valuable Arabian and Egyptian occult instruments (crystal, magic mirror, etc.) I can't complain.

After Lady Burton's death on 22nd March 1896 Miss Freer published two accounts of the affair in *Borderland* in April 1896[1] and January 1897.[2] In view of the theme and contents of these stories it is odd that concurrently with the publication of the first she wrote to Lord Bute on 2nd April 1896, saying:

The S.P.R. folk are greatly excited over the Burton business and want me to speak upon it on April 24th, which postpones my departure for Scotland till the 27th or 28th. Mr Myers is more convinced of the identity of Sir R. Burton than am I. I don't feel that Lady B. was as good a witness as I could wish.

Miss Freer also read a paper on the Burton case, 'Some Recent Experiences, Apparently Supernormal', to the 83rd General Meeting of the Society for Psychical Research at the Westminster Town Hall on 4th December 1896, with the President, William Crookes, in the chair. The address was received with enthusiasm, and at the end of Miss Freer's paper Crookes said 'that he had never heard a paper more scientifically thought out or more clearly expressed'.[3]

[1] 'Some Thoughts on Automatism. With the Story of the Burton Messages. By Miss X', *Borderland*, 1896, vol. III, pp. 157–72.

[2] 'More About the Burton Messages. By Miss X', *ibid.*, 1897, vol. IV, pp. 37–42. W. T. Stead commented with warm approval upon Miss Freer's paper, and it would seem that there was really no limit to his belief in her stories. He wrote, 'Miss X contributes some light upon the famous communications from Sir Richard Burton—communications which, it is curious to know, have excited the liveliest interest in the Vatican, and have led to friendly messages from His Holiness the Pope to Miss X' (*Review of Reviews*, January 1897, p. 56). As the Vatican was on the point of issuing its first condemnation of attempts to communicate with the dead, such a tale seems completely incredible.

[3] *Ibid.*, p. 42, and *Journal*, S.P.R., January 1897, p. 7.

The address was reported at some length in the Society's *Journal*,[1] but the warm approval of the S.P.R. and its President was not supported by the legitimate Press. Sharp criticisms were published, particularly in *St James's Gazette*, the *Westminster Gazette*, and the *World*, this last describing the meeting as a 'peculiarly nauseating recrudescence of offensive spiritualistic balderdash', and Miss Freer's account of the séances as 'vulgar imposture'.

We cannot now determine the precise truth of the matter, for the most important witness, Lady Burton, had died a month before Miss Freer published her first account, and could neither contradict nor confirm its contents. Miss Freer asserted (the reader may think typically) that her story could be corroborated by her friend, 'the Hon. Mrs G., now abroad', but nothing more seems to have been heard about this lady. According to Miss Freer, the first messages from Sir Richard Burton were received on her ouija board on 25th July 1895 when she was 'staying at their country house with Mr & Mrs D'.[2] Who Mr and Mrs D. were, and where their country house was located, Miss Freer did not reveal. Lady Burton was not, of course, present and knew nothing of these sittings. According to Miss Freer's account, the communicating spirit instructed the sitters to inform Lady Burton that messages from her late husband were being received. Miss Freer said that after discussion between her friends and herself it was decided to send a copy of the notes of the sittings to Lady Burton as a matter of duty.

The result could have been foreseen. Miss Freer was invited to Lady Burton's home at Mortlake on 5th August 1895. Sittings were given by Miss Freer with the aid of her ouija board, and Sir Richard obligingly communicated directly with his widow. The rather uninspiring messages did not differ in style from those usually associated with spiritualistic séances. As a variation, Miss Freer changed to crystal-gazing, and described the visions she saw to Lady Burton.

These events were interrupted by Miss Freer's second Scottish tour in the late summer of 1895, and she and Lady Burton never met again. As has been said, within a few weeks of Lady Burton's death in March 1896 Miss Freer published the whole story in *Borderland*, to be followed by her address to the S.P.R. There was, however, another and very different version of the affair, which was to be published a year later.

William Henry Wilkins (1860–1905), of Clare College, Cambridge, as the *Dictionary of National Biography* records, 'came to know intimately the widow of Sir Richard Burton and after her death

[1] 'General Meeting', *Journal*, S.P.R., January 1897, pp. 3–7.

[2] *Borderland*, 1896, vol. III, p. 163.

wrote *The Romance of Isabel, Lady Burton* (1897), a sympathetic memoir founded mainly upon Lady Burton's letters and autobiography.'[1] It is indicative of the friendship and good faith existing between Lady Burton and Wilkins that it was on her directions given during her lifetime that he edited in 1898 a revised edition of Lady Burton's own biography of her husband, *The Life of Sir Richard Burton*, and her *The Passion Play at Ober-Ammergau* (1900), as well as Sir Richard Burton's unpublished *The Jew, the Gypsy, and El Islam* (1898) and *Wanderings in Three Continents* (1901).

Wilkins's book on Lady Burton was dedicated to her sister, Mrs Gerald Fitzgerald, who was involved in his account of the affair of the messages. He first quoted from a letter written by Lady Burton to her friend Mrs Francis Joly on 17th April 1890, in which the former lady's attitude to spiritualism was made extremely clear. Lady Burton regarded the subject as 'a decoy to a crowd of sensation-seekers, who yearn to see a ghost as they would go to see a pantomime', and said that spiritualism, 'when not absolutely farcical, worked for evil, and not for good'. She advised Mrs Joly never to practise or interest herself in such matters, but to debar them from her house. She said, 'There is a spiritualism (I hate the word!) that comes from God, but it does not come in this guise. This sort is from the spirits of evil.' It says much for Miss Freer's ingratiating personality that while holding those views, Lady Burton was nevertheless caught in the toils for a brief period.

Wilkins wrote:

I have dwelt on this side of Lady Burton's character in order to contradict many foolish rumours. During the last years of her life in England, when her health was failing, she was induced against her better judgment to have some dealings with certain so-called 'spiritualists', who approached her under the plea of 'communicating' with her husband, thus appealing to her at the least point of resistance. Lady Burton told her sister that she wanted to see 'if there was anything in it', and to compare it with the occultism of the East. In the course of her inquiries she unfortunately signed certain papers which contained ridiculous 'revelations'. On thinking the matter over subsequently, the absurdity of the thing struck her. She came to the conclusion that there was nothing in it at all, and that, as compared with the occultism of the East, this was mere kindergarten. *She then wished to recall the papers. She was very ill at the time, and unable to write herself; but she mentioned the matter to her sister at Eastbourne, a short time before her death, and said, 'The first thing I do when I get back to London will be*

[1] *Dictionary of National Biography, Second Supplement*, 1912, vol. III, p. 667.

to recall those silly papers.' She was most anxious to return to London for this purpose; but the day after her return she died. Mrs Fitzgerald at once communicated Lady Burton's dying wishes to the person in whose charge the papers were, and requested that they should not be published. But with a disregard alike for the wishes of the dead and the feelings of the living, the person rushed some of these absurd 'communications' into print within a few weeks of Lady Burton's death, and despite all remonstrance was later proceeding to publish others, when stopped by a threat of legal proceedings from the executors.[1]

If this version of the story by Wilkins was the true one, and the messages allegedly from Sir Richard Burton were fraudulently produced by Miss Freer to deceive his widow, it can fairly be said that the imposture was a peculiarly cruel and heartless one. If there was a motive, it was presumably a financial one. Wilkins wrote, six pages before his account of the business of the séances, of Lady Burton's extreme and foolish generosity with money. Such was her enthusiasm for giving to beggars in the street, her biographer wrote, that she frequently returned home with an empty purse. Lady Burton's attitude in the face of criticism of this indiscriminate almsgiving was that she would rather give to ten rogues than turn one honest man away.[2]

The indications are, I fancy, that what Wilkins said was probably accurate. His account was corroborated by Lady Burton's sister. He was right in regard to Lady Burton's failing health, for in her first paper in *Borderland*, before any criticisms were made, Miss Freer revealed that Lady Burton 'had been for some years in a critical state of health',[3] and therefore, the reader may think, especially vulnerable to an approach by Miss Freer on the subject of her husband, her 'least point of resistance', as Wilkins called it. If we seek an explanation for the willingness of Lady Burton, an avowed opponent of spiritualism, to listen to Miss Freer in 1895, we may think that Miss Freer herself supplied the answer when she said that Lady Burton 'had suffered so severely from a sense of giddiness and brain confusion, that she had been to see a specialist'.[4] There is no doubt at all, moreover, that Wilkins was right in saying that Miss Freer rushed the Burton story into print with indecent

[1] W. H. Wilkins, *The Romance of Isabel, Lady Burton*, London, 1897, vol. II, pp. 767–8.

[2] *Ibid.*, p. 761. Another possible motive is suggested by the advice of the spirit of Sir Richard Burton to his widow, through Miss Freer's mediumship, that Lady Burton should employ forthwith a 'capable literary secretary' who was not to be a 'mere typewriting clerk'. *Borderland*, 1896, vol. III, p. 166.

[3] *Borderland*, 1896, vol. III, p. 168.

[4] *Ibid.*, p. 167.

haste within a week or two of Lady Burton's death in March 1896, for the first paper was published in *Borderland* in April. It seems pretty obvious, too, that something very drastic occurred to prevent Miss Freer giving further promised publicity to the case, and the threat of legal proceedings described by Wilkins seems a likely explanation. There is no doubt that Miss Freer, encouraged by the enthusiastic reception of her address to the S.P.R.,[1] *did* intend to publish a paper on the Burton case in the *Proceedings*. She wrote in her second essay in *Borderland* in January 1897, when she was answering the Press criticisms of her address in the previous month, that it was her intention to offer proof of her statements. She wrote, 'That proof will, indeed, be forthcoming in the article that I am about to contribute to the *Proceedings of the Society for Psychical Research*.'[2] It never was, for she was henceforward completely silent on the subject of the Burton messages. Despite Crookes's praise of Miss Freer, the S.P.R. published nothing more. The name of Burton was never mentioned again in *Borderland*, and Miss Freer refrained from any comment on the case in her book, *Essays in Psychical Research*, published in 1899.

The Burton case was probably Miss Freer's first mistake, and it may well be that she realized it. It was not to be the last, however, as the reader will learn. Despite the advantages of her friendship with Lord Bute, her increasing arrogance, coupled with her reckless self-confidence and lack of scruple, was to lead her into a series of difficulties, culminating in the final disaster that overtook her in 1901.

[1] F. W. H. Myers was personally enthusiastic. In an unpublished letter to Lord Bute on 3rd April 1896 he said that the case was 'a very good one' and that he wanted Miss Freer to visit the Burton mausoleum.

[2] *Borderland*, 1897, vol. IV, p. 39.

5

MISS FREER, LORD BUTE, AND THE CLANDON AFFAIR

JOHN PATRICK CRICHTON-STUART (1847–1900), third Marquess of Bute, was the immensely wealthy owner of estates in Scotland and Wales, and the munificent benefactor of both Glasgow and St Andrews Universities, being Rector of the latter ancient and beautiful seat of learning in 1892 and in 1898. His friend F. W. H. Myers described him as 'a great chieftain, a great magnate, a great proprietor, yet withal a figure, a character, which carried one back into the Ages of Faith'.[1] Myers added:

The youth whose vast wealth and eager religion suggested (it was said) to Lord Beaconsfield the idea of his Lothair *had become constantly wealthier and more religious as years went on. Amid the palaces of his structure and of his inheritance, he lived a life simple and almost solitary; a life of long walks and long conversations on the mysteries of the world unseen.*[2]

I have copies of some ninety-five letters written by Myers to Bute from 1890, shortly after Bute had joined the S.P.R., to the end of the Ballechin affair, when coolness developed between the two, exemplified in Bute's last letter to Myers in which he said that *The Alleged Haunting of B—— House* was 'self-defence against imputations publicly made by yourself and others' and that the book 'constitutes an implicit argument against your conclusions'. Myers' letters were, however, ingratiating in tone and contents, and Myers' flattery was often so exuberant that one wonders whether it was not an embarrassment to Lord Bute. Bute was, in Myers' view, an outstanding man of business, yet his nature was unusually kind and generous and his life entirely beneficient and universally valued. He was an outstanding example of thoroughness in all he did, wrote Myers, being gifted with noble perseverance. Bute's letters constituted a wealth of learning. He was a great archaeologist and historian, and he was the one man in the world, Myers considered, who could pronounce upon the relationship between the Catholic faith and psychical research. He was, according to Myers, the only conceivably possible

[1] *Journal*, S.P.R., November 1900, p. 310. [2] *Ibid.*, p. 311.

Rector of St Andrews University. The 'majestic pile' at Mount Stuart, which Bute built and which Myers said he intensely admired, told of a combination of noble qualities in Bute that went far beyond mere wealth and lineage. A photograph of Bute's profile, wrote Myers, was *magnificent* (Myers' underlining), and suggested to Myers a majestic idea of one of the Early Fathers of the Universal Church. And yet, with all these superhuman qualities, Bute could be an exquisite humorist when he chose. His anecdotes, wrote Myers, were intensely funny.

Myers' acquiescence in all Bute said was constant throughout the correspondence. The whole of the opinions of the noble lord were of the utmost value and interest, and had Myers' immediate and unqualified agreement. 'I bow to what you say re Hinton-Ampner [a haunted house],' wrote Myers in February 1893. Bute had *forgotten* more than one unfortunate dissentient *knew*, in Myers' underlined opinion. Myers joined with Bute in wondering how Andrew Lang, who also became Rector of St Andrews and a President of the S.P.R., could write such 'superficial stuff'. If Bute thought there might be something in spirit photography, then so did Myers. On the other hand, although Myers had incautiously told Bute that he had been trying to persuade Miss Florence Marryat, a prolific writer of mediocre fiction and an enthusiastic spiritualist and amateur medium, to give some sittings for the S.P.R., he later obligingly confessed that he did not regard any statement by her 'as worth a moment's consideration'. This obsequiousness was at times faintly ridiculous. To quote one example, Bute took Myers mildly to task for using what he called 'feeble envelopes' for his correspondence; obviously one had burst open in the post. Myers wrote, 'Thank you! I take to heart your warning re feeble envelopes and will remember it to my dying day.'

The object of all this was made pretty clear by the correspondence. Myers was anxious to bring Bute into closer relationship with the S.P.R. and to persuade him to make substantial financial contributions to its work, especially that in which Miss Freer was involved. Bute was made a Vice-President of the Society shortly after becoming a member, and Myers wrote to ask if he would care to join the Council, and become a member of the Literary Committee. Bute wisely refused these two additional distinctions, on the grounds that he was too busy. But the first 'extremely munificent gift' was forthcoming by December 1892, which was later devoted to the Second Sight Enquiry in Scotland. In 1894 'further generosity' was acknowledged, with the encouraging comment by Myers that his mother had left no less than £3,000 to the S.P.R. Myers added that two wealthy members, Lady Caithness and the Duc de Pomar, had made wills 'leaving for a cognate purpose their large possessions'. 'But *that* is very risky,' wrote Myers, 'as the Duc de Pomar is only about forty, and may marry and upset it all any day. Meantime, we rub along with some difficulty and are grateful for whatever adds respectability to our bankers' account.' The implication was clear; the money would be welcome now.[1] Indeed, on 30th July 1896 Myers told Bute that Miss Freer was going to the Highlands again and that the fund was very low, 'so it will be kind if you will either replenish it, or tell us that it is not to be replenished'. By 5th August he was able to thank Bute for his 'very generous reinforcement of the Second Sight Fund'. On 17th December of the same year Myers was thanking Bute again for being willing to meet the cost of the proposed Ballechin House enquiry.

Myers was enthusiastic and persuasive in his letters to Bute on the subject of Miss Freer,[2] which Dr Campbell has quoted in an earlier chapter. She would prosecute the Second Sight Enquiry, said Myers, in exactly the right spirit, 'a spirit at once scientific and sympathetic'. She had certainly, wrote Myers on 16th August 1894, 'thrown herself heart and soul into the task. I think that sooner or later we shall get a conspectus of the Hebridean mind such as we have never had before.' On 8th October of the same year Myers wrote that he was sure that Bute had 'the right woman and in the right place'. Her experience in the haunted house at Clandon was *capital*, wrote Myers with emphatic underlining, and he was sure that Bute himself must be pleased with Miss Freer's vision of the apparition. He assured Bute that he and Miss Freer would do their

[1] The Countess of Caithness was Janet, widow of the sixteenth Earl, whom she had married in 1855. The Duc de Pomar was her second husband, and considerably younger than herself. Both appear in the list of S.P.R. members for the first time in August 1894. The point of Myers' remark seems to be that any money the Countess might bequeath to the S.P.R. was subject to some kind of interest on the part of the Duc de Pomar, who might well survive her and marry again.

[2] This praise of Miss Freer by Myers, of which there was a good deal, did not continue after the quarrel in the Spring of 1897 between Myers and Miss Freer over Miss Chaston, the medium who was with Myers at Ballechin, the few later references to Miss Freer in the correspondence being in very different terms. In his belief (which was entirely erroneous) that his old critic Sir James Crichton-Browne had written the famous unsigned letter to *The Times* in June 1897 that sparked off the Ballechin controversy, Myers wrote to Bute, for example, that Miss Freer had virtually betrayed the S.P.R. to Sir James 'so far as in her lay', just as in May he had intimated to Bute that Miss Chaston was very indignant over Miss Freer's attempt to eject her from Ballechin. These strictures and this change of front were not favourably received by Bute.

'very best' with this important case, of which the reader will hear more.

Miss Freer and Lord Bute first met on 30th May 1894 at her suggestion. Myers had recommended her to Bute as the ideal person to undertake the S.P.R. second sight investigation, and Bute had already agreed. Miss Freer evidently decided, however, that it would be in her interests to make the personal acquaintance of Lord Bute, no doubt confident that he would be quickly charmed by her captivating personality. She accordingly wrote to Lord Bute at his London home on 28th May, using Myers' name as a means of introduction, asking for an interview. The two met, and there is no doubt that Bute was greatly impressed. On 4th June, a few days later, the Rev. Peter Dewar wrote in a letter to Lord Bute:

I am very pleased that your Lordship has had an interview with Miss Goodrich-Freer on the subject of her projected tour of the Western Isles, and that you have formed a high opinion of her gifts and graces. I feel considerably relieved to hear that her association with Borderland *does not imply that she is an adherent of Steadism.*

There is no doubt that Miss Freer very soon exerted very considerable influence over Lord Bute. Their large correspondence, her part of which has been fortunately preserved, shows that she was able quickly to arouse his keen interest in *outré* subjects such as astrological horoscopes, crystal-gazing, clairvoyance (including its alleged value in archaeological research, in which Bute was much involved), and in hypnotism. I have been unable to trace any mention in the literature of Miss Freer's possessing hypnotic skill, although an ability in this direction would undoubtedly help to explain her considerable power to influence others virtually at first meeting. Be that as it may, she wrote to Bute on 6th September 1894:

Last week, however, I visited a haunted house where my human sympathies were evoked to the exclusion of the ghostly—and I hypnotized three of the sufferers, whose lives were literally getting blighted by the terror in which they lived—and suggested that they should be deaf and blind to their visitant. Their instant relief was pathetic to witness!

In earlier pages a number of examples have been given of the extraordinary stories about herself with which Miss Freer regaled Lord Bute, with which the correspondence abounds. She wrote on 19th November 1895 to say that Lord Bute's apparition had appeared to her at Holy Trinity Vicarage, Paddington, the home of her friend Constance Moore, where Miss Freer had become a permanent guest. According to a letter from Lord Bute's daughter, the late Lady Margaret MacRae, Miss Freer told Bute that her phantasm would appear to him in the library at Falkland Palace in Fife at 11 a.m. on a specified day. As Lady Margaret put it, however, 'it never came off'. Miss Freer had a paranormal vision of the original Priory in St Andrews,[1] she told Bute in her letter of 9th October 1895, and was able to hear sounds of worship that 'had no objective origin'. On the evening of the same day, in the same location near the ruined Cathedral in St Andrews, she heard voices and the closing of two invisible doors. She added:

Then came the sound of many feet, and a procession passed me walking in single file; I counted 27 tonsured and robed figures. The doors seemed to remain open for them to pass out at the west end of the crypt—then, I think, across a wide passage beyond, and by another door into a lighted building. I could not see in, and I dared not leave my place, lest all should vanish.

This letter of Miss Freer's is of great interest because of the amusing account given by Lady Margaret MacRae to Dr Campbell of the incident. Lord Bute invited Miss Freer to describe in more detail the habit of the monks of pre-Reformation St Andrews. Her answer was incorrect, but she quickly excused her mistake by asserting that the monks seen by her must have been visitors from another community.

In this connexion it is fair to point out that Lady Margaret and the rest of the family, always excepting Lord Bute himself, were somewhat critical of Miss Freer and her claims. In her letters to her mother and brother Lady Margaret usually referred to Miss Freer with amusement as 'dear Ada' or simply 'the Freer'. Writing to Lady Bute on 26th July 1896, after Miss Freer had been entertained on Lord Bute's yacht R.Y.S. *Kittiwake*, she said:

How did dear Ada enjoy her yachting and the Scilly Isles? I hope she won't send her something or other consciousness, or soul, or whatever she sends about, to see us anywhere![2]

It is clear from the correspondence between Lady Margaret and her brother Lord Colum Crichton-Stuart that they found difficulty in

[1] Miss Freer much enjoyed her visits to St Andrews. Like Andrew Lang, I share her affection for the little grey capital of the ancient kingdom of Fife, which has had associations for me over a long number of years. She wrote to Bute, 'What an interesting place this is! The sky and the sea seem to be among the finest of its many fine shows. I never saw a more magnificent sunset, nor a finer sweep of angry surf.'

[2] Three days later, from Tresco in the Scilly Isles, Lady Margaret wrote, 'I have asked here if Miss Freer came some time ago, and they didn't seem to know about her; perhaps she only sent her ghost or soul or whatever it is!'

believing that Miss Freer had any paranormal powers at all. In a letter passed to Dr Campbell and myself for quotation, a letter which throws light on more than one of Miss Freer's activities and upon Lord Bute's financial support for them, Lady Margaret wrote:

I should think the Freer used Father Allan and got to know him deliberately for that purpose. I am afraid I did not like her and should believe the worst. I don't think she had any second sight or vision herself. I do not know about Swanley. I do not remember when she went to Jerusalem, but saw her there well settled in the early 1900s. Of course, as my Father died in 1900 his help would have ceased by then.

There were other opinions. The Hon. Mrs Stirling of Keir, who was a friend of Lord Bute's daughter, wrote to Dr Campbell to describe her visits to Mount Stuart, the seat of the Bute family. While qualifying her recollections as memories sixty years old, she said that although Lord Bute 'was wax in Miss Freer's hands',[1] and had a touching belief in the findings of the S.P.R.,[2] the rest of the family looked upon Miss Freer as a charlatan. Miss Freer, said Mrs

[1] Despite her influence over Lord Bute, Miss Freer was evidently unable to destroy his interest in the medium Florence Cook, whose materialization 'Katie King' was endorsed as genuine by the chemist and physicist William Crookes in circumstances which most sensible persons, both then and now, consider were dictated by Miss Cook's physical attractions and not as a result of scientific enquiry. Miss Freer wrote to Bute on this subject on 10th December 1894, 'I have asked Florence Cook's sister-in-law (comparatively quite a decent person) to tell me about Katie King's end, but have not heard yet. I think it is as well that Mr Crookes's interest in her *has* ceased. I don't think that his evidence is of great value in that connection. I think Mr Myers still clings to Mrs Mellon! [Mrs J. B. Mellon, formerly Miss A. Fairlamb, had been exposed by Mr Thomas Shekleton Henry while wearing a mask and muslin drapery, impersonating her materialization 'Cissie' two months previously.] It is all so hideously material. Fancy the prospect of returning from "the Rest that remaineth" to have to upset tables and wind up musical boxes in a milieu which we poor mortals wouldn't condescend to enter. Living or dead, fancy voluntarily associating with Mrs Williams or Florence Cook!' Despite these strictures, the correspondence between Mr James Coates and Lord Bute shows that as late as 1899, before the first of his seizures, Bute was interested in Florence Cook (by then Mrs Corner) coming to Scotland for private sittings. The story of Florence Cook and William Crookes is told in my *The Spiritualists*, London, 1962, and Dr E. J. Dingwall's *The Critics' Dilemma*, Crowhurst, 1966. Mrs A. Williams-Ellis included an excellent short account in her *Darwin's Moon. A Biography of Alfred Russel Wallace*, London, 1966, as does Mr Simeon Edmunds in *Spiritualism: A Critical Survey*, London, 1966.

[2] This was only true of the period to 1897, the year of the Ballechin upheaval, the mysterious affair of Miss Chaston, and the quarrel between Miss Freer and F. W. H. Myers. Bute's opinion of the behaviour of the S.P.R., and of Myers in particular, was made very plain in his letter to Myers of 4th April 1899.

Stirling, 'was regarded as a joke, and not a very good one'. Sir William Huggins, F.R.S., the astronomer, writing to Lord Bute on 9th September 1894, referred sarcastically to a hair which had been sent to Miss Freer in order to test her clairvoyant powers. The test was a failure. Huggins said, 'I am sorry the hair did not act as a more potent charm. I hope the golden colour of the hair will not suggest to Miss Freer to ask for a further loan, but rather to pay up the Falkland one.'[1]

The two principal cases in which Miss Freer and the S.P.R. became embroiled to the extent of attracting fierce criticism were those concerning the supposed haunting of Clandon Park, near Guildford, in Surrey, and Ballechin House, near Dunkeld, in Perthshire, in both of which Bute became involved as Miss Freer's patron. The incidents and the controversies which resulted were of the same sort: the investigation by the S.P.R. of allegedly haunted houses by subterfuge contrary to the wishes or consent of the owners. It is not surprising that the owners of Clandon and Ballechin bitterly resented both the deceit practised upon them and the resultant publicity, which they regarded as highly detrimental to the future value of their property. In the case of Ballechin in particular, the owners intensely and understandably disliked any exposure of family scandals, which the ghost-hunters suggested might be the cause of the hauntings.

It is hardly to be wondered at that such methods earned for the S.P.R., Miss Freer, and Lord Bute a growing unpopularity, which ultimately exploded as a violent public controversy in the columns of *The Times* in June 1897. The printed criticisms were so formidable and unrestrained, as will be seen, that the S.P.R. leaders asserted that the Society had no official connexion with these unfortunate and embarrassing affairs. They were not successful, which is not surprising in view of the evidence which demonstrates that the Society had been deeply involved in both cases from the beginning.

Clandon Park was the property of Lord Onslow.[2] Rumours of its haunting had appeared in the spiritualist magazine *Light* in 1895,[3]

[1] Lord Bute was the owner and hereditary keeper of Falkland Palace in Fife. Miss Freer visited Falkland at the end of her Highland tour in 1894 at Lord Bute's invitation, and wrote him a long account of the visions she said she had seen there.

[2] William Hillier Onslow (1853–1911) was the fourth Earl of Onslow, G.C.M.G., P.C., etc. Formerly Under-Secretary of State for the Colonies (1887), Parliamentary Secretary to the Board of Trade (1888), and Governor of New Zealand (1889–92), he was at the time of the Clandon affair Under-Secretary of State for India.

[3] 'Lord Onslow's Haunted House', *Light*, 1895, p. 565.

and in January 1896 Miss Freer wrote an article in *Borderland* about it.[1] The house was let by Lord Onslow at the time, and gossip had been reported from the domestic staff of the tenants, Captain and Mrs Blaine, of the appearance of a female phantom clad in cream-coloured satin. Miss Freer wrote, 'The present writer has had the advantage of being allowed to make some inquiries on the spot on behalf of the Society for Psychical Research, but the amount of evidence so far obtained has not yet justified a formal report to the Society.'[2]

Miss Freer's enquiry was limited to a single visit to Clandon, the unpublished correspondence shows, on 11th December 1895, when she was entertained by Captain and Mrs Blaine overnight. She was accompanied by Mr G. P. Bidder of the S.P.R.[3] In her paper read to the S.P.R. in January 1897 she said, rather typically it may be thought, that her task had been made easier for her by the fact that she had 'been staying in some country houses in the neighbourhood of Clandon, and Mr Bidder was a resident in the same county'. She told Lord Bute in her private correspondence with him that she had obtained an invitation from Mrs Blaine, although in her paper to the S.P.R. she stated that the tenants had not been very ready to give assistance or information in the matter of the haunting, an observation rather contradicted by her letter to Bute of 15th December 1895. She said in this communication that the Blaines had been very kind in giving her every facility for quiet enquiry, adding, however, that 'Mr Bidder's collecting three housemaids to stand in a row and "give evidence" alarmed them back into their shells, and I had to outstay him to restore the balance'.

Miss Freer said that she and the Blaines 'had a bond of sympathy in the stables, and we make ghosts a parenthesis in our talk of horses'. In a later letter in the same month she added that Captain Blaine 'was the best of the lot,—had seen the world and was a gentleman and consequently easier to deal with. One knew his language.' It is of interest to record that Miss Freer told Lord Bute

[1] 'The "Ghosts" at Clandon Park', *Borderland*, January 1896, vol. III, pp. 76–7.

[2] *Ibid.*, pp. 76–7. It is interesting that in this early report, published shortly after her first and only visit in December 1895, Miss Freer put 'Ghosts' in sceptical quotation marks, in the same way as she was later to refer to Myers' friend Iris Jessica Chaston as a 'medium'. Its title can usefully be compared with that of her dramatic account published a year later, 'The Spectre at Clandon House [*sic*] as Seen by Miss X', *Borderland*, 1897, vol. IV, pp. 167–9.

[3] Clandon must have been one of the last cases with which Mr Bidder was concerned. He died on 1st February 1896 as a result of an accident in Manchester on 9th January, when he was run over by a horse and van.

that the main evidence came from the servants, with the exception of her own claim to have seen the apparition herself during this single visit, which she said was corroborative of the servants' stories, and could not have been due to expectation.

Miss Freer never visited Clandon again. In her letter to Bute of 19th February 1896 she said that she had ventured to remind Mrs Blaine of her promise of a second invitation, which had not been forthcoming, and that it would be a pity if the enquiry could not be resumed. On 4th March 1896 in a letter to Lady Bute, written during Lord Bute's illness, Miss Freer said that the Blaines had now left Clandon (Lord and Lady Onslow were taking up residence in the house themselves), but that it was still hoped that Myers might be able to obtain further information from them. Miss Freer was not able to make her way into Clandon a second time because of Lord Onslow's firm dislike of this kind of investigation, as will be seen. It may be thought, therefore, that Miss Freer made a good deal more of the case in her later writings and lectures in 1897 than was justified by the opinion expressed in her first account published in *Borderland* in 1896, when she said that the evidence did not justify a report to the S.P.R. at all.

The same *Borderland* article said that Miss Freer's visit to Clandon had been made on behalf of the S.P.R., while in the later accounts after trouble had developed with Lord Onslow, and notably in the S.P.R. *Journal* of February 1897,[1] it was stated that the investigation had been made at the suggestion of Lord Bute. The matter is confused and it is probably not now possible to ascertain the exact truth. It is not in dispute that Miss Freer was mentioning Clandon in her letters to Lord Bute in December 1895, but as their correspondence was regular and considerable, it would have been most unusual if this had not been the case. On the other hand, it seems that Miss Freer did prepare a report of some sort which she sent to F. W. H. Myers during the same month of December 1895, which demonstrates beyond doubt that the S.P.R. was involved in the matter from the beginning. Myers wrote to Bute on New Year's Day 1896:

Miss X's Clandon experience which she has sent to me is capital!—and the whole thing is quite in your *line—the best, it seems, of the large*

[1] *Journal*, S.P.R., February 1897, pp. 21–5. This was a report of the 84th General Meeting of the Society at the Westminster Town Hall on Friday, 29th January, with the President, W. Crookes, in the chair. Miss Freer read her paper on Clandon, 'A Passing Note on a Haunted House', to an appreciative audience.

haunted houses with 'fine confused feeling' in the way of possible iniquities of bygone members of historical families. May the 'pretty lady' live long and prosper!

It is reasonable to ask why, if the enquiry was initiated by Bute, as was later suggested after trouble had developed with the formidable Lord Onslow, Miss Freer sent her report to Myers, who did not think it necessary to tell Bute about it for a period of some weeks. This unpublished letter of Myers' also throws some light on the criticisms made over Ballechin that the S.P.R. was not averse from publicizing family scandals in connexion with alleged hauntings, whether feelings were hurt or not. After this first letter to Bute on the subject of Clandon, Myers continued to send him items of news about the case. On 4th March 1896 he emphasized again the importance of Clandon and Miss Freer's vision of the apparition, and on 21st April 1896, in connexion with the attempt to obtain further information from the Blaines, Myers informed Bute that 'meantime the Blaines draw in their horns for fear of the Earl! We must wait awhile and see what happens. I will write if there is any new development.' These letters suggest that it was Myers who was conducting the affair.

After Lord and Lady Onslow had taken up residence at Clandon early in 1896, an unsuccessful attempt was made to obtain permission for Miss Freer to visit the house again. Enclosed with Myers' letter to Bute of 9th April 1896 was a letter dated 7th April to 'My dear Mr Myers' and signed 'Winifred Burghclere'. In this letter Lady Burghclere stated that she could be of no use in regard to the Clandon ghost. It was, she said, 'a sorry subject' with the Onslows, who firmly believed that the ghost was invented during the tenancy of the Blaines. Rather oddly, Myers asked Bute to destroy this letter, but Bute did not do so and it has now been discovered among his papers.

This letter from Lady Burghclere to Myers is perplexing, for it seems to contradict an account by Miss Freer in both the S.P.R. *Journal* of February 1897 and in her second paper on the subject in *Borderland* in April of the same year, in which she said that the approach to Lord Onslow through Lady Burghclere was made by Lord Bute. In support of this statement Miss Freer published a letter from Lord Bute to herself, explaining what had happened, dated 9th August 1896. In this letter Lord Bute said that what he had done was upon the advice of F. W. H. Myers. What had been wanted, he wrote, was the permission of Lord Onslow for Miss Freer, a sensitive, as Lord Bute called her, to visit Clandon and for the S.P.R. to publish a report on the case. Bute said that he wrote to Lady Burghclere, with whom he was acquainted and whose husband was Lord Onslow's brother-in-law, asking if she would approach Lord Onslow on behalf of the S.P.R., to ask if these two requests could be granted. Lord Bute said that he did not keep a copy of his letter to Lady Burghclere. Lord Onslow's answer had been 'disappointing and surprising'. He refused both requests, saying that he had no belief in the haunting, and was anxious to avoid publicity becoming attached to his property. It seems rather odd that Lady Burghclere, having already written on behalf of Myers with complete lack of success, should nevertheless apparently have agreed to make a later approach at the suggestion of Lord Bute.

Lord Onslow's refusal to allow Miss Freer to visit Clandon a second time did not prevent her publishing reports on the case both in *Borderland* and in the S.P.R. *Journal* in 1897. She said that she had visited Clandon during the occupation by the Blaines, who had entertained her without the knowledge of Lord Onslow. She had tea with her hosts in the dusk of an autumn day.[1] When, later, she went upstairs to dress for dinner, Miss Freer claimed to have seen the apparition of a female figure, cloaked and hooded, with a dress showing as gleaming yellowish white satin where the cloak parted. The figure, said Miss Freer, corresponded with the descriptions of other unnamed percipients.[2] The phantom vanished as she approached it. Miss Freer's story attracted much publicity.

There is some evidence to suggest that this story of Miss Freer's was a fabrication. Her single visit to Clandon, as we have seen, had been made on 11th December 1895 in company with Mr G. P. Bidder. There was, however, another guest who is mentioned nowhere in Miss Freer's colourful published accounts. This was the Duke of Richmond and Lennox,[3] who was just the kind of distinguished person with whose name, the reader may think, Miss Freer would have made great play in her story if there had not been some compelling reason for her not to do so.

[1] The date of her only visit was 11th December 1895 as has been stated.

[2] The private correspondence discloses that in April 1896 Myers had received a letter from Lord Onslow's secretary to say that Lord Onslow was 'credibly informed that the ghost was due to the maids frightening a footman' during the Blaines' tenancy. This was not revealed in the S.P.R. or *Borderland* reports. In his letter to Bute containing a casual reference to this, Myers said that the story of the footman and the maids did not account for Miss Freer's vision, a suggestion with which the reader may agree.

[3] Sir Charles Henry Gordon-Lennox, K.G., P.C., D.C.L., LL.D. Sixth Duke of Richmond, Duke of Lennox, Earl of March, and Baron Settrington.

The Duke of Richmond wrote to Lord Bute from his house at Guildford on 12th December 1895:

What a pleasant clever woman Miss Freer is! The Blaines asked her to dine and sleep at Clandon last night, and they asked me to come over to dinner to meet her. I found Bidder was staying there too, who is a County Council friend of mine. Owing to Lord Onslow's dislike to a ghost being supposed to appear at his house, the Blaines are very careful to avoid talking about it in public, and they did not wish the fact of Miss Freer's visit being known. So whilst I was there not a word was said about it, and after Miss Freer had sat in the dark in the state bedroom for some time and came back to the drawing room, one tried to glean from her appearance, if she had had any luck.

This morning she has driven over here, and told us that at present she has seen nothing, and that what to her mind is the unsatisfactory thing about it is that no one but servants *has seen the appearance. She is meanwhile making investigation and enquiries amongst the servants who have left, but who were the first people to report what they saw eighteen months ago. She intends to return here next month and stay longer, as she has to go back to town unfortunately this afternoon. She begs me to say that she will write to you tomorrow.*

The Duke of Richmond wrote to Lord Bute again on 26th December 1895:

I have read Miss K's papers which arrived this morning with the greatest interest. Thank you so much for sending them; I am now forwarding them to Miss Freer as requested by you. I do hope she will have an opportunity of going there again before the Blaines give up the house on February 1, when Onslow returns, who said the other day, the first thing he should do, would be to 'clear the ghost out of the house'.

These letters make it plain that on the morning after the only evening she spent at Clandon Miss Freer told the Duke of Richmond that she had seen nothing, which confirms her first published account in *Borderland* in January 1896, when, as we have seen, she initially said that the evidence did not justify a report. The letters of the Duke of Richmond do not confirm at all, it may be thought, Miss Freer's subsequent story about seeing the apparition herself during her single visit to Clandon. They suggest that this alleged experience may have been worked into her later letters to Bute and Myers and into the subsequent reports published both in *Borderland* and in the S.P.R. *Journal* in 1897, to give some support to a case of alleged haunting that would otherwise have depended on mere gossip from the servants' hall.

The publication of the reports in the S.P.R. *Journal* and *Borderland* in February and April 1897 must have justifiably infuriated Lord Onslow. In *Borderland* Miss Freer had been sufficiently impertinent to suggest that he was an obscurantist, obstructing the progress of science.

There is a tide in the affairs of houses and of men, which neglected at the time leads on to the rocks. Lord Onslow lost an opportunity of which he would have done well to avail himself . . . As things stand, the chatter-boxes (and the commercial value of a good many things is in the hands of the chatterbox)—the people who have time to go out to lunch—will soon allow the statement to pass into history, that 'Clandon has been investigated by the S.P.R., but Lord Onslow was afraid to publish the result'.[1]

Lord Onslow took the opportunity two months later to tell his own side of the story. Miss Freer's subsequent enquiry into the alleged haunting of Ballechin House, in which Lord Bute was again involved, had caused a considerable controversy in the correspondence columns of *The Times* in the early summer of 1897, of which the reader will hear more. Mrs Caroline Steuart, the wife of the owner of Ballechin House, had written a letter which *The Times* published on 18th June 1897. Mrs Steuart complained that she 'had not the remotest idea that our home was let to other than ordinary tenants', and that it was not within her knowledge that Colonel Taylor and Miss Freer of the S.P.R. had taken Ballechin House for the purpose of ghost-hunting and the publication of a report. Mrs Steuart added:

In my intercourse with them I spoke as one lady to another, never imagining that my private conversations were going to be used for purposes carefully concealed from me—a deceit I resent deeply.

Lord Onslow at once wrote in support of Mrs Steuart, his letter being published in *The Times* of 19th June, the following day. He said that he did not wonder that Mrs Steuart was resentful over the deceit practised upon her. He wrote that in the case of Clandon Park he had let his house to tenants who were persuaded by the S.P.R. to allow similar 'researches to be conducted by certain highly impressionable ladies'. Lord Onslow added:

Their hallucinations were published far and wide in the local, London and foreign newspapers, but were fortunately so ludicrous as to excite nothing but ridicule; yet, did I ever again desire to let the place, many an intending tenant might decline to take a house with such a reputation.

[1] *Borderland*, 1897, vol. IV, p. 167.

I need hardly add that no other person ever heard, saw or dreamt of a ghost at Clandon. I wish there were some means of making this society responsible in hard cash for the effects of the light-headed nonsense by which they depreciate other people's property.

F. W. H. Myers' letter in reply to Lord Onslow, published in *The Times* on 22nd June 1897, claimed that the S.P.R. had 'abstained from publishing the evidence collected on the subject by two of its members', and that in consequence Lord Onslow's letter seemed 'scarcely fair'. This was feebly evasive, and was not likely to arouse confidence in the writer's *bona fides*, for Myers refrained from mentioning that Miss Freer had addressed the 84th General Meeting of the Society at Westminster Town Hall on 29th January 1897, five months previously, on her experiences at Clandon, and that her paper had been printed in the *Journal* of February 1897.

6

MISS FREER AND THE BALLECHIN INVESTIGATION

NO NOTE upon Ada Goodrich Freer and her activities in psychical research would be complete without some account of the S.P.R. investigation of Ballechin House, 'the most haunted house in Scotland',[1] during which Fr Allan McDonald himself was one of the visitors. This notorious case was the subject of a substantial book by Miss Freer, with the nominal co-authorship of Lord Bute.[2] It has twice been discussed with approval by the late Harry Price,[3] and once with brevity and some scepticism by Dr E. J. Dingwall and myself.[4] A good deal of further information of the greatest interest has since been discovered, however, from two principal sources. First, the previously unpublished letters to Lord Bute from Miss Freer, F. W. H. Myers, Sir James Crichton-Browne, Sir William Huggins, John Milne, Sir John Ritchie Findlay,[5] and some others on the subject of Ballechin have been made available to Dr Campbell and the present writer. Secondly, two copies of Miss Freer's book, extensively annotated by her, have been located and examined.

On 31st January 1931 Miss Freer (then Mrs H. H. Spoer) wrote to Mr John Lewis, the Editor of the *International Psychic Gazette* in London, from St Lukes Hospital, New York, where she had lain ill since Christmas, and where she was to die less than a month later on

[1] This phrase was quoted, with some irony, by Mr J. Callendar Ross in *The Times* of 8th June 1897. There can be no doubt that the late Harry Price used Ballechin as a blueprint for his highly successful book, *The Most Haunted House in England*. Following the procedure adopted at Ballechin, he took a tenancy of Borley Rectory and invited observers to stay there to watch and listen for the alleged phenomena, with printed suggestions as to what they might see and hear. The result was that Borley's previous purely local reputation was enlarged until it became 'the most haunted house in England'.

[2] A. Goodrich Freer and John, Marquess of Bute, *The Alleged Haunting of B—— House*, London, 1899. A second, revised edition was published in 1900.

[3] *Poltergeist over England*, London, 1945, pp. 220–8, and *The End of Borley Rectory*, London, 1946, pp. 294–302.

[4] *Four Modern Ghosts*, London, 1958, pp. 15–20.

[5] The son and heir of the owner of *The Scotsman* newspaper. He succeeded his father in 1898, and received a baronetcy in 1925.

24th February 1931. The letter said that she wished to give her personal copy of *The Alleged Haunting of B—— House* to a library that was on a permanent basis, for she regarded it as a valuable document. It was the second edition of 1900, and had been presented by Miss Freer to her prospective husband, Dr H. H. Spoer, on 6th January 1905, the year of their marriage. Miss Freer's letter to Mr Lewis is pasted on to the half-title of the book, with a note by W. A. Marsden of the British Museum that in accordance with her wishes it was deposited in the Department of Printed Books by Mr John Lewis on 24th December 1931.

At the end of the book a cutting is pasted in from the *International Psychic Gazette* of January 1932. The article is headed 'The Haunting of a Highland House. Psychical Researchers on the Trail of a Ghost', and was by the Editor, John Lewis. In it he described how the book came into his hands. Miss Freer had originally concealed under initials the names of most of the persons involved in the Ballechin drama. In this annotated copy, however, as Mr Lewis put it, she had unveiled for the first time many secrets closely guarded for thirty years, by inserting the names of all the actors, and photographs of most of the scenes.

In the National Library of Scotland is a copy of the first edition of *The Alleged Haunting of B—— House*, also annotated by Miss Freer. It came from the library of Lord Rosebery, to whom it had been presented by Lord Bute. Bute had evidently asked Miss Freer to add to the text the names of the persons concerned with Ballechin for the information of Lord Rosebery, for Bute wrote to him on 12th July 1899 to say that he had invited Miss Freer to prepare the book in this way and send it. The photographs of Ballechin House and its grounds, and of some of the investigators, which Miss Freer inserted into the second edition now in the British Museum, are not present in the Rosebery copy, which, however, gains slightly by having been annotated when the events were more freshly in mind.

In the present work I shall give an account of the Ballechin case for the benefit of those who are not familiar with its previous literature, and at the same time record the identities of the persons whose testimony is to be discussed against the background of the new information which is now available. The unpublished correspondence will, I hope, enable me to throw a good deal of new light upon the whole affair and the bitter controversy that the case aroused, and on the personal quarrel between F. W. H. Myers and Miss Freer at this time.

Ballechin House, situated on the River Tay not far from Dunkeld in Perthshire, was the property of an old Highland family named

Steuart. Like many houses of its kind (and especially Borley Rectory) it enjoyed a slight and merely local reputation of being haunted until scandal-mongers and psychical researchers began to interest themselves in it. Although, according to the biographer of Fr R. H. J. Steuart, S.J., a distinguished member of the family, the ghosts of Ballechin were variously described as those of a big black dog, an old white-haired priest, and a woman in white, the later story of the 'wicked major' with which Miss Freer regaled the investigators was more detailed and exciting.

Major Robert Steuart (1806–76) retired from the service of the East India Company in 1850, sixteen years after he had inherited Ballechin House on the death of his father. He never married. He was regarded as an eccentric because of his excessive fondness for dogs, of which he kept a large number at Ballechin, and his belief in spirit return. It was said that he frequently declared that he would haunt Ballechin after his death, probably in the form of a black spaniel of which he was particularly fond. It was alleged that this was the reason why all fourteen dogs belonging to Major Steuart were killed after his death. Scandal linked Major Steuart's name with that of his young housekeeper, Miss Sarah Nicholson, who died at Ballechin on 14th July 1873 at the age of twenty-seven. According to Miss Freer, Major Steuart, on his death three years later, was buried beside Miss Nicholson.[1] On the other hand, when this story received some publicity, Dr J. A. Menzies, who referred to Major Steuart as 'an old and dear friend', wrote to *The Times* to say that there was not the slightest foundation for the story of the affair with the young housekeeper.[2] 'I can readily believe,' wrote Dr Menzies, 'that people who found his straightforward and uncompromising attitude in public affairs disagreeable should dislike him. Eccentric to some extent he was, but it is a calumny to talk of him as the "wicked major".'

Mr J. Callendar Ross, one of the visitors to Ballechin during the S.P.R. investigation and a leader-writer of *The Times*, wrote in the issue of that newspaper of 8th June 1897:

No haunted house is complete without a legend of a crime, or a tragedy, or a badly-spent life, to explain why the ghost walks. In the drawing-room after dinner we listened to our hostess, who is an excellent narrator, expounding the story of the wicked major. It seems that a former proprietor, who died some twenty years ago, had a standing quarrel with

[1] *The Alleged Haunting of B—— House*, second edition, 1900, pp. 21–8. Unless otherwise stated, all references will be to this later enlarged edition.

[2] *The Times*, 21st June 1897.

Mrs Grundy. He kept his house full of dogs; he did not care for the society of his neighbours; he was rather feared than loved; and local gossip, with reason or without, charged him with unnecessary familiarity with his housekeeper.

Sir James Crichton-Browne, F.R.S., who went to Ballechin with Mr Callendar Ross, wrote:

The legend as to the origin of the haunting of B. was told to us by Miss Freer. It appeared that some twenty years ago the proprietor of B. was a retired major of eccentric habits, who kept the house full of dogs, would have nothing to do with his neighbours, was accused of wicked conduct, and was generally feared.[1]

Miss Freer said on p. 31 of her book that 'there seems to have been no idea of the place being haunted before the deaths of Sarah N—— and of Major S——, whereas since that time the peculiar phenomena have been constantly attested'.

According to Miss Freer, Lord Bute first heard about Ballechin and its ghosts in August 1892, when a priest, Fr Patrick Hayden, S.J., visited Falkland Palace in Fife, of which Bute was the owner and hereditary keeper. Fr Hayden had been staying at Ballechin during the previous month of July, and had heard strange noises and had seen, between waking and sleeping, a momentary vision of a brown crucifix.[2] A year later, in August 1893, Fr Hayden met a Miss Yates, who twelve years previously had been a governess at Ballechin and had left because 'so many people complained of queer noises in the house'.[3] Fr Hayden reported this story to Lord Bute.

In 1896 Ballechin House was let for three months to a naturalized Spaniard, Mr Joseph R. Heaven, of Kiftsgate Court, Mickleton, Gloucestershire, and his family.[4] Mr Heaven wrote to *The Times* during the controversy:

When I went to Ballechin at the beginning of August my family had already been there a few days, and at once they told me they had found out the house was supposed to be haunted and that they had heard most unaccountable noises. I had the greatest difficulty to persuade my people to stay in the place, and after all we left Scotland about the end of September—two months earlier than usual. I personally did not

[1] *The Doctor's After Thoughts*, London, 1932, p. 177.

[2] *The Alleged Haunting of B—— House*, pp. 1–10. [3] *Ibid.*, pp. 10–12.

[4] In a letter to Lord Bute of 21st July 1899 Miss Freer wrote with Victorian insularity of the Heavens that they were 'pleasant and intelligent, and what in English folk would be "barbarous opulence jewel-thick" is less offensive in foreigners'. Their Spanish name was Cielo.

give any importance to the rumours that Ballechin-house is haunted, and attributed the very remarkable noises heard to the hot-water pipes and the peculiar way in which the house is built. In fact, I have to confess I cannot believe in ghosts, and consequently I did my best to persuade everybody that Ballechin was not haunted, but I am afraid I was not always successful.[1]

Mr Heaven's lack of belief in the ghosts of Ballechin and his opinion that the noises were due to the hot-water pipes and the peculiar construction of the house is hard to reconcile with the story of one of his guests, a Mrs Howard, who published her experiences in a magazine article on 9th October 1896 and whom Miss Freer quoted at length on pp. 58–62 of her book:

The haunted room (for so I may justly call it) was inhabited by two or three persons in succession, who were so alarmed and disturbed by the violent knockings, shrieks, and groans which they heard every night, and which were also heard by many others along the same corridor, that they refused to sleep there after the first few nights . . . Even the dogs cannot be coaxed into this room, and if forced into it, they crouch with marked signs of fear. The disturbances take place between 12 and 4.30, and never at any other time. A young lady, of by no means timid disposition, and possessed of great presence of mind, has often heard the swing-door pushed open and footsteps coming along the corridor, pausing at the door. She has frequently looked out and seen nothing. The footsteps she has also heard in her room, and going round her bed. Many persons have had the same experiences, and many have heard the wild unearthly shriek which has rung through the house in the stillness of the night . . . As I write, at the commencement of October, the house on the lonely hillside is deserted; the tenants have gone southwards; an old caretaker (too deaf to hear the weird sounds which nightly awaken the echoes) is the sole occupant. Even she closes up all before dusk, and retires into her quarters below; though she hears not, her sight is unimpaired, and she perhaps dreads to meet the hunchback figure which is said to glide up the stairs, or the shadowy form of a grey lady who paces with noiseless footfall the lonely corridor, and has been seen to pass through the door of one of the rooms. Within the last two months a man

[1] *The Times*, 14th June 1897. On p. 15 of her book Miss Freer said of the Heaven tenancy that Ballechin, with the shooting, was let 'for a year, to a wealthy family of Spanish origin. Their experience was of such a nature that they abandoned the house at the end of seven weeks, thus forfeiting the greater part of their rent, which had been paid in advance.' This was a gross exaggeration, as will be seen from Mr Heaven's letter, which suggests that he might have stayed for a maximum period of four months in normal circumstances. In the earlier part of his letter he refers to 'my tenancy for three months last year'.

with bronzed complexion and bent figure has been seen by two gentlemen, friends of mine. They both describe him as having come through the door and passed through the room in which they were, about three in the morning.

Miss Freer said that Mrs Howard's story was in no sense 'written up', and that it was in any event entirely corroborated by other evidence.[1] I have found little confirmation of this. Two of Mrs Howard's fellow guests at Ballechin were a Colonel Aitchieson and a Major Berkeley. They are picturesquely referred to in her account as witnesses, although not by name:

Those who serve under her Majesty's colours are proverbially brave; they will gladly die for their country, with sword in hand and face to the foe.

Major Berkeley wrote to the Hon. Everard Feilding in January 1897, confirming the fact of the noises at Ballechin, but nothing else:

Between two and four in the morning there used to be noises on the door (of Colonel Aitchieson's room) as if a very strong man were hitting the panels as hard as ever he could hit, three times in quick succession—a pause, and then three times again in quick succession, and perhaps another go. It was so loud that I thought it was on the door of his dressing-room, but he said he thought it was on his bedroom door. One theory is, that it was the hot water in the pipes getting cold, which, I am told, would make a loud throbbing noise. I tripped out pretty quick the first time I heard it, but could see nothing. Of course it is broad daylight in Scotland then.

The same banging was, I believe, heard on one of the bedroom doors down the passage, in the wing on the ground floor, and on investigation I found there were hot-water pipes outside that door as well. There were yarns innumerable while I was there about shrieks and footsteps heard, and bedclothes torn off. But I did not experience these.

Colonel Aitchieson corroborated this account in a letter to Major Berkeley:

You write asking me about Ballechin House and its spook. Well, I never saw *anything, and what I heard was what you heard, a terrific banging at one's bedroom door, generally from about 2 to 3 a.m., about two nights*

[1] *The Alleged Haunting of B—— House*, p. 58. She did not reveal that in her letter to Lord Bute of 15th July 1897 she had said that 'Mrs Howard will not corroborate her statement to me as to the most interesting of Mr Howard's experiences'.

out of three. Of course there were other yarns of things heard, etc., but I personally never heard or experienced anything else than this banging at the door, which I could never account for.

These two accounts, read in conjunction with that of Mr Heaven, suggest that both Mrs Howard's story and that told by Mr Harold Sanders in *The Times* of 21st June 1897 of the events at Ballechin in the autumn of 1896 should be accepted with reserve. Sanders, a butler formerly in the employ of Mr Heaven, had been at Ballechin during the family's stay there. He wrote:

One gentleman (a colonel) told me he was awakened on several occasions with the feeling that some one was pulling the bed clothes off him;[1] *sometimes heavy footsteps were heard, at others like the rustling of a lady's dress; and sometimes groans were heard, but nearly always accompanied by heavy knocking . . . I then retired to my bed, but not to sleep, for I had not been in bed three minutes before I experienced the sensation as before, but, instead of being followed by knocking, my bed-clothes were lifted up and let fall again—first at the foot of my bed, but gradually coming towards my head; I held the clothes around my neck with my hands, but they were gently lifted in spite of my efforts to hold them. I then reached around me with my hand, but could feel nothing. This was immediately followed by my being fanned as though some bird was flying around my head, and I could distinctly hear and feel something breathing on me. I then tried to reach some matches that were on a chair by my bedside, but my hand was held back as if by some invisible power. Then the thing seemed to retire to the foot of my bed. Then I suddenly found the foot of my bed lifted up and carried around towards the window for about three or four feet; then replaced to its former position. All this did not take, I should think, more than two or three minutes, although at the time it seemed hours to me. Just then the clock struck four, and, being tired out with my long night's watching, I fell asleep. This, Mr Editor, is some of my experiences while at Ballechin.*[2]

My view is that the evidence of Mr Heaven, Colonel Aitchieson, and Major Berkeley demonstrates that mysterious noises were frequently heard in Ballechin House, but there is no independent support for the accounts by Sanders of the pulling of bedclothes and the holding of his hand 'as if by some invisible power', nor of Mrs

[1] Colonel Aitchieson and Major Berkeley were the only military members of Mr Heaven's house party. It will be seen that Colonel Aitchieson's unpublished personal account suggests that this incident was probably invented by Sanders. It is interesting to compare Colonel Aitchieson's story of the banging on the door with Professor Balfour-Browne's recollection of the boot marks, see p. 181.

[2] *The Times*, 21st January 1897.

Howard's stories of the hunchback figure, the grey lady, and the man with the bronzed complexion and bent figure. What caused the noises is a matter of opinion. Dr E. J. Dingwall and I have previously and briefly commented upon them in another place.[1] In this connexion the published view of Professor John Milne, F.R.S.,[2] the distinguished seismologist, is of great interest. In a letter published in *The Times* of 21st June 1897 at the height of the Ballechin House controversy, Milne wrote:

I am more inclined to the view that the Ballechin mysteries are to be explained not so much from the character of the noises which have been heard, but rather from the knowledge we possess relating to the seismicity of the district in which they have been recorded. For years past this part of Perthshire has been well known as the hotbed for British earthquakes. Between 1852 and 1890 no less than 465 shocks have been noted there, out of which number 430 are claimed by Comrie. Many of these have been accompanied by sounds and often, as is common in earthquake countries and as I can testify from considerable personal experience, sounds may be heard and no movement can be either felt or recorded by an ordinary seismograph. As early as 1840 the British Association appointed a committee to investigate the Perthshire earthquakes, and instruments were established in the Parish Church at Comrie. In one of the reports of this committee we find a letter from David Milne to the Rev. Dr. Buckland, in which he relates the experience of Lady Moncrieff, who stated that whilst residing in Comrie-house scarcely a day passed without hearing either the rumbling noise in the earth or the moaning in the air produced by a mysterious agent. Many other quotations might be made to show that in Perthshire seismic sounds have been common,[3] *and, because such sounds do not travel far from their origin, they might be heard at an isolated house in the country and nowhere else . . . The Society for Psychical Research when on bogey-hunting expeditions might possibly find that the suggested use of tromometric apparatus might not only lay home-made ghosts but would furnish materials of value to all who are interested in seismic research.*

The reader now has before him the story of the alleged haunting of Ballechin House prior to the S.P.R. investigation in 1897. The

[1] *Four Modern Ghosts*, pp. 17–19.

[2] In 1897 Milne was Secretary of the Seismological Committee of the British Association, a position he occupied until his death in 1913.

[3] Comrie is about 22 miles from Ballechin. The latter lies in the triangle formed by Pitlochry (3 miles distant), Dunkeld (9 miles distant), and Aberfeldy (6 miles distant), all three of which have an earthquake history. Charles Davison, *A History of British Earthquakes*, Cambridge, 1924, pp. 62 and 159.

first firm intention to conduct an enquiry at this time is mentioned in a letter from Myers to Lord Bute dated 17th December 1896. Myers said that he had 'received the papers re the Perthshire haunted house: and I am doing my best to find someone willing to go there'. It is clear that Bute had expressed a willingness to pay the cost of an S.P.R. investigation, for Myers said that since this was so, he anticipated no difficulty in obtaining volunteers to stay in the house. This optimism was well founded, and on Myers' recommendation Ballechin was occupied by Miss Freer, her friend Miss Constance Moore, and Colonel G. L. le Mesurier Taylor from early February 1897 to the middle of May. Colonel Taylor was a prominent member of both the Society for Psychical Research and the London Spiritualist Alliance. Lord Bute paid all the expenses, and the house was staffed with servants.

The tenancy, which was a furnished one, was negotiated in Colonel Taylor's name by agents who were instructed that the house was required by Colonel Taylor and his family, with 'a little winter shooting and some good spring fishing', as was later revealed during the controversy in a letter printed in *The Times* of 16th June 1897 from Colonel Taylor's own agents, Messrs T. and J. Speedy of Edinburgh. This embarrassed communication was in response to an indignant letter, also printed in *The Times* on the same day,[1] from the agents for the owners, Messrs R. H. Moncrieff and Co. of Edinburgh. In their letter Messrs Moncrieff complained that the offer to rent Ballechin House had been accepted on the understanding that Colonel Taylor required the property for his personal occupation with the rabbit shooting and fishing, neither the S.P.R. nor the real purpose for which Ballechin House was to be used, ghost-hunting, having been so much as hinted at in the negotiations. Messrs Moncrieff indignantly concluded their letter:

The damage and injury done to Captain Steuart in the whole matter will be far-reaching and irreparable, and we have on his behalf to intimate that he will hold all those concerned responsible for the loss and damage he is bound to sustain.[2]

Unless a number of persons were to be disbelieved, it would seem that the negotiations by the S.P.R. representatives for the tenancy of Ballechin House were lacking in frankness. Captain J. M. S. Steuart wrote to *The Times* from Paris on 10th June 1897 and his

[1] Messrs Moncrieff and Co. published the whole of the correspondence relating to the letting of Ballechin House in *The Times* on 16th June 1897 in support of their statement that they had been deceived.

[2] *The Times*, 16th June 1897.

letter was printed on 14th June, two days before his agents published the facts. He wrote:

As owner of Ballechin, I desire to state that I had no idea I was letting Ballechin to Lord Bute and the Psychical Society, and would never have done so had I known. I let Ballechin for three months to a Colonel Taylor, with fishing, etc., and it was only at the end of his tenancy I discovered for what purposes and by whom Ballechin had been really rented.

The letter published in *The Times* of 18th June 1897, in which Mrs Caroline Steuart wrote that she deeply resented the deceit that had been practised upon her, has already been quoted in connexion with the Clandon affair. In regard to the reassuring description of Colonel Taylor as a family man interested in shooting and fishing, which his own agents Messrs T. and J. Speedy said had been represented to them, Miss Freer herself disclosed the truth two years later in her book. In trying to support her unlikely assertion that Messrs Moncrieff, the agents for the Steuart family, should have been aware that Colonel Taylor was 'well known as a Spiritualist in England and America', she incautiously revealed that Colonel Taylor 'neither shoots nor fishes', and that he was a widower without family.[1]

In regard to the general involvement of the S.P.R. in the affair from the beginning, which is made perfectly clear by Myers' correspondence, it is of interest to record that Miss Freer said in her book that if Colonel Taylor had not agreed to have the lease put in his name, then either William Crookes, the President of the S.P.R., or Mr Arthur Smith, the Society's Hon. Treasurer, would have done so.[2] And as for Myers' promotion of the affair and his desire and recommendation that she should go to Ballechin, Miss Freer said that Myers 'wrote urgently to her' saying that if she did not get phenomena at Ballechin probably nobody would.[3]

Miss Freer and her friends doubtless found living at Ballechin, with a staff of servants at their disposal and all expenses paid, pleasant enough. Lord Bute described it as 'a luxurious country house, ample, though not too large, in a beautiful neighbourhood'.[4] Miss Freer herself, in a diary which she kept of her stay in the house, said:

[1] *The Alleged Haunting of B—— House*, pp. 75–6.
[2] *Ibid.*, p. 74.
[3] *Ibid.*, p. 76.
[4] *Ibid.*, p. 81. This part of Perthshire may indeed be considered the best favoured district of the Scottish Highlands.

It is cheerful, sunny, convenient, healthy, and built on a very simple plan, which admits of no dark corners or mysteries of any kind. A pleasanter house to live in I would not desire, but it is constructed for summer rather than for winter use.[1]

During the tenancy a number of persons, between thirty and forty in all, were invited to stay at Ballechin for a few nights at a time to experience the alleged phenomena which, as we have seen, had been variously reported in the past as including strange noises, objective manifestations, such as the lifting of beds and bedclothes, the appearance of several spectres of various kinds, and a vision of a crucifix. The distinguished visitors included Professor Oliver Lodge, Andrew Lang, the Hon. Everard Feilding, Archbishop Angus MacDonald,[2] Sir James Crichton-Browne, Fr Allan McDonald, John Ritchie Findlay, Rev. Charles J. M. Shaw, and F. W. H. Myers, the latter in company with a young woman from London, Miss Jessica Iris Chaston, described scornfully by Miss Freer in her book as 'a "medium"'.[3]

It is of great interest that today, seventy years after the Ballechin controversy, new evidence is available from the unpublished papers of Lord Bute throwing fresh light on the mystery. Two letters, substantial in length and written privately to Lord Bute by men of intelligence and substance who were visitors to the house during the S.P.R. tenancy, have been made available to Dr Campbell and myself. One, Mr H. F. Cadell, W.S., an Edinburgh solicitor who had acted for Colonel Taylor in regard to the formalities of the tenancy, had experiences during his stay. The other, Mr (later Sir) John Ritchie Findlay, the son and heir of the owner of *The Scotsman*, had none, but his letter is of considerable value because it contains his private appraisal to Lord Bute of some of the principal persons involved in the Ballechin investigation carried out by the S.P.R.

Mr Cadell, writing to Lord Bute on 8th March 1897 from 19 Ainslie Place, Edinburgh, said:

I went to Ballechin on Saturday last and Mrs Macphail has suggested that I should write to you about what occurred there, during my stay. It was arranged that I was to sleep in Room No. 2, and Colonel Taylor in No. 3—No. 1 being empty. I went to bed about 12 o'clock. I suddenly awoke with the impression that there was someone in the room. I lay still and tried to realise what was in the room but could not do so. There was

[1] *The Alleged Haunting of B—— House*, p. 84.

[2] R.C. Archbishop of St Andrews and Edinburgh, formerly Bishop of Argyll and the Isles.

[3] *Ibid.*, p. 184.

no idea of movement in my mind, but I felt convinced that someone was there. This impression appeared to gradually fade out of my mind after about seven or ten minutes, and I then got up and looked at my watch. The time was 4.40 a.m. I then went back to bed, but did not go to sleep—I heard the clock on the main stairs strike 5.

Shortly after I thought I heard someone moving in No. 1, which I knew to be empty. I listened and I thought someone seemed to be moving round three sides of the room and then coming back again. The movement went on for 3 or 4 minutes and then stopped, but after a pause of some minutes it commenced again. I tried to make out footsteps, and could not do so. The movement was that of a heavy body going round the room, and the floor seemed to shake, as old flooring will when a heavy man walks about. My bed also was shaken. After going on for some time the movement stopped and again after a pause began again. I heard the movements four separate times. The periods for which the movements and the pauses lasted were irregular. After waiting some time and finding that the noises seemed to have stopped altogether, I got up and lit the candle at 5.25 and read for 25 minutes, when I felt sleepy and blew out the candle. I did not however go to sleep, but heard six strike. The day was then dawning. I noticed that the rooks began making a noise about 5.35.

About ten minutes after the clock struck six, I heard a noise like a lightfooted person running down stairs, which seemed to adjoin No. 3, where Colonel Taylor was sleeping, and almost immediately after I heard a loud rapping at the door of No. 1. Then there was a momentary pause, and as I jumped out of bed the rapping occurred again. As I opened the door of my room leading into the passage the rapping occurred again but less loudly. There was no one in the passage, and I went back to bed having shut the door. No sooner had I got into bed than there was a knock at my door, which I thought must be Colonel Taylor coming to speak to me on account of the rapping at No. 1. I therefore called out 'Come in', but there was no answer, and I accordingly went to the door again, only to find no one there.

I heard the servants in the bedrooms above me get up about 6.30, and as 7 struck I heard them moving about the house. Colonel Taylor did not hear anything. There are no stairs coming down to the bedroom storey, where I thought I heard footsteps. The rapping was not in any way an alarming noise. 'Ouija'[1] *had informed us that I was not to be disturbed, and I was not therefore 'expecting'. That night it referred to 'the Major' and stated that he formerly occupied Rooms No. 3 & 8. I could not therefore have expected noises in No. 1.*

Last night I was not so much disturbed, but I awoke at 3.10 and did

[1] It is reasonable to conclude that Miss Freer was the operator.

not sleep after that. I had the same sensation as on the preceding night that whenever I was going to sleep something woke me. At 5.20 I heard three noises very close together, but they were very distant, and sounded from the direction of No. 8.

Everybody in the house has heard noises with the exception of Colonel Taylor. The Butler was an unbeliever until Saturday night, when he heard something that appears to have convinced him.

I was very much interested in what I heard, and I have to thank your Lordship for the opportunity of going to Ballechin.

P.S. I forgot to mention that I do not believe in the screams, which former tenants assert that they have heard. No one has heard them during this year. I heard the owls last night, and in the night their hoots do not sound unlike screams. I am sure there must be two stories in connection with the place—one which has to do with 'the Major', and the other of older date with all sorts of personages connected with it. I ought also perhaps to mention that after hearing the noises at No. 1, I went down the main stair and came back up the back stair. H.F.C.

Mr Findlay wrote to Lord Bute on 3rd March 1897 from 3 Rothesay Terrace, Edinburgh. In a previous short note he had expressed his appreciation of the hospitality afforded him during his stay. He had deliberately slept in Bedroom No. 3, in which both Fr Hayden and Major Berkeley had heard strange noises, but his own experiences 'were absolutely nil'. He added 'that as all that is worth relating rests almost entirely on the testimony of Miss Freer', he did not feel that anything could usefully be printed in *The Scotsman* for the present. Lord Bute had evidently responded to Mr Findlay's first note by sending some papers dealing with the earlier evidence for the haunting. In reply Mr Findlay wrote:

I am much obliged to you for sending me the documents which I return. Some of them Mr Shaw had already shown me but the most of them are new.

In writing before I refrained from indicating what opinion I had formed of the Ballechin investigations, but your letters encourage me to think that it may be of some interest to you to know how they impressed a critical and somewhat sceptical observer. I may say that my natural instinct would be to find a personal explanation of the various phenomena; and to explain the 'ouija' messages as the result of such subconsciousness as Binet has investigated. I am neither nervous nor susceptible to impressions. I am prepared to be told that this amounts to a preconception, which invalidates my testimony, but I submit that it is not more illogical than the desire to see and hear which seemed to be common to most at Ballechin. It is perhaps impossible really to approach any subject with an absolutely empty mind.

I may tell you frankly, though in confidence, that there was hardly a person at Ballechin whose testimony I should set much store by in matters of the kind. They could not stand cross-examination, and in the eyes of common men their testimony would be vitiated by predisposition and inclination. Miss Freer you know better than I do. She knows what she is about, but she is an expert in such matters, and her personal tendencies or 'powers' cannot be ignored. Colonel Taylor is a professed spiritualist—a man of sound common sense but little imagination. He has had no 'experiences' but if he should have any, a supernatural explanation would be the first that would suggest itself, and he would accept it with an alacrity that would only amuse most people.

Mr Powles[1] *was I think the most nervous man I ever met. He seems to live in a world of influences, which are a perpetual source of annoyance to him. He can tell by instinct whether a room or house is haunted and his instinct is confirmed by his experience. He* sees *nothing but is prepared by constitution to feel and hear. Mr Shaw the parson,*[2] *on the other hand, is in the habit of seeing figures outlined in light against a dark background. These he told me he could see at will. He seems to have little critical instinct, and a thorough belief in the supernatural. The first night I was there he went down the avenue in order that he might see the apparition of the nun. He went predisposed to see and he did see what he described as 'something'. The following incident illustrates his attitude of mind. Miss Freer came to meet me in a waggonette. The horse started at the train, and she was thrown out. He saw all that happened, yet he seriously asked her if she thought she had been thrown out by supernatural agencies. These things should be kept in view in dealing with his testimony.*

Miss Langton is a young girl, somewhat hysterical, not strong physically, and strangely susceptible to outside influences. Miss Moore on the other hand struck me as being a person of sound common sense, and her evidence I should value beyond that of all the others who are predisposed by temperament to such experiences. Of course it may be said that it is only persons of this sort, who are competent to investigate such matters, but if you adopt this position you must abandon all hope of convincing the majority of mankind, who I am afraid have little sympathy with such an attitude of mind.

With regard to the sounds heard I can offer no explanation. They may be natural sounds formalised and exaggerated by the imagination of those

[1] Mr Lewis Charles Powles was an Associate of the S.P.R.

[2] Rev. Charles J. M. Shaw was an Associate of the S.P.R.

who heard them. But in the absence of any personal experience I do not put this forward with any confidence.

With regard to the 'ouija' messages I have less difficulty. From your letter I gather that you are inclined to halt between two opinions, the one that they are subconscious dreams, the other that they are communications from a mischievous and ignorant spirit. What strikes me forcibly about them, is their groping and tentative character. The dates have gradually been brought down to present times. It must too, be borne in mind that on the part of those who have been obtaining them there has been a constant effort to verify them by tradition and documents. Burke's Landed Gentry was constantly referred to. The minds of those engaged were thus fixed upon what is true in them and this would almost certainly lead to the elaboration in a halting fashion of a story which bears a strong resemblance to the truth. Another feature of them is that I can find little or nothing of importance in them, which I did not know to be consciously or unconsciously in the minds of those engaged. The Scottish use of 'West' had been discussed when I was there, yet its use in a subsequent 'ouija' message is considered matter for surprise. Similarly the phrase 'ora pro nobis' was in the mind of Mr Shaw. Another criticism which suggests itself is the manner of indicating time, e.g. 10.53. This is of quite modern origin, and even now is not in use among uneducated persons unless they are railway servants. How does the use of this phrase fit in with the hypothesis of an ignorant spirit? In the messages of earlier date, it is a sort of anachronism of the kind that vitiates a document.

Were those at Ballechin kept in absolute ignorance of all the details of family history I should have more confidence in the 'ouija' messages. The date 1880 puzzles me. I have done nothing, and will do nothing to enlighten them as to the details contained in your letters.

I would not have ventured to criticise so freely a party with whom I spent two very pleasant days unless I had thought it might interest you to learn how these things struck an outsider. This too is my only excuse for troubling you with a letter of such length.

I would like very much to go back if I could manage it.

With many thanks for being allowed to read the documents you sent me.

There is another opinion which is not so valuable as those of Mr Cadell and Mr Findlay, merely because it is a recollection recorded now, after an interval of seventy years. It is, however, of the greatest interest; not only because Professor W. A. F. Balfour-Browne is a distinguished entomologist, trained originally as a barrister, whose remarkable memory is well known among his colleagues, but because he is almost certainly the only surviving person who, as a young man of twenty-three, was a visitor at Ballechin during those far-off days of the S.P.R. investigation.[1] On p. 210 of her book Miss Freer describes how near the end of the tenancy Ballechin was visited by Sir James Crichton-Browne, his nephew and a friend. Sir James's nephew was Mr W. A. F. Balfour-Browne of Magdalen College, Oxford, and his friend was Mr J. Callendar Ross, a leader-writer for *The Times*. Dr Campbell has had the privilege of meeting and corresponding with Professor Balfour-Browne, who wrote to him on 29th September 1966:

I knew nothing about the matter until my uncle asked me to accompany him to Ballechin. I think I had just come down from Oxford.

The haunted house was a large one and we three enquirers were bedded in one end of it in three rooms which connected with one another, I having the middle one. I remember my uncle's activity in moving a large wardrobe which covered the door from his room to mine. For the few nights we were there all was peace but one interesting item occurs to me. We three came down to breakfast one morning and only Miss Freer's companion was down, and in answer to our enquiries, she said that all had been quiet at the end of the house where she and Miss Freer slept. Later Miss Freer told us that the ghost seemed to have moved to her end of the house on the previous night!

We examined the whole house, and except for marks on various doors indicating that someone had hit them with some object, such as boots, there was nothing out of the way except that, all round the top floor rooms there was a passage round the house. I managed to crawl along this passage and again arrive at the small door by which I had got into it. The passage might have enabled someone to play ghosts upon the servants or whoever slept in those top rooms and the boot-marks suggested that there had been some joking. Except for these possibilities, it was suggested that the house lay upon a line which had shown signs of earth movement. I need not tell you the impression that my uncle and Mr Ross got of the matter but I felt that Miss Freer had either been sent there to prove *the existence of a ghost or she herself had decided to do so on her own authority.*

I know nothing about Ross except that someone told me he was a leader-writer for The Times. *I never heard of any of the other people you mention. If the row about Miss Chaston was a matter of morals it is possible that I was regarded as too young to be told about it!*"

As in the case of the alleged haunting of Clandon, within a short time of her arrival at Ballechin Miss Freer claimed to see an

[1] Since these words were written, Professor Balfour-Browne died on 28th September 1967 at the age of 93.

apparition, this time of a nun, in a glen near the house one evening in February. Neither of her companions, the Hon. Everard Feilding and Mr Lane Fox, could see anything, a failure which Miss Freer attributed to their temperamental unsuitability for experiences of this kind.[1] Miss Freer was, as we know, an automatic writer, a class of person in whom the S.P.R. was to become increasingly interested from the turn of the century to the present time. She soon obtained information through her 'ouija board' that the name of the nun was 'Ishbel'. She also heard 'Ishbel' speak and weep, and was able to describe her in some detail in a letter to Lord Bute:

'Ishbel' appears to me to be slight, and of fair height. I am unable, of course, to see the colour of her hair, but I should describe her as dark. There is an intensity in her gaze which is rare in light-coloured eyes. The face, as I see it, is in mental pain, so that it is perhaps hardly fair to say that it seems lacking in that repose and gentleness that one looks for in the religious life. Her dress presents no peculiarities. The habit is black, with the usual white about the face, and I have thought that when walking she showed a lighter under-dress. She speaks upon rather a high note, with a quality of youth in her voice. Her weeping seemed to me passionate and unrestrained.[2]

A few days later Miss Freer began to see another apparition in company with that of 'Ishbel', referred to in her account as 'Marget' and heard the two figures conversing in the glen.[3] On a later occasion in company with Miss Freer, her friend Miss Langton heard the sound of low conversation, and Miss Moore heard 'a murmuring voice'.[4] Another visitor, the Rev. Charles J. M. Shaw, saw the figure in the glen on 19th February, and heard a loud groan and saw a momentary vision of a crucifix on the wall of his bedroom at Ballechin on 24th February.[5] On 26th February Miss Freer saw the apparition of a woman with a 'coarsely handsome' face in the drawing-room.[6]

It has to be remembered that in investigations of this kind in allegedly haunted localities the power of suggestion is exceedingly strong. Colonel Taylor himself observed in a latter to Lord Bute:

The clairvoyant visions of 'Ishbel' in the grounds are not of great evidential value for the scientific world in general, and I think that any amount of 'voices' could be read into the noises of the running stream, near where she is seen, by those who 'wished to hear'.[7]

[1] *The Alleged Haunting of B—— House*, p. 92.
[2] *Ibid.*, p. 93.
[3] *Ibid.*, pp. 101–2.
[4] *Ibid.*, p. 108.
[5] *Ibid.*, pp. 112–13 and 121–4.
[6] *Ibid.*, p. 126.
[7] *Ibid.*, p. 145.

The tendency of perfectly honest but impressionable persons, under strong suggestion from a dominating character, towards small hallucinatory experiences is documented in my essay on D. D. Home in my *New Light on Old Ghosts*. I have never doubted Miss Freer's ability to influence those with whom she came in contact. The Rev. C. J. M. Shaw, moreover, was not only an Associate of the S.P.R., but was also a member of one of the spiritualist circles subscribing to the occult magazine she organized and sub-edited.[1]

While all this was going on, Miss Freer's colleague Colonel Taylor unfortunately heard and saw nothing to which he attached any psychical significance, although he repeatedly slept in the most haunted bedroom and paid many visits to the glen hoping to see the phantom nuns. Miss Freer said that this was because 'although a frequent visitor to haunted houses, he has never had any experience'.[2] Colonel Taylor left Ballechin on 16th March, after spending five weeks there 'very pleasantly', as he wrote in his letter to Lord Bute on 19th March 1897. Colonel Taylor went on to say, surprisingly in the circumstances, that he was disappointed in the way in which the 'ghostly influence' at Ballechin had manifested itself during his stay. He thought the vision of the brown crucifix was important, but expressed some scepticism in regard to the whole of the rest of the phenomena. He added:

It is very interesting to note Miss Freer's experiences but in regard to those of others who have something to relate, it is perhaps difficult to determine how much these statements should be discounted for error of observation and self-suggestion. I heard many noises in the night during my stay at B——, but they were of much the same sort I have been accustomed to hear at a similar time in other houses. I think that some of our witnesses may have given them undue prominence, under the influence of their own expectancy.

My discussion of the alleged haunting of Ballechin is intended to be no more than the placing before the reader of some hitherto unpublished information, and to be an introduction to the surprising events that quickly followed the end of the S.P.R. investigation in May 1897. The reader will no doubt have formed a preliminary opinion of the 'phenomena' at Ballechin. In this connexion a comment made by Frank Podmore in his review[3] of the *Alleged Haunting of B—— House* in S.P.R. *Proceedings* is not lacking in interest. It is

[1] 'Our Circles and Members', *Borderland*, 1895, vol. II, pp. 88–92. Mr Shaw's name appears on p. 90.

[2] *The Alleged Haunting of B—— House*, p. 140.

[3] *Proceedings*, S.P.R., 1900–1, vol. XV, pp. 98–100.

true that the Society decided to disclaim Ballechin and throw Miss Freer to the wolves when the storm broke in the columns of *The Times* in June 1897, and that an adverse review could therefore be expected. It was, however, valid for Podmore to say, as he did, that it was somewhat significant that during the investigation it was Miss Freer who first heard the noises, who first saw the apparition, and who was most frequently and most conspicuously favoured with 'phenomena'.

7

MISS FREER AND THE BALLECHIN CONTROVERSY

AFTER THE S.P.R. tenancy was over one of the guests wrote a long account of his experiences at Ballechin, which was published in *The Times* on 8th June 1897. The author, Mr J. Callendar Ross (1844–1913), was a leader-writer on the staff of that newspaper, and his account was unsigned. It was printed under the caption 'On the Trail of a Ghost', which was repeated over the whole of the considerable ensuing correspondence. In his obituary it was stated that Mr Ross was a Perthshire man, from which it is reasonable to assume the possibility that he knew something of the history of Ballechin House before he went there during the S.P.R. investigation. His father was a surveyor in Perthshire, who later became the land agent to Lord Muncaster's estates at Ravenglass in Cumberland. Before joining *The Times* in 1881, Mr Callendar Ross had been a leader-writer for the *Glasgow News* and had edited the *Dumfries and Galloway Herald and Courier*. He was described as having studied medicine, as being interested in scientific subjects, and of being a writer with a 'vigorous, lucid and pungent style'.[1] He went to Ballechin in company with Sir James Crichton-Browne and Mr W. A. F. Balfour-Browne. His account of his experiences during his visit in *The Times* was highly critical of the way in which the S.P.R. investigation had been conducted.

When Mr Callendar Ross's story was published, Myers believed quite erroneously that it had been written by Sir James Crichton-Browne, F.R.S., who had been publicly critical of the S.P.R.'s methods in conducting thought-transference experiments in 1883. Sir James, in company with Sir Francis Galton, F.R.S., and George G. Romanes, F.R.S., had been invited by Professor Henry Sidgwick, the President of the S.P.R., and F. W. H. Myers to witness mental phenomena, which were claimed to be supernormal, produced by two young men, George Albert Smith (mentioned in an earlier chapter in connexion with Miss Freer's abilities in obtaining psychic messages through sea-shells) and Douglas Blackburn. Prior to the

[1] *The Times*, 14th April 1913.

'experiments' conducted by the S.P.R. leaders, Smith and Blackburn had been paid public performers in a 'second sight' act in the music-halls of Brighton. Blackburn later stated publicly in print in 1908, 1911, and 1917 that the 'experiments' were simple trickery, and that the S.P.R. investigators had been as easy to deceive as children. Sir James and his friends knew nothing of these future revelations, of course, but as a result of their own observations and some simple tests, soon became convinced that the whole thing was conjuring, as might have been expected, and said so. Sir James published a detailed account of these events in *The Westminster Gazette*, including the final clash with the infuriated Myers:

The last scene of all, or passage-at-arms, I vividly recollect. Mr Myers, standing in front of the fireplace, said: 'It must be allowed that this demonstration has been a total failure, and I attribute that to the offensive incredulity of Dr Crichton-Browne.' To which I rejoined: 'I hope I always will show offensive incredulity when I find myself in the presence of patent imposture.' [1]

Myers and the S.P.R. hushed up the affair as best they could, and suppressed all mention of the incident in the account of the experiments in their *Proceedings*, and in a privately circulated pamphlet, *Mr Blackburn's Confession*, prepared by Miss Alice Johnson, the Secretary of the Society, in 1909. This pamphlet, issued after Douglas Blackburn had published his first statement in 1908, claimed that the experiments proved telepathy and that Mr Blackburn's revelation that they were simple conjuring was not true.

Sir James's attitude to the experiments with Smith and Blackburn in 1883 still rankled with Myers in 1897. Lord Bute arranged for Sir James to visit Ballechin on the recommendation of Sir William Huggins, to which Myers could scarcely object, since Bute was paying the costs of the investigation. Myers wrote to Bute, however, on 4th April 1897:

Perhaps you will pardon me for saying privately *that I don't think there will be* room *for him when my little group are there! I respect his scientific attainments, but his personal manners are not encouraging to sensitives. I have seen him at it!*

When Mr Callendar Ross's account was published in *The Times* on 8th June 1897 Myers wrote to Lord Bute on the same day:

[1] For an accessible account of the incident see Sir James Crichton-Browne, M.D., LL.D., F.R.S., *The Doctor's Second Thoughts*, London, 1931. In my *The Strange Case of Edmund Gurney* the matter is fully discussed and the relevant extracts from *The Westminster Gazette* and S.P.R. literature of the period are reproduced.

I am sorry, but not much surprised, to see Crichton-Browne's letter in The Times *today, re Ballechin. That a self-invited guest should write this of his host (whose name I presume he had been desired not to mention) and his host's friends, is not alien to the conception which one brief interview with this gallant knight had given me of him. I did warn you, and I warned Miss Freer, of his* animus.

Myers' letter was wrong on both its main points. Sir James did not invite himself to Ballechin, and he did not write the letter in *The Times*. He did, however, include an account of the adventures of Mr Ross, Mr Balfour-Browne, and himself at Ballechin in his memoirs,[1] and the discussion with the driver of the wagonette that brought them from the station is too amusing to omit:

As we made our way to B., I thought it well to ask the driver if he knew what was going on there. 'Weel, sur,' he replied, 'we dinna ken, but I keep drivin' there and back queer-looking folks like you, and I thought maybe they were opening a hydropathic.' I suggested to him that perhaps they were hunting up the ghosts there, at which he laughed heartily, and said: 'Na, na! there are some Roman Catholics, but nae ghosts there; its a' havers!'

Sir James said that Miss Freer told them the story of the noises on their arrival, and regaled them with the history of the 'wicked major'. Despite this conditioning, they experienced nothing at all. 'I lay awake reading till three or four in the morning, and there was not a mouse stirring, and after that I had a tranquil sleep,' wrote Sir James, adding that, 'the breakfast party was evidently disappointed when we came down unscared and with no tale to tell.' On the second evening of their stay Miss Freer gave them some further details of the alleged manifestations:

During the Sunday evening we heard from Miss Freer and her friends further particulars of the noises, of the strange sensations by which they were frequently accompanied, to wit, rocking of the bed, tugging at the bedclothes, a sense of icy chilliness as if entering an ice-house, and of struggling with something unseen, so we went again hopefully to bed, but were again disappointed, for the silence was unbroken, and we slumbered tranquilly. We were evidently immune to ghostly visitations.'

Sir James recorded that he drew Miss Freer's attention to the peculiar construction of the house with its hollow wooden casings, its flimsy rafters, and its vibrating floors, and its situation in a

[1] Sir James Crichton-Browne, *The Doctor's After Thoughts*, London, 1932, pp. 175–84.

particularly seismic area of Scotland. Sir James confirmed in his account that the visit of Miss Chaston to Ballechin with Myers took place when Miss Freer was absent 'on an Easter visit to some friends', and that after first writing a series of letters to Bute about his experiences at Ballechin, Myers had later declined to allow their contents to be published. Sir James wrote that little need be said of the apparitions seen by Miss Freer 'at a time when she was highly strung', and that these were rather obviously 'hallucinatory in character, the offspring of suggestion upon a strongly prepossessed mind'. Sir James concluded his account:

The costly and very generously conducted experiment at B. was a fiasco—an illustration of the growth of a myth and of the magnification and misrepresentation of a few simple natural phenomena by sensitive minds in quest of the supernatural. As an old Highland woman said to Miss Freer: 'There are no ghosts at B., it was just the young callants last year that were having a lark.'

In his account in *The Times* of 8th June 1897 Mr Ross confirmed many of the points Sir James was to record in his memoirs in later years. He said that their visit to Ballechin had taken place after the enquiry 'had been going on for more than two months', *i.e.*, in May 1897 when no progress had been made. He said that the visitors were predominantly members of the S.P.R. or had sympathy with the aims of that Society, and that 'nearly all seems to have begun by assuming supernatural interference instead of leaving it for the final explanation of whatever might be clearly proved to be otherwise inexplicable'. Mr Ross gave a good deal of information about the odd construction of the house, saying that it was 'one huge sounding board transmitting and possibly intensifying certain kinds of noise'. He gave a number of examples of noises heard by him which had been traced to entirely natural origins. He told how Miss Freer was in the habit of entertaining the nervous guests at these 'haunted house parties' with stories of the ghost and its activities, and with her theory about the 'wicked major'. Mr Ross added:

The only mystery in the matter seems to be the mode in which a prosaic and ordinary dwelling was endowed with so evil a reputation. I was assured in London that it had had this reputation for 20 or 30 years. The family lawyer in Perth asserted most positively that there had never been a whisper of such a thing until the house was let for last year's shooting season to a family, whom I may call the H's.[1] *I was told the*

[1] Mr Ross was referring to the tenancy of the Heaven family in 1896. He was presumably unaware of the testimony of Fr Hayden, who had told Lord Bute of noises at Ballechin at an earlier date.

same thing in equally positive terms by the minister of the parish, a level headed man from Banffshire, who has lived in the place for 20 years. He told me that some of the younger members of the H. family had indulged in practical jokes and boasted of them. . . . The steward or factor on the estate concurs with the lawyer and minister in denying that the house had any reputation for being haunted before the advent of the H. family.

Mr Ross concluded his long article in *The Times* with a surprisingly frank criticism of Miss Freer and the S.P.R.

Lord Bute's confidence has been grossly abused by someone, and, what he will probably regret even more, he has been unwittingly led to do an appreciable injury to the owners of Ballechin. It was represented to him by someone that he was taking 'the most haunted house in Scotland', a house with an old and established reputation for mysteries if not supernatural disturbances. What he has got is a house with no reputation whatever of that kind, with no history, with nothing germane to his purpose beyond a cloud of baseless rumours produced during the last twelve months. Who is responsible for the imposture it is not my business to know or to inquire, but that it is an imposture of the most shallow and impudent kind there can be no manner of doubt. . . Without attempting to judge individuals, it must be said that an experience like the present intensifies the suspicion and disgust which close contact with the S.P.R. always tends to excite. I am well aware that among its members are many men of eminence, ability and unquestionable honesty. So on the direction of many a dubious company we find the names of men of honour and integrity. Men do not sufficiently consider the responsibility which they incur, financially or morally, when they lend the sanction of their names to proceedings which they do not control and perhaps never inquire into. Seen at all close the methods of the Society for Psychical Research are extremely repulsive. What it calls evidence is unsifted gossip, always reckless and malignant; what it calls discrimination is too often the selection from gossip, all worthless, of those portions which fit best into the theory it happens to be advocating.[1]

It is almost unnecessary to say that this article created a sensation. Miss Freer, over her pseudonym of 'Miss X', wrote at once to *The Times* to express her anger that Mr Ross, who she alleged had given an undertaking to publish nothing about Ballechin, and especially its identity, had violated her hospitality. She said that it was quite untrue to say that the name and location of the house were known in London before Mr Ross went there.[2] Unfortunately for her, this was

[1] *The Times*, 8th June 1897. [2] *Ibid.*, 9th June 1897.

promptly contradicted in a published letter from Mrs Therese Musgrave, who wrote:

I for one can corroborate the statement made by your correspondent that the name of the house in Scotland and the names of the proposed visitors were known in London as early as March, and were spoken of without reserve.[1]

Nobody wrote in support of the assertion by Miss Freer.

The most surprising reaction to Mr Ross's letter came from F. W. H. Myers. He had stayed at Ballechin House from 12th to 22nd April 1897, during the tenancy but while Miss Freer was temporarily away from Ballechin. Myers had been enthusiastic about the phenomena after reading Miss Freer's journal. He had written to her as early as 13th March, 'It is plain that the B—— case is of *great* interest. I hope we may have a discussion of it at S.P.R. general meeting, May 28th, 8.30, and perhaps July 2nd, 4 p.m., also . . . I will send back the two notebooks after showing them to the Sidgwicks. I am so very glad that you and the others have been so well repaid for your trouble.'[2] While at Ballechin Myers wrote again to Miss Freer on 15th April to discuss her proposed lecture on the case to the S.P.R., which it was agreed should be on 2nd July, but which never took place. Myers said that the noises were still going on, and that he was moving into Room No. 5 to be nearer to them. He said that he was reporting his experiences in a series of letters to Lord Bute. On 21st April he wrote again to Miss Freer in a similar vein suggesting that they should meet in London.[3] They never did, and this letter was, so far as I know, their last communication, for a reason to be discussed later. It can be said that 23rd April was the date of the personal quarrel between Miss Freer and Myers, the cause of which was, I fancy, much more human than the alleged haunting of Ballechin House and only indirectly connected with it. 8th June, when Mr Ross's letter was published, was, however, the significant date of the parting of the ways over Ballechin itself. In this incident Myers seems to have behaved very badly indeed. Whether the reason was purely fear of ridicule in the face of Mr Ross's criticisms, and the public support these received from all sides, or whether in addition the emotional upset with Miss Freer a few weeks previously was still rankling and influenced his attitude in some degree, I do not know.

1 *The Times*, 12th June 1897.

2 *The Alleged Haunting of B—— House*, pp. 183–4.

3 *Ibid.*, pp. 186–7. In transcribing Myers' letters to her, Miss Freer omitted many sentences, which may have been of a personal nature.

When Mr Ross's letter appeared, Myers immediately decided that it would be expedient to disclaim Ballechin. Signing himself as Honorary Secretary of the S.P.R., he wrote to *The Times* at once and said that while he had visited Ballechin representing the Society, he had decided that there was no evidence worth reporting.[1] He did not say that he had stayed in the house for as long as ten days, accompanied by his medium Miss Chaston. He did not mention his eulogies of the case to Miss Freer. He did not reveal that he had reported his own experiences there in a series of letters to Lord Bute.[2] Nine days later he persuaded Henry Sidgwick to support him in view of the continuing public criticism. Sidgwick wrote to *The Times* to confirm that Myers had formed an 'unfavourable view' of the investigation at Ballechin, and that he and the S.P.R. Council had agreed that there was nothing worth publishing.[3] It had evidently been decided that Miss Freer should be thrown to the wolves to save the face of the Society.

Another visitor to Ballechin, signing himself 'One of the Witnesses', was highly critical of Myers' action. He wrote that from his personal knowledge he could say that Myers had testified in writing to his own experience of the phenomena, that Myers had made himself acquainted with but a very small part of the evidence, and that in repudiating the case on behalf of the S.P.R. he had not revealed his omission to place any of the evidence before the Council.[4] Miss Freer made use of this letter when defending her position in *Borderland*. She said that Myers' letter, which was lacking in both courtesy and chivalry, needed no comment from her. It was, she wrote, 'sufficiently and effectively answered by that of One of the Witnesses'.[5] Of Sidgwick's letter supporting Myers, she said that if the Council of the S.P.R. shared Myers' view, then the letter should have been written by the President, William Crookes. Sidgwick's letter was, she wrote, 'a masterpiece of saying nothing'.[6]

The next criticism of importance came from Sir James Crichton-

[1] *The Times*, 10th June 1897.

[2] According to Miss Freer, Myers wrote to Bute to say that his letters must 'be in no way used' (*The Alleged Haunting of B—— House*, p. 186). The private correspondence shows that Myers asked that Bute return the letters to him, which Bute did with the request that Myers should not destroy them. They were never published.

[3] *The Times*, 19th June 1897. In her letter to Lord Bute of 29th August 1897 Miss Freer said that this was not true, and that Myers had acted on his own responsibility without consulting the S.P.R. Council.

[4] *Ibid.*, 12th June 1897.

[5] *Borderland*, 1895, vol. IV, p. 307.

[6] *Ibid.*, p. 308.

Browne, who also flatly contradicted Miss Freer's allegation that the guests had agreed not to reveal the identity of the house. Sir James wrote, over the signature of 'A Late Guest at Ballechin':

In my case there was certainly no such stipulation, and had any condition of the kind been attached I should not have accepted the invitation sent to me. Science knows nothing of secrecy, which is, however, the life-blood of quackery and imposture. I went to Ballechin as an investigator on the distinct understanding that I was to assume a critical and sceptical attitude and was to have an absolutely free hand. There was, however, no call for either scepticism or criticism, as my experiences, during the two nights I spent there in one of the haunted chambers were of the most common-place description. I heard no sound of the supernatural and saw no glimmer of a ghost.[1]

Sir James said that what had struck him as so extraordinary was that even at the time of his visit, when the tenancy of Miss Freer and Colonel Taylor had been going on for so long, no attempt at experiment or research had been made. The residents and visitors, he said, 'had been sitting there all the time, agape for wonders, straining on the limits of audition, and fomenting one another's superstitions without taking any precautions to prevent deception'. He added that practical joking, hallucination, and fraud would account for the bulk of the 'phenomena', while what remained, if any, could be explained by earth tremors and by 'the creakings and reverberations of an old and somewhat curiously constructed house'. Sir James concluded his letter by observing that in regard to the Ballechin affair the S.P.R. was 'a household divided against itself', which was true.

In the same issue of *The Times* as Sir James's letter other damaging criticisms appeared. Mr John MacDonald, a former butler at Ballechin, wrote to say that he had never heard any noises for which he could not account during the whole time he lived there, and would have no hesitation in sleeping alone in the house. A correspondent signing himself 'H. R.' said that the performance of the S.P.R. at Ballechin was 'a caricature of a legal inquiry and the parody of a scientific investigation'. He added that the Society, in his view, could not have 'the remotest idea of the legal or scientific meaning and value of evidence'.[2] Two days later Mr Joseph Heaven, the previous tenant of Ballechin, wrote to *The Times* saying that he had attached no importance to the stories of the house being haunted, and that he had attributed the noises heard during his occupancy to the peculiar way in which the house was built, and to the hot-water

[1] *The Times*, 12th June 1897. [2] *Ibid.*, 12th June 1897.

pipes. Mr Heaven said that he had no belief in ghosts.[1] His letter has already been quoted. The same day Mr Heaven's letter was published another correspondent, signing himself 'L. E. B.', wrote to say that the S.P.R.'s methods of reporting its cases brought its operations into discredit. If the Society was to invite scientific attention, said this critic, it must 'eliminate root and branch such childish methods'.[2]

The criticisms were coming thick and fast, for concurrently with the letter from Mr Heaven and 'L. E. B.' the letter from Captain J. M. S. Steuart was published, revealing his annoyance over the deceit practised on him in obtaining the tenancy, already quoted.[3] This, as we have seen, precipitated the publication of the whole of the correspondence, some half-dozen letters, between the agents for the Steuart family, Messrs R. H. Moncrieff and Co., and the agents employed by the S.P.R. representatives, Messrs T. and J. Speedy,[4] to which reference has already been made. Messrs Speedy made it clear that they had been deceived by their own clients.

18th June 1897 was an embarrassing day for the S.P.R. *The Times* published the letter from Mrs Caroline Steuart, already quoted, complaining of the deception practised upon her. Worse still, from the point of view of the exposure of Myers' part in the affair, a further letter appeared from Sir James Crichton-Browne:

Surely Mr Myers' memory is at fault when he says that he decided when at Ballechin that the evidence collected there was not of such a character as to justify its publication by the Psychical Research Society? I visited Ballechin after Mr Myers, and I was there told that he insisted on the publication of the whole transaction. I was indeed, consulted as to the propriety of including in the publication called for by Mr Myers the testimony of one witness whom there were grave grounds for discrediting.[5]

On the following day the previously quoted letter from Lord Onslow was published. This was mentioned in the discussion of the Clandon case. It was in this letter that Lord Onslow sympathized with the Steuart family and wished that 'there were some means of making this society responsible in hard cash for the effects of the light-headed nonsense by which they depreciate other people's property'.[6]

The issue of *The Times* of 21st June contained the very interesting

[1] *The Times*, 14th June 1897.
[2] *Ibid.*, 14th June 1897.
[3] *Ibid.*, 14th June 1897.
[4] *Ibid.*, 16th June 1897.
[5] *Ibid.*, 18th June 1897. It seems probable from the private correspondence that the dubious witness was Myers' friend Miss Chaston.
[6] *Ibid.*, 19th June 1897.

letter from Professor John Milne, the seismologist, which has already been discussed. On the same day appeared a letter from Dr J. A. Menzies, an old friend of the Steuart family, who said that there had been a legend of the apparition of a white lady, who used to appear once or twice a year in one of the rooms. This had been exploded by a member of the family:

His common sense told him that there must be a reason for this; and he very soon discovered that when the moon was in a certain position, her image reflected from one mirror to another bore a certain resemblance to a white figure. So that ghost was laid. I may say in conclusion, that I have stayed often in the house, and never heard any noise of the sort mentioned as ghostly; and I never heard that the house had the reputation of being haunted.[1]

Finally, on 23rd June two letters were published which some might regard as bringing down the curtain on the alleged haunting of Ballechin House. Mr C. L. A. Skinner wrote:

I have slept at Ballechin many nights during the last 20 years and in more than one room. I have spoken to eight members of my family and friends who have also passed many nights there, and not one of us has ever seen anything or heard any strange noises. I was there a fortnight in 1879, in August and September, and again in 1883, and I never even heard talks or reports of supernatural noises.

I remember the late Mr John Steuart telling me that when he succeeded to the property, he found that the house needed a good deal of repair and that, from some cause or another, the result of the repairs was to cause a good deal of reverberation in the house. The stories about the 'wicked major' are untrue. His property was left by will to his nephew, Mr John Skinner, who took the name of Steuart, and his chief eccentricity lay in keeping a number of dogs in the house.[2]

Major S. F. C. Hamilton, of the 4th Lancashire Fusiliers, wrote with military brevity:

I have slept in Ballechin, the house of my late father-in-law, hundreds of times. I have never seen or heard a ghost or had my sleep interfered with. Ballechin has been in the family since the 15th century, and it has now been left to the Research Society to discover a ghost![3]

Ballechin was summed up in a long leading article in *The Scotsman* of 18th June 1897. After an epitome of some of the most interesting

[1] *The Times*, 21st June 1897.
[2] *Ibid.*, 23rd June 1897.
[3] *Ibid.*, 23rd June 1897.

and amusing criticisms, the writer gave his own impression of the controversy:

The secretary of the Psychical Society, Mr Myers, wrote repudiating on behalf of the Society, all connections with the Ballechin investigations. He had been down there with a medium, whose discoveries according to a statement made by Miss X to the reporter, were of no value. One is inclined to ask if any medium's discoveries could be of any value, and how the public can be expected to give any credence to investigations which, though professedly scientific, are conducted with such assistance. At any rate, Mr Myers made up his mind that there was nothing good enough for his Society. One of the witnesses wrote challenging Mr Myers' right to arrive at any such decision, and stated that not only had he not examined the evidence on which the phenomena were supposed to rest, but he had himself personally testified in writing his experience of them. The anxiety of the secretary of the Psychical Society to clear himself of the Ballechin Ghost does not speak very well for the methods of his Society. Ill-natured people may think that if the name had not come out, he would not have been so ready to repudiate responsibility, and would have been less critical of another of these anonymous stories of anonymous ghosts which adorn the pages of the Society's Proceedings . . . If Miss X and her associates can prove that there are sounds and sights to be heard and seen at Ballechin for which it is impossible to find any natural explanation, she may earn the medal of the P.R.S., but she will have done irreparable injury to the property. A house that is said to be haunted is bad enough, but a house that is proved to be haunted by systematic observations would not be fit for habitation. If, on the other hand, she merely confirms the account given in The Times, *there may be less to complain of. But whatever effect the business may have upon the reputation and value of Ballechin, it will certainly not make the public more enamoured of the methods of these pseudo-scientific ghost hunters. A method of investigation which begins with deception and must be conducted in secrecy is not very likely to lead to truth. Even if the veil had not been drawn from the Ballechin investigations would any one have accepted a collection of anonymous testimony as being of the slightest scientific value? And the light which has been thrown by the letters in* The Times *on the manner in which these so-called investigations were conducted is not calculated to inspire confidence. It is true that they have been repudiated by Mr Myers on behalf of the Psychical Society, but no doubt Miss X and the Ballechin party would be equally ready to repudiate the results obtained by him and his medium Miss ——. The general public have never quite taken these psychical investigators at their own valuation, and now that they have fallen out among themselves it will probably think less of them still. The only person for whom it is possible to have much sympathy in connection with the business is Mr Steuart, whose property has acquired such an unfortunate notoriety owing to the doings of these ghost hunters.*

Against the background of this assembly of contemporary comment, the most recently published assessment of the case by a modern writer is of interest. On the cover of the second edition of his *Between Two Worlds* (New York, 1967) the late Dr Nandor Fodor was described as 'the most amazing psychic investigator of our time'. On pp. 222 ff., after some criticisms of *The Haunting of Borley Rectory. A Critical Survey of the Evidence* (London, 1956) and my co-authors and myself, Dr Fodor turned his attention to Ballechin:

> The only point on which I wish to take issue with Harry Price in [is?] his claim that Borley Rectory was the most haunted house in England. Nothing but the 'most' could satisfy Harry Price's narcissism. For the sake of truth I want to state that the most haunted house in England (of which Harry Price must have been well aware, from extant literature) was Ballechin House in Perthshire.

This claim for the supremacy of Ballechin over Borley by Dr Fodor, whose lack of knowledge of both cases seems to me to have been profound, was based on Miss Freer's book and some inventions of his own, including an assertion on p. 224 that the house was haunted by 'a pack of phantom dogs'. He confessed (p. 229) that when he 'wrote to the family for information whether the house is peaceful or not, [he] received a very curt non-informative answer'.

Another modern writer, Dr Alan Gauld, makes no mention of Ballechin at all in his *The Founders of Psychical Research* (London, 1968). The omission is not an isolated one, for in this account of the activities of the S.P.R. and its leaders from the first beginnings to the early 1900s the author equally makes no reference to the Burton and Clandon affairs, nor to the Scottish second sight enquiry. Dr Gauld does not comment upon the several hundred letters to Lord Bute from Myers and the other persons involved in the matters discussed in the present work, whom it might be thought are inextricably involved in any balanced account of the early history of the S.P.R.

8

MISS FREER AND THE MEDIUMS

THERE CAN be no doubt that Miss Freer was angry with F. W. H. Myers for his desertion of her during the Ballechin upheaval which started on 8th June 1897. Apart from the evidence already adduced, she went to considerable lengths to prove that Myers was not to be trusted when she published her book on Ballechin in 1899. In the centre of an otherwise blank page following the title-page she printed the following:

I visited B—— representing that Society [*S.P.R.*], . . . *and decided that there was no such evidence as could justify us in giving the results of the inquiry a place in our* Proceedings.—The Times, *10th June 1897.*

FREDERIC W. H. MYERS
Hon. Sec. of the Society for Psychical Research

Compare pages 189 *et seq*

The pages quoted showed first, by reproducing Myers' letters, that he had enthusiastically believed in the worth of Ballechin as a case of haunting, and that it was his wish that Miss Freer should lecture to the S.P.R. on the subject. Miss Freer showed that Myers had described his experiences in the house in a series of letters to Lord Bute, afterwards withdrawing this testimony. She quoted Myers' expressed pleasure that her work had been so amply rewarded. The comparison which Miss Freer invited the reader to make, in the most prominent possible position in her book, could not fail to throw the gravest doubts on Myers' honesty of purpose. She had reason for her displeasure, but it may be thought that the extreme lengths to which she went in her book to denigrate him went deeper than the Ballechin affair itself.

I believe that Miss Freer was furious with Myers from 23rd April 1897, the day she discovered that a woman friend of his, Miss Jessica Iris Chaston, described by Miss Freer as 'a "medium" ' (the sarcastic inverted commas were hers), had been a member of the party during Myers' stay at Ballechin from 12th to 22nd April. The other members of Myers' 'little group', as he termed it in his letters to Lord Bute, were 'an intimate friend' named Colin Edmund Campbell, Miss Chaston, and a woman referred to in the correspondence as 'Mrs Loof', who like Miss Chaston is mentioned nowhere in the literature of psychical research and spiritualism. She was described as Miss Chaston's attendant. In addition, Dr (later Sir) Oliver Lodge and Mrs Lodge were there, but left Ballechin before the others.

Miss Freer had temporarily absented herself from Scotland on 9th April, and did not return until 28th April. Myers had no idea that she was coming back at all, as he revealed in his letter to Bute of 23rd April, in view of the fact that the tenancy was nearing its end. On 12th April, three days after he believed Miss Freer had left the house for good, Myers arrived at Ballechin. He returned home on 22nd April, leaving Miss Chaston behind with the intention that she would stay until Monday, 26th April, in company with Mr Campbell and Mrs Loof, because the weather was especially beautiful and beneficial to her health.

It would appear that Miss Freer heard of Miss Chaston's presence at Ballechin in a letter from Lodge written on 22nd April, after his return home, and which she received the following day. On Friday, 23rd April, Miss Freer telegraphed from London to the butler at Ballechin to say that Miss Chaston, Mrs Loof, and Mr Campbell 'must leave today without fail'. The pretext for this 'peremptory notice to quit', as it was described in the correspondence, was that another visitor, Mr Macphail, was coming to Ballechin as an observer. As the house was a large one with a full staff of servants, and had accommodated sizeable groups of observers throughout the period of the Enquiry and would in fact be without guests if Myers' 'little group' left, and as Mr Macphail was not expected until the afternoon of Monday, 26th April, it may be thought that the reason given by Miss Freer for the summary ejection of Miss Chaston was not the real one. It may be thought, too, that the procedure of telegraphing instructions to the butler to dismiss Miss Chaston and the others from the house was deliberately impolite. It was stated in Myers' letters to Bute of 2nd May 1897 that 'Miss Chaston is very indignant at Miss Freer's procedure'. Saying with embarrassment that he felt he owed Bute some account of the incident, Myers added that he would 'prefer not entering upon the matter with Miss Freer',

[1] This was C. E. Campbell of Ardpatrick (1870–1951), a Fellow of Trinity Hall, Cambridge, and a member of the S.P.R. See contemporary issues of Burke's *Landed Gentry*.

which was no doubt prudent in the face of this sudden appearance of the tigress' claws.

The private correspondence shows that Sidgwick was invited to intervene, but he was not successful. The most he could ascertain from Miss Freer was a denial of any personal antagonism towards Miss Chaston. This the reader may doubt, for in her book on Ballechin Miss Freer not only violently attacked Myers, but also included some singularly unpleasant passages about Miss Chaston.

Who and what was Miss Chaston? In Miss Freer's book she is simply referred to as 'a Miss C——', and we should not have known her name, other than from the personal correspondence, if it had not been inserted in the annotated copies of *The Alleged Haunting of B—— House*. In his letter to Bute of 2nd May 1897 Myers described her as 'a middle-aged lady, head of a hospital'. Both these statements were misleading, and one is entitled to speculate on the reason for this. Jessica Iris Chaston was thirty-three, some seven years younger than Miss Freer, and was therefore hardly middle-aged. She was the proprietress of an establishment described as a small private nursing home at 36 Devonshire Street, London, which was certainly not a hospital.

If she was a medium, which was ostensibly the reason why Myers took her to Ballechin, it is remarkable that so far as I am aware her name is mentioned nowhere in the literature of spiritualism and psychical research. It is difficult to understand, moreover, why Myers selected her for the séances he wanted to hold at Ballechin. The S.P.R., and Myers in particular, were in close touch with a number of well-known mediums at this period, and it therefore seems odd that Myers should have chosen an unknown young woman for his purpose.

Was Miss Chaston even a nurse, qualified to superintend a nursing home? Doubts were raised about this at the time, and these do not seem to have been fully resolved. After her visit to Ballechin, Lord Bute seems to have been sufficiently curious to question Myers about her, and afterwards to seek the opinion of Sir James Crichton-Browne. The latter in a letter to Lord Bute of 28th May 1897 commented upon some information given by Myers about Miss Chaston's supposed antecedents. This was capable of being checked, a task to which Sir James devoted some attention.

The correspondence makes it clear that Myers had said that Miss Chaston had previously been a nurse at Chelsea Infirmary and at Addenbrookes Hospital in Cambridge. As one of the leading medical authorities in the country, Sir James was in a favourable position to ascertain whether these assertions regarding Miss Chaston's respectability had any foundation in fact. On 6th June 1897 he wrote to Lord Bute to say that he had satisfied himself that Miss Chaston was not a state registered nurse, and had never been a member of the Royal British Nursing Association. He enclosed letters from the Matrons at both Chelsea and Addenbrookes, both of whom had searched their records and declared that they had never heard of Miss Chaston. What Sir James did discover was that Miss Chaston had probably been employed for three years at Fulbourn Asylum, Cambridge.

The circumstances of Miss Chaston's subsequent career were as unusual and obscure as those surrounding her stay at Ballechin. In 1900 Jessica Iris Chaston left 36 Devonshire Street and went to live with a gentleman calling himself Earle Wellington Jenks at 38 Ashworth Mansions, Elgin Avenue, Maida Vale. In her will made on 21st April 1902 she left all her estate (amounting to about £300) to Mr Jenks. She died on 17th November 1903 at the age of thirty-nine, being described on her death certificate as Jessica Iris Trevor, the wife of Earle Wellington Jenks Trevor, although she and Mr Trevor (or Jenks, as he had previously called himself) were never married. The cause of death was mitral disease of the heart, established for several years, general oedema, which she had contracted four months previously, and acute oedema of the lungs, from which she had suffered for ten hours.

In his letter to Bute of 23rd April 1897 before the storm broke, Myers said of the visit to Ballechin, 'It so happened that both Miss Chaston and Mrs Loof were much out of health at the time and were greatly benefited by the change.' This remark does not fit very well with the comment by Miss Freer (who does not seem to have met Miss Chaston) in her book that Miss Chaston 'was described as in weak health and partially paralysed'.[1] Even if this description was true, which we are entitled to doubt, it was a singularly unkind remark to record in print. Miss Chaston was evidently not in robust health, but she was quite well enough to make the long journey from London to Perthshire. Both she and Mrs Loof 'were much out of health at the time', according to Myers, but their indisposition seems to have been such that a change of location and country air were very beneficial. Miss Chaston's later association with Mr Jenks (or Trevor), moreover, does not suggest that she was suffering from any permanent disability other than a heart condition.[2]

[1] *The Alleged Haunting of B—— House*, p. 185.

[2] It is odd that at least two other women with whom Myers had associations did not enjoy good health. Mrs Marshall, the wife of his first cousin, who committed suicide in 1876 after a three-year affair with Myers, was 'constantly in ill-

Miss Freer's printed comments on the psychic messages received, through Miss Chaston's alleged mediumship at Ballechin, the details of which had first been sent by Myers to Bute and then withdrawn, were sarcastic and scathing:

These remarkable disclosures included, among other details, the murder of a Roman Catholic family chaplain, at a period when the S[teuarts] were and had long been Presbyterian, the suicide of one of the family who is still living, and the throwing, by persons in mediaeval costume, of the corpse of an infant, over a bridge, which is quite new, into a stream which until lately ran underground.[1]

She remarked in print, too, that after her return to Ballechin on 28th April 1897 she enquired of the servants what had occurred during her absence. They had, she wrote, 'very definite views as to the nature and causes of the phenomena during the visit of Mr Myers' party'.[2] All this makes it clear that Miss Freer regarded Miss Chaston's mediumship, if such existed at all, as entirely fraudulent, and was prepared to say so in print in terms which seem to me to have been both malicious and defamatory.

It is of some interest in this connexion to notice that Miss Freer was also to criticize Myers bitterly in print in 1899 in her book on Ballechin over his partiality for 'the experiences of female mediums, whether hired or gratuitous', and for introducing with approval into S.P.R. *Proceedings* 'reports of spiritualist phenomena, and the lucubrations of mediums',[3] in a tirade in which the emotional overtones were very obvious.

This attack had, of course, to await the publication of *The Alleged Haunting of B—— House*, which in 1897 had not yet been written. We may notice, however, that Miss Freer found something unpleasant to say about her former friend Myers in print in *Borderland* within a few weeks of the Ballechin quarrel. In July 1897, in an article 'Psychical Research in the Victorian Era',[4] she wrote that Myers, who she coldly described as this 'important official', was imposing his influence upon the S.P.R. literature to such an extent 'that one can no longer allege that the S.P.R. is not committed to Spiritualism'. She regretted the 'loss of freshness and vigour' of the Society compared with its work in early years, and said that the

[1] *The Alleged Haunting of B—— House*, p. 192. [2] *Ibid.*, pp. 199–200.
[3] *Ibid.*, p. 183. [4] *Borderland*, 1897, vol. IV, pp. 247–53.

health' according to Dr Gauld, as was Mrs Constance Turner, who died in August 1890 at the age of twenty-five, a matter of four months after her meetings with Myers at Folkestone (*Journal*, S.P.R., June 1964, pp. 318 and 320). Miss Freer, who outlived Myers, was an exception.

present organization under the direction of Myers had 'nothing corresponding to the S.P.R. of old days', which, she said, used to publish excellent papers by a number of notable members. These she listed by name, mentioning Edmund Gurney and Professor and Mrs Sidgwick among others, but pointedly excluding Myers.

It is of additional interest to notice that within a few months of the Ballechin affair her new-found hatred of mediums spilled over into a public attack in a lecture actually delivered to an audience of spiritualists. On 17th December 1897 Miss Freer gave an address to the London Spiritualist Alliance at St James's Hall in London. The Chairman was Col G. le Mesurier Taylor, her colleague at Ballechin, who incautiously introduced her (without knowing what was to come) as 'a most acute and sympathetic observer of psychical phenomena'.[1] In her talk, which she entitled 'Hauntings', she defended the investigation of Ballechin House, which she said had been ignored by the Society for Psychical Research, despite the fact that Myers had recorded experiences during his stay there. She said that it was a matter of the deepest regret that a Society which existed for the purpose of investigation should have washed its hands of a case 'with the most complete and best authenticated record of alleged haunting which it was possible to obtain'.[2]

It was at the conclusion of her remarks that Miss Freer made her bitter observation in regard to mediums. She had previously devoted many pages of *Borderland* to a consistent support of their claims, writing, for example, in most favourable terms of the mediumship of Mrs Leonore Piper, W. Stainton Moses, and Eusapia Paladino. She was now reported as saying to an audience of members of the London Spiritualist Alliance that she strongly dissented from their practice of employing such mediums, 'a class with which she had no sympathy whatever, and for which she wished to express an entire lack of toleration'.[3]

From one who had herself been the actual medium at the Burton seances, such an outburst to a roomful of believers might be thought to be both unbecoming and most unwise. It was, moreover, a complete change in the public attitude she had maintained so consistently and successfully during many years of sitting on the fence, by displaying, on the one hand, a respectable but tolerant agnosticism

[1] *Light*, 1st January 1898, p. 7. [2] *Ibid.*, 8th January 1898, p. 17.

[3] *Ibid.*, 8th January 1898, p. 17. Miss Freer had previously mildly dissociated herself from spiritualism when it suited her to do so. In her letter of 8th October 1896, printed in the *Oban Times*, she wrote of 'the superstition of spiritualism', while earlier in the same year she had denied she was a medium in a letter to the *Inverness Courier* on 8th May.

towards spiritualism, while, on the other, claiming supernatural powers of her own and acting as the paid assistant editor of an occult periodical. It may be thought, too, that this sudden and reckless abandonment, in circumstances that could hardly have been less appropriate, of her previous position in which she had obtained the best of both worlds, displayed a motivation that was almost certainly emotional in its origins. The lecture was reported in successive issues of the spiritualist periodical *Light* of 1st and 8th January 1898, accompanied by fierce criticism of Miss Freer's disparagement of mediums. The leading article of 1st January was wholly devoted to this, accompanied by the publication of hostile and sarcastic correspondence, but this did not prevent Miss Freer from returning unrepentant to the attack as soon as an opportunity publicly to do so presented itself.

On 5th December 1898 Frank Podmore, the Joint Honorary Secretary of the S.P.R., gave an address to the Sesame Club in London on the Society's experiments with the medium Mrs Leonore Piper.[1] Miss Freer rose to speak during the discussion and was reported as saying:

She had known many mediums, and she had disliked them all. They were emotionally flabby, coarse and irreverent, much given to inflict upon you morality of the copy-book order.

She then extended her criticism to include the S.P.R. (and, of course, Myers) for experimenting with Mrs Piper, causing pain and suffering to the wretched medium. She was reported as actually saying:

Her strongest reason for objecting to the Piper experiments was the gross brutality of the whole thing. Had they a right to subject a fellow-creature to such convulsions—apparently epileptic fits—as Mrs Piper exhibited in her trances, even for the purpose of scientific discovery? She had had Mrs Piper at her feet in tears, begging to be saved from the kind of life she was leading.[2]

It is hardly necessary to say that this outburst created an uproar.

Mrs Bessie Russell-Davies made a spirited and caustic reply to Miss Freer's attack on mediums. She (Mrs Davies) was a Spiritualist, and not only a Spiritualist, but one of those vulgar and degraded mediums.[3]

The controversy thus started by Miss Freer continued for many

[1] 'Parleying with Spirits', *Light*, 17th December 1898, pp. 612–13.

[2] *Light*, 17th December 1898, p. 613.

[3] *Ibid.*, p. 613.

weeks in the pages of *Light*. Dr Richard Hodgson of the S.P.R. wrote that Mrs Piper 'was indignant at Miss Freer's remarks as reported in *Light*'. He said that no such incident between Mrs Piper and Miss Freer, as described by the latter, had ever occurred, and that Mrs Piper had never suffered at the hands of the S.P.R. He inferred that there had been little personal contact between the two ladies at all, and that 'the starting point for Miss Freer's misrepresentations' was probably an occasion when both had been in Cambridge and had been walking through the College grounds (presumably Trinity) with Myers and a friend, who had momentarily walked on in front leaving Mrs Piper and Miss Freer together. Hodgson quoted from a letter written to him by Mrs Piper on 5th January 1899 after the incident at the Sesame Club, in which the medium said that she had never suffered pain during her trances, and had never told anybody, including Miss Freer, that she did.[1]

In her reply, published a week later,[2] Miss Freer said that it was Dr A. T. Myers[3] of the S.P.R., the brother of F. W. H. Myers, who had asked her to visit Mrs Piper in London, 'where, not at Cambridge, the incidents to which I have referred took place'. As for Mrs Piper's denials that she had suffered 'gross brutality' at the hands of the S.P.R., Miss Freer wrote, 'It does not surprise me that Mrs Piper's memory should appear to be affected by her experiences.'

At the end of her reply Miss Freer declared that as regards the remarks attributed to her at the Sesame Club, she could not hold herself responsible for a newspaper report of anything she said. The room was crowded, she wrote, and hearing was difficult. This was instantly seized upon by her critics. A correspondent wrote to say that he had been sitting close to Miss Freer and 'heard all too plainly the words which fell from her lips. They do not look pretty in print, but Miss Freer must take their entire responsibility.'[4] The Editor added that the report in *Light* was perfectly accurate.[5] This giving of the lie to Miss Freer was supported by Mrs Bessie Russell-

[1] 'Miss Freer and Mrs Piper', *Light*, 4th February 1899, pp. 55–6.

[2] *Ibid., Light*, 11th February 1899, p. 67.

[3] As the reader knows, it was not Miss Freer's habit to reveal the actual names of the witnesses she claimed were involved in her stories. The example of her friend 'the Hon. Mrs G., now abroad', who she declared could corroborate her account of the Burton sittings, will be recalled. She was safe, however, in the case of Dr A. T. Myers, who had died of a self-administered overdose of narcotics on 10th January 1894, five years previously (*The Strange Case of Edmund Gurney*, pp. 12, 16, and 199).

[4] 'Miss Goodrich-Freer and Mrs Piper', *Light*, 18th February 1899, p. 83.

[5] *Ibid.*, p. 83.

Davies, who wrote to say that she had been present at the Sesame Club, and assured her readers that all that Miss Freer 'had to say in regard to Mrs Piper, and her abuse of other mediums, was very distinctly heard by myself and your very trustworthy reporter, who sat on the chair next to me, and I made it my business to ask him if he heard distinctly'. Mrs Davies concluded her remarks by saying:

I know her [*Miss Freer*] *personally, and believe her to be distinctly incapable of forming a reliable opinion on psychic subjects from* her own observation—*what she may have read or gleaned from others' experience does not count for anything. Her patronising pity for 'poor Mrs Piper' is wasted, and I cannot help feeling sorry for her when I see that she has to resort to throwing doubts on your reporter to escape the consequences of her attack on Mrs Piper, Spiritualism, and 'all mediums'. I very much regret that 'all mediums' were not present to hear her opinion of them; if they had been I fancy she would in future have to depend entirely on her own 'mediumship' for something to talk about, and the result would then be very small indeed.*[1]

The dispute spread to America. Miss Lilian Whiting of the American branch of the S.P.R., writing from Boston, Mass., said:

It is amazing to all those who are familiar with the trance phenomena exhibited through Mrs Piper, and with the earnest, sincere, and most faithful and enlightened work of Dr Hodgson, in the patient investigation of years, that any intelligent person can make the singularly reckless statements regarding Mrs Piper that appear over the signature of Miss Freer.[2]

The year 1899 marked a climacteric in Miss Freer's career, and no doubt she took stock of her position. The Ballechin quarrel with Myers and her emotional reaction to it had lost her at one stroke the sympathy of both the spiritualists and the S.P.R., the two main classes of credulous persons upon whom she had relied over the years for part of her living and her literary ambitions. She had deserted her benefactor W. T. Stead in favour of Lord Bute, and *Borderland* had ceased publication two years before. Her comfortable home with her friend Constance Moore's family, with whom she had first lived at Holy Trinity Vicarage, Paddington, and later at 27 Cleveland Gardens,[3] had ceased, and Miss Freer and Miss Moore had set up

[1] 'Mrs Piper and Miss Goodrich-Freer', *Light*, 25th February 1899, p. 95.

[2] 'Miss Goodrich-Freer and Mrs Piper', *Light*, 11th March 1899, p. 112.

[3] Although Miss Freer was only a guest at 27 Cleveland Gardens, she invariably referred to this address as 'my London house' in her letters to Lord Bute.

house together at The Laurels, Bushey Heath. In April 1899 Miss Freer and Miss Moore had relinquished their part-time appointments at Swanley Horticultural College, following a difference of view with the governing body. On 31st July Miss Freer wrote to Lord Bute that she had 'lately given away a psychic library', presumably her own, suggesting that her interest in the subject was ending.

On the other hand, Miss Freer had the invaluable folklore material she had obtained from Fr Allan McDonald during the second sight expeditions to the Highlands and the Isles in previous years, of which she was already making free use in her career as a writer and lecturer. Preparations for what was ultimately to be virtually a complete change from psychical research to folklore as the subject for her literary work had already begun concurrently with her first attacks on Myers and the mediums in July and November 1897. From the last months of 1897 to her departure from England at the end of 1901 she was to lecture on Hebridean folklore and history to the Viking Club, the Folklore Society, the Scottish Society of Literature and Art, the Gaelic Society of Glasgow, and similar institutions, and articles over her name on these subjects were published in *The Contemporary Review*, *Blackwood's Edinburgh Magazine* and other journals of the period.[1]

The other important advantage she still enjoyed in 1899 was the continued patronage of Lord Bute, who took the side of Miss Freer in the quarrel with Myers and the S.P.R., and it was his help that enabled her to publish her book on the case in 1899 with his name on the title-page as co-author. Unfortunately for her, Lord Bute was to suffer his first apoplectic attack in August 1899, to be followed by a second seizure on 8th October 1900, to which he succumbed the next day without rallying.

Miss Freer's first book, *Essays in Psychical Research*, a collection of material previously published in periodicals, appeared in May 1899. It was scathingly reviewed by Dr Richard Hodgson of the S.P.R.[2] Hodgson said the book dealt with its subject in the popular manner of *Borderland* rather than in any scientific way, which would reduce its value and interest for many readers. He complained that in her essay on the divining rod she had used material of Sir William Barrett, previously in S.P.R. *Proceedings*, without acknowledgment. But Hodgson had most to say about Miss Freer's 'misrepresentation of fact' regarding Mrs Piper, and brought out again the whole of the controversy in *Light*. The reviewer implied, with perfect truth and

[1] For a list of these articles and lectures see p. 227.

[2] *Proceedings*, S.P.R., 1899, vol. XIV, pp. 393–6.

possibly with inside knowledge, that on the subject of mediums Miss Freer's views were emotional and obsessional.

Miss Freer is evidently labouring under an idée fixe, *which perhaps began between two and three years ago, and has become more strongly established since.*

In my opinion Dr Hodgson's dating of the beginning of Miss Freer's obsession in regard to mediums is correct, in that it commenced at the time of the quarrel with Myers over Miss Chaston in the spring of 1897.

A few weeks later *The Alleged Haunting of B—— House* was published. The S.P.R. review by Frank Podmore[1] was seriously critical, as could have been expected. Podmore said that Miss Freer's 'laborious journal' of her stay in the house was 'quite unimpressive', although conceding that if experiments in other allegedly haunted houses had been described in a similar way 'they might be found to make even duller reading'. The reviewer complained that no attempt had been made to ascertain the source of the sounds, or 'even to have determined whether or not the sounds which they described day after day were objective'. Podmore added:

But, after all, the main reason why the recital of these various manifestations fails to impress us has still to be told. It was Miss Freer who first saw a ghostly figure; it was again Miss Freer who first heard ghostly noises, and throughout these records it is Miss Freer who is most frequently and most conspicuously favoured with 'phenomena'. Miss Freer has shown that she knows how to observe clearly and how to record accurately, but, for all that, her testimony in a matter of this kind carries very little weight.

Podmore, after commenting upon Miss Freer's unusual liability to hallucinations, although conceding that she was 'not of course responsible for this mental idiosyncrasy', said that it must seriously impair the value of her testimony. He thought that the apparition of the nun Ishbel 'had her birth in the percipient's imagination'. Podmore said that of the remainder of the odds and ends of reported phenomena 'it is hardly necessary to speak'. It is odd that nowhere in the review did Podmore mention the name of Miss Freer's co-author, Lord Bute.

[1] *Proceedings*, S.P.R., 1900, vol. XV, pp. 98–100.

9

MISS FREER, SWANLEY, AND THE LAST YEARS

DURING HER last years in England Miss Freer maintained a correspondence with Fr Allan McDonald, most of which has unfortunately been destroyed. His diary, however, kept from September 1897 to June 1898, shows that it was extensive. One of her objects seems to have been to obtain his help in translations from Gaelic, a language with which she was not familiar, for her purpose in making use of his folklore material over her own name. From his side there seems to be little doubt that Fr Allan had 'fallen' rather badly for Miss Freer, as most men she met seemed to do in one way or another. A sentimental attachment of this kind, entirely innocent in its nature, would be quite normal in Fr Allan's circumstances. He was living in isolation and celibacy and was not in good health, and to have an attractive and intelligent woman arrive in Eriskay and tell him that his folklore collection was of scientific value and encourage him to collect more would mean a very great deal to him. It seems fairly obvious, however, from his diary entries that his emotions were involved. If an expected letter from Miss Freer did not arrive, he was acutely disappointed and entered the fact in his diary. He wrote that his friendship with Miss Freer had been 'an education of mind and soul, and has thrown sunshine over the last two years of my life'. In his diary he called her sometimes the 'lady of the ghosts', but more often simply 'the little lady'. He wrote, 'The more I know of Miss Freer the holier she seems. May God ever guide her and have her in His keeping.' Miss Freer does not seem to have returned this affectionate regard, for on occasions Fr Allan noted ruefully in his diary that she sometimes even confused him with Fr MacDougall, the parish priest of Benbecula, and that letters from her went astray in consequence. But there can be no doubt that she kept Fr Allan's nose to the grindstone in connexion with the work that she invited him to do, and that Fr Allan willingly followed her instructions. His diary records *inter alia* that he spent many hours answering lists of questions sent to him, gathering information which she required for papers and lectures, lending her his MSS., and translating material for her that had been written in Gaelic.

A few surviving letters from Miss Freer to Fr Allan McDonald throw some light on her life at this period. She and Miss Constance Moore were still living together at The Laurels, Bushey Heath, in 1900, the year in which Miss Freer's book on Ballechin House had evidently been sufficiently successful to justify a second and revised edition. Despite this, there seem to have been financial difficulties. As Lady Margaret Macrae wrote in a letter already quoted, Lord Bute died in 1900 and his help ceased in that year. Doubtless to her surprise and disappointment, Miss Freer was not mentioned in Lord Bute's will. Miss Moore had to take a job in London to make ends meet. 'Alas! I am tied to work in town now, and only get week-ends of holiday,' she wrote to Fr Allan in June in response to his suggestion that she might revisit the Hebrides.[1] The two friends were looking for a smaller house ('the object of moving is economy,' wrote Miss Freer to Fr Allan in October), but without success.

Miss Freer had suffered a severe breakdown during the winter of 1900–1, and 'was very ill for some months' as she wrote to Fr Allan on 28th August 1901. One wonders what was the cause of this collapse on the part of a woman who had always boasted of her exceptional health and vigour. 'I am *so tired*,' she wrote in the same letter to Fr Allan. She had, of course, expended much energy in the preceding years in writing, lecturing, ghost-hunting, touring the Highlands and the Isles, and in public controversy. On the other hand, she was only forty-four, and was still sufficiently youthful in appearance to pass as at least ten years less than her real age.[2] The breakdown was, moreover, a temporary one despite its evident severity, as was demonstrated by the active life of travel and literary activity she was soon to resume.

If one looks for some special cause for Miss Freer's breakdown at this time, it is reasonable to recall that F. W. H. Myers died on 17th January 1901. On the assumption that there had been a relationship between Myers and Miss Freer from the days of her introduction

[1] Miss Moore's letters to Fr Allan, her only personal papers I have seen, suggest that she was a very sincere, sympathetic, and rather colourless person, completely dominated by Miss Freer. It is interesting that she never joined the S.P.R., despite her companionship with Miss Freer over many years, including the expeditions to the Hebrides and the stay at Ballechin. The reason is presumably that stated by Miss Freer in her letter to Bute of 25th January 1896 in which she said that Miss Moore 'scorns the whole subject' of psychical research.

[2] Four years after Myers' death Miss Freer married Dr H. H. Spoer, who was sixteen years her junior yet who seems to have believed that his wife was about his own age.

to the S.P.R., then the death of possibly the first man in her life could have been a sufficiently severe shock to precipitate her illness. Her emotional attacks upon him after the Ballechin quarrel over Miss Chaston would, I fancy, support this view rather than the reverse, as would the coincidence of her breakdown with the time of Myers' last illness and death and a remark in her letter to Fr Allan McDonald that if it were not for Miss Moore she would seriously consider retiring into a convent.

Another mystery connected with Miss Freer's health, and possibly her sex life, at this precise period, is contained in a single letter passing between two ladies who knew her well, and who shall be nameless. The letter is dated 28th February 1901, six weeks after Myers' death.

She [Miss Freer] talks of coming to live in London, and asked me if I would go and 'stroke' her sometimes as it does her good. I don't think that can all be flattery, because she couldn't stand it if it didn't do her some good, but on the other hand she must know I should enjoy immensely doing anything of the sort.

Dr Campbell is of the opinion that this letter means that Miss Freer wanted her friend to soothe and flatter her during this period of disturbed health and low spirits. Dr E. J. Dingwall, on the other hand, takes the view that Miss Freer was seeking the pleasures of flagellation, as demonstrated by the suggestion that the experience would be one Miss Freer would find difficulty in enduring but for the benefit it brought her, and that her partner in what was proposed would herself obtain immense enjoyment from beating Miss Freer. The word 'stroke', placed in quotation marks by the writer of the letter, would lend itself to either interpretation.

Whatever the answers to these questions may be, it is clear that in the early months of 1901 Miss Freer was not her usual self, and had been through a period of ill-health and mental depression. The point is a not unimportant one, because there seems to be no doubt that during the summer of 1901 something occurred that irretrievably damaged Miss Freer's reputation as a psychical researcher and clairvoyante. There is some evidence to show that she was detected in fraud for the first time since the commencement of her career in the late 1880s. She had previously avoided exposure over this long period by shrewdly confining her activities to crystal-gazing, shell-hearing, clairvoyance, the seeing of apparitions, and so forth, all of which relied entirely upon her own plausibility and the avoidance, as we have seen, of any investigation of her stories by the consistent concealment of names and locations in her accounts. An explanation of her downfall at this time could be that her normal extreme caution had been impaired by ill-health.

I believe that the incident, the occurrence of which has been concealed until now, took place shortly before 13th August 1901. On that day Alexander Carmichael, who had spoken in earlier days in such glowing terms of Miss Freer, wrote cautiously to Fr Allan that he thought it right to tell him that news had reached him from London 'that Miss Freer is not altogether what she seems, and draws upon her imagination a good deal for her facts. I deem it right to tell you this much, my dear friend'. It may be thought that it would be a considerable embarrassment to Carmichael to make even this small preliminary disclosure to a close friend in the far-away Hebrides, for he knew that Fr Allan had an affectionate and high regard for Miss Freer, an opinion that Carmichael had previously shared with enthusiasm. But Carmichael was a conscientious person, no doubt concerned, in the light of what was being whispered in London, at the influence he knew Miss Freer could exert over the unsuspecting Fr Allan in distant Eriskay. 'I fear', wrote Carmichael to Fr Allan, 'that I think less of Miss Freer than I did.' Having broken the ice, Carmichael followed the matter up with a more positive statement in a further letter to Fr Allan on 7th October 1901.

We hear from various sources that Miss Freer is not genuine and some call her a clever imposter. I never got my wife to believe in her. In London it is said that one society after another, and one man after another, have thrown her off.

Finally, on 25th March 1902, Carmichael made specific reference to the incident and disclosed in his letter to Fr Allan that it had occurred in the village of Swanley in Kent, where 'they turned upon her for her lies, pretence and imposture', and Miss Freer 'had to clear out'. Most unfortunately, Carmichael gave no other details or identification of the occurrence, merely adding, 'Quite a number of her friends in London have found her out and will not have anything to do with her'. It seemed probable from this, but not certain, that this ostracism stemmed from the Swanley exposure.

The suggestion that Carmichael's letters constituted a developing account of the embarrassing discovery of Miss Freer in fraud is possibly confirmed by her own letter to Fr Allan already quoted of 28th August 1901. This was written a matter of only two weeks after the first letter from Carmichael. It clearly referred to some recent disturbing episode, for she apologized for not writing for so long, and gave as the reason that she had experienced 'much anxiety and uncertainty about various matters'. She said, moreover, that Mrs Jenner, the wife of Henry Jenner of the British Museum, the authority on the old Cornish language and a near neighbour at Bushey Heath, was saying that Miss Freer and Miss Constance Moore had quarrelled after living together for twenty-one years. The truth of the matter, explained Miss Freer, who did not deny the fact of the parting, was that Miss Moore had had 'severe family troubles', that it was now 'necessary for her to be much in London', and that it would be better for her to be 'among her relatives which is what *they* want'. Miss Freer said that she and Miss Moore were disposing of The Laurels, for which they had received a satisfactory offer,[1] and Miss Freer was accepting an invitation to visit the Holy Land.

What was the incident at Swanley? For some time I thought that it might be connected with Miss Freer's resignation of her post as a joint secretary, with Miss Moore, of the women's branch of the Swanley Horticultural College in April 1899, but I now think this improbable for four reasons. First, the resignation had taken place over two years before Carmichael's letters to Fr Allan on the subject of the downfall of Miss Freer at Swanley, the whole tone of which suggested a recent occurrence. Secondly, the notion that Miss Freer had been discovered in lies, pretence, and especially *imposture*, in carrying out her prosaic part-time duties on the secretarial staff of a horticultural college, seemed divorced from reality. Thirdly, Miss Moore also resigned on the same date from her similar position, which indicates that the reason was one which concerned both joint secretaries, who could scarcely have both been detected in imposture and lies. Finally, Carmichael's quotation of the expressed opinions that Miss Freer was 'not genuine' and was 'a clever imposter', and his reference to her consequent ostracism by her friends in London, point clearly, or so it seems to me, to Miss Freer's activities in psychical research, a subject in which imposture and lack of genuineness are unfortunately exceedingly common.

It follows that I believe that the Swanley location was coincidental, and that the disaster that overtook Miss Freer in that village in the summer of 1901 had nothing to do with her appointment at the horticultural college in earlier years. If this is accepted, then it can be said at once that the hypothesis that Miss Freer was exposed as a fraud in psychical research activities at Swanley would offer a more adequate explanation than that given by Miss Freer for the parting

[1] An attempt to discover whether The Laurels was jointly owned by Miss Freer and Miss Moore or, as seems more probable, was the sole property of Miss Moore, has not been successful.

with Miss Moore. It would account for Miss Freer's decision to leave England and the cessation of her membership of the S.P.R., and would provide a reason for the disappearance of all the files dealing with her affairs from the Society's archives. It would explain the suppression of all approving references to her in the publication of Sidgwick's 'Journal' in *Henry Sidgwick. A Memoir* five years later, and the surprising fact that after 1901 Miss Freer's name was scarcely ever mentioned again in S.P.R. literature, despite her large and enthusiastically praised contributions to the early volumes of *Proceedings*.

I told Dr Campbell, when he posed the problem of Swanley in his first letter to me, that there was no mention of any such incident in the entire published literature of psychical research so far as I was aware, and that an investigation of such a postulated event of over sixty years ago, mentioned only once and without details in private correspondence of the period, might well present insuperable difficulties. It was a sobering thought that our knowledge of the matter was limited to the occurrence of the presumed incident in the small village of Swanley during the summer of 1901, although it was a reasonable inference from the disappearance of the S.P.R. files that the Society was involved, and had hushed the matter up because of Miss Freer's prominence in that organization. These were the only slender leads we possessed.

An examination of the published work of the S.P.R. leaders at this period produced one very interesting clue. In 1902 Frank Podmore's book *Modern Spiritualism* appeared. To his discussion of the mediumship of Mrs Leonore Piper in the second volume he had added a footnote, presumably at a late stage in the preparation of the MS.

So far as I am aware, no other clairvoyant medium of note since 1848 has failed at one time or another to exhibit physical phenomena, if only to the extent of table-rapping, as part of her mediumistic gifts.

Podmore added that sometimes these physical phenomena, which, according to him, *all* clairvoyant mediums except Mrs Piper had exhibited, 'have not been made public at all'. It seems to me that the addition of this footnote by Podmore, buried though it is in a book of nearly seven hundred pages, is of the highest importance in connexion with the mystery before us. Miss Freer had been one of the most prominent clairvoyantes ever associated with the S.P.R. in its early years, sponsored by Myers and enthusiastically commended by Sidgwick, Crookes, and others. Podmore knew her well, and it

[1] *Modern Spiritualism*, London, 1902, vol. II, p. 332, n. i.

is impossible to believe that he had forgotten about her when he wrote this footnote. Yet Podmore, having just completed *Modern Spiritualism*, the most complete survey of the subject ever attempted either then or now, was the one man who knew better than anyone else that there was *nothing in the published literature* that even hinted that Miss Freer had ever departed from her chosen and safe field of clairvoyance, visions, telepathy, shell-hearing, and the like. We may therefore think, on the basis of this footnote, that Podmore had become privately aware, some time shortly before 1902, that Miss Freer had indulged in table-rapping, the crudest of all forms of fraudulent spiritualist phenomena, or had exhibited some other alleged manifestations of the séance room. Was this the postulated incident at Swanley? It can at least be said that the dates coincide, and it may also be thought that if Miss Freer did try her hand at table-rapping without the advantage of experience, at a time when her physical and mental health was not good, these could well be the circumstances in which she was at long last caught out in trickery.

Carrying the argument further, it may be thought that the inner circle of the S.P.R. would be aghast at the discovery of Miss Freer in fraud. Previous disasters, like the enforced printed withdrawals in *Proceedings* of the ludicrous stories of Sir Edmund Hornby and 'Mr X.Z.', the exposures of the Society's pet mediums Miss Wood and Miss Fairlamb, the confession of trickery by the 'mind-reading' Creery sisters, the suicide of Edmund Gurney in 1888,[1] and the subsequent upheavals over Clandon and Ballechin, had made the S.P.R. sensitive and vulnerable over any further embarrassment in connexion with its published work. The panicking by Myers and Sidgwick and the immediate desertion of Miss Freer in the face of the first criticism of Ballechin had been entirely symptomatic of this anxiety. It is obvious, moreover, that the silence over Swanley, the obliteration of Miss Freer's name from the S.P.R. literature after 1901, the disappearance of all the files of matters with which she had been concerned, and the suppression of Sidgwick's early praise of her qualities are facts which must have *some* explanation.

All this pointed in one direction, and that was to Swanley. The theory now to be put to the test envisaged that there was in Swanley a house in which Miss Freer had been caught in fraudulently producing physical phenomena, of which Podmore had specifically mentioned table-rapping, and that as a result Miss Freer had been forced to 'clear out'. The circumstances also suggested the possibility that it was from Miss Freer's disillusioned host that Podmore received the private information on which his guarded footnote was

[1] These affairs are discussed in my *The Strange Case of Edmund Gurney*.

based. Since, however, the S.P.R. was able to keep the matter secret to some extent, an additional inference might be that the unknown person in Swanley, despite his or her annoyance, had reason not to be anxious to have the matter noised abroad. It seemed increasingly clear that we were looking for someone in Swanley who knew both Miss Freer and Podmore, and membership of the S.P.R. seemed the most obvious connexion between them and the postulated unknown person. The List of Members of the S.P.R. dated February 1901 was consulted and showed only one name in Swanley, the Rev. Charles J. M. Shaw, living at a house called The Orchard. This discovery was of extreme interest, for it will be recalled that the annotated copies of *The Alleged Haunting of B——* reveal that the Rev. Shaw had been one of Miss Freer's visitors at Ballechin House; he had also been a member of one of her *Borderland* spiritualist circles. According to John Ritchie Findlay Mr Shaw had 'a thorough belief in the supernatural'.

The Rev. Shaw's connexion with Podmore was of equal interest. At some time prior to May 1900 Mr Shaw had invited a professional medium, Alfred Peters, to be his guest at The Orchard, where demonstrations of clairvoyance were given. A second visit to The Orchard was paid by Peters in May 1900 for further clairvoyance, which was however followed by an exhibition of physical phenomena, this having been forecast by Mr Peter's 'Hindu control' at the séances.

The Rev. Shaw decided that as an S.P.R. member he should give an account of these sittings, which had greatly impressed him, to the Society. He evidently thought that Frank Podmore was the appropriate person to whom the story should be told. Podmore recorded that Mr Shaw first gave him a verbal account of the sittings with Peters in November 1900 and later sent him a detailed written statement on 6th February 1901. This was published by the S.P.R. with an introductory note by Podmore in July 1901.[1] Podmore repeated the story in *Modern Spiritualism* (vol. II, pp. 259–62) without, however, revealing that the séances took place at Swanley, so that this place-name does not appear in the book or its index. The account was mainly devoted to the physical phenomena exhibited by Peters.

In July 1901 Miss Freer was without a patron, and on the evidence of her correspondence with Fr Allan McDonald was short of money at the time. In July 1901 Miss Freer would learn from her

[1] *Journal*, S.P.R., July 1901, pp. 104–9. In his account Mr Shaw made it clear that he had 'engaged the services' of the medium, from which it is proper to conclude that Peters was paid a fee.

S.P.R. *Journal* that the Rev. C. J. M. Shaw, her supporter at Ballechin and a member of one of her Borderland spiritualist circles, had twice hospitably entertained a professional medium as a guest at his home and had been much impressed by the phenomena he had seen.

Miss Freer would also know, having been acquainted with the Rev. Shaw since the Ballechin affair in 1897, that he was no ordinary vicar. She had described him, indeed, four years earlier in her letter to Lord Bute of 17th March 1897, as a man of means and position. He was a member of the great Kentish family of Shaw of Eltham, and became the eighth Baronet in 1909. He had married Elizabeth Louisa Whatman Bosanquet, the daughter of J. E. Bosanquet of Pennenden and Claysmore, and of Lombard Street. To Miss Freer, who had lost the patronage of Lord Bute by his death in the previous year, Mr Shaw might well seem to be a useful person to be cultivated by an early visit to The Orchard at Swanley.

All this was, of course, an elaborate inference from the few facts available. I suggested to Dr Campbell that the theory could be confirmed or otherwise by an approach to the ninth Baronet, Sir John Best-Shaw, to enquire whether he knew that a Miss Freer did in fact visit his father at The Orchard, Swanley, in 1901. If that was established, then it might be thought that the Swanley mystery was explained.

Dr Campbell accepted my suggestion and has both visited and corresponded with Sir John, who was born in 1895 and was therefore a boy of six in 1901. His evidence has been given most conscientiously, and is strictly limited to his positive recollections. It amounts to the following:

> *1. Sir John remembers Miss Freer coming to stay with his parents at The Orchard in 1901. He cannot recall the season of the year.*
> *2. He remembers that his mother told him long afterwards that Miss Freer was the author of the book on Ballechin House, which his father had visited.*
> *3. He remembers that his mother told him that his father had detected 'a lady' faking table-rapping at a séance somewhere. He cannot positively recall that his mother said that it was Miss Freer although he can say that no other name was mentioned.*

The reader may think that it is of some interest that although Sir Charles Shaw remained a member of the S.P.R. until his death in 1922, no further accounts of psychical phenomena from his pen were contributed to the Society's literature after July 1901. It may be thought, too, that as it was Frank Podmore to whom Sir Charles first gave his verbal account of Alfred Peters' phenomena in November 1900, and it was again to Podmore that Sir Charles sent his written statement in February 1901, it would be to Podmore that Sir Charles would confide the story of what Miss Freer had done at Swanley. Sir Charles's position would be an embarrassing one. He had supported Miss Freer's accounts of her experiences at Ballechin, and had allowed his testimony to be printed in the book published only two years previously. He knew now that she was a fraud. From his point of view he would doubtless wish for as little publicity as possible. On the other hand, as a conscientious man, he doubtless felt that he had a duty to inform a leading member of the Society for Psychical Research. Podmore was the obvious choice. This would fully explain the discreet footnote added to p. 332 of the second volume of Podmore's *Modern Spiritualism*, which was to be published in the following year.

For obvious reasons Podmore would have to inform the Society's Council of what had happened. For one thing, in her books published only two years previously Miss Freer had claimed to be a member of several S.P.R. committees and to be an official of the Society. Whatever the truth of these statements may have been, she was certainly no longer a member of any of the four committees of the Society by the time she left England in December 1901,[1] and not long afterwards her connexion with the Society ceased altogether, despite her claim to be a member to the end of her life.

It can hardly be doubted that in the nature of things the story would have leaked out to some extent[2] by the late summer of 1901, and it seems significant that Carmichael told Fr Allan in the first two of his three letters about Miss Freer that his information came from London, where the S.P.R. had its headquarters. 'In London it is said that one Society after another and one man after another have thrown her off', wrote Carmichael in October 1901.

[1] *Journal*, S.P.R., March 1902, pp. 195–7.

[2] The S.P.R. has always had its gossips. It will be recalled, for example, that after the opening of F. W. H. Myers' sealed 'posthumous message' on 13th December 1904, for comparison with the hoped-for divination of its contents in the automatic writings of Mrs A. W. Verrall, the matter was reported in the national Press. Sir Oliver Lodge, after opening the sealed message before a selected audience, lugubriously conceded that the 'experiment has completely failed, and it cannot be denied that the failure is disappointing'. The 'leaking' of this disaster to the Press was regarded with severe displeasure by the S.P.R. leaders. 'It has become necessary to reiterate this caution,' it was stated, 'because a flagrant violation of the rule has recently occurred in the unauthorised communication to the public press of the essential part of a statement that appeared in the *Journal* for January' (*Journal*, S.P.R., January 1905, p. 13, and February 1905, p. 32).

The subsequent career of Miss Freer is not a matter for detailed discussion here. In December 1901, a few months after the Swanley episode, she left England to live in Jerusalem, and it was there that she wrote the preface to her *Outer Isles* in May 1902. Her *Inner Jerusalem* was published in 1904. The break with psychical research and her former life and interests in England was complete.[1]

In her letter of 28th August 1901 to Fr Allan McDonald, Miss Freer said she had received an invitation to visit the Holy Land for a year. As might have been expected, she refrained from giving any other information, but it is reasonable to suppose that among Miss Freer's circle this suggestion could scarcely have come other than from the widowed Marchioness of Bute and her family. They were property owners in Jerusalem, and had fulfilled the late Marquess's instructions to bury his heart on the Mount of Olives in the early winter of 1900. Later correspondence in the Bute family papers indicates in fact that Miss Freer was employed by the Butes as their agent in Jerusalem, and that in the event she did not revisit England for nearly ten years.

It is possible that despite lack of belief in Miss Freer's alleged powers as a clairvoyante, *etc.*, the Butes may have felt some sense of obligation towards her as a friend of the late Marquess. If it be assumed that the family had been informed of the Swanley affair, however, an alternative and more likely possibility is that Miss Freer's departure from England at this time, if it could be arranged, would not be unwelcome to them. They would be acutely conscious that her name had been prominently associated with that of their late father in psychical research matters. Although Swanley, with its embarrassments for both the S.P.R. and the Rev. Charles Shaw, had received no publicity, there was no guarantee that this situation would necessarily continue. An offer of paid employment far away from England at this special time seems a considerable coincidence if it was not connected with Swanley.

Miss Freer continued to live in Jerusalem, and in 1905 married there a German–American, Hans Henry Spoer, an authority on the language of the Near East. We have no information regarding her conjugal relations with her husband, but the difference of sixteen years in their ages must have made it no ordinary union, despite Dr Spoer's apparent belief that his wife was about the same age as himself.

Miss Freer's *In a Syrian Saddle* was published in the year of her

[1] Apart from the publication by her of some psychical documents, originally given to her by F. W. H. Myers, under the title 'Some Leaves from the Note Book of a Psychical Enquirer', in the *Occult Review* in 1906.

marriage, and books from her pen appeared at intervals for the rest of her life. Among others, *Things Seen in Palestine* was published in 1913, *Arab in Tent and Town* in 1924, while her final work, *Things Seen in Constantinople*, was published in 1926 when she was nearly seventy. In the light of what we know about her earlier literary activities in psychical research and folklore, any claims implicit in these books that Miss Freer was an authority on the Near East can, I fancy, be regarded as doubtful. It seems probable, indeed, that her writings at this period owed much to her husband.

The life of the Spoers was a wandering one. In 1909 Dr Spoer came to England to study at Lichfield Theological College. Miss Freer's address in the membership list of the Folklore Society in 1911 was given as 53 Bath Road, Wolverhampton. Her husband was ordained in that year and went as a chaplain to Cairo, Miss Freer's address in the records of the Folklore Society in 1912 and 1913 being Church House, Cairo. Her *Who's Who* entries from 1913 to 1916 give her address as Heliopolis, Egypt, while in the Folklore Society membership list from 1914 to 1917 she is shown as at Box 104, Austrian P.O., Jerusalem, which may have been a forwarding address. In her entry in *Who's Who* in 1925 she said that she had been, from 1918 to 1920, the 'Assistant to Dr Spoer; District Commander under U.S.A. High Commissioner, Armenia, 1918–19', although this was not mentioned in the earlier entries from 1918 to 1924. In the Folklore Society membership list of 1923 she was shown as being at the American Bible House at Stamboul.

In 1923 Dr Spoer was appointed director of the Foreign Born American division of the Diocese of Michigan, U.S.A., and he and his wife went to live in America, Miss Freer's entry in *Who's Who* for 1925 showing her address as 68 East Hancock Avenue, Detroit, Michigan. Dr Spoer occupied this position for three years. In 1926 he became the rector of St Peter's Episcopal Church and head of the English Department at St Albans School at Sycamore, Illinois, and lived with his wife at St Peter's Rectory in Sycamore. This was the last address given by Miss Freer in *Who's Who*, but in fact yet another and final move was made after Dr Spoer had held these appointments for only one year. In 1927 he became the Chaplain of the New York Mission Society, and the couple removed to 2540, 30th Road, Astoria, New York. It was from this address that Miss Freer, fatally ill, was taken to St Luke's Hospital, New York, on 20th December 1930. She lay in hospital for nine weeks waiting for the end which she knew was inevitable, if we can assume this from her anxiety in January 1931, some weeks before her death, to ensure that her 'personal copy' of the *Alleged Haunting of B—— House* came back to England and the British Museum. She was an elderly woman of seventy-three, despite her successful claim to be only fifty-six, and had enjoyed a long and eventful life.

One wonders what ghosts of the past gathered round her bed. Did she think of her brothers in far-away Rutland, the companions of those first beginnings of long ago she had so effectively obliterated, or of the kindly relative who had brought her up in Yorkshire and of whom she had recorded not a single word of appreciation or even of identification? Did she see again the face of the generous and credulous W. T. Stead, the mentor and benefactor of *Borderland* days, whom she had criticized and disowned when it seemed an advantage to do so? Had she a thought for the faithful Constance Moore, whose devoted friendship of over twenty years had provided both a home and daily companionship to the formidable orphan who would otherwise have walked alone? Did she think of Lord Bute, who had believed in her when the spiritualists and psychical researchers had united against her, or of the gentle and noble Fr Allan McDonald, whose work of many years she had used? Did she remember the Rev. Charles Shaw, who had supported in print her account of her experiences at Ballechin, and whose hospitality she had rewarded by disillusionment? Or were her last thoughts of the intimacies of those early S.P.R. days with Frederic Myers, her equal, it might be thought, in the exploitation of the kindly and the trustful, and who at the end had deserted and disowned her as she had deserted and disowned others?

She died on 24th February 1931. As has been said, the only obituary of her so far discovered is that which appeared in *Folklore*, in which it was deplored that no biography of a woman of such remarkable and varied achievements had been written.

III

Ada Goodrich Freer and Fr Allan McDonald's Folklore Collection

1

MISS FREER AND HEBRIDEAN FOLKLORE

IN HIS obituary of Miss Freer in *Folklore*, already quoted by Mr Trevor Hall earlier in this book, A. R. Wright, F.S.A.,[2] Vice-President of the Folklore Society and editor of the journal in question, wrote of Miss Freer that:

The list of her published works shows her remarkable range of knowledge and experience. Those of the greatest folklore importance are Outer Isles *(the Outer Hebrides, 1903);* Inner Jerusalem *(1904); and* Arabs in Tent and Town *(1924)* . . .

Wright goes on to write of Miss Freer's 'inherited Highland sympathy with the mysterious', further evidence of the myth of her Scottish ancestry.

Miss Freer's book *Outer Isles*, which was published in London in 1902, not 1903, contains 427 pages of text divided into eighteen chapters, several of which had earlier appeared as lectures or magazine articles. Of these, six chapters, amounting to 142 pages, a third of the book, are devoted to South Uist and Eriskay, and consist nearly entirely of local folklore and tradition. Yet Miss Freer's own letters to Lord Bute prove conclusively that she was ignorant of Gaelic and had only spent a few days in South Uist and Eriskay in the course of much wider travels in the Highlands in 1895, 1896, and 1898. The total time she spent in South Uist and Eriskay on these three visits combined cannot have been more than six weeks and was probably considerably less. It would have been miraculous if any one, even a Gaelic-speaker knowing something of the oral tradition, had succeeded in gaining such an intimate knowledge of the folklore and traditions of a Hebridean island in such a brief space of time. In fact, the source of the information used by Miss Freer in these six chapters and sporadically elsewhere in her book was Fr Allan McDonald's notebooks, which had first come into her hands under the circumstances described here on pp. 72–77, and the last two of which, as well as the one he called 'Strange Things', after which this book is named, may have been covered by the agreement reached to collect on behalf of Lord Bute made in November 1895.

There is no record of the original first impression Miss Freer made on Fr Allan McDonald at their first meeting in September 1895. It was no doubt a good one. Miss Freer excelled at making good first impressions. We know she did so in the cases of W. T. Stead, Lord Bute, the Rev. Peter Dewar, and Alexander Carmichael. There is evidence that Fr Allan McDonald himself came to feel a deeply affectionate regard for her. On 7th September 1897 he wrote in his diary:

The more I know of Miss Freer the holier she seems. May God ever guide her and have her in His keeping. My acquaintance with her has been an education of mind and soul, and has thrown sunshine over the last two years of my life. The jottings I made of folklore and kindred stuff I am glad please her, and I hope this winter to continue collecting.

This was written in spite of the fact that his diary reveals that Fr Allan McDonald was a reader of the weekly edition of *The Times*, and must therefore have known something of the hostile criticism that had been provoked by the Ballechin House ghost-hunt, for the weekly edition of *The Times* had reprinted Ross's original anonymous attack on the Ballechin investigation, and the subsequent letters of Miss Freer herself, of F. W. H. Myers repudiating the investigation on behalf of the S.P.R., and of 'Tenez-le-Droit' defending it.[1]

Miss Freer's letters to Lord Bute and to Lord Bute's secretary, already quoted, reveal a rather different attitude. To her, Fr Allan McDonald was a 'poor priest' whose collection of folklore was 'somewhat confused', but out of which material useful to her and to the S.P.R. Second Sight Enquiry might be extracted if they were edited by a clever person like herself, Fr Allan McDonald being retained 'at our service' to collect more such stories by an expense grant from Bute which at her suggestion was reduced from £50 to £10. It is probable, in fact, that Miss Freer exercised her very considerable charm upon Fr Allan McDonald for the purpose of getting what she wanted for the Second Sight Enquiry and her folklore writings and lectures out of him. A further indication of her attitude towards him is revealed in the entry in his diary for 3rd March 1898, when he records that the picture of Fr George Rigg which she had sent him had been delayed in reaching him because she had addressed it to him c/o Fr Samuel Macdonald, then parish

[1] A reader of the weekly edition of *The Times* would not have realized the amount of hostile criticism the Ballechin affair had provoked, nor how the owners of the house had been led to believe that it was only being let for sporting purposes.

priest of Daliburgh in South Uist, and had written Fr Allan's name as 'MacDougall' instead of 'McDonald'. 'She is always making it "MacDougall",' wrote Fr Allan in his diary, which was kept for this month in Gaelic.[1] Fr, later Canon, A. MacDougall was at this time parish priest of Benbecula. Miss Freer had visited him in September 1895 and he had accompanied Fr Allan McDonald on a visit to Ballechin House at the end of April 1897. Fr Allan McDonald could hardly have made the same impression on her as she had on him if she thus confused the two.

Fr Allan McDonald and Fr MacDougall had been guests at Ballechin House from 29th April to 6th May 1897. On 30th April Miss Freer recorded in her journal that 'the priests both looked very weary. They were not frightened, but the sounds have kept them awake all night.' In *The Alleged Haunting of B—— House* their names are disguised as the 'Rev. A. MacD——' and the 'Rev A. MacL——'.[2] A photograph of Ballechin House, pasted inside the cover of Fr Allan McDonald's notebook entitled 'Strange Things', is reproduced among the illustrations in this book. This is the notebook already referred to in which Fr Allan McDonald began entering second sight stories, with circumstantial details, on 26th November 1895, and the fact that the last entry of this kind is dated 5th June 1897 strongly suggests that it was the controversy over Ballechin and the quarrel between Miss Freer and the leaders of the S.P.R. over their failure to support her in it which brought the Second Sight Enquiry to its real end.

Miss Freer herself had been elected a member of the Folklore Society in London in 1893. In an article in *Borderland* she had replied to Edward Clodd's attack on the S.P.R. in his presidential address to the Folklore Society, given in January 1895.[3] In this article, which has already been quoted by Mr Trevor Hall, she asserted that she had been familiar with the rich folklore of a northern English village from childhood. It is therefore surprising that when she started to lecture and write about folklore, it was not about the rich and varied traditions of the unnamed northern village in which she had alleged she was brought up, but about the folklore of the Outer Hebrides, part of Scotland with which she only had the superficial acquaintance of two or three brief summer visits, and the language of which she did not know and never learnt. It is even more surprising that the Folklore Society, which had

[1] See *Gairm*, vol. I, p. 72.

[2] *The Alleged Haunting of B—— House*, p. 202. The identities are confirmed from the annotated copy of the book in the National Library of Scotland.

[3] *Borderland*, vol II., pp. 263–4.

already published good material from the Highlands contributed by such persons as Dr R. C. Maclagan and the Rev. Malcolm MacPhail, should have been so ready to accept Miss Freer as an authority on the subject.

The first intimation of Miss Freer's intention to write about Hebridean folklore was given in a brief report printed in the *Glasgow Evening News* of 21st October 1896. This report, which was obviously inserted in order to counteract the article on 'Ghost Hunting in the Highlands' which had appeared in that paper two months before, and has been already quoted, was couched in such flattering terms as to make it appear probable it was either contributed by Miss Freer herself or by some close personal friend. It reads:

That seeker of the supernatural Miss Goodrich Freer, has just returned from her now annual tour in the Hebrides. No one who has met Miss Freer can be surprised at the courtesy and kindness with which the people of the Isles have treated her. She is indeed an extremely charming personality without the faintest look of the 'new woman' about her. Early this year she lectured before the Inverness Gaelic Society, and greatly impressed the members of that body with her sincerity and her desire to get at the truth. Her sympathies are all with the Highlands and the Highlanders and she is a keen Jacobite. Though not a Gaelic speaker, she can read the language. By the way, she is not merely a 'supernaturalist', she is deeply interested in folk-lore, and her investigations are likely to result in a work on that subject.

The assertion that Miss Freer was able to read Gaelic is belied by the fact that she admitted in her letter published in the *Oban Times* of 10th July 1897 that she could not judge the merits of the Gaelic essays written by the Tiree schoolchildren for her competition. In the winter of 1897–8 Fr Allan McDonald recorded in his diary that he was doing translations for Miss Freer. The assertion that she could read Gaelic was unfounded.

Yet between April 1897 and November 1901 Miss Freer was to give lectures to five learned societies and publish articles in three substantial journals on Hebridean folklore, much of which was reprinted in 1902 in her book *Outer Isles*, and to acquire the status of an authority on the subject, as is evident from the remarks of Professor Magnus MacLean, in his *Literature of the Celts*,[1] and of

[1] P. 324 (1902). Miss 'Goodrich Frere' is named along with other 'writers of distinction', including Andrew Lang, Douglas Hyde, and Miss Eleanor Hull, who have done much of recent years to popularise the Celtic lore and literature, and to extend its sway over English letters'.

A. R. Wright, F.S.A., Vice-President of the Folklore Society and editor of its journal, in his obituary notice of her, already quoted. These lectures and articles may be listed as follows:

1. Short address to the Folklore Society on 'Folklore of the Hebrides', given at the meeting of 27th April 1897.[1] The address (it is not called a paper) may have been extempore, and was probably of a general nature. It was not printed in the Society's journal, *Folklore*. It can only have been a short address, as four other persons read papers at the same meeting, which 'concluded with a hearty vote of thanks being accorded to Miss Freer for her address' (*Folklore*, 1897, vol. VIII, p. 194).
3. 'The Norsemen in the Hebrides', a paper read to the Viking Society in London on 26th November 1897, and later published in their *Saga Book*.
3. A paper 'On the Folklore of the Outer Hebrides', read to Section H of the British Association for the Advancement of Science at Bristol on 13th September 1898. An abstract of this paper, which was very comprehensive, appeared in the 1898 Report of the British Association.[2] The lecture was also reported in the *Oban Times* of 24th September of the same year.
4. 'Christian Legends of the Hebrides', an article published in the *Contemporary Review* of September 1898 (vol. LXXIV, pp. 390–412).
5. Paper on 'The Powers of Evil in the Outer Hebrides', read to the Folklore Society on 15th February 1899, and published in *Folklore* in September of the same year (vol. X, pp. 259–82).
6. Article on 'Eriskay and Prince Charles', published in *Blackwood's Edinburgh Magazine* of February 1901 (vol. CLXIX, pp. 232–41).
7. Paper on 'More Folklore from the Hebrides', read to the Folklore Society on 6th November 1901, and printed in *Folklore* in March 1902 (vol. XIII, pp. 29–62).
8. Paper on 'Footprints of the Past in the Outer Hebrides', read to the Gaelic Society of Glasgow on 12th November 1901, and reported in the *Oban Times* of 16th November.
9. Paper on 'Second Sight in the Hebrides', read to the Scottish Society of Literature and Art on 14th November 1901; reported

[1] It is characteristic of Miss Freer's secretiveness that she could not tell readers of *The Alleged Haunting of B—— House* that when she left Ballechin House on 9th April 1897 for three weeks, one of the reasons for her return to London was to give this address to the Folklore Society.

[2] *Transactions of Section H.*, p. 1020.

in the *Glasgow Herald* of the 15th and in the *Oban Times* of 23rd November 1901.

10. Her book *Outer Isles*, published by Archibald Constable & Co Ltd of London in 1902 (not 1903 as stated in her *Who's Who* entries). In this book some of the Tiree schoolchildren's essays are published as Chapter IV, 'The Ceilidh in Tiree', and papers numbers 2, 4, 5, and 6 described here are reprinted, with minor alterations, as Chapters XIII, X, XI, and XII respectively.

It is to be observed that the full texts of papers numbers 1, 3, 8, and 9 do not seem to have been preserved anywhere.

Readers who are acquainted with the Hebrides will be well aware that to collect the amount of information contained in such a series of lectures and articles as this would necessitate both prolonged residence in the islands and a knowledge of the language of the people. How then had Miss Freer, ignorant of Gaelic as she was, managed to make such a collection in the course of a few short visits made to the Isles since the summer of 1894?

2

THE DEBT TO FR ALLAN McDONALD

EXAMINATION OF Miss Freer's articles and lectures reveals several acknowledgments, sometimes apparently generous, to Fr Allan McDonald for help received in gathering her material. The general impression given is that Fr Allan had assisted her by giving her introductions to reciters and tradition-bearers in Eriskay and South Uist, and had sometimes accompanied her on visits to their houses and helped her to note down information.

As both his letters to her (including items he had translated for her) and the copyings she made or had made for her from his notebooks have disappeared, any assessment of the precise extent of her indebtedness to him was impossible until a substantial amount of his literary remains had been traced, listed, and catalogued, a process which was not complete until the mid-1950s. When this had been done, the suspicion already formed, that Miss Freer's dependence on Fr Allan McDonald's notebooks as a source of information about the folklore and local history of the southern Outer Hebrides had been almost total, was fully confirmed. Further evidence of her indebtedness was found in Fr Allan's 1897–8 diary, which has already been alluded to.

We do not know what information was given in Miss Freer's address to the Folklore Society on 28th April 1897; being short, it was probably a general account of the subject. The lecture to the Viking Club is indebted to Fr Allan McDonald for a good deal of information on Eriskay and other place-names, and on words of possible Norse origin currently used in Uist Gaelic; the lecture is referred to in Fr Allan McDonald's diary for 18th November 1897: 'The Norse lecture is on the 26th. Set to gathering more information on the subject.' The next day he wrote, 'engaged with the Norsemen all day, and scribbled till I was tired. How little it takes to upset me if the subject be interesting!' (He was in poor health at the time.) On 20th November he wrote, 'sent off . . . a budget of Norse scribblings to Miss Freer. I was lucky in having a chance to send them across [*i.e.* to be posted in South Uist]. The messenger I sent with the last lot lost three days over his errand with bad weather and want of a ferry.' On 30th December: 'I see from [the] *Oban Times* that Miss Freer gave the Norse lecture.'

The lecture shows that Miss Freer had done some reading in translations of the sagas and in works on Hebridean archaeology into which Fr Allan McDonald's philological material was set. In the course of her remarks she made the following allusion to Fr Allan's collection:

While speaking of literature, one's mind naturally turns to the question of folklore. It would be an interesting point to analyse the folklore of the Hebrides, much of which has been most ably collected by the Rev. Allan Macdonald, so as to ascertain how much it has in common with that of Ireland and Scandinavia respectively.[1]

This sensible suggestion is immediately vitiated by the remark that 'The Fingalians are, doubtless, to a great extent, of Norse origin'—this assertion apparently based on the opinion of one of Fr Allan McDonald's informants that the Fiantaichean (Fingalians) and the Lochlannaich (Norsemen) were the same people, a notion with which the great majority of Uist tradition-bearers would never agree.[2]

In the course of her published writings Miss Freer does not refer to Fr Allan McDonald's collection of Hebridean folklore again. Her next article, on 'Christian Legends of the Hebrides', published in the *Contemporary Review* of September 1898, begins with a general religious history (now, of course, out of date) of the Catholic Hebrides,[3] and continues with a number of legends and traditions condensed from Fr Allan McDonald's notebooks. No acknowledgment is made at all. On p. 391 she writes that the 'stories were mainly collected' on a bare island with a weekly postal service. 'From a great quantity of folklore collected in these islands I have selected a few stories bearing on the life, especially the childhood, of Our Lord'[4]—the reader would naturally think she was the collector, and this impression would be strengthened by her remark later on that: 'I give, as far as possible [the stories] in the words of the narrators, who used mainly the colloquial Gaelic, but sometimes quoted fragments of old rhythmical versions, and now and then one

[1] *Saga Book of the Viking Club*, p. 59.

[2] *Op. cit.*, p. 62. The original entry is in Fr Allan McDonald's South Uist dictionary, under FIANTAICH.

[3] It is likely that even this was written by Fr Allan McDonald, as in his diary on 9th June 1898 he wrote that he was doing a resumé of 'Island Church history' for Miss Freer.

[4] *Op. cit.*, p. 391.

or two of them, sailors for the most part, translating into their quaint, imperfect English'.[1]

There follows immediately the folk anecdote of our Lord curing his stingy host of the colic by rubbing 'it' [*sic*] three times with hut straw with the grain and three times against the grain, reciting the following words as recorded by Fr Allan:

> *Bean chiùin 's duine borb*
> *'S Crìosda 'na laigh' air a' cholg.*
> (A mild wife and a wild husband
> And Christ lying on the beard [of barley].)

This story is taken, practically word for word, from Fr Allan's Notebook VI, item 239. Miss Freer, however, does not give the Gaelic words used, which Fr Allan McDonald did not translate, but says that Christ 'said certain words which are still, it is said, used as a charm for colic, but I have not been able to recover them'!

The remainder of the article is similarly based on material in Fr Allan McDonald's notebooks, and it may be fairly said to initiate free use of his material under Miss Freer's name, which his friends so much resented, once they realized what was going on. On p. 401 Miss Freer had the impertinence to 'correct' Martin Martin's Gaelic in a footnote.

The article on 'Eriskay and Prince Charles' in *Blackwood's Magazine* is equally without any acknowledgment of the source of Miss Freer's information. A very bad instance of this is the description of a visit to 'Maighread Mhór', 'Big Margaret', an old lady on Eriskay who 'can speak no word of English'.[2] Big Margaret sang Miss Freer a lullaby, of which she could not (of course) write down the words, 'but not even one or two of the islanders whose aid we invoke can make much of them. Either the sense has been lost, or they are baby-nonsense rhymes pure and simple.'

Miss Freer says Big Margaret went on to sing her a waulking song, the words of which the singer ascribed to Flora MacDonald. Twelve lines of this are given by Miss Freer in translation, together with comments by the singer on it. These include the lines:

> I was at Mass in the yellow wood with thee;
> I was in —— and I was in Uist with thee;
> I was in Kildonan of the pine with thee;
> I was in the land of the black nuns with thee.

Miss Freer explains the missing word by saying, 'Margaret is too deaf to converse with, and we fail to recover the missing word'.

[1] *Op. cit.*, p. 394. [2] *Blackwood's Magazine*, February 1901, p. 239.

The song in question is that known by the name of the subject, 'Seathan' ('John'). Quite a number of versions have been recovered in the Hebrides, see *Carmina Gadelica*, vol. IV, pp. 60–83. Fr Allan himself took down another version on Eriskay from Mrs Donald MacEachen in January 1897 (Notebook V, 194). I have recorded versions in Uist, Barra, and Vatersay myself. The song is a passionate lament for Seathan, son of the King of Ireland, by his sweetheart. None of the other singers Carmichael quoted, or whom I have heard, ascribed it to Flora MacDonald or thought her husband was the subject of it. The twelve lines quoted in English by Miss Freer correspond exactly with twelve lines of a version taken down by Fr Allan McDonald in Gaelic in March or April 1897, and they are entered in his Notebook VI, 29, together with the singer's ascription to Flora MacDonald and her disapproving comment on the concluding line, 'I would not give thee to Jesus Christ', that was quoted by Miss Freer. The original of the line with the missing word was '*Bha mi 'n Ile 's bha mi 'n Uithisd leat*'—'I was in Islay and I was in Uist with thee'. Miss Freer may indeed have visited Big Margaret along with Fr Allan McDonald, but she certainly depended upon him to translate the song, and Big Margaret's comment on it, for her. The reason she failed to recover the missing word was not Big Margaret's deafness but the difficulty of reading Fr Allan's handwriting.

In her concluding paragraph Miss Freer stated she had learnt to know the island well, had photographed it 'a score of times' (where are these photographs now?), had classified its flora (this Fr Allan and Miss Constance Moore had done), and had 'learnt its songs and its traditions'—but here again there is no mention of the actual source of her information.

The two papers read to the Folklore Society in 1899 and 1901 were prefaced by something of an acknowledgment to Fr Allan McDonald, but it is far from unequivocal. In her introductory remarks to the first paper, that on 'The Power of Evil in the Outer Hebrides', Miss Freer said:

These stories are all recent, and in nearly every case the name of the informant and the approximate date of any incident has been recorded. The language used is, as far as possible, that, or a translation of that, of the informants, and variants have always been carefully noted.

Such gatherings are not easily made. The Celt must know and trust well those whom he admits into his inner life, and though in our wanderings in the islands we have long since learnt to feel at home and among friends, I could never myself have accomplished such a collection, and have to acknowledge most cordially and fully the help of the Rev. Allan MacDonald [sic], *Priest of Eriskay, to whose patience, erudition, and perhaps even more his friendship with the people, these records are mainly due.*[1]

In the introductory remarks to the second paper, that on 'More Folklore from the Hebrides', which is docketed 'Copyright reserved by the Author', Miss Freer said that she believed she could claim that much of the folklore contained in her paper

has never before been printed, and that even in the case of such traditions and beliefs as are so far widespread as to have been gathered together elsewhere, that, at all events, they are here given for the first time as collected in the islands of South Uist and Eriskay. In the very few cases in which I have presented examples already published by Mr Carmichael in his Carmina Gadelica, *it is because we have both borrowed from a common fount, the Rev. Allan MacDonald* [sic], *who has long had access to sources of information entirely inaccessible to all others, and to whom I acknowledge the deepest obligation. As priest, and even more as friend, to a people whose hearts can never open fully but to one of their own faith and living in their midst, he has had, and has used to the full, opportunities that are in the most literal sense unique, and without him—his knowledge, sympathy, and erudition—the folklore, songs, hymns, customs, and tales of these islands could never have been collected.*[2]

Miss Freer concluded with the following words:

The above miscellaneous gatherings are, so to speak, the flotsam and jetsam of the wild seas of the Outer Hebrides. They present, I believe, considerable material for the commentator and the comparative folklorist, but the task of discussion is one for which the present writer lacks —among other things—at this moment, leisure, though she looks forward to the attempt on some future occasion.

Could it be that Miss Freer had spotted a Gaelic-speaker, with some first-hand knowledge of the oral traditions of the Hebrides, perhaps a personal friend of Fr Allan McDonald's, in the audience, and had feared that embarrassing questions might be asked? Or was it because she had already arranged to leave England the next month for the Near East?

The first of these two papers, some material from the second, and the articles in the *Contemporary Review* and *Blackwood's*, were

[1] *Folklore*, vol. X, p. 259. [2] *Folklore*, vol. XIII, p. 29.

reprinted in Miss Freer's book the *Outer Isles*, published in London in 1902. In the preface to this she wrote:

To name all who have facilitated our enquiries, and added to the pleasure of our wandering, would be impossible in a country where courtesy, hospitality, and even friendship, have never failed. I must, however, mention, with especial gratitude and esteem, the Rev. Allan MacDonald, Catholic priest, of Eriskay, whose practical kindness and companionship alone made possible some of the more difficult of our journeyings, and without whose help much of this book (especially chapters VII–XIII [the reprinted paper and articles referred to]) *could never have been written.*[1]

Mention is also made of the 'stimulus' provided by Lord Bute to visit the Isles in the first place: not a word is said of the original mission, to collect evidence of second sight on behalf of the S.P.R.

No reader of Miss Freer's remarks I have quoted from *Folklore* and her *Outer Isles* would reach any conclusion but that she had visited Eriskay and the neighbouring islands and there made a collection of local folklore with the invaluable help of Fr Allan McDonald. They would also receive the impression that where Miss Freer had not given the actual words of the reciters, she herself was responsible for translating them from the original Gaelic. Had she honestly acknowledged her obligations she would have said that she was going to read to her audience folklore collected, and where necessary translated, by her friend Fr Allan McDonald of Eriskay, who had had a remarkable (though not a unique) opportunity to make such a collection. All she was responsible for was its arrangement. In the event Fr Allan's name was not even mentioned in the Indexes of the volumes of *Folklore* (X and XIII) in which these papers were printed.

I have already demonstrated Miss Freer's almost total dependence on Fr Allan McDonald's notebooks as the source of her information,[2] and more instances are discussed in this introduction and in the Appendix and Notes to this book. The diary which he kept from 1st September 1897 to 30th June 1898 makes the nature of the work he was doing for her quite clear. Entries referring to his help with the article on the Norsemen in the Hebrides have already been referred to. On 3rd March 1898 he records a letter from her saying, among other things, that she had sent him her paper on the Norse-

[1] *Outer Isles*, p. xi.

[2] 'The late Fr Allan McDonald, Miss Goodrich Freer and Hebridean Folklore', *Scottish Studies*, 1958, vol. II, pp. 175–88. A substantial number of offprints were printed, and copies can be supplied to anyone interested who sends me a stamped addressed half-quarto envelope.

men for him to correct the Gaelic 'names' in it,[1] presumably with a view to its being printed in the *Saga Book*. On the 4th March he writes he was doing this, and that he hoped she would be able to read his handwriting, which she had found difficult to do before.

On 22nd September 1897 Fr Allan McDonald recorded that he had sent a letter to Miss Freer 'in answer to eight interrogatory statements which took me half a day to write'. On 1st December 1897 he wrote that he had written to Miss Freer a letter on general topics and sent her a volume of his folklore notebooks (number not stated). On 17th February 1898 he regretted he could not help Alexander Carmichael, who was 'in the throes of publishing his *Or* and *Ob*' [*Carmina Gadelica*], as 'my MS. are with Miss Freer'.

On 19th May he wrote 'Letter from Miss Freer—great letter. She is in quite high form. How she can turn the notes to such account I can't make out. A bee is skilful to extract honey from many strange flowers.' On 29th May: 'I wish Miss Freer would send me the work she wishes me to do. I sent her the seventh book of notes on Sunday last . . . I fully expect a letter and work this week.' On 9th June 1898: 'Letter from Miss Freer with work she wishes me to do—translations of a variety of short Gaelic passages i.e. a resumé of Island Church History and Notebook [number] I. returned.' Presumably this was wanted for the article on 'Christian Legends' already referred to.[2]

This last entry completely disposes of any suggestion that Miss Freer may have known Gaelic well enough to collect this folklore herself, as her own writings frequently imply.

Fr Allan McDonald had also sent Miss Freer the diary, letters, and photograph of his great friend Fr George Rigg, who died a heroic death in the Uist fever epidemic of 1897. Miss Freer had intended to write a brochure on Fr Rigg.[3] The photograph was returned wrongly addressed; there is no record of the diary and letters having been returned.[4] Miss Freer's own story was that the brochure had been burnt when a lamp exploded and burnt her and nearly set the house on fire.[5]

[1] The entries for March 1898 were written in Gaelic. This reads: 'Chuir i hugam blaigh de'n phàipeir a sgrìobh i air na Lochlannaich 'sna h-Eileanan an Iar air son nan ainmnean Gàidhealach a bha air fheadh a chur air dòigh dhith'.

[2] See p. 230.

[3] *Borderland*, vol. IV, p. 47: 'It was during her sojourn among the remote islands of the Outer Hebrides in search of folk lore and Borderland lore, that Miss X had unique opportunities for observing the self-sacrifice of his life in that forlorn Country of which the English reader knows so little.'

[4] Diary entries for 8th, 9th, 14th, and 16th September 1897, and 17th March 1898.

[5] Diary entry for 3rd March 1898.

It is typical of Miss Freer that when she came to relate the story of Fr Rigg's death in her book *Outer Isles* she gave the date of it incorrectly as 1898 (it was 1897), and made no mention of Fr Allan McDonald being the source of her information, giving only 'a priest on a neighbouring island', described as the predecessor and faithful friend of Fr Rigg, as the writer of a letter on the subject which she quoted at length.[1] Nothing was said of Fr Rigg's diary or of the project of writing a pamphlet about him.

[1] *Outer Isles*, pp. 155–6.

3

DISILLUSIONMENT

MISS FREER had made such a good first impression on her male acquaintances and her audiences in Scotland that it was a long time before anyone questioned the use she was making of Fr Allan McDonald and his folklore collection. Her use of Dewar's second sight material was never questioned at all. Fr Allan McDonald himself had implicit faith in her. Who, in his position, would deny such a charming, intelligent, sympathetic, still-young lady of supposedly Highland ancestry material for her lectures and articles in the south, which he probably thought were designed to instruct and inform the ignorant Sassenachs and win friends for the remote and neglected Hebrides in influential quarters? The only signs of any misgivings about Miss Freer's use of Fr Allan McDonald's folklore collection before the spring of 1902 were shown in two letters from George Henderson written on 21st December 1897 and 23rd January 1901, expressing concern about the return by Miss Freer of Fr Allan's notebooks on account of the valuable Gaelic folk-tales which they contained, and in which Henderson had a particular interest.[1] As regards the character of Miss Freer herself, there is in Fr Allan's diary an account of a conversation about her which he had with Fr MacDougall, parish priest of Benbecula (who had gone with Fr Allan to Ballechin in April 1897), in which Fr Allan records that he could not get Fr MacDougall to commit himself to an opinion of her. The date of this entry was 10th January 1898. But there is ample evidence from the diary itself that Fr Allan had both sentimental admiration for, and every confidence in her during the period it was kept, 1st September 1897 to the end of June 1898.

When doubts were first expressed about Miss Freer's integrity, it was in London in the summer of 1901, and it was her reputation as a clairvoyante and a psychical researcher which was in question, as has already been described. As has been said, the matter was hushed up, but the news must have come as a shock to those of her Scottish

[1] Notebook II contains a series of stories about the youthful exploits of Fionn MacCumhail and the foundation of the Féinn, taken down from Alasdair Johnston on Eriskay, whom Henderson had met in 1892, see *Celtic Review*, vol. II, p. 262, where these stories are printed.

acquaintances, such as Fr Allan himself, to whom it was conveyed confidentially. Indeed, the tone of Alexander Carmichael's letter of 7th October 1901 suggests that Fr Allan may have tried to defend Miss Freer against the accusation conveyed in Carmichael's preceding letter of 13th August, when he had written that people in London were saying that Miss Freer was 'not altogether what she seems'.

When it began to dawn on Fr Allan McDonald's friends a few months later that Miss Freer intended to republish several of her lectures and articles based on Fr Allan's folklore collection under her own name in her forthcoming book *Outer Isles*, strong feelings were aroused and expressed in private correspondence, and were later echoed by some of the book's reviewers and by the writer of the obituary of Fr Allan in the Scottish *Catholic Directory*.

It is as well to set down here the sequence of events connected with the growing feelings of disillusionment felt about Miss Freer in 1901 and 1902. On 8th June 1901 the *Oban Times* reported that Miss Freer and her friend Miss Ruth Landon (spelt 'Loudon' in the report) had been staying on Tiree for some little time. In his letter to Fr Allan McDonald of 13th August Carmichael mentioned that his wife had seen Miss Freer at the Exhibition in Glasgow, and in that of 7th October he said that he had seen Miss Freer in Glasgow, presumably on the same occasion, 'and she told us that she missed seeing you in Oban'. Since Fr Allan McDonald used to take his annual holiday regularly in July, going to stay with a sister at Helensburgh, this must mean that somehow Miss Freer had just missed seeing him at Oban on her return from Tiree, Oban being the mainland port for both Tiree and South Uist. This failure to meet is also mentioned in Miss Freer's letter of 28th August to Fr Allan; in this she also says that she returned to Bushey Heath three weeks ago. All this suggests that her debacle at Swanley must have occurred in July or early August 1901.

Whatever had happened at Swanley became known to only a few people. It did not deter Miss Freer from lecturing to the Folklore Society in London on 6th November on 'More Folklore from the Hebrides', to the Gaelic Society of Glasgow on the 12th on 'Footprints of the Past in the Outer Hebrides', and to the Scottish Society for Literature and Art on the 15th on 'Second Sight in the Hebrides' in the same city. The first of these three papers consisted entirely of material from Fr Allan McDonald's notebooks, particularly V and VI, written after January 1896; the other two do not seem to have been indebted to him.

It is immediately striking that none of these three papers was reprinted in her Hebridean *magnum opus Outer Isles*, which appeared in the summer of 1902, though isolated items used in her last folk-lore lecture can be found there. The fact is that by the beginning of November 1901 the manuscript of *Outer Isles* must already have been in the hands of the publisher, and also in those of the printers, for on 15th December, when Miss Freer was already on her way to Port Said, Ruth Landon wrote to Fr Allan McDonald from 34 Carlton Road, Putney, enclosing 'slips 44–51' (presumably galley proof sheets) which Miss Freer had written to tell her that she could not find among her own proofs. Miss Landon asked Fr Allan to correct her corrections if necessary, and remarked that it was possible that Miss Freer might have 'already corrected another set of the same sheets' and returned them to the publisher, 'but in case this is not so I should be responsible'. It is therefore clear that Fr Allan McDonald never saw a complete set of the proofs of *Outer Isles* at all—something that is confirmed by the gross errors that occur in the printing of Gaelic words and phrases in the book. From two of the four questions enclosed with Miss Landon's letter, the galleys she sent to him probably corresponded to pp. 92–104 approximately, part of the chapter called 'Miscellaneous notes on the Islanders'.

It seems not to have been until March 1902 that Fr Allan McDonald's friends realized that Miss Freer had a book in the press in which a large amount of Fr Allan's material previously used in her lectures and articles was to be reprinted under her name. On 18th March Fr Allan's friend, Walter Blaikie, one of the directors of the Edinburgh firm of T. & A. Constable Ltd, which had published Carmichael's *Carmina Gadelica* two years previously, and who was author of a volume on the itinerary of Prince Charles Edward in the Highlands which had been published by the Scottish History Society in 1897 (he had met Fr Allan through his travels in connexion with this work), wrote that he was strongly suggesting to an unnamed moribund society in the possession of some money that this should be used in an attempt to

collect and publish every piece of Celtic lore, ancient and even comparatively modern, connected with the history, the Church, the customs, superstitions, the wars, the dress, the manufactures of the Highlands. Especially the poetry from oral sources and folk lore.

Now dear Father Allan I know that you have collected much; more probably than any man living. I know that many people have had the use of your matter, sometimes without suitable acknowledgment. Now I think this is the very opportunity for letting the world know your work, and that this may be the chance for producing a worthy work in your own name and with some remuneration for it.

The implication is clearly that there had been no remuneration for what Fr Allan had put at the disposal of others. Such a project as this demanded that Fr Allan McDonald's notebooks be submitted for scrutiny and report to a professional scholar. We shall see how Miss Freer's use of them affected that report presently.

On 25th March Carmichael wrote to Fr Allan:

I hope you are keeping well and that you have weathered the winter well. I saw some time ago that you and Miss Freer were collaborating on a work which you are bringing out jointly. I hope we shall see it soon. Who is your printer? It is not your warm friend *Mr Blaikie or we would have heard of it. I hope the work is progressing well and rapidly. Well, my dear friend, all that I will say is this. I thought much, very much, of Miss Freer. I think less, much less, of her now. My wife and daughter thought her very clever, very plausible, and very pleasant, but they were not at all enamoured of her very much, very much less than enamoured of her, the reason being, as they said themselves, that a woman can see through a woman better than a man can.*

Carmichael went on to refer to the affair at Swanley; this part of his letter has been quoted already by Mr Trevor Hall in an earlier chapter.

On 1st April 1902 George Henderson wrote to Fr Allan:

I suppose you have got your Gaelic *MSS. with the tales on Fionn* [i.e. *Notebook II*]. *I have strong thoughts of completing an English account of the Fionn Saga begun by Campbell of Islay and trust you won't give your Gaelic MSS. out of your hand to any unsafe source. Mr Blaikie writes me he has your MSS. I suppose your folk-lore ones in English. I do not know what his view is, but I'll do what I can to urge his project to a successful issue. The matter is* private. *Has Miss Freer re-published your articles? I think she is rather bold in writing her name over them with such meagre acknowledgment to you; of course I know you well, but I don't admire that sort of thing.*

The book *Outer Isles* was published in July 1902 (not in 1903 as is stated in Miss Freer's *Who's Who* entries), the Foreword having been written by Miss Freer in Jerusalem in May. The acknowledgment given to Fr Allan McDonald in it has already been quoted. The opening paragraph of the first chapter, which describes Miss Freer's journey with Miss Moore to Tiree in 1894, clearly infers that she was 'a woman of leisure'. Nothing is said about the journey having been undertaken on behalf of the Society for Psychical Research, which in the index is called the 'Society for Physical Research'. Nothing is said about Dewar. The book was widely reviewed, and often admired, though considered by some critics to be biased politically in favour of the crofters and against the landlords, and to paint too gloomy a picture of life in South Uist.[1] An attack made by Miss Freer on the administration of Tiree under the Duke of Argyll's estate management was answered in a letter to the *Oban Times* of 30th August 1902 by Lady Victoria Campbell, who said she had been resident in the island for part of every year since 1891, and wrote:

At the request of the late Marquis of Bute I gave Miss Freer an introduction to some few people on the island who might assist her in her folklore. I cannot remember her asking me a single question regarding land or industry questions, nor have I heard of her interesting herself in any of these matters. I am quite certain, if she had informed herself of facts, she could never have penned such a statement of Tiree and its inhabitants . . .

There is a wide field for women of leisure and culture to help our people in industries and other modes of self-help, and I am glad to say it has been my privilege to know such English and Scotch ladies whose time and energies have been fully occupied in doing something practical to help real need; thus avoiding the temptation of being a 'busybody' in other matters such as, I fear, Miss Freer has become.

At least two Scottish reviewers were aware of the extent to which Miss Freer depended on Fr Allan McDonald for her folklore material. In a long review in the *Oban Times* of 9th August 1902 Mrs Blair, better known later as Mrs Macaulay and subsequently to become the owner of the paper,[2] after remarking that various chapters in the book consisted of articles and lectures already

[1] Miss Freer saw South Uist through the eyes of Fr Allan McDonald at a time when he was a sick man and bitterly distressed by the death of his friend and successor at Daliburgh, Fr George Rigg, of fever caught when attending an old woman whose own relatives, Fr Allan felt, should have looked after her, having recovered from the fever themselves. A very different picture of Uist can be found in F. G. Rea's *School in South Uist*, Routledge & Kegan Paul, 1965. Rea was headmaster of Garrynamonie School in the same parish from 1890 to 1894 and from 1903 to 1913, knew Fr Allan McDonald, and had a much more intimate knowledge of South Uist than Miss Freer.

[2] The review was not signed, but Mrs Blair's name is written over it in blue pencil in the bound copy in the *Oban Times* office.

printed in the *Contemporary Review*, the *Folklore Journal*, the *Saga Book of the Viking Club*, and so on, went on to say:

Impatiently we ask at this point, the Rev. Father MacDonald of Eriskay, how many times more is he going to allow the field of folklore and traditions to be ploughed by his oxen?

She then quotes the 'Sassenach lady's' acknowledgment in the Foreword to the book, and says:

Father Allan, gentlest and most retiring of men, is the greatest living authority on that body of knowledge, in which is comprised Hebridean tradition and literae humaniores. *We do not quarrel with Miss Goodrich-Freer for accepting the aid Father Allan has rendered. This is only one small service out of the numberless instances where Father Allan has stood aside and let others step forward to cull the fruit which by right of research is his. Or put it another way: he has gathered, it may be, from his flock, that which he and they would never have offered to a passing visitor. The sympathetic personality of the priest has drawn to him that which would not have been accorded to a stranger. But much, nevertheless, has passed into the possession of strangers.*

Similar remarks appeared in a review in the weekly Church of Scotland magazine *Saint Andrew* on 14th August 1902 by a writer who signed himself 'Quille Penne'. He wrote:

Last year in the course of a prolonged sojourn in the Outer Hebrides I found myself continually coming on the tracks of Miss Goodrich-Freer, the Psychical Society lady, whose first interest in the Highlands confined itself mainly to spooks, and the second sight. Her new book, 'The Outer Isles' [sic], *just issued in the most handsome print, paper and binding, is doubtless the result of her prolonged residence in Tyree and the Island of Eriskay, Sound of Barra. She has been wise not to give much space in her volume to the spooks that first excited her interest, for there an investigator who knows the people but superficially and is unacquainted with the language is usually hoaxed by some hamlet humorist, or treated with the utmost suspicion and distrust by the natives generally.*

Miss Freer's best chapter appeared a year ago in Blackwood's Magazine, *and treats of Eriskay, the little island where Prince Edward Charles* [sic] *first set foot in Scotland on his hopeless mission of 'Forty-Five'. To the priest of Eriskay (the island is, of course, Roman Catholic) she has confessedly been indebted for the greater part of her information regarding the folklore, religious customs, etc. of the Outer Hebrideans. The priest in question—Father Allan MacDonald—has in recent years collected a great body of such material, and it is the eager wish of all who know him, that instead of generously throwing his collected notes open to everyone who asks, he should publish them himself.*

This last paragraph was quoted by the Eriskay correspondent in the *Oban Times* of 13th September 1902. 'Quille Penne' went on to say that the people of Uist would not thank 'the English lady' for her comments on the poverty and desolation of their island. 'A traveller fresh from London is apt to be a poor judge of what comfort and content are in spots less blest.'

How had Fr Allan McDonald got into the position that most of the general folklore in his magnificent collection had been given to the public in lectures, articles, and a book under Miss Freer's name? It is clear that the process involved had been a gradual one; as time had gone on, more and more material, latterly collected with Miss Freer's encouragement, had been communicated to her for her lectures and articles, and had been used by her with occasional acknowledgment. But it is very unlikely that Fr Allan had had any idea that nearly all this material was to be reprinted in a book of which Miss Freer was to appear as sole author.[1] It is certain that he never saw some of her lectures in print until long after publication, and very doubtful if he ever saw them in manuscript. This can be proved in the case of the two lectures given to the Folklore Society. The first, on 'The Powers of Evil in the Outer Hebrides', was read to the Society on 15th February 1899 and was printed in the September issue of their journal that year; but Fr Allan did not see it until late April 1902, when Ruth Landon sent him a copy, saying she was sure Miss Freer would like him to have it. Fr Allan's immediate reaction was strong disapproval of a certain statement on the opening page. Miss Landon replied on 23rd May saying:

I am writing to tell you how sorry I am that I sent you the Folk-lore paper before waiting Miss Freer's permission to do so, which would have saved you the annoyance of seeing the mistake at the beginning. She is grieved that you should have been caused it.

That passage does not occur I believe in Outer Isles *but I have asked Mr Kyllman to make certain of it, he being the publisher responsible.*

A comparison of the versions of the lecture as printed in *Folklore* in September 1899 and in *Outer Isles* in July 1902 shows that the statement to which Fr Allan took exception was:

[1] It is true that the lecture on 'More Folklore from the Outer Hebrides', given to the Folklore Society on 6th November 1901 and based entirely on Fr Allan's material, was not reprinted in *Outer Isles*, but Miss Freer claimed copyright in it when it was printed in *Folklore* in March 1902.

Moreover, these stories are all recent, and in nearly every case the name of the informant and the approximate date of any incident has been recorded.[1]

This was not true of material recorded in Fr Allan McDonald's first two notebooks at any rate, but Miss Freer had even tried to make it appear true by altering what Fr Allan had originally written. In the winter of 1887–8 he had recorded an item about 'framing witchcrafts' by crossing threads of various colours, and how a man who tore up such a device had later been drowned in a storm, concluding, 'This occurrence did not take place within the memory of the present generation.' This sentence Miss Freer altered to 'The story is not only true, but of recent occurence'.[2]

As has been said, the lecture on 'More Folklore from the Outer Hebrides' was not reprinted in *Outer Isles*, though some of the material in it is used there, in Chapters VII, VIII, and IX. But although this lecture was given to the Folklore Society in November 1901 and printed in their Journal in March 1902, Fr Allan McDonald did not see it until Alexander Carmichael's daughter Ella sent him a copy on 23rd December 1902 to draw his attention to her father's annoyance at Miss Freer's assertion that Fr Allan McDonald had been a common source for both his *Carmina Gadelica* and her lectures.

This shows that Fr Allan McDonald had not known or realized what Miss Freer was actually doing with the material he was putting at her disposal. The upshot came in the report from George Henderson on Fr Allan's notebooks, scrutinized regarding possible publication as suggested by Walter Blaikie. This was conveyed to Fr Allan in a letter from Alexander Carmichael written on 6th January 1903:[3]

Mr Henderson says that Miss Freer has made such free use of your MSS. in her various publications that she has not left much of much value. This is very vexing, for both Mr Henderson and Mr Blaikie were very desirous that all your MSS. should be published in full and in your own name. Both were prepared to do all in their power towards accomplishing this, and I was equally prepared to give you all from my gatherings that would help you in any way. And so was Ella prepared to render all the help she could to you in the way of reading the proofs near

[1] See *Folklore*, vol. X, p. 259; *Outer Isles*, p. 229.

[2] Fr Allan McDonald, Notebook I, 67; *Folklore*, vol. X, p. 282. See also *Scottish Studies*, vol. 2, pp. 180–1; and pp. 310–11 here.

[3] The date written on the letter is 6th January 1902, but a reference to the Gaelic Mòd at Dundee proves this this was a mistake for 1903. The Mòd had been held at Dundee in the autumn of 1902.

the printers. Mr Blaikie will be vexed and disappointed as we all are here . . .

Eventually it was proposed that a Gaelic Texts Society be founded and that the first volume published by it should be a book of waulking songs collected and translated by Fr Allan: but this idea was dropped in favour of the foundation of the *Celtic Review*, which appeared from 1904 to 1916.[1] As for Fr Allan's folklore collection, that had been gutted as far as general folklore was concerned, and there would be no chance of publication under his own name until *Outer Isles* and the September 1899 and March 1902 numbers of *Folklore* were out of print and forgotten. But before that time Fr Allan himself had died and his notebooks had disappeared.

If ever any book should have been published as the admitted result of a collaboration it was *Outer Isles*. Published under Miss Freer's name alone, it set the seal on her almost totally undeserved reputation as a Hebridean folklorist. Fr Allan McDonald is not even mentioned in the Indexes to Volumes X and XIII of *Folklore* in which the lectures based on his material are printed. Miss Freer had a highly flattering obituary in that journal on her death in 1931; Fr Allan McDonald's death in 1905 passed entirely unnoticed.

When sending the March 1902 number of *Folklore* to Fr Allan McDonald with her letter of 23rd December, Ella Carmichael wrote:

It will be very kind of you to write as you propose. The sting of the sentence [*quoted in Fr Allan's letter printed below*] *lies in its being said in opposition to what my father himself says in his introduction to Carmina which I cannot suppose that Miss Freer did not see—in fact as she speaks of the similarity of their material it is natural to suppose she read the introduction.*

On 7th January 1903 Fr Allan McDonald wrote the following letter to the editor of *Folklore*:

In a paper entitled 'More Folklore from the Hebrides', by Miss A. Goodrich-Freer, read at a meeting of 6th November 1901, and published 25th March 1902, occur the following words: 'In the very few cases in which I have presented examples already published by Mr Carmichael in his Carmina Gadelica, *it is because we have borrowed from a common fount, the Rev. Allan Macdonald, etc.*

I should be guilty of an injustice to my good friend Mr Carmichael if I were to allow the statement to pass without comment. The author

[1] See J. L. Campbell and F. Collinson, Introduction to *The MacCormick Collection of Waulking Songs*, Clarendon Press, 1968.

of Carmina Gadelica *borrowed nothing from me. I did put a book of notes at his disposal,*[1] *as he courteously mentions in the introduction to his great work, but, as he tells us in the same paragraph, he was unable to make use of these notes, having so much material of his own. Mr Carmichael has done more for the collection of Island folklore than any living man.*

Allan McDonald

Eriskay, South Uist, 7th January 1903

This letter was printed in *Folklore* of March 1903, Volume XIV, p. 87, under the heading 'Folklore from the Hebrides: A Disclaimer'. It marked the formal and final ending of a friendship that had lasted for more than six years, greatly to Miss Freer's advantage.

[1] This was Fr Allan McDonald's MS. collection of hymns. Carmichael did not use any of Fr Allan's material in his first two volumes, published in 1900; but other volumes published after Carmichael's death do contain some of Fr Allan's material.

IV

'Strange Things'

1

STORIES FROM FR ALLAN McDONALD'S EARLY COLLECTION

THESE ARE ghost and second sight stories from Fr Allan McDonald's first two folklore Notebooks, I and II. They were taken down, together with a great deal of other folklore material of all kinds, between 1887 and 1893; the two notebooks are Fr Allan's 'folk-lore MSS.' referred to by the Rev. Peter Dewar in his letter of 17th March 1894 to Lord Bute, and studied by Dewar on his visit to Eriskay early in August the same year. They must have been seen by Miss Freer on her visit to the Outer Isles in the autumn of 1895, and were afterwards borrowed by her.

Fr Allan McDonald's habit was to carry a small notebook with him and there enter the stories which he was told, and afterwards to copy these in fair hand into the quarto notebooks already described. Marks and remarks in Miss Freer's handwriting frequently occur in them. In the case of Notebook I she completed the list of contents from No. 331 to the end. Many items, including all the stories printed here, are marked with ticks in her hand, either in the list of contents or in the text, presumably to indicate they were to be copied. In the list of contents of Notebook I the following marks also occur: SS, presumably for 'second sight'; H, presumably for 'historical'; ?, presumably meaning that an English translation or explanation was required.

Except in one or two instances, the stories are printed here in chronological order. In most cases the titles given in Fr Allan McDonald's list of contents are used, marginal comments by Miss Freer are reproduced, and references are given in the cases of stories that were used by her in her publications. Apart from a small batch of stories about the *Fuath*, or spirit of panic, and another about the importance of cock-crow and the part poultry sometimes were said to play in preternatural warnings, second sight stories are sporadic, until No. 209, between which and No. 265 there is a large batch of second sight stories likely to have been of interest to the S.P.R. Second Sight Enquiry, nearly all of which were marked by Miss Freer with SS in the list of contents.

TRADITIONAL GHOST STORIES

The following items would have had little or no evidential value for the Second Sight Enquiry; they are included to give an idea of the folkloric background to psychical phenomena noted later.

1. 'My Grandfather is Arising'[1]

About one hundred and fifty years ago there lived at the back of Ben More in Uist a family of the name of MacPhail. They are supposed to have come from Glenelg and were not Catholics. In the house there dwelt the old man MacLeod,[2] his son and wife, and a girl. The girl was seven years of age and had never spoken. The old man died, and the son went to the Baile (Township) for the usual funeral arrangements, leaving the corpse in the house with his wife and child. The corpse was laid on a plank as usual, when of a sudden the hitherto dumb girl said distinctly, '*Tha mo sheanair ag éirigh*', 'My grandfather is arising', and the mother said, 'if these are your first words of speech it is time for us to retire' ('*Ma 's i sin a' chiad chainnt a fhuair thus*', *tha 'n t-am againn a bhith gluasad*'). Thereupon they retired hastily to the *cùl-tigh* (upper end of the house) and closed the door, barricading it with two querns and other articles. The speech of the child proved true, for the corpse rose and pushed against the door, but finding it impossible to force an entrance, began to dig the ground under the doorpost with his nails, and, having forced himself halfway through the opening thus made, he cried, '*Thugad mi! Thugad mi!*' 'I am getting at you!' Shortly after the cock crew, and he became motionless, and was found in this position when his son came back from the Baile in the morning. After the body was placed in the coffin it was almost impossible to carry it, and this unnatural weight was felt by the bearers until the Baile was sighted, when the weight became suddenly the weight of an ordinary corpse. Several descendants still survive in Uist. Many of them emigrated to America. Those in South Uist are, I think, all Catholics. [I 20]

[1] This story is still told in Uist. See Margaret Fay Shaw, *Folksongs and Folklore of South Uist*, p. 10. I heard the late Seonaidh Caimbeul, South Lochboisdale, tell this story in 1935 and took down the Gaelic.

[2] *Sic.*

2. *A Story of Loch Skipport*[1]

A skipper of a vessel put into Loch Skipport, and as he was pacing the deck during the night, he on three successive nights observed a singular phenomenon. On the coast opposite there was a dwelling-house, and towards this house he observed coming from the north a ball of fire. This ball of fire always turned back without doing any injury whenever the cock crew.

The skipper went ashore and asked the people of the house to spend that night with him on board, and at the same time made a bargain for the purchase of the cock. To these proposals the people of the house agreed, and proceeded to the vessel which lay at anchor. As they were walking the deck they all saw the ball of fire coming from the north, and proceeding to the house as usual. This night the ball entered one end of the house and came out at the other end, and then re-entered the dwelling, which was consumed by flames before the eyes of the owners. The skipper asked if they could give any explanation for this strange occurrence. 'The only explanation I can give,' said the man of the house, 'is that this has happened as a punishment for some wrangling that took place between my wife and me during the last few days.' [I 28]

3. *Lachlann Mac Mhaighstir Alasdair and the Shinty Game*

Lachlann mac Mhaighstir Alasdair, ['Lachlan son of the Reverend Alasdair', *c.* 1700–70], brother of our most famous bard,[2] was tacksman of Draemisdale in South Uist. He was a Catholic at one time of his life, but afterwards forsook the faith. When dying he sent for Fr Campbell's great-grandfather to get a priest for him, but the family of Arivullin would not allow the priest near, and so the man died without the rites of the Church, though it is hoped in the hands of Charity.

There are many remarkable stories told of his appearing after death to various persons, to several of whom he is said to have declared that he is to wander through the world till the day of Judgment as a punishment for neglecting his religion.

[1] This story was used by Miss Freer in 'The Powers of Evil in the Outer Hebrides', *Folklore*, vol. X, p. 263, and in her book *Outer Isles*, p. 233. The Editor of *Folklore* added the footnote; 'This curious story is widely spread in Scotland. See Hugh Miller, *Scenes and Legends*, p. 72; *Notes and Queries*, 7th series, vol. XI, p. 95.' In *Outer Isles* Miss Freer reprinted the footnote as if it were her own.
The story is, or was till very recently, current in South Uist.

[2] Alexander MacDonald, whose ghost is said to have been seen in Uist in recent years.

Iain mac Dhòmhnaill òig 'ic Nìll [John, son of Donald, son of Neil], who died about twenty-five years ago [*c.* 1863], of Dalibrog, and whose daughter still [1888] lives at Kilphedir, was when a boy playing shinty on a Sunday evening by moonlight on the strand of Dalibrog. There was a dispute about a goal, and questionable language was used in the course of the dispute. In the midst of the uproar a being appeared at the tide-mark. His stature was great and his appearance familiar to none present. The boys were terrified and ran away.

When grown to manhood this Dalibrog boy engaged as farm-servant with Rev. Mr Munro of Draemisdale, and it was his duty to keep watch during the night and pound the cattle that strayed into the corn. On a certain night Angus Munro, the son of the minister, came to the bothy and told the man to hurry up as the cattle were devouring the hay. He had one object of his own in view at the time. The man went out to look for the cattle, and encountered an unknown man of great stature, as he was going in one direction. He turned then in another direction and met this strange being again. A third time, as the farm servant was crossing a clachan, or stepping stones, the unknown being stood once more in his path. The man was terrified and uttered the exclamation, '*A Dhia 's a Mhoire, glacaibh m'anam*', 'God and Mary, preserve my soul!' The unknown answered, '*Tha sin glé mhath, ach cha b'i sin a' chàinnt a bh'agad 'n uair a chuala mise mu dheireadh thu*', ['That's all very well, but that wasn't your language when I last heard you'], and at the same time he told the man that he was the being who terrified him and others while playing shinty on the Dalibrog strand. After this he appeared several times to the same person, and told him that he was Lachlann mac Mhaighstir Alasdair.[1] [I 49]

(From Rev. A. Campbell)

Later, Fr Allan McDonald noted that:

A stone forming goal was taken up in the hand and put round the head three times, saying, '*Dà choilleag dhiag eadar mi is Dia gun deach i mach no nach deach*' ['twelve goals between me and God whether it went out or not'].

[This was] said in shinty match, till Lachlann Mac Mhaighstir Alasdair appeared at Bruthach na Saile-daraich. This was the old way of settling a dispute. It is a gross enough violation of the Second Commandment. [I 196]

[1] Story I 49 is marked 'H' by Miss Freer in Fr Allan McDonald's list of contents, and was presumably referred by her to local history.

THE FUATH OR EVIL SPIRIT

Stories about the *Fuath* or evil spirit belong perhaps to folklore rather than to psychical phenomena, but as these stories, though second-hand, are told with some circumstantiality, they are included here.

As J. G. Campbell remarked,[1] the attributes of the *Fuath* are different in different tales. He does not have any stories about the *Fuath* being associated with rivers.

Miss Freer used all of these *Fuath* stories (I 21–6), first in *Folklore*, vol. X, pp. 273–4, where I 22 and I 26 appear verbatim, and in *Outer Isles*, pp. 244–6, where they are somewhat condensed, and the names of persons and places are omitted. In consequence of the reproduction in *Folklore* of I 22 in the first person, where Fr Allan McDonald's 'I've met men who would not go to catch fish' is rendered 'I have met men who would not dare to go to catch fish', the reader of *Folklore* would be left with the impression that the anecdote had been directly told to Miss Freer.

4. Dangerous to Kill Fish at Spawning Time

It is believed among the people that a curse follows the occupation of killing fish in spawning time, and that those who follow the occupation are apt to encounter a '*fuath*' or evil spirit, and I've met men who would not go to catch fish at that time from the fear of encountering this *fuath*. [I 22]

5. An Encounter at Spawning Time

Ronald Macdonald was farm servant with Rev. John Chisholm, priest of Bornish. He had set a net in the spawning time across the little stream to the west of the house. At midnight he went to pull the net. He saw a man of gigantic stature at the other end of the net, and retired in terror to the house. He was pursued by the gigantic figure till he entered the house.

He verily believed he had encountered the *fuath*. [I 26]

6. 'Time to Share'

A story is told in Uist of one Alasdair Mór Mac Iain Làidir, who lived at some undated epoch, having gone to kill fish in a stream by night at spawning time, and while so occupied being joined by a

[1] *Witchcraft and Second Sight in the Scottish Highlands* (Glasgow, 1902), p. 188.

fellow labourer to him unknown. They agreed to work in partnership and to share the catch equally. After landing a great quantity of fish the unknown was incessantly urging Alasdair to proceed to the distribution of the spoil, saying: "*S mithich roinn! 'S mithich roinn!*' '*Cha mhithich, cha mhithich,*' *os Alasdair*, '*tha tuilleadh éisg air an abhainn fhathast.*' 'No, no, there's lots of fish in the stream yet.' At last the moorcock crew, and Alasdair's fellow-labourer vanished in a flame of fire and to his astonishment Alasdair found that his fish were only phantoms.[1] [I 21]

7. *Dangers of Nocturnal Fishing*

Subjoined is a further example connected with the *fuath* and untimely nocturnal fishing.

Alex. Walker of Buaile M[h]ór above Milton, South Uist, about sixty years ago [*c.* 1827] was engaged catching fish by night at Leacach, Staolaval. When so engaged he perceived a man coming down the stream. He himself told the man to step aside so as not to frighten the fish. The person so addressed obeyed. Mr Walker had caught a good quantity of fish by this time and while following up the sport, he was astonished to see something like a mill-wheel rolling down towards him.[2] He thought that things did not look altogether canny, and he deemed it prudent to decamp with all speed. He picked up his fish hurriedly and put them on a withe with the exception of one fish, which he had decapitated accidentally by tramping upon it with his boot. As he was going away he stowed the fish away in a nook where he could afterwards easily find them, and then hurried off to the nearest dwelling, which was at Lochboisdale, the house of Roderick son of Dougal Steele. On his way over the moor he was frequently thrown to the ground. On asking his pursuer if he had any part with God, '*Am beil pàirt agad do Dhia?' Ma tha, bruidhinn rium,*' he got no answer. In the morning he returned for his fish and got none but the headless one. The above narrative is true. [I 23 and 24]

8. *Story of the Three Men from Kildonan*

Three men, one from Kildonan, the other from Milton, the other from either of these townships in all likelihood, went to fish by night,

[1] As Duncan Macdonald, Peninerine, told me this story (1951), the point was that the fish were to be assigned to each party in turn, and to make up the number Alasdair himself would have been assigned to the Evil One last of all. He saw that, and so kept putting off the final division until the cock crew.

[2] *Cf.* Story No. 28 (I 237) for reference to a similar object.

as usual on Abhainn Hornary. They had cabers for splashing and terrifying the fish into the nets. They also used these cabers as vaulting poles when crossing the stream, and in one spot where there was a stone standing in the middle of the stream it was their custom to vault towards this stone, and afterwards by another leap get across. On the night in question as they were going to cross the stream they perceived a man standing on the stone, who stretched out his hand and helped the first two comers over. As the third who expected to meet with the same courtesy was addressed in the following terms by him who stood in the middle of the stream: '*Cha tàinig t'uair-sa fhathast*' ['Your time has not come yet'] and he got no assistance. The two men who were helped over soon after fell into decline and used to exchange visits during their illness, remarking, '*B' fhurusd' aithneachadh gun robh rud-eiginn tighinn oirnne bho oidhche Abhainn Hornary*,' ['It was easy to see that something came over us from the night at Hornary River.'] They both died shortly after.[1] [I 25]

SECOND SIGHT, PREMONITIONS, UNCANNY NOISES, POLTERGEISTS, AND OTHER HAUNTINGS

The remaining stories in Fr Allan McDonald's Notebook I must have been a discovery of considerable interest to the persons associated with the S.P.R. Second Sight Enquiry. They are printed here in the order in which they occur, except that anecdotes connected with teleportation by the host of the dead, which is rather a different subject, have been separated.

All these anecdotes were ticked by Miss Freer, presumably for copying, but I have not been able to discover that she ever published any of them, apart from numbers 10 and 11 here.

9. *A Lamb seen in a Coffin*

A carpenter named Alex. Steele says that when making a coffin for the daughter of Angus M., Garrynamonie, who was of feeble intellect in life, he observed a lamb surrounded with rays of light standing in the coffin. What struck him particularly was that the coffin was in a dark part of the house.

He observed exactly the same phenomenon while making a coffin for Neil Campbell (Malcolm's son) of North Boisdale, who died in 1867. [I 11]

[1] I have heard Duncan Macdonald, Peninerine, tell this story also.

10. A Cock Forewarns of Drowning[1]

John Morrison, joiner, Kilphedir, was playing the bagpipes in his house on a winter's evening, while there was a terrible snow-drift outside. The cock suddenly came down from his roost and began to crow and to leap up, flapping his wings at the piper. His wife, who herself narrated me the incident, told the husband to cease playing, as the action of the cock boded some untoward occurrence. In the lull that followed the shrill notes of the pipe, the group around the blazing turf fire began to meditate on what mishap had occurred, or was likely to occur that night. The violence of the storm without, and the blinding and deceiving nature of the snow-drift made it quite certain to their excited minds that some evil was abroad. They thought perhaps that the priest who had been seen to pass south may have succumbed to the storm while returning home. In the midst of their surmises a rap was heard at the door and the voice of the priest was distinguished asking for the goodman of the house. He went to the door, and being taken a little apart by the priest, he was told that his brother Malcolm had met with his death in the storm, being deceived by the drift, and had [walked] into Loch nam Faoileann, where, falling through the ice and being speedily benumbed, he was unable to extricate himself. The brother John heard the news with surprising composure, his mind having been previously prepared for the worst. [I 27]

11. Confusion amongst Poultry Foretells a Death[2]

(1) Mrs A. Walker, Dalibrog, told me a singular story. She had gone to visit a sick old woman who was a Protestant. She was alone with the sick woman whose relatives were seated round the fire at the other end of the house. The woman was not thought to be in any immediate danger of death. All of a sudden all the fowls on the roost descended to the floor, and a great deal of confusion ensued among them. They rushed about from corner to corner of the room as if pursued by an enemy. Mrs Walker was astonished and frightened, and could not explain the extraordinary occurrence, when she suddenly turned her eyes to the sick woman, and beheld her a stark corpse, to her horror. It is needless to say that she regards the whole incident as 'uncanny'. [I 30]

[1] This story was used by Miss Freer in *Folklore*, vol. X, p. 264, almost verbatim, and in *Outer Isles*, p. 233.

[2] These stories were used by Miss Freer in *Folklore*, vol. X, p. 264, and *Outer Isles*, p. 234.

(2) A tailor in South Boisdale told me of an experience of nearly a similar nature that he had while working [for] a Protestant. He is fully convinced that there was nothing natural to account for the extraordinary commotion among the fowls. [I 31]

12. Ghostly Warnings not to break the Sabbath[1]

A man named Dougal MacKintosh from Keanovay, Loch Eynort, was engaged a few years ago working at a pier at Loch Skipport, and it was his custom to come home to Loch Eynort on Saturday and to return to his work crossing the hills before dawn on Mondays.

On Monday morning as he was crossing the moor between the High Road and Abhainn Ghaetraic, the tie of his shoe became loosened, and he stopped to tie it. On raising himself up again, he beheld a strange man standing before him and before he had time to think much of the matter the stranger addressed him thus: '*Na biodh eagal ort romhamsa, ach thoir an aire nach brist thu 'n Dòmhnach tuilleadh.*' 'Be not afraid of me, but take care that you do not break the Sunday again.' The old code was to observe the Sunday '*bho dhol fodha na gréine Di-Sathurna gus an éireadh i Di-luain*', 'from sunset on Saturday to sunrise on Monday', according to *Duan an Dòmhnaich*, 'the Ballad of the Lord's Day'.[2] [I 69]

13. A Death Light

Towards the end of August 1888 I was called to attend a dying woman at South Lochboisdale. After administering the rites of religion, a crew and boat were procured. As we were nearing Strom Dearg, one of the rowers drew attention to a light playing on the shore just at the spot where we had embarked. It continued for some time, but its appearance did not cause much astonishment, only we could not imagine what objects any person would have in being in such a spot at such a time.[3] We thought the dying woman would live till morning, but when the boatmen returned home, the woman was dead, and they were told she was dead just at the time we should have been approaching Strom Dearg. The men spoke of the light and made diligent enquiry if any person had been to the shore, and

[1] This anecdote was not ticked by Miss Freer. In the list of contents it is marked with a question mark.

[2] 'Which find on next page' wrote Fr Allan. There follows a version of this ballad which he had taken down from Mrs D. MacCormick, North Lochboisdale, in 1887. Other versions can be seen in *Carmina Gadelica,* I 216; *An Ròsarnach*, IV 64 (version contributed by Donald Sinclair from Fr Allan McDonald's missing papers). See also *Eriú,* III 143.

[3] 'Time?' written by Miss Freer in the margin.

it was found out that no person was there. The coincidence was remarkable. The woman was one Mrs John Currie, a saintly woman, who bore a long illness with uncomplaining fortitude, and would not allow the people of the house stay up to watch her. Her illness was cancer in the stomach and she endured tortures without ever groaning, saying God would be better pleased with her for suffering in silence. [I 140]

14. Voices at Glaic Chàrnan an t-Seirm

A spot in Eriskay is called Glaic Chàrnan an t-Seirm. Voices were frequently heard in this spot, and a *càrnan* [cairn] was set up to mark the spot. 'And there was little wonder that voices should be heard, considering that so many people were to come to stay in the island afterwards'. The sounds were only a *manadh* or warning, foretelling of future events. [I 159]

15. Voices heard at Carshaval

Two brothers Donald and John MacCormick of Kilphedir were during spring this year 1889 working at Carshaval. The night was setting in, and the other workers had gone home. They wished to stay longer to finish some work they had begun. They heard a voice between the road and the Loch saying to them, '*Tha 'n t-am agaibh a dhol dhachaigh*' ['It is time for you to go home']. They paid no attention. The warning was repeated and they went home. This hill is said to be haunted. [I 209]

16. Screams Heard at Carshaval

Alex. MacIntyre, Buail' Àrd, Kilphedir, three years ago, 1886, was returning on a Sunday night from the house of a neighbour Alex. MacLellan. On his way between the two houses, he heard great cries coming from Carshaval. He went into his father's house and asked the inmates to go out. They also heard the turmoil.[1] [I 210]

17. Noises like Carts Clattering at Carshaval

Mrs Hector MacPhee [Bean Eachainn Dhùbhghaill], Garrynamonie, was proceeding past Carshaval one night and heard a most tremendous uproar as if all the carts in the country were clattering over the stoniest of places at once. She saw nothing extraordinary. [I 211]

[1] Miss Freer wrote in margin, 'Any coincidence since?' and below, presumably after getting a reply from Fr Allan McDonald, 'no coincidence—up to February 1899'.

18. Noise Heard on Eriskay

In Eriskay half way between Baile and Coil[l]eag a' Phrionnsa there is a path leading through a wide gap in a sandhill. John (son of Michael) with other schoolboys were playing at shinty in this place about eighteen or nineteen years ago [*i.e.* about 1870]. It was in winter time and there was a fine moonlight. A cloud came over the face of the moon, and the players retired to the side of the sandhills. There was a dog with them. 'Look at the dog,' said one of the company. The dog appeared to be in great terror with his hair standing erect. Suddenly they all heard a rumbling noise as if all the iron sheets in the ships of the Kingdom were being jolted over the ground and rocks into the sea proceeding from East to West. The boys scampered and were not philosophical enough to examine into possible natural causes for the occurrence.[1] [I 212]

19. Voices of Dead Person at Iochdar

Widow Ronald MacDonald, Dalibrog, went one day to Iochdar to see friends. At night they sat up late talking over the news of friends far and near. She was overcome with sleep owing to her fatiguing walk. Her companion pulled her dress to awaken her. She was awakened but fell asleep immediately. After a while her companion wakened her again and insisted that she should go to bed. Next morning her companion told her that the first time she awakened her she had just heard a voice saying, '*Éiribh agus gabhaibh a chadal*' ['Get up and go to sleep'], and the second time '*Éiribh as a sin agus gabhaibh ur n-ùrnaigh agus gabhaibh a chadal air neo bithidh 'n t-aithreachas oirbh*' ['Get up out of there and say your prayers and go to sleep, or else you'll repent of it']. She said she thought the voice belonged to a neighbouring woman who had died shortly before, and so suddenly that a pot of water she had put on the fire for washing was used for the washing of her corpse. [I 213]

20. Noise in a House in Iochdar

Mr MacEachen of Iochdar was a merchant and had made a fair amount of money. He built a new house and an excellent one comparatively, but he never entered it alive. His body was laid out in it, however. There were rumours about its being haunted. Mrs Ronald MacDonald, Dalibrog, spent a night in it, and she declares that the whole night—which was a calm one—doors were banging,

[1] 'Is this where you found some signs of human occupation?' added by Miss Freer at the end.

footsteps were trampling up and downstairs, blows were given to the floor as if stones were falling. '*Gu dearbh fhéin, cha do chòrd an turtaraich a bh'ann ach miadhoineach rium*' ['Indeed, the uncanny noises there didn't please me very much']. One Archibald MacDonald (Beag), an emeritus Ground Officer, is said to have left the house on account of disturbances said to occur there. [I 214]

21. Noise in a House in Kilphedir

A very parallel case existed in Kilphedir. One Alex. Steele a joiner, lived in it along with an old man called John Steele. The report was current that noises were heard in it. Mrs Ronald MacDonald accompanied Mrs Steele on her way to Lochboisdale pier as the latter was emigrating with husband and family for Manitoba. She asked her if it was true about the house being disturbed. 'O yes, I often heard strange sounds and *turtaraich* [uncanny noises], but we never saw anything; but I believe old John Steele saw things as well.' After Steele went away, the house was vacant for a year, when it was taken by the present [1889] holder Widow C. MacKinnon. She had a son by her first husband called Angus Walker. This son with the rest of the family spent a day in July 1886 in transferring furniture to Steele's house. Angus then went to look after some kelp he was making on the machair and became very ill, so ill that he could not be taken to the new house, and he died the very night he meant to [have] gone to stay in the new house. No voices have been heard since. [I 215]

22. Woman struck by something uncanny in Dalibrog

Widow John MacMillan of Dalibrog, was at the township road one evening struck by something, and thrown to the ground, about two or three years ago. She did not deem the occurrence natural. A few days after, a woman in the neighbourhood died, and some planks belonging to her were put into requisition for making the coffin . Singularly enough, the lads who came for the planks threw them all down in the place where she had been thrown to the ground. [I 216]

23. Haunted House and Writing in Iochdar

Uisdean Mac Thormoid's case in Loch Carnan, Iochdar, was peculiar. Two women were carding, and they observed what they took to be writing on the ashes. They asked the invalid abovenamed to get up and read the writing. He would not get up. One of the women looked out and she saw the priest, Rev. MacColl, coming; and going into the house she said, '*Coma leibh, tha fear a' tighinn a leughas an sgrìobhadh*' ['Never mind, there's a person coming who can read the writing']. But when the priest came in, the writing was removed, and not by any party visible. Showers of stones etc. were frequent. [I 217]

24. '*The Little Ghost of Angus, son of Neil*'

A Poltergeist in Benbecula [1]

Bòcan beag Aonghais 'ic Nìll [the little bogey of Angus, son of Neil]. In Lianiclet, Benbecula, there lived a man well known as Aonghas MacNeill. He built a new house, and was digging a potato pit when a neighbour remarked to him, '*Tha e cho math dhut gabhail ealamh ris an àite sin agus duine air a thiodhlacadh ann*' ['You'd better leave that place alone; a man is buried there']. He merely laughed and proceeded with his work. After that, as the people of the house sat by the fireside, '*bhiodh cuifeannan 'gan caitheamh air fheadh an taighe*', bits of sticks and peats used to be thrown about the house and fire, and a shinty in the house was used by an invisible hand to belabour the feet of all[2] present. A friend of the man of the house, a Protestant, undertook to allay the spirit, but in his contest [fared] very ill. '*'S gann a fhuair e a bheatha leis*' ['He hardly got away with his life']. It was singular that no matter where the shinty was hidden, it was always found by the spirit and used as above related. One day the man of the house going to the shore for weed took the shinty with him, and going out to a point, hurled it into the sea as far as he could, saying, '*Théid mise 'n urras nach cuir an caman dragh tuilleadh oirnn*' ['I'll bet the shinty won't trouble us any more']. There was a strong east wind at the time.[3] However, the shinty was to the fore that night as usual. After some time the '*cuifeannan* and the shinty' were laid aside and a new mode of procedure adopted. A small hand would be seen playing with a switch (*steafag*) and it would come through the boarding at the bedside. This continued for a year, when a voice said, 'I will not come any more.' The disturbance thereafter ceased.

The *tobhta* or ruined walls of the house, are still standing, and the following story is told regarding them. Two girls were with the cattle at the fold, and a shower of rain coming on they took shelter at the ruin and began plucking grass growing within for their cows. '*Dé*

[1] I have heard this story discussed quite recently in Benbecula.

[2] 'old' in MS. [3] Which should have carried the shinty out to sea.

nan tigeadh Bòcan beag Aonghais 'ic Néill?' ['What if Angus MacNeill's little bogey were to come?'] said one. '*Seadh! Seadh! Seadh!*' ['Yes! Yes! Yes!'] three times responded a slender shrill voice.[1] [I 218]

25. *A Ghost seen at Peninerine*

Cuidhe Pheighinn-an-Aorainn. A tall female in black is said to haunt this spot. Donald MacCormick,[2] Kilphedir, was once riding past and she appeared by his side quite as tall as himself on horse-back. [I 230]

26. *Mrs D. MacKinnon and Lachlan MacDonald (decd.)*[3]

Mrs Donald Roy MacKinnon of North Lochboisdale was going home from Dalibrog one evening in the winter of 1887. When approaching the little stream called Abhainn Cham she was passed by Ronald MacDonald, crofter, Garryhillie, and by the factor's machine [*i.e.* trap] returning from Lochboisdale. These people had not gone far past, when she perceived herself accompanied by a person she did not know. It was her intention to call at some house on the way, but the stranger reading her mind told her that it would be better not to call. He accompanied her to the neighbourhood of her house when she became so overcome with terror that she fainted. Her son Malcolm found her in a fainting condition. It was fully a week before she got over her fright. The stranger said many things to her, and said that she should tell Gilleasbuig Ruadh's sister at Lasgeir not to be going out of doors at night. He said other things too, which she did not believe herself at liberty to divulge. He told her also that he was to meet her yet. [I 231]

27. *John MacKinnon, Eriskay, and Voice Warning*

John MacKinnon, Eriskay (Iain beag mac Iain 'ic Mhurchaidh), had gone to bed and after sleeping for some time wakened and continued awake. He heard the door of his house open and a man rushing in hurriedly, saying, '*Iain bhig! Iain bhig! greas ort!*' ['Little John! little John! Hurry up!']. He knew the voice to be that of his nephew Malcolm MacKinnon who lived in the next house. He

[1] A Gaelic version of this story, taken down by D. J. MacDonald from Donald Allan MacQueen in Iochdar, is printed in Gordon Mac Gill-Fhinnein's *Gàidhlig Uidhist a Deas*, p. 58. Here the incident is said to have happened at Cill Amhlaidh in South Uist.

[2] Donald MacCormick was the school attendance officer. There is an interesting description of him by Frederick Rea in *A School in South Uist*.

[3] So titled by Fr Allan. For Lachlan MacDonald see p. 251.

got up as quickly as he could, and went over to Malcolm's house, but found it closed, and no person awake. He walked round the house but there was no sign of a light or any person being up. He could not get into the house. He went back then to his own house and busied himself raising the fire, awaiting Malcolm's return, thinking by this time that Malcolm may have gone down to look after boats and that he would call again on his way back. He waited, but in vain. He asked the wife if she had heard the call. She said she didn't. Two days after, Malcolm rushed into the house, hurriedly exclaiming, '*Iain bhig! Iain bhig! greas ort!*' He was not in at the time. A brother-in-law of his called Donald (Bàn) Currie, was being drowned out in front of the house. He was returning with a boat load of sea-weed. This occurrence explained the matter. The voice was considered a '*manadh*' or warning. [I 232]

28. A Wheel-like ghost[1] *at Lag nam Bòcan, Dalibrog.*

Between the house at Dalibrog of Widow Stewart and Widow J. MacMillan, Marion MacKinnon declares that she has observed a strange being as also something like the iron rim of a cart wheel rolling past her, and will on no account take that road alone after dark. Donald MacMillan also heard a strange noise there, which he was not able to account for satisfactorily. [I 237]

29. Uproar on hill at South Lochboisdale[2]

Mrs Ewen Morrison, South Lochboisdale, when herding cattle on the hill above the townland fell asleep and was awakened by what she took to be some one calling out to her. On wakening she heard a great uproar but could see nothing and she hurried home in alarm. [I 241]

30. Ghost seen at Bàgh Hàrtabhagh[3]

One stormy night, several men from Eriskay were fishing for herring at Bàgh Hàrtabhagh about eight years ago [*i.e.* around 1880]. They were Alex. Campbell, John MacInnes, Alex. MacInnes, Archibald MacDiarmid and Alex. O'Henly. The night was very rough and coming ashore they had no fire in their shieling, so they started for South Lochboisdale, joining hands so as not to go astray from each other in the bogs. One of the party saw a being like a man walking on a hillock a little apart—'*spaidsearachd air a' chnoc,*'—and asked if

[1] *Cf.* similar object described in another anecdote on p. 254.
[2] This item was not ticked by Miss Freer.
[3] Fr Allan McDonald's title is 'Meeting a Mysterious Man'.

all the party were together. They answered that they were. He then asked if they saw anything, and they said they did. They hurried on to South Lochboisdale in terror in the most unclement weather, and three of them came to Donald Campbell the mason's house where they related the adventure. The others found shelter elsewhere. [I 242]

31. Eriskay Alarm Bird[1]

In Eriskay in the spring of 1887, a bird with a terrible scream was observed to flit across the Island from time to time at night. None of the natives ever saw its like before. One man Angus Johnston told me he heard it at his house, and what was more that it seem[ed] to push against his door and to make as much noise in moving about his door as a man would. It was no natural bird he felt convinced. Singularly enough, the autumn of that year was sadly memorable for the number of young people who died through measles in Eriskay, among whom was the only daughter of Angus Johnston. He was telling me about this bird before the illness of his daughter. [I 243]

32. Neil Bowie's Experience

Neil Bowie of Eriskay was returning one evening about five o'clock with his daughter Flora aged about fourteen from Baile to the Harbour. When at Abhainn 'ic Cuithein the girl observed a man with his back towards them moving towards the sea. She did not recognise the person and she asked her father who it was. He could not make out who it was. The person was represented as being clad in the ordinary fisherman style and is said to have red braces over his blue shirt or jersey. They kept gazing at the man and were astonished to see him go to the sea and wade out as he was, and after wading out he dived under the water and was not seen again by them. Whatever the whole apparition meant is not at all clear. Up to this date nothing has happened at the spot. It will be interesting to see if the case is a case of second sight. The occurrence took place about five years ago. The girl Flora is since dead, but Neil is hale and strong. [I 244]

33. An Experience at Bàgh Mór Òdhalaig

Neil (Ruadh) MacPhee, John (Roy) MacPhee, and Dembric [Dominic] Martin were fishing at Bàgh Mór Òdhalaig one evening. It was cold and they went ashore to warm themselves. Neil MacPhee set fire to a tuft of heather near immediately after landing. The others

[1] I have heard stories about this bird, which is said to have been a portent of the aeroplane.

were proceeding in his direction when they perceived by the light of the fire another man quite close to Neil. They shouted to Neil to return to the boat. He did not know what they meant by going away so suddenly, and paid no attention to them. They shouted again and again, saying that they would go away without him if he did not come at once. He went down to the shore, and then they told him what they had seen. He said he saw nothing. The result was that they took the boat [out] at once and in such alarm that they fought to untie the rope ashore fastening the boat, and as no one would venture to go ashore again, the rope was cut. [I 247]

The reason that they took to the boat so eagerly was that the sea is felt to be safe from the ghosts of the land. Fr Allan McDonald makes this clear in an earlier entry, I 37, which reads:

Sea Blessed

The sea is considered much more blessed than the land. A man will stay all night alone in a boat a few yards from the shore without fear, yet he would not stay an hour in the darkness alone on the shore so near him. The boats of course are always blessed and holy water is kept in each boat as a rule. On one occasion going to Eriskay after nightfall I was made aware of this idea of the sea's blessedness. I asked the man who came for me what place on shore would his companion be in, who was awaiting us. He won't be on the shore at all, by the book. He will be in the boat itself. The sea is holier to live on than the shore.'

It is interesting to compare this with what Miss Freer made of it in *Folklore*, vol. X, pp. 260–1, and *Outer Isles*, p. 231:

The sea is much more blessed than the land. A man will not be afraid to stay all night in a boat a few yards from shore, but he would not stay an hour alone in the dark on land.

A priest told me that one day he was crossing the dangerous Minch, which lies between Uist and Eriskay, on a dark night to visit some sick person. He asked the man who had fetched him where his companion, who was awaiting them, would shelter on the shore. 'He won't be on the shore at all, by the Book! It is in the boat itself he will be. The sea is holier to live on than the shore.'

She did not use I 247.

34. A Poltergeist[1] *at Bàgh Hàrtabhagh*

Malcolm MacDonald, then living at South Lochboisdale, now at North Lochboisdale, was fishing with an Eriskay crew at Bàgh

[1] Fr Allan has 'An Experience at Bàgh Hàrtavagh'.

Hàrtabhagh. The Eriskay crew went home on Saturday but said they would be at the shieling on Sunday night. Malcolm said he would be there too. One of the Eriskay men, Archibald MacDiarmid (dead two years ago) came over on Sunday evening with an Eriskay boat alone of the crew [the only one of the crew to do so], and was landed at Hàrtabhagh. He expected Malcolm to be there, but couldn't find him. After some time, he started to light a fire in the sheiling and was struck by a piece of stick thrown in by the *luithear* [hole in the roof which served as a] (chimney). He uttered no very choice exclamation, to be sure, at what he took to be Malcolm's practical joking. Another piece of stick hit him then. At last he got up and began to look for Malcolm, by whom he felt convinced the sticks were hurled. But no Malcolm could be found. He divined at last that the whole affair was uncanny, and set off for Glendale. [I 248]

35. A Second Sight Experience at Kilphedir

James MacPhee of Kilphedir had an inn at the time of the incident to be narrated. Margaret MacDonald, Dalibrog, was servant there. One evening when coming from [the] stack with [an] armful of peats, she met a man at the door, whom she had never seen before. She told him to go in. He said, '*A bheil iad a stigh?*' 'Are they in?' She told the people inside about him, but as he didn't come in, they laughed at her. She recognised him afterwards in the person of 'Mac Sheumais 'ic Lachlainn' who came from America. The gold watch guard and dress were identical. The gold chain is now in Allan MacDougal, merchant, Lochboisdale's possession. [I 265]

36. Story of Collecting Driftwood

A man from Borve was in the habit of scouring the shore early every morning and often during the night, for driftwood. One night he found a neat little deal of wood on the shore, and remarked to himself that his luck was not so bad. He left it where he found it and went on his rounds, and returned in due course for the board. He found it now to be all gnarled and knotted, and gazed at it in astonishment. The transformation was extraordinary. Another transformation began forthwith, and the board became a dog with its tail curled over its back. The man went homewards in terror, but seeing a light in the priest's house, he thought he would go to him (Rev. Donald MacDonald[1] of Bohuntin, who died in Lochaber afterwards), and narrated the occurrence. The priest who was as much addicted to hunting as his caller to scouring the shore, was making shot at the

[1] Rev. Donald MacDonald was priest of Barra from 1839 to 1851.

time. The priest said it was a warning to both of them not to be so often on the shore.

Right to driftwood, at the time we speak of, was let. [I 319].

(D. MacCormick, Kilphedir)

TELEPORTATION

'Being carried away by the host of the dead' is something of which there were many stories in the Highlands. I have added here some items on the same subject from Fr Allan McDonald's sixth notebook, taken down between January 1897 and June 1898. The reader is also referred to anecdote No. 52 of 'Strange Things' (p. 297 here).

37. Being spirited away by the dead

Another belief among the people is that the dead come at night and take a living person away in their company often a great distance, and return with him before morning. This is called *Falbh air an t-Sluagh.* A dismal sound is said to precede the grim procession. One Eóghainn mac 'ic Iain Bhàin of the South End of Uist is believed to have been borne to Canna in this way and to have eaten potatoes and saithe there. A young man from Iochdar called Iain mac Uisdein 'ic Iain, who went some five years ago to Manitoba,[1] is also believed to have been spirited away in this way. His complexion was very pale and awestricken. His brother is still in Iochdar. [I 224]

38. An Experience at Garryhillie

Three men from Dalibrog about eight years ago ([*i.e.* 1881] went one evening to see a tailor MacCaskill in Garryhillie who had got a severe bruising some time before. When it became late, about ten o'clock, Donald MacMillan, one of the trio, started for home alone. He had not proceeded far when at a spot where there are large white stones on either side of the road—opposite Widow MacIntyre's Croft (Garryhillie)—he heard a sound as if a flock of plovers (*sgaoth fheadag*) were passing. He looked to the East whence the weird sound proceeded and beheld a man moving towards him and then passing by him across the road. The being had not the solidarity of an ordinary body, but stole past as if floating in the air. He could not say whether it was a man or a woman for certain, but he thought it was a man. He did not know what to think of it unless it was the '*sluagh*' on one of their grim processions. It was the strange

[1] See also p. 298.

whistling sound that drew his attention to the matter first as he had never heard stories about the spot before.

It is said that several people have found the same spot uncanny since that date. [I 225]

39. An Experience of Fr. Campbell's[1]

Rev. Alex. Campbell has still the most vivid recollection of an incident of somewhat the same nature that occurred in his boyhood when living at Garryhillie. A rushing sound as if of rushing wind on which were borne wailing sounds was heard as if coming from the Graveyard and rushing to their dwelling. The doors were thrown in and screams were heard, and all the inmates were struck with terror. It was at night time the incident occurred. All who heard the uproar were convinced that it was nothing natural. [I 226]

40. An Experience at Carshaval

Mary Currie and her sister were coming home by Carshaval,[2] and when at the end of the hill they saw a very dark showery cloud (*meall*) coming over the *Lùb* of Kilphedir shore. Her sister asked her to stay till the shower would go past. She was rather insisting on going home, however she yielded to her sister's persuasion. The sound of the Shower going past was terrible and alarming. That same night her father (dead) appeared to her after she went to bed and said to her, '*Bha thusa cur an aghaidh do phiuthair a bhith fuireach an diugh, ach nan robh sibh air dol air adhart bha sibh an cunnart ur beatha chall. B'e sluagh a bha 's a mheall dubh a chunnaic sibh.*' ['You were against your sister waiting today, but if you had gone on you would have been in danger of losing your lives. The black shower you saw today was the host of the dead'.] [I 249]

41. Sluagh seen near South Lochboisdale[3]

Hector MacIntyre of South Lochboisdale saw one evening bright with the moonlight two females swimming in the air past him. They were erect and near the ground. It was shortly before Roderick Gillis's death [in] 1886. [I 293]

[1] Written *c.* 1889. Rev. Fr Alexander Campbell was a native of Uist. The incident would have taken place in the late 1820s.

[2] Carshaval hill, about two miles south of Dalibrog, has a bad reputation for ghosts. See stories on p. 258.

[3] Fr Allan McDonald titled this 'Death Warning'; but it seems to have more in common with the 'host of the dead' stories.

The following items are added from Fr Allan McDonald's sixth notebook:

Unsafe to leave Windows on west side of house open

The window on the west side of the house should never be left open after sunset as that is the side from which the '*sluagh*' or the processions of dead come, and they might be troublesome. [VI 206]

(Taken down December 1897).

It wasn't safe to leave a window facing the West open after sunset. If a woman were milking a cow in the house and a window open, a small arrow might enter and strike the beast dead. The arrows were thrown by the '*sluagh*'—the dead multitude. [VI 345]

(Taken down *c.* April 1898)

How to Avoid the Sluagh

If a person were to go out at night with a sieve in the hand he would require to have a piece of coal in the other hand to prevent his being spirited away by the *Sluagh* or the crowd of dead who wander about in large bands. [VI 145]

(From Marion MacLennan, December 1897)

Name of the Leader of the Sluagh

'*Niall Sgrob*' is the name given to the person who went at the head of the procession of the '*sluagh*'. '*Niall Sgrob air thoiseach an t-sluaigh.*' [VI 346]

(Taken down *c.* April 1898)

THE SECOND NOTEBOOK

Fr Allan McDonald's second quarto notebook was begun at the end of 1889 or the beginning of January 1890, as is proved by the dating of No. 13 (Story No. 44 here), which he says he entered on the night of 6th January 1890. It cannot have progressed at all quickly at first, as No. 60 (Story No. 49 here) was taken down exactly a year later. Following No. 74 of the notebook comes the first six and a half verses of Fr Allan McDonald's Gaelic poem on the Last Day of the Year 1892,[1] but this must have been entered later, as No. 82 is the beginning of the Fionn stories, taken down from Alexander Johnston, Coil(l)eag, Eriskay, 18th December 1892; a large part of these are written in George Henderson's handwriting; as has already been

[1] See *Bàrdachd Mhgr Ailein* (1965), p. 28.

described, he was visiting Uist and Eriskay in November and December 1892.

Fr Allan McDonald called the notebook 'Miscellanea Vol. II'. On the flyleaf he wrote, presumably for Miss Freer's information in connexion with the Second Sight Enquiry, 'In this volume and the preceding I didn't take names and dates always. It never occurred to me to do so as a general rule. To some things however I attached the names of my informants.'

Fr Allan McDonald made no list of contents for this volume, but Miss Freer made an index under classified headings, such as religious stories, historical, plants, etc., with reference to the item-numbers, and the remark 'those crossed I have not copied. A.G.F. June 1899.' This was presumably in connexion with her lectures to the Folklore Society. No. 1 in the notebook, about the sister of St Columba, appears in *Folklore*, vol. X, pp. 271–2; No. 41, the charm for curing cattle, in translation, in *Folklore*, vol. X, p. 279; No. 59, about the house in Morvern where no cocks ever crow, in *Folklore*, vol. X, p. 263. No. 10, about its being lucky for an engaged couple to have their banns called first, appears in *Folklore*, vol. XIII, p. 33.

At the foot of the page Miss Freer wrote,'* said by Fr Allan to be not worth translation'. This * mark is applied against numbers in the text, not in Miss Freer's index of contents. We know from Fr Allan McDonald's diary that it was he who was doing the translating.

Twelve numbers are listed by Miss Freer under the heading 'Second Sight etc.' All were ticked for copying: all are printed here for the first time, so far as I know.

42. A Saw Rising on its End

Donald Campbell, a carpenter living at Arivullin, came into the house of Neil Campbell and said to him, 'It will not be long till I have to make a coffin, for the little saw rose up by itself on the work table today.' In three or four days he was making a coffin for a brother of his own.

This phenomenon was not uncommon, as also the hearing of disturbances among the tools and boards that happened to be in a carpenter's shop. One Alex. Steele said that he did not feel anything of the kind among his tools, but he attributed this fact to his blessing his tools every evening with holy water when leaving the workshop. [II 3]

43. A Plank gave a Moan

Rev. Alex. Campbell and Angus Walker now of Dalibrog, and Dougal MacCormack now in New Zealand, were when children amusing themselves sliding on a plank. Suddenly the plank gave a moan and the terrified children ran away. The wood was used for making a coffin a few days later. [II 4]

(Rev. A. Campbell)

44. *Wailing at Trossary*[1]

On the last Saturday of the year 1889 John Steele, carpenter, belonging to North Boisdale was returning from the house of a tailor called Donald MacIntosh near Trossary with clothes made for him by the said tailor, when he heard weeping and wailing at Trossary. He heard particularly an old man and a young woman wailing. He was so convinced that some person about the place had died, that he was astonished on Sunday to hear no new name read out on the List of the Dead by the priest.

He is now convinced it must have been a warning of death.

I have entered this fully here on the night of 6th January 1890 and it will be interesting to observe how the 'warning' will be accomplished.

It was John Steele himself who related his experience to me on the day succeeding the occurrence. [II 13]

45. *Ghostly Helpers at Sea*[2]

Dougal Campbell of South Lochboisdale owned a smack. To assist him in the management of his craft, he employed Donald MacInnes, Ru' Bàn, Eriskay, an experienced mariner. They were sailing round the Mull of Kintyre on a stormy night, and as the wind blew hard it was found necessary to furl some of the sails. The crew consisted of the two men already named only. They observed two other men standing on the deck in the forepart of the vessel, and overheard them speaking in an unknown tongue. Whenever the crew set to work pulling down the sails or tightening ropes the two strangers were always seen giving a helping hand, and when the men ceased working the strangers also ceased, and stood by talking together in the unknown language. Though both men witnessed these strangers and observed their actions and heard their conversation neither the one nor the other spoke about what he observed until next morning when the day broke [and] they found themselves in smoother water. They could not exactly recognise the strangers, but thought that they bore a resemblance to two uncles of Campbell who had been

[1] Fr Allan's title was 'Trossary warning'.

[2] First line of story used as a title in Fr Allan McDonald's notebook.

drowned some time previously, and they considered that the assistance given them by the strangers was an intervention of Providence in their behalf.

One of the men on seeing the apparition did not deem the matter altogether canny, and proceeded to sprinkle the apparition with holy water, but on his way towards it he fell on the deck and broke the bottle which contained the holy water. He noticed that the strangers did not avoid the spot blest by the holy water, and from this he judged that the coming of the strangers was for good. One of the strangers was dressed in a long black dress like a cassock.[1] [II 22]

> This story is substantially true. I got it from Dougal Campbell afterwards. The cassock is an addition. He said the men seem to have had an Ulster on, and he thought that might be the man who bought the boat afterwards. Others said that they were two deceased uncles of Dougal's.
>
> A. McD.

46. A Light on the Sea[2]

Dugald MacInnes of Village, Eriskay, was fishing on the coast of Skye near Glendale, when one moist night the lookout said he saw a steamboat coming. They were on the lookout at once, and saw the light approaching as if hung to the mast of a steamboat. But there was no steamboat, and strange to say the light proceeded to the shore and rose over the land and seemed to cross the Island of Skye, keeping always at a little elevation above the land. The witness[3] of the phenomenon regarded it as uncanny. The light was red and went against the wind. The night was wet and stormy. The size of the light was like a ship's lamp light. [II 23]

47. Phantom Ships

Phantom ships have been [seen] several times on the coast of Uist and also out at sea at some distance from the land. It is difficult to get the people to believe that the phenomenon is not supernatural. One man who was told by a clergyman that it was only a natural occurrence, answered, '*'S fhad' bho chuala sinn gun dianadh sgoil amadan de dhuine*' ['It's long since we heard that schooling would make a fool of a man'], and he went away maintaining that he had seen the

[1] Items Nos. 19, from the seventh line onwards, to the end of No. 22 were copied into this notebook in the handwriting of George Henderson, presumably from Fr Allan McDonald's rough notes.

[2] This kind of thing is now considered to have been a foresight of aircraft.

[3] Miss Freer wrote in margin 'any other witnesses?'.

seldom-seen 'Flying Dutchman'. Others explain it as a presage or *manadh* of a shipwreck. [II 32]

As Fr Allan does not record any anecdotes of these, I add a story I heard myself from the late Seonaidh Caimbeul in 1935. Seonaidh was born in 1859, the same year as Fr Allan.

On New Year's Day my companion and I were returning home from fishing. We had been staying in a sheiling at Caolas Staolaidh. We were sailing home to Lochboisdale, and the wind was against us. We put the boat about to enter Lochboisdale and I looked out at the time and saw a fine big ship coming northwards past Rubha na h-Òrdaig; she was a very fine big ship, and I watched her constantly, and I told my friend that they had a fine New Year Day after the bad weather they had had on Hogmanay night last night. She was coming straight towards our boat, and we said to each other she must be coming in to anchor in Lochboisdale and she was getting closer to us all the time. She came so close to us that we could have read her name, but it was not on her bows; she was so close to us that we could have made out something as small as a little dog, if such had been on her bridge; and I would say she was deeper in the water than if she had been merely in ballast, but she was not as deep as she would have been fully laden. When she had come as far north as where we had put our boat about, she turned out to sea, and we said to each other that she had only been taking a look at the land, because the day was so fine. There were no lifeboats to be seen on her. She sailed out then about two miles.

Then we saw that more coal had been put into her fires, as a big puff of smoke came from her. I was keeping an eye on her all the time, and I noticed she was getting deeper in the water. Then she drew away straight towards the north and after a short time we saw white smoke come out of her funnel, and I said that she was settling in the water, and looked like sinking. 'Is she?' said my friend. 'Indeed she is,' I said. There were big clouds in the sky, and one of them obscured the sun, and afterwards the sun came out stronger again, and I saw her more clearly some distance away. 'She's going down beyond a doubt,' I said. 'What a calamity,' said my companion. I was watching her all the time. Her gunwhale was painted white and I saw her gunwhale at the water, then she went under. She had four masts and I only saw them for a couple of minutes before they went out of sight, and nothing more was seen or heard of her. When we reached land we told people we had seen this sight, and the Wreck Receiver came to question us about it, and I told him exactly what we had seen and I had nothing more to tell him than that. The Wreck

Receiver said to me, 'I'm not sure you won't see the Tower of London in consequence of this.' But nothing happened afterwards, and we never heard any more about her, or what ship she could be.

48. The Doubles of Sweethearts[1]

(i) A curious phenomenon which seems to have undoubtedly occurred at different times to different persons is that men have been met and struggled with or threatened by the phantoms of women to whom they were engaged to be married, or by whom they were eagerly sought as husbands. This phenomenon occurred principally in cases where there was talk of a breach of the engagement.

John Bàn mac Dhòmhnaill 'ic Fhionnlaigh who lived at Buaile Mhór, Milton, and emigrated to America in 1827, had occasion to rise at night out of bed. The moon was shining brightly through the window at the time, and he saw standing in the moonlight a certain female figure—one of the women of the township, whom he readily recognised. He was much alarmed about the occurrence and consulted afterwards an old man of the township about it. He advised him to speak severely to the woman in question or else that she would cause him trouble. This he did and she admitted that she was thinking of him at the time, though she had not gone out of her own house. He was never afterwards troubled by her. [II 55]

(Told by the Rev. A. Campbell)

(ii) Alex Steele, carpenter, and a companion were going together in the interests of the said companion to arrange a contract of marriage with a certain girl in Boisdale. However, they did not go, and spent the night together. When they had gone to bed, they both observed the said woman looking over them, and both gave a scream of fright. The man never made any more advances to the said party. [II 57]

(iii) A certain man in Morar—a shepherd—used frequently to be confronted by the phantom of a woman when going about his work, and especially at night. She threatened him several times, and were it not for his dogs she might have injured him. The dogs invariably set upon and wounded her and drove her off. After several years he married the woman whose phantom he had encountered so often. [II 58]

49. Cries Heard on the Sea

Towards the end of 1890 cries of people as if drowning were heard from the shore at Pollacharra in the direction of Lingay Island in the Sound of Barra. So distinct were the cries that a boat proceeded im-

[1] No title in MS.

mediately in the direction. One of these in the boat (Rory Morrison, Smerclet), gave me the narrative. After proceeding on their way for some time the crying and shouting ceased, and the men in the boat were thinking of turning back to shore and had actually turned round the boat when the shouting began again, and they speedily pulled round and hastened forward. After a short time the shouting ceased again and the men once more thought of returning, and as they were preparing to do so the shouting was renewed again and they went forward once more, but after doing their best to find anyone in distress, they were obliged to give up and go home. All the crew heard the shouts distinctly. No one was lost at the spot at the time. The shouting is supposed to be a warning of something untoward going to happen at the spot in question.[1] [II 60)

(Rory Morrison, Smerclet, 6th January, 1891)

50. *Train or Engine Seen*[2]

One Norman MacLean, a miller in Smerclet, was on the road above South Boisdale, when he saw at night approaching what looked to him like the engine of a train. It seemed so palpable that he came off his horse's back and held the said horse by the bridle when the apparition passed, as he was afraid the pony might be frightened. It went noislessly past as he held the horse's head.

I heard the incident from himself. This incident occurred in 1890. [II 61]

51. *A Singular Light in the Heavens above Fuday*

On the night of Christmas Day 1890, a singular phenomenon was seen from Eriskay by several people, among whom were John MacKinnon Sr and his wife, Village, [and?] John MacKinnon (John Mór's). In the heavens over above Fuday Island they saw a bright light about the size of a lamp light appearing and disappearing like a lighthouse revolving light. It lasted each time about a minute. It was seen at least three times. The colour of the light was white and bright. The night was a bright moonlit night. Was it possibly a reflexion of some lighthouse?[3] [II 62]

[1] The following comments are added in Miss A. Goodrich Freer's hand: 'Any coincidence yet?' and then 'The Rev. A. Macdonald wrote to me in November 1898 in answer to above query. "An Eriskay boat struck on a rock about this spot this last October, and the crew ran a great risk of being drowned."'
See 'Strange Things', No. 41.

[2] This kind of thing is now considered to have been a foresight of a bus.

[3] A note in Miss Goodrich Freer's hand adds: 'Is the island inhabited?' To which Fr Allan replies: 'One family in it'.

PROPHECIES

52. *Prophecies about Bornish House*

A prophecy existed for about a hundred years that Bornish House was to go on fire, and so much anxiety did this prophecy cause old Mrs Macdonald, Bornish, that she every night personally superintended the extinguishing of all lights about the premises. When the last Bornish left the house he remarked, '*Falbh, tha e coltach gum beil an fhaisneachd gun reachadh an taigh 'na theine briagach.*' [Go, it seems that the prophecy that the house would go on fire was a false one.]

The old house was afterwards roofed anew, and is now occupied by Mr J. Ferguson. The prophecy has not yet been fulfilled, unless the fire which occurred in the farm steading during Mr Ferguson's occupancy be considered a sufficient accomplishment of it. [II 5]

The last [MacDonald of] Bornish was urging some of his tenants to go and work at kelp for him to the detriment of their own tillage work. One of the men quarrelled with him and said, '*Tha iad beò na chì fhathast an càl a' fàs 's an* "dining-room" *agaibh.*' [They're alive who'll yet see cabbages growing in your dining-room.]

This strange prophecy was fulfilled. Neil Campbell who was on the same land with Bornish (when reduced to poverty) actually planted cabbage [*sic*] in the old dining-room. [II 6]

53. *Signs of the Changes that were to happen in South Uist*[1]

The following signs of the changes to take place in Uist were given me [*i.e.* Fr Allan] by Angus MacInnes, October 17th 1896 (Smerclet).

'*Tòiseach nan turragan fitheach geal fhaicinn.*'

'The beginning of the troubles was to see a white raven.' Aonghus òg, Arivullain, saw this bird at Coilleag a' Rògha, and killed it. He was drowned in Loch Eynort not long after, and the family of Arivullain faded out of sight. [V 132]

The next sign was to see a '*Feannag Gheal*', 'White Crow'. Angus himself saw this, and Kilbride, where it was seen, was lost to the family who had it. He says it was not snow-white but very white compared with any other crow he had seen, that it lived with the

[1] These prophecies are included, although those from Fr Allan McDonald's Notebook V do not belong to his early collection. All of them were utilized by Miss Freer, except the last, in *Outer Isles*, pp. 179–80.

other crows, and had the same style of speech—or rather *conversation*—as they had. '*An aon seòrsa còmhraidh aice 's a bh'aig càch.*' [V 133]

Bithidh farmad aig a' bheò ris a' mharbh, 'The living will envy the dead,'—and that happened when they were putting the men out into the sea (*mach air a' mhuir*) at the time of the evictions and forced emigrations, when the emigrants would prefer to be dead in their graves in Hallan than going alive out of the country. [V 134]

Cuiridh mac na mnatha caoile duibhe cas gacha taobh 'an Rògha Ghlas, 'The son of the slender black wife will place a foot on each side of the Rògha Glas.' This was verified when the small tenants were cleared away, and the land on both sides of the Rògha Glas were made into one large farm as it is today. The first who had the farm on both sides of Rògha Glas was [left blank in MS.]. [V 135]

Angus old [also?] gave the following proverb: *Ged is tu mo mhàthair teann o' mhaodail* [*sic*]. A saying of prophetic import as to Uist, signifying that the character of the people would be so selfish, that the daughter would refuse necessaries to the mother. It is one of several other Uist prophecies. Oct. 16, 1896. [V 127]

54. *The Prophecy of the End of Boisdale's Family*

Colin of Boisdale was at a funeral in Hallin beyond Dalibrog. There was a man who had the reputation of being a seer in Garryhillie called Aonghus Mac Iain (Angus says that Donald MacLean's (miller, Garrynamonie) wife is a granddaughter of his (?)). Boisdale sent for him and asked him to tell him the future about himself and family.

'I'd sooner not,' said the *fiosaiche* [seer], 'as you may not care to hear it.' 'Come,' said Boisdale, 'it can't be very bad, and I insist on hearing it.' Angus then said, '*Bithidh thusa* [*sic*] *glé mhath fad do laithean. Bithidh do mhac glé mhath as do dheoghaidh, ach cha mhór as fhiach t'ogha. Agus mu dheireadh thall bheireadh* skiff *Lochlannach a h-uile diar dha t'fhuil seachad air an Rubha Mhurchanach.*'

'*Och, a bhodaich*,' *arsa Cailein*, '*cha bhi mo chuid fearainn-sa mar sin gu bràch.*'

'*Ach nach robh*,' says Angus MacInnes quietly.

['You will be very well off all your days. Your son will be very well off after you, but your grandson will be worth little. And at the end a Norwegian skiff would be able to carry every one of your descendants past the point of Ardnamurchan.'

'Och, you old fool,' said Colin, 'my estate will never be like that.'
'But wasn't it,' says Angus MacInnes quietly.] [V 139]

55. *The Barra Seer*

The name of the fiosaiche or Wizard [*sic*] that the old MacNeils of Barra had was 'Mac a' Chreachainn'. Can it have been Mac Neachtain or MacNeacail—the latter a common enough name in Barra today. 'The son of the scallop shell' seems a strange name. He said, '*Bithidh Barraidh fhathasd fo rodain 's fo gheòidh ghlasa*'—'Barra will yet be under rats and grey geese.' The prophecy is true as to Eoligarry, around which was the home of the people before they were evicted.[1] Eoligarry is proverbial for its rats today. [V 138]

[1] Eoligarry was resettled after the First World War.

2

'STRANGE THINGS'

'STRANGE THINGS' is the title of the notebook whose first pages contain fifty-eight anecdotes which almost certainly must have been taken down by Fr Allan McDonald in connexion with the S.P.R. Second Sight Enquiry. The reasons for supposing this are, first of all, the dates on which the items were recorded, and secondly, the fact that the anecdotes are very carefully written, the names of the sources and the dates are always given, and many of them were told to Fr Allan McDonald at first-hand.

The first batch of anecdotes was entered by Fr Allan on 26th November 1895, not long after Miss Freer had paid her first visit to Uist; by 25th February 1896 forty-eight such stories had been recorded. The next entry is dated 25th May 1897; there are nine others, the latest date noted being 5th June. After that date Fr Allan McDonald recorded no more evidential ghost or second sight stories, a fact which supports the supposition that it was the attacks on the Ballechin House investigation in the London *Times* which started on 8th June, during which the S.P.R. leaders Myers and Sidgwick dissociated the Society from that investigation, which brought the Second Sight Enquiry to an end.

The gap between 25th February 1896 and 25th May 1897 can be partly accounted for by ill-health: on 2nd July 1896 Carmichael wrote to Fr Allan McDonald mentioning that Miss Freer had told him Fr Allan had been very ill. By then his health was improving. During 1896 Fr Allan McDonald was also engaged in noting general folklore and folk-tales in his Notebook V; in this case out of 196 items, only 30 were entered between 26th February and 8th October (Nos. 52–81 inclusive). At the end of 1896 Fr Allan had a visit from George Henderson, who was the source of six items entered in the notebook at the beginning of January 1897.

The fact that Fr Allan entered anecdotes connected with ghost and second sight stories in a special notebook during the winter of 1896–7, when he was also engaged in recording general folklore, is additional evidence that 'Strange Things' was intended for a special purpose. It contains no marks made by Miss Freer, but a photograph of Ballechin House is pasted inside the cover. After 5th June

1897 there are no more entries for over a year, the next being the place-names of Mingulay, taken down on 20th June 1898. These are followed by fifty items of general folklore, after which most of the notebook is filled with Fr Allan McDonald's original Gaelic verse.

'Strange Things' is printed here in exactly the order of the manuscript, one anecdote often leading directly to another. There is no list of contents or index in the original MS., so I have had to provide the titles. Fr Allan McDonald's reference numbers are retained.

The notebook was obviously in Fr Allan McDonald's possession when Miss Amy Murray visited Eriskay in September 1905, as several tunes of Gaelic folk-songs, of which Fr Allan had taken down the words, were written into it by her, and several items contained in the notebook are mentioned by her in her book *Father Allan's Island*, including an anecdote about a human appearing in seal form (footnote to p. 235: this is No. 112 from this notebook).

1–12 Portents[1]

(*1*)

Mrs Oighrig MacCormick,[2] Dalibrog, saw a trunk open of itself. The lid rose up about a foot.[3] It was in her own house. Others heard the noise it made when closing. The trunk was not locked at any time—only closed. It was the year a girl called Mary MacAllister died. This Mary lived in the next house to Mrs MacCormick and was an invalid for years. The opening of the trunk was not more than three months before Mary MacAllister's death. When Mary died a towel belonging to the MacAllisters but at this time in Mrs MacCormick's trunk was taken out of the trunk at the time of washing the corpse.

Mrs MacCormick says she often heard knocks given to trunks—not as if given by a man's hand but hard as if struck by a hammer, and that some trifle or other, perhaps only a pin or needle or whisky glass that would be required in connexion with the corpse or funeral was sure to be taken out of the trunk. This happened so often that she has kept no distinct and separate remembrance of individual cases.

(*2*)

Mrs MacCormick when a servant in John Morrison's (Barrach) Smerclet (while Mr Morrison and his wife were out of the house, at

[1] Anecdotes 1–12 from Mrs MacCormick, Dalibrog, 26th November 1895.

[2] MS. 'MacCormack', but spelt with an *i* in Uist. 'Oighrig' is usually turned into 'Euphemia'.

[3] *Cf.* Amy Murray, *Father Allan's Island*, p. 163.

a ball as far as she remembers, and she and the children were in bed) heard a large saw that was placed above the bed give three blows, and then come down from the top of the bed so that one end of it nearly touched the ground, and then saw it go up and down twice and heard it as if sawing. She put her head under the blankets. She doesn't remember which coffin was made first after this by her master Mr John Morrison. This happened 25 years ago or perhaps before that. There was a *crùisgein* [crusie] lit the whole time.

(3)

Mrs MacCormick saw a plank that stood between the stalls of the cattle in her own house, have a bright light shine upon it.[1] The light shone on about three feet of the plank. She told it at once to those in the house. They said, '*Fada goirid gum bi e, théid e timchioll air marbh fhathast*'—'Whether a long or short time elapse before it happens it is certain that it will be used about the dead yet.' About a month after a poor man called Alexander MacDonald (Lobban) died, and as he had no near relatives to provide a coffin some person came to the MacCormick's house for a plank, and the plank that had been pointed out so significantly before was given with a good will. (about 8 years ago.)

(4)

Mrs MacCormick says that her husband found fault with her for letting people have the use of his horse creels. She made up her mind that if ever they were allowed to go out of the house for the use of others, that it would be only when her husband himself gave them out. She placed them in the sleeping room near the bed. One night, after she and her husband had gone to bed, but she does not recollect whether she had slept for a time and then wakened or whether she had never slept, she heard a noise as of a very dry old creel being broken bit by bit. There were occasionally perceptible intervals of silence. This went on altogether for about a quarter of an hour, she thinks. She nudged her husband and asked him if he heard it. He asked her in reply if she heard it herself. At last there was a big crash of twigs crackling, and the thing ceased.

Next morning or the morning after that (she is not certain which) a man called Ronald MacDonald, plasterer, whom she did not know, came to the house and he asked her if her husband Roderick was in. Roderick was working outside, but she soon fetched him. This man told Roderick that his cousin John, the little plasterer, had died

[1] *Cf.* Amy Murray, *Father Allan's Island*, p. 164.

during the night, and he asked Rory to go to Bornish to fetch carpenter Steele to make the coffin. Rory went to Bornish and got the carpenter and went with him to Lochboisdale where he stayed that night to make the 'corpse'. Next morning Roderick came home and asked the wife to get ready the horse and the creels to carry the biscuits and whisky to the graveyard. Mrs MacCormick thinks the little crackling as of twigs at first meant the rattling of the biscuits in the creels afterwards.

(5) *A Corpse Candle*

When living in Loch Eynort South Uist at a place called Rubha nan Clach, a young man called Mac Iain 'ic Fhearchair went out of the house to go and fish trout. That evening Oighrig and her mother were carding wool. A delicate brother was in bed. The mother saw a 'candle' of light pass by her to the upper end of the house. She thought it was a sign that the sick brother was in danger and she called out to him, and he shouted in reply that he was all right.

Next day a brother of the young man who had set out to fish from Oighrig's house, came to get two square little jars as he was going for whisky for his brother's funeral. The lad had been found dead at the side of a stream and his catch of trout was found near him on the ledge of a rock. Oighrig was 13 or 14 years old then.

(6)

A Mrs Morrach Campbell was coming along with Oighrig then about 11 years old from Northbay, Barra, to Eoligarry, when they reached the Tràigh Mhór or Great Strand. Both heard the pipes playing behind them. Both of them were afraid. The piping continued the whole way till they reached Eoligarry. They both thought it the warning of a funeral at which the pipes would be played coming to Kilbarra graveyard in front of Eoligarry house. Mrs Campbell died a good long time ago.

(7)

Mrs MacCormick says that her sister Mary MacMillan, still alive in Eriskay, when at service in Kilbride farm South Uist at night-fall at the Cnoc-a-deas saw a phantom funeral, and that [she] went aside out of the way, and that she heard the creaking of the coffin passing. She thinks that Mary recognised the people attending the funeral. (To be inquired into from Mary herself when I see her.)

(*8*)

Widow Angus MacLeod, Dalibrog, told Mrs MacCormick that two or three years before Malcolm Morrison was found in Loch nam Faoileann, Dalibrog, she heard a loud cry (*ràn*). It was so distinct that she came out of her house. When the accident happened she recognised the cry as that of Peggie the daughter of John MacKay, Kilphedir, and of a sister of the deceased Mrs Neil MacCormick.

(*9*)

She says that Neil James McLeod saw something this last autumn on the high road not far from his own house. This Neil James McLeod lives halfway between Dalibrog and the pier at Lochboisdale.

(*10*)

She says that her brother Alexander MacMillan still alive in Eriskay (1895) saw a spar of wood in the boat rise two or three times by itself, and that it was afterwards used for carrying a coffin.

(*11*)

She had heard that somebody (she could not tell who) had seen planks leaping by themselves[1] from the ground at Donald MacDonald's (joiner) Dalibrog. She acknowledged that she did not like to take the road past the house at the time she heard this. Donald MacDonald made a coffin since for Kate MacKygan who died in the hospital and it is probable that he also supplied the wood.

(*12*)

She was under the impression that her maternal uncle Iain MacNeill saw the *Bean-Nighe*[2] at the edge of a loch at Smerclet. I asked her how the *Bean-Nighe* or 'washing-fairy' was dressed according to what she had heard. She had a *còt uachdar* [top coat] and a large brooch on her breast. She had never heard of any particular colour that the *Bean-Nighe* seemed to wear in preference.

13. Evil Eye

Mrs Catherine MacDiarmid who died about four years ago in Eriskay had a great fund of folk-lore. She gave the following story as

[1] *Cf.* Amy Murray, *Father Allan's Island*, p. 164. [2] See No. 27.

a personal experience. She was at service down in the middle of Uist. A man was passing as she was milking a cow. She gave a drink of milk from the cogue. No sooner had the man left than the cow became obstreperous and began to rush about wildly. Next morning the cow was equally wild. She consulted an old man about it. He told her to put a pair of trousers on the horns of the cow. She did this, and the cow started southwards and she after the cow. The cow never stopped till it stopped at the door of the house of the man who had got the drink of milk the day before. (I have no doubt that the man in question was contumeliously spoken to.) The cow returned quietly and gave no further trouble.
(Annie MacIntyre—who heard it from herself—2nd December 1895)

14

Neil MacIsaac's experience at the Sound of Eriskay.[1]

15

Mrs John MacDonald's (Murdoch's) experience.

16

The spinning wheel that worked by itself at night.

17. The Evil Eye

Annie heard of a woman in Eriskay who would not milk her cows in the presence of her own husband because he had the evil eye.[2] (They are chary of mentioning names in this connexion and I have a delicacy in asking. Though I have often heard of the evil eye I am never told of any special people who have got it.)

In 1898 Fr Allan McDonald entered the two following anecdotes on the same subject in this notebook (Nos. 63 and 64):

(1) The belief in the evil eye is universal, and it is all a question of evidence whether its existence is admitted or not. I must take evidence upon it and if the evidence prove satisfactory I will believe

[1] Stories 14–16 are left blank in MS. It is possible that these and other items of which only the titles are entered in 'Strange Things' were left blank for the stories to be copied into this MS. from Fr Allan McDonald's other notebooks. *Cf.* No. 27 here, which refers to an incident Fr Allan wrote down in 1889 in his Notebook I.

[2] *Cf.* Amy Murray, *Father Allan's Island*, p. 162.

in it. Though I have heard much about it I never get to gathering evidence on the subject in a formal way.

Dougal MacMillan, Postmaster, says that he once went to a house, and he had not long been in it till he suddenly felt unaccountably ill. He had to go home and went straight to bed and began to vomit till he was nearly dead. He knew that it was said that one at least in the house had the evil eye and he conscientiously can attribute no physical cause to his sudden illness that he knows of. He believes it was the evil eye that made him ill. Neither on sea nor land had he been troubled with vomiting for years before or after this. (So many people say that they had an attack of vomiting after the evil eye.)

(2) An odd occurrence took place when Miss Freer was here. The whole thing is characteristic. Women always, never men, go with the cow to the bull. Two women in Eriskay, whose names and addresses I know but will suppress here, went each with a cow to the bull about the same time. One naturally remarked that it would be best to leave the bull and the cows together and leave the priority of selection to the bull. The other, near whose house they were at the time, scorned the suggestion and forcibly drove the bull into her stockyard along with her own cow. The bull found himself no sooner penned in than he broke out of the pen and forsook this cow for the other. On his way to the other cow he fell down as if dead, and remained so until water in which a silver coin had been placed was sprinkled over him. He then revived! One of the women has more than a slight reputation as to being possessed of mystic powers in the way of withdrawing the milk produce of her neighbours' cows to her own. She is the one from whose cow and from whose pen the unfortunate bull broke loose. At the present moment the occurrence is the subject of the suppressed talk of the natives. It is an incident I heard of only by the merest chance, as they do not like to ventilate their feelings of this kind in the hearing of the clergy.

18. Strange Creatures

Duncan MacInnes, Ru' Bàn, tells me that he was told in Barra that a party had gone out to Currachan Rock east of Barra to catch cormorants. They used to muffle the oars and take off their boots so as to surprise the cormorants asleep. On landing they saw some unnatural creature or perhaps some unusual creature on the rock. This was last year and since then nobody has gone to kill cormorants on the Currachan.[1]

(5th December 1895)

[1] It is possible this was a walrus.

19

Duncan also tells that at Hallowe'en 1894 Lachlan MacNeil (Mac Chailein 'ic Dhòmhnaill Roger), Castlebay [Barra] and two other lads were pursued by a creature that changed shapes. When it got near any of them a little bird got between it and its victims whereupon it rushed after another of them. The little bird acted as guardian to them.

20–1. Revenants

(*20*)

Mrs Donald MacInnes a native of Barra living in Village Eriskay says that there was a man in Barra called Angus. His wife died leaving one child. He married again. The second wife was very good to the child. Somehow a shirt belonging to the child disappeared, and the husband upbraided her for letting it be lost, and he said that if she cared for his child she would have been more careful. He was always charging her unjustly with neglect of the child. The second wife in course of time had a baby, and after the baby was born a warm drink was being prepared at the edge of the fire for the mother. The vessel containing this drink was twice quite unaccountably overturned and the drink spilt. The third time the drink was duly prepared and brought without mishap to the young mother. Some time after the birth of the child when the husband was out of the house, the deceased wife—the mother of the little child to whom the lost shirt belonged—came to the house and told the second wife not to be afraid of her, that she was as kind to the child as if it were her own, and that she often felt annoyed at the manner in which the husband spoke to her (No. 2 wife) and that the little shirt that was lost had been inadvertently picked up with some straw by the husband himself and placed in *torcadh na h-àmhadh*, the hole in the kiln, and that it was she who had overturned the vessel with the drink in it twice the time the second baby was born, and that if she had not done so wife No. 2 would have died like herself whose death was caused by getting a draught after childbirth made on peats emitting too much smoke and little heat (*deoch far bàrr an deathaich*) and that she turned over the first two draughts as they were made with such a fire, but that by the time the third draught was being prepared the fire was at a proper heat without much smoke.

(5th December 1895, Duncan MacInnes, Ru' Bàn)

(21)

Duncan then told of a Barra man called Alex. B. who was married three times, and left a family by his first two wives. There was a wild evening and the third wife sent out one of the first wife's family to look after a cow. The child went unwillingly. A child of wife No. 2 had a sore foot and she was bathing his foot, and he was crying. She put him to bed and as he was weeping she scolded him. She heard a rap then at the window and saw wife No. 1 looking in, and at the partition beside she saw wife No. 2 and heard her say, '*Tha e glé ghòrach dhut a bhith coirbte ri m' phàiste-se. Cha bhi thu fada 'na chùram uile gu léir.*' 'It is foolish of you to be cross with my child. You won't have him long under your care in any case.' She died not long after.[1]

(5th December 1895, Duncan MacInnes)

22. Transformation

John Smith, South Boisdale, says that he heard that Norman MacLean (now miller in Smerclet) and other boys were at the Hallin machaire near where there are the ruins of a hut. They saw a raven at the hut, and they began to wave their arms to frighten the raven. The raven leapt down in the shape of a little man and began swinging his arms as if pulling rags of clothing from here from there from everywhere. The boys scampered. J. Smith said heard this from Norman MacLean's brother Donald who lives in Garry-namonie.

(John Smith, South Boisdale, S. Uist, 5th December 1895)

23

Donald MacLeod (Mac Iain Aonghais) now in Castlebay, had an experience with a woman on MacCuish's croft, Eriskay.[2]

24

Man seen at Haun on hillock between Stephen M. MacIsaac's house and the store, by Donald MacInnes (Duncan's father).[3]

25. Second Sight

Calum Dhòmhnaill (MacKinnon), [the] Bard, Bruernish, Barra about 17 years ago was going to settle an account for lobsters with

[1] This story was used by Amy Murray in *Father Allan's Island*, pp. 161–2, where the Gaelic is quoted with several misspellings.

[2] Rest left blank in MS. [3] Rest left blank in MS.

Allan Steele, Merchant, Northbay Inn. A woman, Mrs Rory MacDonald, Bruernish, gave him a bottle to take back full of paraffin in her own house. His Uncle (still alive in 1895) John MacKinnon, Bruernish, was in at the time. When the woman gave Calum the bottle he looked at the bottle and told me not to take it at all with me. Calum said, 'Why will I not take the bottle?' 'Because your Uncle wishes you not to take it and the night dark.' But Calum thought nothing of it and took the bottle with him. A little after leaving the house, his uncle asked him, 'Have you the bottle yet?' Calum said he had. He told me to throw the bottle away because the bottle would do harm to me or to somebody else. 'What proof have you that it will do harm to me or to somebody else?' asked Calum. He said, 'When the woman gave you the bottle I saw the glass of the bottle and blood on it.' When he said this, Calum threw the bottle away to a side, because he himself had told me before that he used to see things. It was on a flat rock that the bottle fell and it was broken, a good way from the houses near Gàradh Bhruthairnis. We walked to Northbay and settled the account. We returned, and we saw a light at Gàradh Bruthairnis coming towards us. There were lads from Eriskay going to Northbay Inn and lads from Bruernish with them. A lad from Bruernish asked me if I had a clout or handkerchief in my pocket when we met them. The lad's name was Samuel MacKinnon[1] (still alive), Bruernish. I asked him why he wanted it. He said that when they were coming at the top of Bruernish my foot slipped on a flat rock and I fell forward. I stretched my hand before me falling and I put my hand upon a bottle that was broken on the rock. Look at my hand how it is so badly cut, he said. The little finger and the next were badly cut and the blood flowing. We (my uncle and I) parted with them. My uncle said, 'Did you notice what he said? Didn't I tell you that the bottle would do harm to you or to somebody else?' 'You did,' said I, 'but I didn't believe it till now.' 'After this, you will pay heed to what your father's brother will ask you of the kind.' To confirm the truth of the thing I (Calum) went to the place where I broke the bottle next morning to see if I could see blood about it. I got to where the bottle was, I saw the blood on the rock and on the glass of the bottle.

(Taken down from Calum at present 17th December 1895.
Malcolm MacKinnon, Donald's, Bard, Bruernish, Barra)

[1] Malcolm MacKinnon (Calum Dhòmhnaill) died in 1932. He was a well-known bard in Barra, where some of his songs are still popular. Seven of them were printed by Colm Ó Lochlainn in *Deoch Slàinte nan Gillean* (Dublin, 1948). Samuel MacKinnon was living in the 1930s; his wife, well known as 'Bean Shomhairle Bhig', was a famous singer of traditional waulking songs, and had sung for Mrs Kennedy-Fraser.

26

Dougal MacIntosh Loch Eynort and his sister at Loch an Tràigh Bhàin.[1]

27

Story[2] of the man Johnston who caught the *Bean Nighe* (Fairy Washerwoman).[3]

30–3. Uncanny Boats

(*30*)

Yesterday, 12th February 1896, a boat popularly called the 'Horse' left Eriskay for Lochboisdale on her way to Benbecula. The boat had been bought by Mr Bain of Creagorry from Mr A. MacLennan merchant of Eriskay and is to be used it is understood for conveying materials to the new pier being erected at Petersport, Benbecula, by Mr Bain, contractor. The boat has been considered uncanny in Eriskay for some time. On the evening before she left after she had been pushed out to sea, I happened to be in the midst of a group of the fisherman and we began talking of the boat. One of these present, Angus MacIsaac, Haun, said that one day a year or two ago (I can't remember which) Neil Bowie, Harbour, a seer was coming down to Haun and asked him what pretty boat that was which lay at anchor and he said it was the 'Atlantic'. He then asked Angus what other boat lay by the shore near him and Angus said it was a boat called the 'Horse'. Neil Bowie then said, 'I would advise you never to go into her by day or by night.' So far nothing has happened to the boat unless a little damage that was done to her against the shore on a stormy night, since the seer spoke. It will be interesting to note her future history. All in Eriskay are glad that she has gone. Some say that it was not fair to sell her without telling that she was thought uncanny. (13th February 1896)

[1] Left blank in MS.

[2] This story was actually taken down by Fr Allan McDonald in 1889 (I 228). This reads: 'A Johnston from the middle district of South Uist was passing by a lake at night at Snushaval, when he heard a splashing in the water by his side. He did not know what it was, and he grasped at it, and seized a diminutive being in human shape engaged with washing. He understood it was the *Bean-nighe* preparing the death-shirt and he asked her who was going to die. She is said to have told him that it was some relative of his own.'

[3] Rest left blank. Nos. 28 and 29 are completely blank in the MS.

(31)

As we were talking, a young man called Roderick MacDiarmid told the company that his own father Archibald, and Alex O'Henly, Eriskay, and Alexr. MacIntyre of South Lochboisdale (all since dead) were fishing lobsters for Mr Ferguson, merchant, South Lochboisdale, in the one boat. They were ashore in South Lochboisdale and went to a *luadhadh* or fulling of cloth in Allan Gillies' house there. They went to see their boat at the spot called Port Ruairidh 'ic Iain 'ic Fhionnlaigh, and were astonished to see the boat which was at anchor turn right over three times and to see a dark thing which looked like a dog on the keel when the keel was uppermost. Next day they took their creels and pots ashore and pulled up the boat. They were asked by Mr Ferguson why they did so, and they told him with reluctance. 'Don't speak of it,' said he, 'to the people.' The boat was sold and went to Loch Evart, North Uist. Some time after a schoolmaster's son was at the steamboat with this boat and the rope of his boat got entangled with the propeller of the steamer and was tossed about and the lad was found drowned on the back of the boat.

(Roderick MacDiarmid, 12th February 1896)

(32)

This led to talking about a boat in Barra in which last year a young man was accidentally killed by a gun. They said that noises were heard in the boat on her way home to Barra via the Caledonian Canal from the East Coast where she was bought. This year it is said that the boat was launched for the ling[1] fishing and Donald MacIsaac said he saw her out all ready for the fishing. Since then it is said that she has been pulled up on the beach once more, as more noises have been heard in her and she is considered as destined to do more harm.

(33)

Then the story of a newish boat, of the Highland skiff style that was in Barra, was told. There had been warnings given about the boat either by noises or a seer. The boat was taken ashore and burned to falsify the predictions. The anchor belonging to it was taken by another boat and that boat was swamped and the crew lost.

(12th February 1896, Stephen MacIsaac's House, Eriskay)

[1] 'spring' deleted.

34–5. Second Sight

(34)

Marion MacRury, Ru' Bàn, Eriskay, about 12 years ago when only a child was in the enclosure in front of the School House door Eriskay with Margaret MacAskill a sister of the interim teacher Harriet MacAskill—the head teacher Miss MacKay having had to go home to Buckie in bad health. It was broad daylight on a Saturday. She noticed the head of a man and a woman outside the wall coming round on the south side. She asked Maggie MacAskill who they were. Miss MacAskill said she didn't see anyone. Marion MacRury then noticed them come in by the east gate and the man had a waterproof and the woman had a grey shawl on her arm. She had never seen either of them before. She saw them pass a yard or two from her into the School House front door and she drew Maggie MacAskill's attention to them again. Maggie didn't see them but rushed into the house to tell her sister Harriet. They found nobody in, and Marion MacRury was taken in and told she had seen a *taibhse* and Harriet MacAskill got a bible and closed it to Marion's face so that the wind might go in her eyes. If it wasn't for that says Marion I might be as bad as the Red Tailor (Bowie), Harbour, but I never *saw* anything since. Miss MacKay the teacher died a month or two after leaving Eriskay for her home. Maggie MacAskill and Marion MacRury were in the school enclosure another day and saw two people coming round just as the other two she had seen had come. They turned out to be real characters this time, viz. an uncle of Miss MacKay's and Mrs Malcolm MacAskill from Pollacharra, South Uist. The man came across to see about the effects of his deceased niece and Mrs MacAskill came to see her daughters. At the most there could not have been more than three months between the vision and the realisation. I can't find out if the vision was prior to Miss MacKay's death or not.

(Marion MacRury, 19th February 1896)

(35)

Marion MacRury says that she did not *see* anything after the bible ceremony. But I know that she heard and felt on two subsequent occasions. One of these I mentioned before. The other was this. She had gone when it was dark to fetch a pail of water from a well at the end of Donald MacInnes' house (Land Constable). Donald was ill at the time. She filled the pail, and when returning had gone only a few steps till she heard a sound as of a flock of birds. She saw nothing but felt she could not get away, and felt as if her feet were trampled on and hurt. The pail she felt swinged to and fro till only a little water was left in it. She began to cry, but could not move home for some time. When she did get home she expected to find her feet cut and badly bruised but there was nothing to be seen on them. Donald died in a few days and his funeral in starting made a circuit round the spot where Marion had her experience and she says she watched to see if it would go in that direction. This happened about six years ago. The date can be ascertained as Donald MacIsaac's funeral was the day before[1] Malcolm MacIntyre, Haun's, marriage.[2]

(Marion MacRury, 19th February 1896)

36. Portents

Neil Johnston, Haun, Eriskay, aged about 60 says that when he was a little boy (about 7 or 8) he saw a trunk in the house open and heard bagpipes that were in the trunk give a groan as bagpipes give when being blown up. His mother said that it would not be long before the pipes would be taken out for a funeral. As far as he can remember they were taken out for the funeral of a grand-aunt of his called Catherine.

(Neil Johnston, February 1896)

37

Neil Johnston says that he heard that Alex. MacDonald, piper, Kilphedir, still alive in 1895, had prepared a sheepskin as a bag for his pipes and had laid it aside on the top of a bed.[3] and that the wife one day heard this skin give a groan and asked her husband if he had been putting wind into it and that he said that he had not. Not long after the skin in question had to be got ready for the funeral of a brother of the piper called Malcolm, belonging to North Lochboisdale, who shot himself accidentally while hunting ducks.

38. A Taibhse

He also said that Archibald MacDiarmid, since dead, when going to the strand met a tall lady dressed in dark clothes about 30 yards to the north east of the north east corner of the school wall and that when he looked again she was gone. He recognized the person he had seen when Mrs Robertson (a widow) came a year or two afterwards to

[1] 'before' pencilled over 'after' in MS.

[2] This story and the preceding one were used by Amy Murray in *Father Allan's Island*, p. 163.

[3] *Cf.* Amy Murray, *Father Allan's Island*, p. 163.

teach in the Island of Eriskay. At the time mentioned (if the date be at all near the mark) she was living with her husband in Mauritius.

39. A Mysterious Light

Neil Johnston says that on the night of Lady Cathcart's last wedding,[1] he with others had returned from Dalibrog to their boat at Ru' na Mòna, Eriskay Sound. John MacDonald (son of Angus son of Ewen) said to him, 'Look at the light out at Sgala nan Cat!'[2] We went over, but when near it went out. When we got into the boat it appeared again.

(Neil Johnston, February 1896)

40. A Forewarning

John MacDonald (son of Angus son of Ewen), Eriskay, says that he was going to fish flounders in the Oitir between Eriskay and Barra. There were with him in the boat John Morrison (son of Neil) and Colin MacInnes with others. John Morrison could *see* things. When opposite Village, Eriskay, Morrison said to Colin that it would be better for him to go ashore. The other asked why. 'Because you don't look well.' Colin replied with a little indignation, 'Do you look well yourself?' There was no more said and they went on to fish, and after catching some fish they landed at Ben Stack, Eriskay, and began to roast some on the heather. Colin stayed in the boat. Those who were cooking came down to the boat with some for him, and he was resting over an oar, and said *Mo chridhe!*—'My heart!' He never spoke again. A lad was despatched by land to have something warm in readiness for him when the boat would reach near the houses. He died that night. (I told this before[3] but this is from as near an eyewitness as I can get.)[4]

(John MacDonald, 15th February 1896)

41–2. Mysterious Cries[5]

(41)

John MacMillan, aged 70, Smerclet, who says he never saw anything, tells the following. There were two boats fishing, said he, near Lingay, opposite Kilbride. It was a calm evening—so calm that they had to row going home. When between Lingay and Pollacharra but

[1] This took place in 1880. Lady Gordon Cathcart was the then proprietrix of South Uist.

[2] 'The Rock of Cats'.

[3] Not in this notebook.

[4] This story was used by Amy Murray in *Father Allan's Island*, pp. 162–3.

[5] See also the Early Collection, No. 49 (II 60).

nearer Lingay they heard a cry as of people in distress in the direction of a little island east of Lingay, called Grianamul. The crew of the one boat called to the other boat and asked if they heard the cry. They said they heard it. John MacMillan was in one of the boats. One boat had not good oars. The other with the good oars went towards where they heard the cry. They heard the cry repeatedly. John MacMillan who was in the boat that was making for home says that he heard the cries repeatedly till he reached Pollacharra and after dragging the boat up the beach, and while standing at the little wall at the east corner of Pollacharra. After that they went down and pulled up the second boat and went home. The boat that had gone in search were hearing the cry repeatedly but when they got close to Grianamul they heard the cry to the west side of them. No accident happened at the time or since. I asked MacMillan if the cries might not have been the howling of seals that were common in the Sound. He said that they had thought of that but that they knew the cry of the seal well enough and that it was far more like the cry of people in distress.

(J. MacMillan, Smerclet, February 1896)

This happened about Xmas 1890.
Fr Allan McDonald added: I am informed that this warning was verified. A Uist fishing boat struck on a skerry near Lingay and the crew began to cry out, but they got off safely and no person was lost. I do not know what boat it was but I will mark it down when I hear and also the date.
(Added in pencil) An Eriskay boat, October 1898, struck on a rock here on a wild night and was nearly lost. Some of her timbers were broken—boat called Helen Ann . . . . . . (?)

(42)

Angus MacIntyre (Bàn) (Aodh's son) says that one night while crossing from Barra to Eriskay he and all in the boat with him twice heard the shout of a human voice. I asked him if he recognised the voice and he said he didn't. It wasn't particularly stormy though there were gusty showers. He doesn't know what it meant.

(26th February 1896)

43. A Mysterious Light

About four years ago he saw a large flame of fire light after dark as he was coming from Harbour to Roshinish as he was behind John MacDonald's, Haun, in the direction of Rory MacCaskill's house. He thought it meant that someone was to die in MacCaskill's house soon. No death occurred there since, but the wife of one Ewen

MacMillan died to the North East of MacCaskill's half a year after he saw the light. He says he could have seen a fire at MacMillan's from where he was and that it would appear to be at MacCaskill's as the two houses were in a line.

(25th February 1896)

44. A Ghost at Loch Scavaig

These were the only personal experiences he had but he began then to speak of Donald MacEachen, Harbour, [Eriskay], who is said to see things but is very reticent. Last Autumn (1895) while at the Loch fishing in Scavaig, Skye, Donald MacEachen, who was in the same boat with MacIntyre, was sent to fetch a stone from the shore as they were ashore in a little island in Loch Scavaig after dark. When he returned, he had no stone and didn't answer questions put to him for some time. A brother of Donald's said, 'Donald has seen something, but he will be all right presently.' When Donald spoke, he told them to put off the boat from shore. They did this. They asked him what he saw and he said he saw a man with a hard black hat and a long coat reaching half way between knee and ankle, and that he passed so near that he could have touched him with his hand stretched out. He didn't see him till he raised up his head from trying to find a stone among the seaweed. The man he saw passed up a most steep piece of the shore without any difficulty.

(Angus MacIntyre, 25th February 1896)

45. Apparitions of the Living

He heard Donald say (and he and those present in the house all bore testimony to Donald's exceptional truthfulness) that at the time of the East Coast fishing, between the end of June and September when in Ben Stack, Eriskay, he had seen by a peat stack an Eriskay man who was at the East Coast at the time and another who was in Eriskay talking together.

(Angus MacIntyre, 25th February 1896)

46

Neil Johnston[1] then said that he had heard Neil Bowie, Harbour, say that he saw a man belonging to Howmore who had died in Dumfries and another who had died in Howmore itself walking along shoulder to shoulder and talking together.

(Neil Johnston, 25th February 1896)

[1] Pencilled note in margin 'Neil himself told me this afterwards'.

47. A Phantom Funeral

Angus MacIntyre says that Donald MacEachen told him that he was going to Donald MacLellan's one evening and that he saw a coffin coming, and that he stepped aside to avoid it. As far as he remembers, it was Donald MacInnes, Ru' Bàn's, coffin (about six years ago).

48. A Taibhse

He says that Donald MacEachen told him that as he and his brother Angus were coming from the west side of Eriskay where they had gone for bait, when they were passing the pool at the back of Malcolm MacKinnon's, Harbour, he saw a grey haired man resting his hand on his palm and lying stretched at the side of the pool and that he was so near he could have touched him with his foot.

(Angus MacIntyre, 25th February 1896)

49–50. Prophetic Day-dreams

(49)

Father James Chisholm, Castlebay, was coming from Craigston to Castlebay and at a certain part of the road he saw himself in a day-dream as it were on a part of the road nearer Castlebay and meeting at that spot a priest from the mainland saluting him familiarly with the Spanish phrase, 'Que tal hombre?' There was a considerable rising ground between the place where Fr Chisholm was and where he fancied himself to be so that it was impossible for him to see physically the spot where he fancied himself as meeting the priest. He moved on towards Castlebay amused with the absurdity of his dream, but yet it was realised in every particular. He met this priest (who was taking a cruise round the Island in the 'Dunara Castle') at the spot a few minutes after his vision, and was saluted in the identical phrase he had previously imagined. He had heard nothing about his clerical friend, the Rev. George Ritchie now of Shieldmuir, intending to take this circular cruise.

(25th May 1897)

(50)

Father Chisholm also tells me an experience he had when Miss Freer was in Barra in Autumn 1895. He had daydreams that were realised afterwards, but his impression was that these were extraordinary coincidences rather than that he had any second sight himself. He tells me that he is apt to have these day dreams if he reads and his eyes become tired. He is shortsighted and wears spectacles. When his eyes become tired he says he is apt to become dazed. He says he frequently falls into a 'brown study'. His story is this. Miss Freer and he intended to come to Eriskay. That morning Fr Chisholm saw himself and Miss Freer meet the Doctor of Barra at a certain spot. He saw Miss Freer stop on the way and felt impressed that it could be only to speak to[1] a friend, he foresaw there would be confusion before embarking, that he would lose the way or track in Eriskay, and that the housekeeper at the Chapel House, Eriskay, would give him a bottle with a white label. He did not speak of it to Miss Freer at the time. He says he did not realise that it was of any importance. The incidents seemed trivial. He understands now better that the importance[2] of the incident is of real importance. They proceeded on their way and met the Dr at the spot foreseen. Miss Freer at one place stopped to speak to a native and Father Chisholm expressed surprise and Miss Freer said he was a friend, that she had met him before. Before embarking it was discovered that a small handbag had been sent to Northbay Inn instead of to Bruernish. On getting to Eriskay Fr Chisholm found himself off the track among the corn and potatoes and asked somebody what was the right way, and if he was confident of anything before starting it was that that part of his daydream could not be realised. On reaching the Chapel House I was absent and the housekeeper gave him the bottle with a white label, but he could not remember whether it was whisky or altar wine.[3]

(From Fr Chisholm 22nd May 1897.
I heard him speak of it before, once or twice.)

51

On a recent occasion Fr Chisholm had occasion to sleep in a house in a bed the previous occupant of which had a short time before met with an accidental death by drowning. During the night he felt the end of the bed rise and fall back with a heavy lurch. This happened only once. The incident occurred a few weeks ago.

52. Teleportation

Falbh air an t-sluagh or being borne away by the dead was an experience more common formerly than now. When I ask about it now, I am always referred to the case of a man MacPhee from

[1] MS. 'by' altered to 'to speak to'.
[2] 'class' deleted, 'importance' substituted in MS.
[3] Words after 'label' added in pencil.

Iochdar who emigrated to Manitoba with the Uist colony in 1884. Today I have had a visit from a Uist man who has come back from Manitoba to spend a holiday with his friends. I asked him if he knew MacPhee and he gave me this short account.

John MacPhee from Iochdar lives about a mile away from John Morrison's (my informant) in the St Andrew district. He is about 40 years of age. John Morrison knows him intimately and he heard him tell the following story of his being spirited away. When in Iochdar he was standing at the end of the house between 9 and 10 p.m. He heard a loud sound from the West, which seemed something like the sound of the sea breaking on the shore. He listened to it attentively to make out exactly what caused it. He saw a mass (small) as of men coming in a crowd from the West. He felt hot as if oppressed by the warm breath of many people. He felt himself going away being sped away with rapidity as if he were riding a horse at a furious speed, and he could feel the hair of his head brushed aside by the rapidity of his movement through the air. He alighted on the ground only once and that would be for a minute or half a minute, and then he found himself in the Dalibrog graveyard in the space between the higher and lower graveyards. He had never been to the Dalibrog graveyard before (I don't know if he has since though he may have seen it from the High Road passing about 1½ miles East of it.) When he alighted the heat that oppressed him was gone and he felt himself freed. He looked round and he saw a man at his back with his back to him. He did not know him nor speak to him. The 'dead' came again. He felt the heat and the hot breath again and was whisked away without any further incident till he was left at the spot from which he had been taken at the end of the house. Dalibrog graveyard is about 17 miles from the house. The time he took in going to and fro was very brief. The pot for supper was on the fire when he went to the end of the house and when he went into the house it was being taken off the fire. He was not in the Dalibrog graveyard before but he has yet the liveliest picture of the two graveyards in his mind and he could place his foot on the spot where he alighted. His age at the time would be 25 or 26 years. He felt the wind or rather air cold against his face. He had no fear of such an occurrence afterwards, though he could not help thinking about it, and he became thin and sickly looking after it. John Morrison often heard him tell this story, and is convinced that the man was candidly narrating a true experience. He heard MacPhee tell also of other somewhat similar experiences that he had, but he does not remember the particulars distinctly enough to give them to me in the way of evidence of *Falbh air an t-sluagh* or being spirited by the dead.

He says that MacPhee was so carried away on four or five other occasions at least. He asked him if he had been carried away in Manitoba. MacPhee smiles and says nothing because people laugh at him for speaking of such things.

(John Morrison, son of Ronald, St Andrews, [Manitoba], 5th June 1897)

53. Second Sight in the Uist Settlement in Manitoba

I asked John Morrison if the people had second sight among them in the Uist settlement. He said he didn't think there was much. (Among strangers the people would in any case be chary of telling experiences that would earn them the contempt of neighbours more ignorant than themselves.) There was a young woman Joanna MacDonald in the settlement to whom the following incident occurred 14 years ago—a year before the Uist larger colony went out. She was 13 years of age at the time. On a little rising ground near the edge of her father's lot she saw a very tall gentleman or man dressed in black—a large black coat and a black hat. He was very tall. She thought he was a stranger who wanted some information and she went up to speak to him. He disappeared instantaneously. The first little Chapel of the Colony was built at the spot 4 years after this but the young woman has not yet seen the person that appeared to her about the spot. Another chapel was built in another spot afterwards and those buried near the first chapel were taken up and reburied at the New Chapel. Even then she did not see the mysterious stranger about.

54. Apparitions near the Abhainn Mhór

John Morrison then gave me the following interesting story which he heard over and over again from a man Lachlan Steele who lived along with Morrison's family in Manitoba. Lachlan Steele died nine years ago in Manitoba. He hailed from North Boisdale, South Uist, and went out to the North West [of Canada] in 1884. Some time before going to Manitoba he (Lachlan) and a neighbour and companion Colin O'Henly had gone to Pollachara to procure a bottle of whisky each. They drank two glasses each and no more at the Inn and proceeded home by the Machaire or seaside road. When approaching the Abhainn Mhór ('Great River', 3 to 4 ft wide—ideas relative) and (a notorious spot for experiences, one of which like this I have noted previously) they both saw on the strand two women with black hoods and black cloaks near the sea. These women walked alternatively—one would get 50 yards in advance of the other while that other stood, then that other would advance to her companion and pass her by 50 yards and then stand, and so on. Colin O'Henly asked Lachlan to come along with him and see who they were, that they were probably some people playing a joke. Lachlan would not go and looked at his watch and said it was about one o'clock and that nobody would be larking them (I wonder if this watch incident is a natural interpolation). Colin prevailed upon him to go along with him towards them. The two darkly clad females then stood side by side near the sea and faced round towards Lachlan and Colin. They would be 100 yards or so away. They could not distinguish the faces clearly enough though the night was bright. Lachlan and Colin advanced once more and then the dark females turned round about and went off together towards the sea and seemed to walk on the surface of the water. When the investigators observed this development they did not wait to make any further observations.

(John Morrison, 5th June 1897 [Manitoba]. Colin O'Henly the partner with Steele in this experience is alive in North Boisdale still [1897], and when I see him I must ask him if he ever had an experience of this kind.)

55. *A Water Horse*

Ewen MacMillan, Bunavullin, Eriskay, of Skye descent, aged about 50 tells me that four years ago at the end of May or beginning of June he had gone to look after a mare and foal that he had at about nine or ten o'clock p.m. He went up to Loch Duvat (Eriskay) to see them. There was a foggy haze. He passed at the west end a horse belonging to John Campbell, Bunavullin, and a horse belonging to Duncan Beag MacInnes ditto. He saw an animal in front of him on the North side of the lake which he took to be his own mare and was making up to it. He got to within twenty yards of it but he could not distinguish the colour on account of the haze, but in size it appeared to be no larger than a common Eriskay pony. When he came to within twenty yards of it the creature gave a hideous or unearthly scream (*sgiamh grànda*) that terrified not only MacMillan but the horses that were grazing at the West end of the lake, which immediately took to flight. MacMillan ran the whole way home and the horses did not stop till they reached home. These horses were not in the habit of coming home though they might come home of their own accord occasionally.

(Ewen MacMillan, 5th June 1897)

56. A Mysterious Light

Ewen MacMillan says that when fishing for herring he and the crew with him saw on four or five occasions spread over a year or two a mysterious light on the face of a rock called Sgala Mhór Gleann a' Mhill Mhóir[1] on the East side of Eriskay. It would continue for two or three hours. The men with him on some of these occasions were Alex. and Angus his brothers and John MacIntyre (mac Dhòmhnaill na Càrnaich deceased) and Rory MacCaskill.

57. A Dog's Warning

Ewen MacMillan and his brother Angus about 26 or 27 years ago were in winter at about 1 a.m. going to scour the coast for wreckage. There was a strong South East wind. They had a large dog with them belonging to their father—a large dog he used to have for driving cattle. They were at Gleann a' Mhill Mhóir and were descending the Ceum Cas (or 'steep path') when the dog seized Angus by the back of the neck by his collar and knocked him down. This happened three times and Ewen said it would be better to return home. They were returning and on beginning to return the dog began to fawn and play about them with evident pleasure. When approaching Sloc an Ime[2] (a gully on the rocky coast) the dog which was preceding then gave a bark which Ewen thinks should have been heard in Uist (*Leig e comhnart 's chanainn gun chluinneadh iad an Uibhist i*). Neither of the brothers saw anything at Sloc an Ime or at the spot where the dog made them turn back.

58. Foresight of a Fire

Ewen MacMillan and his deceased sister Mary were returning from Widow Cath. MacDiarmid's house, Ru' Bàn, and when going down towards Haun, Ewen saw a large flame of fire rising over the roof of the Store (now Angus MacIsaac's house). It would be from 2 to 3 yards high. He thought it was the Store on fire. He would have been about 30 yards from the Store at the time. Many did not see it. The time of year was a little after St Brigit's (1st February). He does not know what it means unless it was a warning of the burning of the bed of Mrs Murdoch MacDonald, Haun, who died a few weeks later. (It was customary to burn the straw or sea-grass making the bed if the person died in bed. Mattresses were then not used.) The flame of the burning bed might have been seen by him over the top of the Store from the spot where he was at the time.

(Ewen MacMillan, 4th June 1897)

[1] 'The Big Rock of the Glen of the Big Mound'. [2] 'The Butter Gulley'.

3

FR ALLAN McDONALD'S OWN EXPERIENCES

IT IS generally believed in the Isles that Fr Allan McDonald himself had second sight, or rather that he developed it. Mention of this is made by Amy Murray in her book *Father Allan's Island*,[1] the fruit of a folk-song collecting expedition to Eriskay in September 1905, the month before Fr Allan died. This book contains more personal information about Fr Allan McDonald than any other written at that time.

Miss Murray says:

Fr Allan himself had seen *but once, he said, and that nothing more than the corpse-candle (a sight nowise out-of-the-way), and in another island. Looking down from a hill-side by night, he saw it move across the plain, then down a glen, to a house where he knew a man was dying: walking homewards, met a messenger to say, The man was dead.*

This story suggests Fr Allan's experience in August 1888, which he wrote down at or near the time,[2] but there the light was seen on the shore and the person whose death it was felt to have presaged was a woman.

Amy Murray continues:

But at Dalibrog, on a night before one of his young men was drowned, he lay awake a long time, hearing outside a low murmuring as of a multitude. Father Chisholm, a priest (and seer as well[3]*) from another parish, was in another bed in the same room and asleep, or so Father Allen thought. But presently he spoke out, saying, 'Do you hear anything?'*

'It might be the wind.'

'You know it is not *the wind,' rejoined the other.*

They got up and looked out at the window, which gave on the gravelled doorland of the chapel, but saw nothing.

[1] Published in New York in 1920. The quotation here is from pp. 200–1.

[2] The story is No. 13 of the Early Collection (I 140).

[3] See 'Strange Things', Nos. 49–51. Fr, later Canon, Chisholm was then parish priest of Castlebay, Barra.

Next day Father Allan was in the same room while they were carrying the drowned man into the chapel; and when he heard them underneath the window, speaking low amongst themselves, he knew that sound for what he heard the night before.

It is possible that this incident is the subject of one of Fr Allan McDonald's Gaelic poems, *Bha ceothragach mìn am muigh*, 'There was a fine mist outside'.[1] Translated this reads:

There was a fine mist outside, and the sighing of the wind could not be heard; the light of the day was obscured, and I could not perceive human voices. Despondency possessed my soul, I raised my head from the pillow; my breath came seldom and my heart was beating strongly. There is a sound in my ear and in my head that fills my heart with dread, a sound like the footsteps of thousands marching in the fresh snow, going to a struggle from which they will not return.

But this may have been a premonition of the First World War. Its presence in one of Fr Allan McDonald's later notebooks argues against its having been made while he was at Dalibrog, unless he entered it long afterwards.

Fr Allan McDonald himself left a diary in which one or two incidents of this sort were recorded. The first is from the entry for 6th February 1898:

At 10.45 to 50 p.m. when saying my Office [I] heard a loud (feminine?) call just as if in front of my house. It was clear and bright at the time, nearly as bright as day with the moon, and calm at the moment. I looked out and saw nobody. One of the servants heard it also from her bedroom as if it was in front of the house, and said it sounded like Trothadaibh*!* *or* Trothad mar seo*!*[2] *She declares that it must be a* manadh *or forewarning or presage. We shall see.*

This reminds me of an occurrence that took place on the Sunday evening previous to Fr Rigg's death on 15th August 1897.[3] *I was in the enclosure north west of my house in Eriskay. The evening was delightfully warm with hardly any wind. I heard what I took to be the prolonged hurrah! of say a hundred children out in the open air. It seemed to be at [a] distance from me in some part of Uist across the Sound. I heard the same sound about six times in succession with little intervals between as much as would allow one or two remarks to be made to provoke the children to another hurrah. I looked across the Sound to Uist especially to the east of Glendale, but saw nobody. I thought it must be the children of Garrynamonie school out on picnic somewhere in honour*

[1] *Bàrdachd Mhgr Ailein*, p. 94.
[2] *i.e.*, Come here!
[3] The 15th August 1897 was a Friday.

of the Queen's Jubilee. I called the servant out, and she heard it four or five times. That was after the six times or so I heard it alone first. I could make nothing of it but that we thought it the sound of many voices.

Mrs Robertson [*the*] *late teacher here who was in Pollachar was returning to Eriskay that evening, and I could find out from her all about the Uist Jubilee picnic, for so I had explained the phenomenon to myself. Two hours or more after* [*wards*] *I met a man who told me that Fr Rigg had caught the infection*[1] *and was in bed. Mrs Robertson came later and confirmed the news. I asked her about the picnic. She said there was no such thing at all. The very next Saturday was the day of Fr Rigg's burial. I don't know why I connect the two things. The cry did not convey to my mind anything melancholy, and sounded so far off as to have no more expression than the ringing cheers of children heard at a great distance away from them.*

On 13th March 1898 Fr Allan McDonald wrote in Gaelic, which I have translated, that:

About midnight I was going to sleep. As I often do, I looked out of my bedroom window to see whether everyone else had gone to bed. There was not a light to be seen in any house. Around the church[2] *as far as I could see—but I could not see the church itself though it was not very dark around it—I'd say it was just about as high as the window in the near end of the church, I saw a little red light, no bigger than the light of a candle with a red flame, remain for about three minutes in the same place. It would then go out for about a minute, at least it went out of my sight. I saw it again there.*

I watched it carefully, and I could not say whether it went to the west or to the south west from the spot where I saw it first. The night was not so dark then anyway that anyone would need a torch,[3] *and I can hardly believe that anyone who belonged to the island would have taken a torch with him last night. Hitherto the sky had been clear with stars. At the moment the sky began to get cloudy. The light was not unlike the little light that comes from an ember fallen from a peat torch. I called to the servants, who had gone to sleep, to get up to see it, but they did not take the trouble. 'It's only a* manadh *(forewarning),' said my housekeeper. 'It's a long time since people first saw that light at the church.'*

'Perhaps it's a will-o'-the-wisp?'

[1] Probably typhus, caught when administering to the stricken occupant of a house which no one else dared to enter.

[2] The building formerly used as a church on Eriskay, some distance from Fr Allan's house.

[3] Made in those days by two burning peats held together on a stick.

'Indeed no, it was a forewarning of some sort.'

After I had put out my light and gone to bed, I noticed the match-box on my mantlepiece, which was of a bright ——[1] *colour, which makes it slightly luminous in the dark, I noticed that it was a good deal more bright than I ever remembered its being before. The light at the church was red. I wouldn't swear to it but that the light around the church was a little higher and a little further to the south than the church. Since I couldn't see the church, I can't be sure.*

Some interesting material connected with another of Fr Allan's experiences, which is still talked about and which has undergone some embroidery, were communicated to me by the late Rev. Dr Kenneth MacLeod. I give first an account of this matter which Dr MacLeod says was 'written by some lady or other whom Mrs Kennedy-Fraser knew or at any rate had met. It was meant either for a magazine or a lecture.' (It may be said right away that the hand in which the account is written is not that of Miss Goodrich Freer.) 'You will notice that I have stroked out the reference to myself, as the only thing I could corroborate was the general impression that Father Allan had the gift of second sight. Personally I believe he had, though he was silent about it himself. He often told me stories about other people who had the gift, but never any about himself.'

Acting on Dr Kenneth MacLeod's advice, Mrs Kennedy-Fraser sent the account to the Rev. Fr John Gray, of St Peter's Church, Edinburgh (1866–1934), the person who was involved in the story, for confirmation of its details. His comments on its inaccuracies, as well as a note of mine, follow the narrative itself, which is an interesting example of the way in which such anecdotes get added to. The anonymous writer says:

Fr Al[*l*]*an MacDonald who was for many years priest in Eriska* [sic] *one of the Outer Hebrides belonged to the mainland and did not believe in the phenomena known as second sight. Before his death however he had the gift himself. Communication with the island is uncertain, by fishing boat etc. and there is no telegraph but when two ladies went there to collect Highland music Father Al*[*l*]*an knew of it and expected them though no message had been sent. One of these ladies told me this instance of his foreknowledge *and it was corroborated by the Revd. Kenneth MacLeod now minister of Crianlarich*.*[2] *Mrs Kennedy Fraser, the lady in question, said she had also heard the story in Edinburgh*

[1] An illegible word here.

[2] *. . .*. The words between asterisks were deleted by the Rev. Dr Kenneth MacLeod, whose remark that he could not corroborate the statement is printed above.

from the Polish gentleman who figures in it but who had not then been in Scotland.

All the people in Eriska belong to the Roman Catholic Church, but the church was too small for the congregation and had also fallen into disrepair, and it was Father Al[*l*]*an's great wish that a new church should be built. So when a good fishing year came and his people had money from the herring he said, 'Now is the time to build' and the work was started, but before it was finished the money came to an end and work had to cease. Father Al*[*l*]*an was much concerned and very anxious that the building should be finished before the winter storms should set in. He held special services and made special intercession that the money needed might be sent to him.*

At this time a lady was dangerously ill in Paris, and a great friend, an Austrian Pole by birth who was also a devout Catholic made a vow that if she recovered he would he would give a certain sum to God. The lady recovered and her friend dreamed of an unfinished church on an island and a voice of intimation [*was*] *made to him that his gift was to be made to this church.*

I do not know why he associated the island with Scotland, but he wrote to a friend in Edinburgh telling him the circumstances and asking him to make inquiries as to the place intended. Mr Gray was advised to consult the fathers in the monastery at Fort Augustus and went there, when he was told of Father Al[*l*]*an and his special need. He inquired how the island was to be reached and was told to go straight down to Oban where he would be just in time to catch the steamer for the Outer Isles; that he could land either in Barra or South Uist and must then hire a fishing boat to take him across to Eriska. This programme he carried out, and as the fishing boat came alongside the pier, a priest came down to meet it saying, 'Where is the Mr Gray who is bringing me money to finish my church?'*

On this story Fr John Gray wrote the following comment in a letter to Mrs Kennedy-Fraser dated 15th December 1911:

In the summer of 1899, I think, I was in Scotland, a stranger and a layman (being then only tonsured) but wearing clerical dress as the mark of what I hoped would be. I asked a friend in Fort William what was the poorest mission in the county. He replied: go to Eriskay: Donald and Alfred are just starting. I went. At Fr Allan's table, where we sat down on arrival, he asked us: 'Have you seen a man named Gray anywhere?' I said, 'I am he,' not a little astonished.

He said, 'It isn't you: the man I mean is a layman.' We were leaving with the tide and I went with him into another room and mentioned some business I had with him, about which no one but myself knew. He said,

'You are the man I was expecting.' I was a little ruffled and asked what he meant. He said, 'I had a telegram.' I understood this to [be] a joke as he had just said there was no station on the island. Al[l]an said nothing more of this subject, and I was naturally mystified.

Returning to Fort William I mentioned to my friend there that Fr Al[l]an was expecting me. He told me Al[l]an was possessed of second sight: and since I have considered the explanation lost in that limbo of conflicting evidence. All the particulars in the MS. of which I have first-hand knowledge are inaccurate: except those which relate to myself which you see are passably correct, with a little good will.

Many of my brethren have heard Fr Al[l]an yarn half the night and remember well the weird effect of his stories. *And all add that whatever it is, he had the gift of second sight. He told me there will be no one but himself upon the rock in fifty years* i.e. *1949.*[1] *But I think that was a reasoned prediction: and I know he had arranged for his burial.*

The 'Austrian Pole' referred to in the anonymous lady's narrative was Marc-André Raffalovich (1864–1934). He was not an Austrian Pole but a Russian Jew, born in Paris.[2] He settled in London in 1884. He and John Gray were friends and minor literary figures in London in the 1890s. Gray was received into the Catholic Church in 1890, Raffalovich in 1896. In the autumn of 1898 Gray entered the Scots College in Rome as a student for the priesthood, and he was ordained on 21st December 1901, afterwards being appointed to a curacy at St Patrick's Church in Edinburgh. Raffalovich himself settled in the Morningside district of Edinburgh in 1905, and soon afterwards built at his own expense St Peter's church near by, of which Fr John Gray was appointed the first parish priest in 1906. The date of Fr Gray's ordination has some bearing on the date of his visit to Eriskay. It will be noticed that Fr Gray says nothing in his letter to Mrs Kennedy-Fraser of his reasons for asking a friend in Fort William what was the poorest mission in the country, nor does he make any reference to Raffalovich's alleged vow.

It was certainly not the case that work on the building of Eriskay church came to a halt in the summer because funds had run out.

[1] The 1951 Census gave the population of Eriskay as 330!

[2] Fr Brocard Sewell, O. Carm., *Two Friends, John Gray & André Raffalovich*, St Albert's Press, 1963, p. 10. Raffalovich's parents are described as natives of Odessa. This book is the authority for the other information about André Raffalovich and Fr John Gray given here. There is no allusion to Fr Gray's visit to Eriskay in it.

It is characteristic of the confusion that has attended this story that Amy Murray writes: 'Money came in even from Russia, from some titled man (who was it? I forget), who happened to hear of the poor mission' (*Fr Allan's Island*, p. 218).

The accounts for the building have been preserved, and they show that the first purchase of material for the church, thirty barrels of lime, was made on 17th February 1902, before when a total of £302 5*s* 0*d* had been collected, in three deposits of £102 5*s*, £180, and £20. There is no sign whatever in the accounts that work was held up at any time through lack of funds: the church itself was opened on 7th May 1903, and the last account was paid on 4th March 1904. Raffalovich was certainly a generous contributor: on 5th February 1903 there is an entry 'Seb. A. Raffalovich, £75'. There is also the following letter from him in Fr Allan McDonald's papers:

My dear Father,

I am indeed delighted to be of some use to your mission. How would you like the hundred pounds paid to you? A cheque sent to you? or the money paid into a bank? Please answer to the Caledonian Hotel, Inverness, where we shall be for a week.

A friend of mine says she would like to give £25 towards the altar when the time comes for you to get the altar.

Will you say a novena of masses (for John Gray's ordination) beginning on December 16th and ending on Dec. 24th? If so I will send you 45 shillings.

Believe me
very sincerely yours
André Sebastian Raffalovich

19th August

The year of the date is not stated, but the reference to Fr Gray's ordination shows it must have been 1901, and assuming that the letter was written as soon as Gray had informed Raffalovich that financial aid towards the building of Eriskay church would be very acceptable, Gray's visit to Eriskay must have been in 1901 and not in 1899. Presumably Raffalovich's £75 in February 1903 was an additional contribution, made when funds were running low. It may be noticed that a donation of £20 was received by Fr Allan from Miss Gribbell on 26th September 1902: she was Raffalovich's chatelaine and an old family friend.

As regards the assertion that Fr Allan 'foresaw' two ladies who visited Eriskay to collect Highland music, Dr Kenneth MacLeod has already told us he is unable to corroborate this, nor is there any confirmation of it in Mrs Kennedy-Fraser's chapter on her visit to Eriskay in her book *A Life of Song*,[1] nor does Amy Murray mention any such thing in her *Father Allan's Island*, where many conversa-

[1] London, 1929.

tions with Fr Allan McDonald are recorded: in fact, she writes that 'Father Allan himself had *seen* but once . . . and that nothing more than the corpse-candle'[1] which bears out Dr Kenneth MacLeod's remark about Fr Allan's being reticent about discussing his own experiences. Finally, it must be said that there was no occasion on which two lady folk-musicians visited Eriskay together; Evelyn Benedict (who says nothing about second sight in her letters to Fr Allan), Amy Murray, and Mrs Kennedy-Fraser all found their way separately to Eriskay in the summer of 1905 and at different times.

With regard to Fr Allan McDonald's experience at Ballechin House, there is an interesting, but unconvincing, account of these in an obituary which appeared in the Glasgow *Observer* of 14th October 1905, in which Fr Allan was described as a "Seer and Psychologist":

Some years ago the late Lord Bute assembled a house party at Ballechin—which had the reputation of being a haunted house. The party comprised a number of persons interested in psychological phenomena, and Father Allan was one of the group. Very frequently he spoke afterwards of his experiences in the house that night. He described certain pheonomena which he himself witnessed, and stated, among other events of the night, that at one time he was conscious of a bed-curtain being moved in his room by a hand which was quite visible, while he was satisfied that there was not a living person near but himself.

As has been stated on page 225, Fr Allan McDonald was a visitor at Ballechin from 29th April to 6th May, 1897. If he actually had such a vision as is related here, it is very surprising that Miss Freer did not mention it in her book *The Alleged Haunting of B—— House*. All she recorded was that Fr Allan and his fellow guest Fr MacDougall were kept awake all the night of 29th–30th April by the sounds in the house.

[1] *Op. cit.*, p. 200. See p. 257 here.

APPENDIX A

1. *Examples of Miss Freer's dependence on Fr Allan McDonald's Folklore Notebooks*

SOME OF these have already been given in my article on 'The Late Fr Allan McDonald, Miss Goodrich Freer and Hebridean Folklore', in *Scottish Studies*, vol. II, pp. 175–88 (1958). More examples are added here, and attention is drawn to Dr George Henderson's *Survivals in Belief among the Celts* (Glasgow, 1911), where items can easily be found, of which Fr Allan McDonald is there acknowledged as the source, and which coincide with items in Miss Freer's lectures printed in Volumes X and XIII of *Folklore*, and there implied to have been of her own collecting.

While the full extent of Miss Freer's dependence on Fr Allan McDonald's notebooks could be demonstrated only by the publication of Fr Allan's collection in full, the examples given here ought to prove this dependence beyond the possibility of any further argument.

Fr Allan, Notebook I, item no. 67:

> A man Campbell was going to Mass early one Sunday morning to Kildonan. On the strand he found a woman and her daughter actively '*a deilbh buidseachd*' framing witchcrafts, by crossing threads of varied colours in various manners just as is done when threads are arranged for the loom. He tore up the whole apparatus and chid them with their breach of the Sunday and their malice. The witches entreated him not to mention what he had seen them doing, and they promised him immunity from injury. After Mass he told all the people about the matter, and shortly afterwards, when about to sail to the mainland a crow stood on the mast, and after they started from shore a storm arose in which he perished. This occurrence did not take place within the memory of the present generation.

Miss Freer, *Folklore*, vol. X, p. 282; *Outer Isles*, p. 253.

> I will conclude with a warning against lightly meddling with matters so serious as these. A man named C. was going to Mass early on Sunday morning to Kiloanan [*Sic:* this is what the word looks like in Fr Allan's writing, but anyone who knew Uist would have known 'Kildonan' was meant.] As he crossed the strand, he found a woman and her daughter actively engaged in framing witchcrafts by means of pieces of thread of various colours. He tore up the whole apparatus and rebuked them for malice and for breach of the Sunday. They entreated him not to reveal what he had seen, and promised their protection in return for his silence. Never-

> theless after Mass he told the story. Shortly after, when he was about to sail for the mainland, a black crow settled on the mast of his boat and a storm arose in which he perished. The story is not only true, but of recent occurrence.

The whole story suffers through Miss Freer's condensation, and her last remark is the entire contrary of what Fr Allan himself wrote, and produces a misleading impression as to the contemporaneity of witchcraft in South Uist. This is omitted in *Outer Isles*, as is the man's initial and the name of the locality, doubtless owing to Fr Allan McDonald's protest to Ruth Landon in May 1902, see p. 239.

Fr Allan, I 170:

> On Hallowe'en six plates were placed on the floor each with separate contents and the girls of the house were blindfolded and led to the spot where the plates were laid down, and the first she touched foretold her fate
>
> *Uisge glan* — A husband against whom nothing could be said
> *Salann* — A sailor
> *Min* — A farmer
> *Uir* — Death
> *Uisge salach* — A disreputable husband
> *Eanghlas bhainne* — Foretold adultery.
> *Cf. page 97* (on which page Fr Allan noted the story of the Adultery of Cu-Chulainn and Bláthnat as recounted by Rhys.)

Following the first five Gaelic entries are the English equivalents in Miss Freer's handwriting, 'Pure water, salt, meal, earth, dirty water.' A question mark in her hand follows *Eanghlas bhainne*, and after it Fr Allan has added the explanation 'milk and water mixed'.

In *Folklore*, vol. XIII, p. 53, this divination is given by Miss Freer as follows:

> On Hallowe'en six plates were placed on the floor each with separate contents, and the girl [*sic*] of the house came blindfolded. The first she touched foretold her fate. 1. Pure water portended an unexceptionable husband. 2. Salt, a sailor. 3. Meal, a farmer. 4. Earth, a death, 5. Dirty water, a disreputable husband. 6. An empty plate, no husband.

The sixth divination given by Miss Freer here is quite in keeping with the others; but it is certainly not what Fr Allan McDonald, from whom she copied this item, noted down. The impression given is one of bowdlerization.

This item was not used in *Outer Isles*.

Fr Allan, I 480:

> When Cuchulainn was dying it is said that the host of his enemies despatched a crow *feannag* to see if he were dead. His dying attitude was so life-

like being propped up by spears as related in the narrative supplied by Alex. Carmichael to the Gaelic Society of Inverness. (*Vide* Transactions.) [Vol. II, p. 25. A version of *Tòirioc na Tàine*, taken down by Carmichael from Hector MacIsaac in Benbecula in 1873] that

The *feannag* returned and said:

Chaog an t-suil,
'S cham am bial.

And thereby intimated that his life was extinct.

Fr Allan, VI 258 (from Miss Christina MacInnes, Coilleag, Eriskay):

The raven is not liked because he did not come back to the ark but remained eating the carcases he found floating and lying about, and he acquired such experience then in finding out carcases, that ever since he always knows where a carcase is and has meat (flesh) always. This knowledge of his is proverbially known as '*fios fithich*' the raven's knowledge.

Fr Allan, VI 259:

To bestow[1] Raven's knowledge (*fios fithich*) on a child one should give a draught out of the dry skull of a raven to a child and he would ever after know where a beast (that was missing) was lying down to die (and become food for ravens).

'*Nan tugte deoch do phàiste a claban fithich, bhiodh fios aige càite 'm bitheadh am beathach 'na shìneadh.*'

In her article 'Christian Legends of the Hebrides', in the *Contemporary Review* of September 1898, Miss Freer reproduced these two latter items as follows (p. 400):

The reason, by the way, that the raven did not come back to the Ark was that he was eating the floating carcases. The knowledge of the whereabouts of a dead body is hence called 'raven's knowledge'. A child can be initiated into this by giving him to drink out of the dry skull of a raven. He would ever after be able to find where any missing beast was lying down to die.

This passage was reproduced in *Outer Isles*, p. 224. But in her lecture to the Folklore Society on 6th November 1901, Miss Freer fused the first two items quoted together, suppressed Fr Allan McDonald's reference to Alexander Carmichael, and produced the following:

Knowledge of the whereabouts of the lost, if dead, is called 'raven's knowledge'. When Cuchullin was dying the host of his enemies despatched a crow (*fiannag*) [*sic:* this is what Fr Allan's handwriting here would suggest to a person ignorant of Gaelic] to see if he were dead. His dying

[1] 'aquire' first written, deleted.

attitude was so life-like, propped up with spears, that the raven [*sic*] returning, could only say:

The eye looks askance,
And the mouth is awry.[1]

The reader will notice that as usual Miss Freer makes no attempt to define the context of the tradition described in the two latter paragraphs quoted, so that a person unfamiliar with Uist could not tell whether it was joking, fantasy, or something taken seriously.

Fr Allan, V 162:

> *Iubhair-Beinne* or yew, is kept in a house as preservative against fire. Was it ever used for 'Palms' on Palm Sunday? If so the custom is the same as the Spanish one of placing palm branches on balconies against lightning. (Noted from Dougal MacMillan, Eriskay, on 11th November 1896).

Miss Freer, *Folklore*, vol. XIII, p. 32:

> Branches of yew are kept in the house as a preservative against fire—it may be a survival of keeping the Palm Sunday boughs. (In Spain they are placed in balconies against lightning.)

The way that this item of folklore is presented by Miss Freer illustrates several of the shortcomings of her method.

(1) A botanical error made by Fr Allan is copied. *Iubhair beinne* is not yew, but the creeping juniper that grows in some inaccessible places in the isles. No doubt by now this item has been incorporated into the general folklore of the yew-tree by copyists!

(2) 'Kept in *the* house' is substituted for 'kept in *a* house', and thereby a custom, learnt of from only one informant and probably by no means universal, is generalized and presented as part of a system of Hebridean folk-belief.

(3) Fr Allan's speculation upon the origin of the custom, and his allusion to a foreign parallel, are included as if they were Miss Freer's own comments.

This item was not used in *Outer Isles.*

Fr Allan, I 83 (taken down in 1887 or 1888):

> It is customary on New Year's Eve for the children to go and ask their Hogmanay. From the fourth line of the subjoined rhyme it seems that the custom was kept formerly on the Eve of Xmas, as the Spaniards keep their 'Noche Buena'.
>
> *'S mise nochd dol a Chullaig*
> *Dh'ùrachadh eubh na Calluig*
> *A dh'innse 'mhnathan a bhaile*
> *Gur e màireach latha Nollaig.* [etc.]

[1] *Folklore*, vol. XIII, p. 35.

Miss Freer, *Folklore*, vol. XIII, p. 45 (the translation of the Gaelic is of course by Fr Allan, and unacknowledged):

> Hogmany [*sic*] Night has naturally its special customs. The children go round to the houses on New Year's Eve to ask their Hogmany. It appears from the fourth line of their rhyme as if the custom obtained formerly on *Christmas* Eve, as among the Spaniards,[1] who keep then their *Noche Buena.*
>
> I tonight am going a Hogmanying,
> Going to renew the shout of the Kalends,
> To tell the women of the township
> That tomorrow is the Day of Christmas. [*etc.*]

This item was not used in *Outer Isles.*

Fr Allan [II 77]:

Our Blessed Lord and his Holy Mother once met an orphan girl who was a drudge working for others for her hard earnings. The narrator gave a rhythm [*sic*] in describing her labours, but when I requested her to repeat it, she could only give the narrative in prose.

Our Blessed Lady asked Our Lord to help the girl, and he put it into the mind of a miller who was also a carpenter to marry the girl. (Probably in this connexion comes in *Eòlais a' ghràidh* or *a' ghaoil.*[2]) She soon forgot her poverty and gave herself great airs. Our Blessed Lord and his Virgin Mother came one day to her house and sat in a far corner from the fire, but tho' it was cold she never spoke to them nor asked them to approach the fire, but fussed about the house.

At last the poor visitors said it was time to go and she asked whither. '*A dh'iarraidh na déirce*' [to seek alms], they said. She then gave them a *lodar*[4] of grain. They went to the mill and asked the miller to grind it for them. The miller said the quantity was so

Miss Freer, *Contemporary Review*, 1898, p. 395; *Outer Isles*, p. 216:

Another day, the holy wanderers met a poor orphan girl who was working in hard drudgery. In the original this part of the story is in rhyme, and her labourers are described in much detail.

Our Lady asked her Son to help her, and He put it into the mind of a miller, who was also a carpenter (a common combination in the Hebrides) to marry the girl, who soon forgot her poverty and gave herself great airs; and when the Mother and Son came to see her[3] she hardly spoke to them, but gave them a place far from the fire, and went on fussing about her housework.

At last they rose to go, and all she gave them was a ladleful of grain.

Then they went to the mill, and asked the miller to grind it for them, but he said there was so little of it that

[1] Fr Allan McDonald had been trained for the priesthood at Valladolid. Here again Miss Freer reproduces Fr Allan's allusion to a foreign parallel as if it were her own comment.

[2] *i.e.* the Love Charm.

[3] Miss Freer misses the point completely, which is that the orphan girl, now married and prosperous, did not recognize Our Lord and His Mother when they happened to come again later.

[4] 'ladleful' is written above 'of grain' in Fr Allan McDonald's text.

small that it would break the mill-stones. 'It is food for the needy,' said Christ, 'and no harm will arise if you grind it.'

The miller set to grind it and then went on with his carpentry till God put it into his mind to look to the grist, and he found the ladle of grain had filled the large chest with the most beautiful meal.

They took part and went away, and it occurred to the miller that they were the Son of God and his Mother. He went to his house and asked the wife if any people had called to-day. The wife said there was no day but people called and that she was

Air a nàrachadh,
Air a sàrachadh,
'S air a bleideachadh
[= shamed, harassed, pestered]

every day with beggars, and that two had called this very day. He told her it was the Son of God and his Mother who had called, and told of the miracle he had witnessed.

The woman felt ashamed of herself and ran after the visitors . . .

Ending taken from another version of the story, Fr Allan [*VI 264*]:

. . . saying she did not know who they were, and Christ said: 'When you saw my poor did you not see me?[3] I saw you an orphan and I gave you plenty.' 'But thou didst not give a heart in proportion.' 'May you have a heart and plenty then.' And she was ever after kind to the poor.

it would break the quern[1] (mill-stones). 'It is food for the needy,' said Christ, 'and no harm will arise if you grind it.'

So the miller gave the stones a turn or two, and then went on with his carpentering. After a little while God put it into his heart to look to the grist, and he found that the ladleful of grain had filled the chest with meal of the finest quality.

The travellers took part, and went on their way, and the miller went into the house to ask if any one had called 'the day'.[2] His wife said there was no day but people called, and that she was wearied and annoyed with beggars such as had come that very day. (This part of the story is also in verse.)

Then he told her of the miracle that had been done,

and she was filled with shame and hastened after the Mother and Son, and

said she had not known them. 'When you saw my poor did you not see me?' said Our Lord. 'I saw you an orphan and I gave you plenty,' and ever after that she was good to the poor.

[1] Miss Freer is completely off the rails here. The miller would not be working a quern (hand-mill). People did that in their own houses: the miller was working a water-mill, grinding oats and barley for people who brought him grain in quantity. The miller did not, therefore, 'give the stones a turn or two' and go on with his carpentering. He set the water-mill to work. With such a small quantity of grain of course there was a risk of the big millstones being damaged.

[2] Expression introduced by Miss Freer to give the impression of Highland English used, as if it had been apoken to her!

[3] The first part of the story reproduces a version taken down by Fr Allan McDonald from Cairistiana nighean Dhunnchaidh in South Boisdale, probably in 1894. The ending used by Miss Freer is taken from a version Fr Allan took down on Eriskay in March 1898 from Christina MacInnes. There is no justification for fusing the two versions.

Fr Allan [VI 282]:

It is 'crossed' (banned) to place a peat broadwise at the back of the fire. The peats should be placed face to face. It is said that Our Lord was passing a house and He said that there was either a corpse in the house or a peat broadwise on the fire.

It is also 'crossed (*Tha e air a chrosadh*—such is the wording of all such precepts) to turn the red side of an ignited peat on the fire outwards and the black side inwards. (It is stupid to do so in any case tho' the temptation to do so may be strong, for the fire will ignite more quickly and surely if the ignited faces of the peats are kept facing each other. *Experimentia docet.*)

Miss Freer, *Contemporary Review*, 1898, p. 397; *Outer Isles*, p. 220:

It is 'crossed'—*i.e.* unlucky—to put peats on the fire the wrong way. Our Lord was one day passing a house, and He said there was either a corpse in it or a peat broadwise on the fire.

It is also 'crossed'—such is the literal wording of all such precepts—to turn the red side of a peat outwards and the black inwards. It is a stupid thing to do in either case.

Fr Allan [VI 310]:

The story of the peat broadwise on the fire or against the fire and what Our Lord said about there being either a corpse or a peat broadwise on the fire she [Christina MacInnes] explains thus. Our Lord wished the houses to be cheerful, and to compare the cheerlessness of a house where the peats were not properly arranged in making the fire (and where there would be neither warmth nor light) with a house with a corpse in it (*cho mi-thuarail*). Of course He knew what was in the house, whether a corpse or a peat badly placed on the fire, but He wished to impress on them what a little thing would make a house look as cheerless as if it had a corpse.

The interpretation given to the story is that Our Lord wishes things to be cheerful and liberal, and it is a churlish thing to economise the peats thus, so as to give neither warmth nor light.

Fr Allan [VI 257]:

An old cailleach had a sick cow and our Blessed Lord was passing the way, and she went out and asked Him to make a charm for the cow (*eòlas a*

Miss Freer, *Contemporary Review*, 1898, p. 398; *Outer Isles*, p. 222:

An old woman had a sick cow, and she went to ask Our Lord, as He passed by, to make a charm for the cow. But He returned with her, and,

dhianamh 'na bhoin). He followed the old woman, and when He came to the sick cow He struck her with His staff and said:

> *'Ma bhios tu beo, biodh,*
> *'S mura bithear, cailltear thu.'*[1]

The cow became well, and He went His way. Some time after a priest or some other great person for whom the old woman had an especial regard was very ill with quinsy. The old woman bethought herself of Our Lord's charm for her cow, and she came to see the sick man and struck him with a stick she had and said the words as above. The sick man laughed at the seeming ridiculousness of the charm, and the swelling in his throat burst, and he was cured.

(I asked Christina MacInnes if she heard of Our Lord curing any other animals and she said No—that it was Calum Cille [St Columba] who always cured the animals.[3])

when He came to the beast, touched it with His staff, saying certain words.

The cow was healed, and Our Lord went His way. Soon after, a priest, or some other great person, came by,[2] for whom the woman had a special regard, and he was ill of a quinsy. The old woman struck him with the staff and repeated the charm, but he only laughed at its absurdity.

However, the laugh was his cure, for the quinsy burst.

The sequel to the story has so very modern a tone that it is quoted mainly for the sake of adding that the old woman who told it said she knew of no other case of Our Lord healing animals. It was always St Columkille who did that. There are, in fact, an immense number of stories, some very quaint, as to the healing miracles of St Columba.

Fr Allan [I 73]:

It is said that the beetle (*daol*) tried to betray our Lord in his flight to Egypt. Herod's men were in pursuit of him and came to Egypt and were inquiring of the people if they had observed the Holy Family pass that way.

Miss Freer,[4] *Contemporary Review*, 1898, p. 399; *Outer Isles*, p. 223:

The blackbeetle is universally detested and trampled upon, but the sharded beetle, called Ceardobhan, is a favourite. The blackbeetle tried to betray Our Lord in His flight to Egypt. Herod's men were in pursuit of Him, and came to Egypt, and were

[1] The words of the 'charm' mean 'if you are going to live, may you live, and if you are not, you will die.' It is of course an absurd charm, judged by the wording of charms that were in actual use, by its meaning, and by the fact that Our Lord was capable of miraculously curing the cow without using any kind of charm anyway. But Miss Freer, whose ignorance of Gaelic is again exposed here, was quite incapable of appreciating the subtlety involved in the story.

[2] The person who was suffering from quinsy did not 'come by'. The old woman went to see him, as one might expect. The story has been carelessly transcribed by Miss Freer here.

[3] St Columba was the patron saint of cattle in the Highlands and Islands, see *Gaelic Words from South Uist*, p. 86, under *Crodh*.

[4] This story illustrates again Miss Freer's habit of combining different anecdotes on the same subject in Fr Allan McDonald's notebooks. In this case the information came from different reciters in different places at an interval of ten years.

inquiring of the people if they had seen the Holy Family pass that way.

The person particularly addressed said he observed a group pass that would correspond to the description given. Being further asked when they had passed, he replied that they passed when the corn which was now yellow in his field had been sown. The seed had been sown only the previous day, but a miracle had been wrought in favour of the owner of the field on account of some kindness shown to the Holy Family. As the soldiers were departing in the furtherance of their search a black beetle crept across the path and said, '*An dé, an dé, chaidh Mac Dhé seachad.*'[1] The sharded beetle called '*Ceardobhan*' with less regard for truth than for charity said, '*Briag, briag, a bhradaig!* [sic] *Seachd bliadhna thun an dé chaidh Mac Dé seachad*'[2] The *daol* is universally detested and trampled to death when seen, but the '*ceardobhan*' is a favourite.

The person particularly addressed said he had observed just the party described; and on being asked when he had seen them, he said it was when the corn, which was now yellow in the field, had been sown. The seed had been sown only the previous day, but a miracle was wrought in favour of the owner of the field on account of some kindness shown to the Holy Family. As the soldiers were departing a blackbeetle crept across the path, and said, 'Yesterday, yesterday, the Son of God passed.' The large sharded beetle, however, called out, 'Whisht, you imp, a year from yesterday the Son of God passed,' and so put the pursuers off the scent.

Fr Allan [VI 256]:

Beetles (*daolan*) are seen everywhere during Lent and it is believed this restlessness of theirs at this time is a curse upon them. I cannot make out the connexion between beetles and Lent. One woman says that it was at this time of the year—when the grain was being winnowed that the beetle nearly betrayed him, her version being that He was hiding under a heap of chaff as His enemies came up and asked if He had been seen passing and the beetle said, '*An dé, an dé, chaidh Mac Dé seachad,*'—which saying of hers under the circumstances had the

Beetles are seen everywhere during Lent,[3] and it is believed that they are specially restless at this sacred time on account of the curse upon them.

Possibly because this is about the winnowing time and they are disturbed in their winter quarters.[4]

[1] See a very similar version of this story in *Carmina Gadelica*, IV 3, also II 188, 248, and 267. Alexander Carmichael translated *daol* as 'gravedigger beetle' and *cearrdobhan* as 'sacred beetle'. The *cearrdobhan* appears to be the dor-beetle (*Geotrupes* sp.), the *daol* one of the burying beetles (*Necrodes* or *Necrophrous* sp.).

[2] This passage means 'A lie, a lie, you thief! Seven years ago yesterday the Son of God went past!' 'Seven years' of the Gaelic somehow becomes 'a year' in Miss Freer's précis. In the second version collected by Fr Allan, it is 'seven weeks'.

[3] Presumably because they emerge from their pupae or from hibernation around this time. There is no reason for connecting Lent with the winnowing of corn particularly.

[4] This sentence occurs as a footnote in Miss Freer's article and book.

same merit tho' not to the same extent as that of the *Ceardubhan* [sic] who said, '*Seachd seachdainean thun an dé chaidh Mac Dé seachad*'—the greater merit of the *Ceardubhan* (sharded beetle) being that he told the biggest lie. The beetle is in consequence always killed, and the stone used in killing it is placed on its squashed remains. If not killed outright it might go into a child's ear at night. (C[hristina] MacInnes, Coil[l]eag.)

The stone with which they are crushed should always be left upon the remains, otherwise they may get into a child's ear at night.

Fr Allan [V 49]:

To eat the head of an eel is considered dangerous, as being apt to produce madness. It is believed that the eels are apt to be infected with madness and may thus communicate it to men.

I asked if my informant if [*sic*] he knew any person who became mad in this way and he mentioned the case of a person of his acquaintance who nearly went mad after eating an eel's head but was saved by being able to vomit just as he felt his head beginning to go wrong.

Then there was the story of the man who killed a trout and an eel, and gave his wife the trout and ate the eel himself, and who went mad and told his wife to fly just as he felt the insanity come upon him. She escaped to her husband's brother's house. Next day this brother found his insane brother eating the raw flesh of a horse he had killed, and to prevent further mischief shot the unfortunate maniac. The surviving brother afterwards left the mainland and settled in S. Uist, where there are still descendants. I had this story from one who belongs to the stock. (Cf. 26.)

Miss Freer, *Folklore*, vol. XIII, p. 36; *Outer Isles*, pp. 192–3 (text of latter reproduced here):

Another prejudice, commonly held, is that it is dangerous to eat the head of an eel, for eels are subject to madness and apt to communicate the disease.

Our informant was asked if he had met with any case of such infection, and he instanced a friend of his own who was saved only by being caused to vomit just when his head was beginning to go wrong.

He also told us a story of a man, who, having killed a trout and an eel, gave the trout to his wife and ate the eel himself. He forthwith became insane, but not before he had warned his wife to escape for safety from him to her brother's [*sic*] house. The brother went next day to visit his afflicted relative, and found that he had killed his horse, and was eating the raw flesh, so to prevent further mischief he shot him. It was considered advisable that he should leave the country, and that is how

No. 26 in this notebook, against which there is a tick and 'see 49' in Miss Freer's handwriting, is one of a number of Uist genealogies, and reads as follows:

Iain mac Eachainn ic Iain ic Iain ic Dho(mh)naill Ruaidh nan each [*i.e.* John, son of Hector son of John son of John son of auburn-haired Donald of the horses] said [*i.e.* Donald] to have killed mad brother eating horse. Eel and trout wife yarn.[1] (From mainland). Came to Ben More in Uist and lived there.

he came to Ben More, in Uist, where his descendant still lives, and is known as Ian, son of Ian, son of Donald 'of the horse'.

Who would not think, on reading Miss Freer's careless condensation of Fr Allan McDonald's transcript, that this story, or rather these two stories, had not been told to her and Fr Allan McDonald together? It is clear from Fr Allan's transcript that the stories came from different persons, and that the second, which relates to something supposed to have happened on the mainland four generations earlier, does not relate to the folklore of South Uist but to the class of story connected with people whose ancestors were said to have got into trouble on the mainland and taken refuge in the Hebrides. Nor was it the case that the descendant of Domhnall Ruadh nan Each was still living at Ben More at the time Miss Freer was writing. Fr Allan McDonald himself says that Domhnall Ruadh *lived* there. His descendants, like the other crofters living in the Ben More district of Uist, had been evicted from it before Miss Freer's time, and had either settled in Eriskay, or gone to America.

2. *Items from Fr Allan McDonald's Collection common to George Henderson's* Survivals in Belief Among the Celts *and Miss Freer's articles in* Folklore

Confirmation of the fact that Fr Allan McDonald's notebooks were the source for Miss Freer's information on the folklore of South Uist and Eriskay can be found in Dr George Henderson's *Survivals in Belief among the Celts*, published in Glasgow in 1911. As has been stated in this book, Henderson was a personal friend of Fr Allan McDonald's and had access to his notebooks both before and after Fr Allan's death in 1905.

On p. 293 of *Survivals* Henderson wrote: 'Here is a series of things Taboo which the Rev. A. Macdonald tabulated for the Isle of Eriskay and its neighbourhood.' There follow an account of twenty-

[1] Word uncertain.

five prohibitions of which no fewer than nineteen had been published by Miss Freer under her own name as if of her own collecting, eleven in her 'Powers of Evil' article, in *Folklore*, vol. X, in 1899, and eight in her 'More Folklore from the Hebrides', in *Folklore*, vol. XIII, in 1902. These twenty-five prohibitions occupy pp. 293–7 in Henderson's book, and it is significant that no reference whatever is made to the previous publication of any of them by Miss Freer. It is also interesting that all but two of the twenty-five items here apparently come from Fr Allan McDonald's missing Notebooks III and IV, with which Henderson as well as Miss Freer must have been familiar.

Two examples may be given. It will be seen that Henderson appears to be quoting Fr Allan McDonald verbatim, whereas Miss Freer condenses.

Folklore, vol. XIII, pp. 29, and 30 (but separated by other material):

> It is not right to mend clothes while upon the person. It is an interference with the rights of the dead, to whom alone belongs the privilege of having the clothes stitched upon the body . . .
>
> It is not right for a person to cut his own hair. There is a saying about 'raising scissors above one's breath'—possibly some allusion to cutting the breath of life.

Survivals (1911), p. 295 (consecutively):

> It is not right to mend or stitch clothes while the clothes are on the person. It interferes with the rights of the dead, to whom alone belongs the privilege of having their death linens sewed upon the body (Mary Ann Campbell, 1895).
>
> It is not right (*ceart*) for a man to cut his own hair or even part of it. Whatever it means the meaning has reference 'to raising the scissors above one's own breath' (*togail an t-siosar os cionn analach*). Perhaps it refers to cutting the breath of life which is the thread of life (do., do.).

It may be noted that Henderson takes the trouble to quote the name of Fr Allan McDonald's informant, and the year the information was given: something that should have been expected of Miss Freer as a trained psychical researcher, but which she did not do.

In the whole of Miss Freer's folklore writings derived from Fr Allan McDonald's collection, nothing betrays both her ignorance of Gaelic, and her general lack of first-hand acquaintance with the subject, more than her repeated misunderstanding and misspelling of the word *toradh*. *Toradh* means 'produce'. Milk is the produce of cows, and butter, cream, and cheese are more particularly the produce of milk, and represented wealth in the old days of Highland pastoral economy. Hence the *toradh* or produce of milk was what witches were often suspected of stealing in various paranormal ways. In the winter of 1887–8 Fr Allan McDonald recorded that:

> A plant called *caoibhreachan* was considered lucky and a sufficient protection against witchcraft. They say it is impossible that any milk or *toradh* can be bewitched out of a house, where the *caoibhrichean* is kept under an upturned vessel. (I 86)

In *Folklore*, vol. X, p. 275, Miss Freer has:

> The marsh-ragwort (*caoibhreachan*) is valuable against the *torradh* and Evil Eye generally.
>
> Of all forms of evil influence none is more dreaded than this *torradh*, or the charming away of milk from cattle.

That Miss Freer must have got the idea that *toradh*, which she misspells with a double *r*, meant 'the charming away of milk from cattle', from a careless misreading of one of Fr Allan McDonald's notebooks, is proved by comparing another passage on the same subject as it occurs in her article in *Folklore*, vol. X, and in Henderson's *Survivals*:

Folklore, vol. X, p. 278; *Outer Isles*, p. 249:

> If a person is very much afflicted in regard to the *torradh*, he is wise to adopt the following remedy. 'Whenever' (*anglicé* = as soon as) one of his cows has a calf, to take it away before any milk is drawn. Then, taking a bottle, he is to draw milk from the four teats, kneeling. The bottle is then tightly corked; this is important, for carelessness in this respect might give access to the *torradh* and upset everything. Another method is for a man—a woman won't do—to go [to] the house of the person suspected, and pull off from the roof as much thatch and divots as his two hands will hold, and over this to boil what little milk is left, until it dries up. Another informant[1] advised burning the thatch under the churn, instead of under the milk.

The same item is given on p. 28 in *Survivals* by Henderson with direct acknowledgment to Fr Allan McDonald on the preceding page. It is placed within inverted commas, and is obviously quoted directly from Fr Allan's notebook. I italicize the passages in English omitted or suppressed by Miss Freer:

> If a person were much afflicted by the *toradh, or 'milk produce', being taken from him,* he was advised to adopt the following remedy: Whenever[2] one of his cows calves, to take away the calf immediately before he draws milk *from his dam,* then to take a bottle and draw milk from the four teats *into the bottle,* the person so doing being on *one* knee, *and saying*:

[1] The informant of course was Fr Allan McDonald's, not Miss Freer's.

[2] 'Whenever' here means 'whenever', and not *anglice* 'as soon as', or anything else.

Gum beannicheadh Dia na cuilean so
The mise 'g iarraidh so 'n ainm Dhia
S cha n eil mi 'g iarraidh ach mo chuid fhein.[1]

The bottle is then tightly corked *and hidden in a safe place.* Here is a magic way of retaining the whole by keeping the part. If the cork were to be put in loosely, it is feared that the *toradh would be at the mercy of any one who had the faculty of filching it.*

Another *Uist* informant, *Duncan M'Innes,* said that *he heard* the effective way of recovering the *toradh* was to snatch a bundle of thatch from the threshold of a suspected person and to burn it beneath a churn.[2]

It is therefore clear that Miss Freer (or whoever copied Fr Allan McDonald's notebook for her) overlooked the words 'or milk produce, being taken from him' after *toradh* in the first line of the passage quoted here, and got the idea that *toradh* meant the affliction of having one's milk, etc., filched from one by witchcraft! As regards the precaution described, it must be considered a comparatively modern one, as bottles with corks must have been comparatively rare in the Highlands until about 150 years ago, the traditional vessels used being made of wood, and covered with sheepskin.

[1] This verse, not quoted by Miss Freer, who would no t have understood it unless Fr Allan McDonald had provided a translation, is rendered by Henderson: 'May God bless the cattle-folds! This I am asking in the name of God, nor am I asking but for mine own.'

[2] The Gaelic is quoted as *Tubhadh an fhardoruis a thoirt leat s a losgadh fo thòin a chrannachain* [sic]. See also *Survivals,* p. 295.

APPENDIX B

List of Folktales and Ballads taken down in South Uist and Eriskay in 1892 by George Henderson

THESE ARE listed in Henderson's letter of 26th December 1892 to Alexander Carmichael as follows:

Sgialachds

1. *Caracher Mac Righ Eirinn*
2. *Nighean Chlair Ourlair* [sic]
3. *Sgeul Mu Righ Uilleam* (old)
4. *Ciad Mac Righ Africa*
5. *Sgialac a Ghamhna Dhuinn*
6. *Sgialac Mu Riogh*
7. *An Righ agus an Sagart*
8. *Sagart O' Crà*
9. *Nighean Gruagach na Tiobairt no Fear na Haibeid* (*Righ na Beul Dearg*)
10. *Sgialac A Chait Chaoich*
11. *Triùir Mhac A Ghairneileir*
12. *Sgialac Cath Buail An-Aoin-Doruis*
13. *Mac O Cròlagan*
14. *Sgialac Diol Chaich*
15. *Sgialac Iain Saighdear*

Duans

1. *A Mhuileartach* (2 versions)
2. *Laoidh Dhiarmaid* (2)
3. *Laoidh An Amadain Mhoir*
4. *Bas Oscair* (2)
6. *Laoidh na h-inghinne*, with prose *Suspac* (introduction)
6. *Laoidh Ghille Chinn Choin Fhinn*—with *Suspac*
7. *Comhrag A choin duibh is Bran*
8. *Am Bròn Binn* (touching and beautiful)
9. *Laoidh Chaoilte*—with *suspac*

Henderson added: '5, 6, 8, I do not recollect ever reading in print.'

There is a notebook in Henderson's papers in Glasgow University Library which contains fair copies of most of these stories and ballads, but it has been mutilated. The list of contents shows that it did not contain stories Nos. 3, 7, 8, and 10 here,[1] but on the other hand it had *Murchadh Mac Brian* and *Aoidheach Chlann Uisneach*, both of which have been cut out, as well as Nos. 4, 6, 9, and part of 5 here. There is no indication in the MS. of the identity of the reciters, but in vol. XXV of the *Transactions of the Gaelic Society of Inverness* Henderson said, 'I have taken down romances from the late Domhull Chailein [Donald MacInnes] in Eriskay, of considerable length . . . wherein Brian and Murrough his son and others figure' (p. 180).

As for the ballads, No. 6 and part of No. 9 here have also been removed from the same notebook. The same Donald MacInnes in Eriskay, who Henderson notes was 60 years old in 1892, is given as the source of versions of Nos. 1 and 2. The other versions of No. 1 were taken down from 'D. MacCarmaick, North Lochboisdale: aged 61. Xmas 1892', and from John Smith, South Boisdale. (There are three versions of this ballad here.) The other version of No. 2 was also taken down from John Smith, as was No. 3. The version of No. 8 written in this MS. is not the same as that which Henderson took down from Mór Nic Fhionghain in 1892 and printed in the *Miscellany Presented to Kuno Meyer* (p. 29).

This interesting collection made by Henderson in South Uist deserves to be rescued from oblivion, and the missing stories and ballads traced; I cannot find that he ever published them himself.

[1] Fr Allan MacDonald preserved versions of stories No. 9 and 10 here

MOTIF-INDEX OF THE STORIES

EC = Fr Allan McDonald's early collection, made between 1887 and 1894.
ST = 'Strange Things', the second sight stories recorded for the S.P.R. Enquiry between 1895 and 1897.

[1] The Evil Eye and fairy stories in 'Strange Things' do not by any means comprise the whole of the material Fr Allan McDonald collected on these subjects, but as they belong to folklore rather than to psychical research, the other stories he collected about them are not included here.

(*For list of other folklore items see the General Index under* '*Folklore*')

INDEX

* Indicates that the person is actually named as an informant of Fr Allan McDonald.

† Names so marked are also to be found in *A School in South Uist* by Frederic Rea (Routledge and Kegan Paul, London, 1964.)[1]

[1] Frederic Rea was headmaster of Garrynamonie school in Fr Allan MacDonald's parish of Dalibrog, South Uist, from 1890 to 1894 and again from 1903 to 1913. He was thus unfortunately away from Uist at the time of Miss Freer's visits, otherwise we might have had an interesting description of her. As it is, his book gives a sympathetic description of contemporary life in South Uist, of Fr Allan McDonald, Donald MacCormick, and of some other persons and places mentioned in the stories published here.